Why Governments Waste Natural Resources

Why Governments Waste Natural Resources

POLICY FAILURES IN DEVELOPING COUNTRIES

William Ascher

THE JOHNS HOPKINS UNIVERSITY PRESS
Baltimore & London

© 1999 The Johns Hopkins University Press
All rights reserved. Published 1999
Printed in the United States of America on acid-free paper
9 8 7 6 5 4 3 2 1

The Johns Hopkins University Press
2715 North Charles Street
Baltimore, Maryland 21218-4363
www.press.jhu.edu

Library of Congress Cataloging-in-Publication Data will be found
at the end of this book.
A catalog record for this book is available from the British Library.

ISBN 0-8018-6095-4
ISBN 0-8018-6096-2 (pbk.)

To Diana, Julie, and David

Contents

Preface and Acknowledgments   *ix*

CHAPTER 1   *Introduction   1*

CHAPTER 2   *Anatomy of Resource Policy Failures and Their Linkages to Programmatic Strategies   32*

CHAPTER 3   *Oil and Timber Abuses to Fund Off-Budget Development Programs in Indonesia   59*

CHAPTER 4   *Development Programs through Natural-Resource Abuses   85*

CHAPTER 5   *Distribution through Resource Abuses   144*

CHAPTER 6   *Raising Revenues through Resource Abuses   190*

CHAPTER 7   *Conclusions and Recommendations   244*

Notes   *281*

References   *303*

Index   *319*

Preface and Acknowledgments

For most of its very long gestation period, this book had an unseemly working title: "Why Governments Screw up Natural Resources: It's Not Just Greed, Power, Stupidity, or Ignorance." Clearly, this was not appropriate as a formal title, yet it did reflect my major preoccupation. While many of the disciplines contributing to natural-resource management have made great strides over the past several decades, the political analysis of why policies often fail to incorporate these improvements remained basically primitive. Resource economics, ecology, and resource engineering have matured and flourished. Experts from these fields have spent enormous energy trying to press their technical insights onto government officials of developing countries, very often coming away in frustration with the seemingly cynical, selfish, or bumbling reactions of these officials. The apparently obvious explanation has been that government officials are too jaded or too incompetent to take good technical advice.

This perception is, unfortunately, reinforced by much of the political science applied to natural-resource issues. Of course, there are exceptions, such as insightful applications of collective-action theory to common-property management, and some of the more contextual political-economy analyses of regulatory enforcement. Yet the easiest way for a political scientist to seem penetrating and tough-minded is to "model" the behavior of political leaders as self-interested people out for power, personal financial gain, or both. This presumption has arrested the development of political analysis of natural-resource policy failures, because the "easy" explanation of resource destruction as the result of pandering for political support or simple corruption is all too easy. Someone benefits from virtually every government policy or action, so it is easy to dismiss unsound policies as politically or financially motivated payoffs. This approach is largely a dead end for policy reform, because the premise of the completely selfish government leader admits of very little opportunity to work with these leaders for sustainable development and the common good.

The trick is to grapple with the much more complex reality that government leaders have complicated programmatic objectives, while not being so naive as to ignore their self-centered political motivations. This means going into detail rather than putting the bulk of the effort into formalizing at the level of highly aggregate, stylized facts, which means a case-study approach that tries to infer programmatic, as well as political, motives from events, policies, actions, and statements. For moderately broad conclusions to be drawn from such cases, they must be numerous — not to fit into a statistical analysis, but to distinguish rather common patterns from idiosyncratic ones.

The importance of looking at many cases creates a tremendous debt to the scholars who have assessed specific cases in far greater depth than a synthetic study like this could ever hope to accomplish. For each case it will be obvious how reliant my interpretations are on the solid work of a handful of country experts.

By the same token, my debt to research assistants is profound and long, as might be expected for a work that encompasses cases from more than a dozen countries. In fact, some of the research that underpins this study was begun so long ago that these research assistants now have very distinguished careers: Anjali Acharya, Maya Ajmera, David Ascher, Kevin Cook, Louise Davidson-Schmich, Suzanne Duryea, Marcelo Fava, Chris Greenwald, Christopher Jones, Cathy Karr, Endalkachew Kidanewold, Barbara Kohnen, Jennie Litvack, Patrick Pickett, Monica Rios, Junko Saito, Donna Slawson, Sonal Tejani, and Laura Ziff. Former fellows of our midcareer Program in International Development Policy wrote papers that are important for the case studies: Arnulfo Cruz, Carlos Gieseke, Tomoo Mochida, Abubakar Nuhu-Koko, and Ramiro Tovar.

I will be eternally grateful to Garry Brewer, William Overholt, and Toddi Steelman, brave souls and loyal friends who read an earlier draft "from cover to cover" and took painstaking care to save readers from incoherence and stilted language. Other practitioners and scholars who provided crucial reactions to earlier drafts of this study are Yair Aharoni, George Busenberg, Peter Cleaves, Malcolm Gillis, James Hamilton, Raymond Hopkins, Katrina Smith Korfmacher, Francis Lethem, Jennie Litvack (as a World Bank economist, a far cry from the undergraduate research assistant who started on this project some years ago), Gordon Means, Jack Montgomery, Theodore Moran, Elinor Ostrom, Visvanathan Rajagopalan, Laura Randall, Dennis Rondinelli, Michael Ross, Adam Schwarz, Narendra Sharma, Tom Tietenberg, Angelica Toniolo, Raymond Vernon, and Christopher Welna. Unfortunately, all errors of fact and interpretation remain my own.

Financial support for various components of the research that supported this book came from the U.S. Agency for International Development, the World Bank, and the International Center for Self-governance of the Institute for Contemporary Studies. None of the opinions reflected in this book necessarily reflect the positions of these institutions.

The staff and faculty of Duke University's Center for International Development Research (CIDR) have provided the context and continuity to work on a project of this scope. The stimulating environment of CIDR and the first-rate contributions of the fellows of CIDR's Program in International Development Policy have provided a bridge to developing countries that ensures a two-way flow of knowledge and insight.

The greatest continuity and support have come, as always, from Barbara Ascher and from our children Diana, Julie, and David. For providing incentive for my concern for long-term sustainable development, I also thank Ariana Storm Ascher.

Why Governments Waste
Natural Resources

CHAPTER 1

Introduction

FOCUS AND SCOPE

This book is about the role of governments in wasting natural resources and what can be done about it. Problems of unsound natural-resource exploitation occur in both developed and developing countries. Many rich countries, including the United States, have wasted natural resources and continue to do so: pastures erode from overgrazing, soils become contaminated, and forests are leveled, often without offsetting benefits for society. Yet the focus of this book is on the developing nations because they often have the greatest reliance on natural resources — and can least afford to squander them. These countries, whether in Africa, Asia, or Latin America, depend heavily on the resource base to stimulate economic growth, to provide livelihoods for low-income people, and to maintain the environment. Because the stakes are so high and the resource policy failures in developing countries are often so extreme, we can more easily detect the dynamics that lead governments to squander natural resources.

The cases covered in this book, developed over a decade of individual and collaborative research on forestry, oil, mining, land, and water sectors of selected developing countries,[1] are the following:

Agriculture, Irrigation, Forestry, and Land	*Oil and Mining*
Brazil (Amazonian land; esp. forests)	Chile (copper)
Cameroon (land, forests, and parks)	India (copper)
Costa Rica (land and timber)	Indonesia (oil)
Ghana (cocoa)	Mexico (oil)
Honduras (timber)	Nigeria (oil)
Indonesia (timber)	Peru (oil)
Mexico (irrigation)	Venezuela (oil)
Sabah (Malaysian state) (timber)	
Sarawak (Malaysian state) (timber)	

This is by no means a random sample; it reflects a commitment to look at very important resources for each country included in the studies, but it also reflects where research funding and happenstance permitted sufficient examination. Clearly, there is no claim that the specific patterns found among these cases can be extended to all cases of natural resources in all developing countries. Indeed, such a claim would probably be foolish even if an effort at random selection had been made. Nevertheless, it is fair to say that the patterns found to be common among such a diverse set of countries and resource sectors have to be taken seriously when considering other cases.

The waste and degradation of natural resources in these countries can most commonly be traced directly to government policy failures. These failures cause resource depletion that cannot be justified by the societal gains achieved by such depletion. As forests disappear, petroleum and minerals are squandered, land erodes, water systems deteriorate, and wildlife becomes scarce, we can almost always find a faulty government policy lurking in the background. The question is Why?

The depressing conclusion too often reached is that the unsound policies are simply a matter of greed or ignorance. When governments squander natural resources, critics usually assume that government officials are selfish, shortsighted, corrupt, incompetent, or poorly trained. Scientists often reinforce this perspective by lamenting our general ignorance in the face of the mysteries of nature. Edward O. Wilson writes that

> governments everywhere are at a loss regarding the best policy for regulating the dwindling forests reserves of the world. Few ethical guidelines have been established from which agreement might be reached, and those are based on an insufficient knowledge of ecology. Even if adequate scientific knowledge were available, we would have little basis for the long-term valuation of forests. The economics of sustainable yield is still a primitive art, and the psychological benefits of natural ecosystems are almost wholly unexplored. (1998, 42)

It is certainly true that the ethics of balancing economic development against the noneconomic values of ecosystems remains a thorny problem. Yet the premise that resource managers and government officials are at a loss to choose and implement better policies for forests and other ecosystems is unfounded. The "primitive art" of sustainable yield may not be able to gauge precisely how much resource can be extracted without risking future yields,[2] but it is certainly robust enough both to identify the many resource policies and practices that are unsustainable and to guide resource managers to moderation when the level of sustainable yield is not certain. The essential point, demonstrated time and again in the case studies, is that many natural-resource policies are known to be clearly in error, by government officials as well as by outside observers. They are in error in the crucial sense that they do not husband natural resources in ways that further society's welfare, whether or not they are political errors on the part of the government officials that choose them.

This leads, of course, to the view of policy failures as just politics. This is an equally dangerous, and — fortunately — falsely simplistic view that implies that we should just throw up our hands and dismiss sound resource use as hopeless as long as it remains in the hands of politicians. Even if we concede that politics drives politicians, this does not mean that politics always calls for bad policies. The real challenge is to create conditions in which government leaders can gladly embrace sound natural-resource policies and conservation.

Indeed, the explanations for unsound government resource policies are much more subtle, and much more hopeful, than the standard diagnosis that governments misuse resources out of a combination of greed, politics, and stupidity. As we get to the core reasons why governments waste resources, we will discover many points of leverage for policy and institutional reforms.

The Stakes

It may seem peculiar to some readers that natural resources would even require attention on the brink of the twenty-first century. After all, we are supposed to be in the midst of the "high-tech era," the "information age," the "postindustrial society." The production of physical goods is supposed to be less important than providing services, and greater efficiency and miniaturization are supposed to reduce the demands for raw materials.

The opposite is true. Despite all the predictions that the importance of natural resources would recede rapidly in our increasingly technological world, our industrial and agricultural bases are still firmly rooted in raw materials. Most important, because of population growth and rising incomes, the demand for manufactured goods, food, housing, and energy has continued to soar. These all require greater quantities of raw materials, both renewable and nonrenewable. The increasing demand for natural resources easily outstrips the capacity of new technologies to reduce the need for natural-resource inputs. Technology that miniaturizes devices to save on resource inputs, or that substitutes lighter or more abundant materials for traditional ones, has had negligible impact on the total volume and value of raw-material inputs.

For example, the world demand for industrial wood has been projected to increase from 1.7 million cubic meters in 1987 to 2.0 billion in the year 2000 and to 3.1 billion in the year 2025. Wood for farms and households — that is, wood for fuel, building houses, and fencing poles — may increase from 2.6 billion cubic meters in 1987 to 3.1 billion in the year 2000 and to 4.0 billion in the year 2025 (Sharma et al. 1992, 29).

Similarly, for all of the promise of energy conservation, responsible projections of world energy consumption foresee increases of 30–45 percent per decade through the year 2020.[3] The demand for oil, the most easily transportable of fuels, is expected to grow by 25–35 percent over the next fifteen years (Crow 1996).

Food demand will continue to expand more rapidly than will population, because higher incomes permit greater food consumption. Greater food supplies require more water (despite the promise of drip irrigation systems, which are quite expensive) and, therefore, an expansion of irrigation systems. It has been estimated that half of the expected increase in crop production between 1995 and 2010 will come from the expansion of irrigation systems (Mannion 1997, 255). Fertilizers, the other crucial raw-material ingredient for higher agricultural yields (the so-called Green Revolution), are still based on natural deposits. The UN Food and Agriculture Organization has projected that nitrogen fertilizer demand will increase at a rate of more than 20 percent each decade, whereas potash and phosphate fertilizer demand will increase at a rate of nearly 35 percent each decade (FAO 1994).

While the world's continued dependence on raw materials poses some risks for continued economic growth throughout the world, it also represents enormous opportunities for developing nations that can husband natural resources effectively. Although a few developed countries such as Norway, Canada, and the United States benefit greatly from raw material exports (oil, timber, and food, respectively), it is the developing world that relies most heavily on natural resources for domestic production and crucial foreign-currency earnings through export. Table 1.1 displays the proportions of export earnings for the countries examined in this book, as well as several others.

This table quickly dispels any illusions that the developing world has "graduated" from its reliance on natural-resource-based exports.[4] The countries with the largest populations, such as China, India, Indonesia, Brazil, and Mexico, have relatively lower portions of export earnings coming

Why Governments Waste Natural Resources

Table 1.1 Raw Material Proportion of Merchandise Exports, Selected Developing Countries, 1995 (unless otherwise indicated)

Country	Agriculture and Livestock	Forest Products	Seafood	Minerals, Metals, and Fertilizer	Hydrocarbons	Total Raw Materials
Algeria	—[a]	—	—	—	96%	98%
Argentina	52%	—	4%	3%	12	73
Bangladesh (1993)	6	—	9	3	—	19
Bolivia	23	6%	—	43	15	87
Brazil	29	5	—	17	3	55
Cameroon	34	24	—	9	29	97
Central African Republic	21	3	—	69	—	93
Chile	17	13	6	51	2	89
China	8	—	2	6	4	20
Colombia	32	—	2	9	30	75
Costa Rica	64	—	5	2	—	72
Ecuador	33	2	20	2	38	95
Egypt	15	—	—	10	38	63
Ghana (1992)	27	10	—	53	2	93
Honduras	83	4	6	—	—	93
India	13	—	4	20	3	39
Indonesia	8	15	4	11	26	63
Kenya (1993)	57	—	2	7	9	75
Malaysia	9	9	—	2	8	28
Mexico	7	—	—	5	11	23
Morocco	17	—	16	14	14	63
Mozambique (1994)	33	2	46	3	10	95
Nicaragua	56	3	20	3	—	82
Pakistan	26	2	2	9	4	41
Paraguay	81	9	—	—	—	91
Peru	26	—	4	51	5	87
Philippines	11	—	3	6	2	22
Saudi Arabia (1993)	—	—	—	—	95	97
South Africa	8	3	—	25	11	49
Sri Lanka (1994)	20	2	2	8	—	33
Thailand	11	5	8	3	—	28
Trinidad and Tobago	5	—	—	7	59	70
Tunisia	8	—	—	10	12	32
Turkey	18	—	—	8	2	29
United Arab Emirates (1993)	5	—	—	36	6	48
Uruguay	63	2	4	—	—	71
Venezuela	2	—	—	8	78	88
Zambia (1993)	4	—	—	91	—	95
Zimbabwe	49	2	—	25	2	78

Source: Calculated from 1997 figures provided by the United Nations International Trade Centre (UN Conference on Trade and Development and General Agreement on Tariffs and Trade), "International Trade Statistics: Exports for Country," Geneva, 1997.

[a] Dash signifies less than 2%.

from resource-based exports, in part because industries from developed countries have chosen the larger countries as the sites for labor-intensive, export-oriented manufacturing. Some of these countries, particularly China and India, have already largely exhausted their natural-resource-based exports. Even so, many countries, both big and small, still owe much of their production and exports to natural resources, going far beyond agricultural products.

Is Natural-Resource Wealth a Curse in Disguise?

What of the common complaint that dependence on natural resources relegates developing countries to the poverty of digging and hoeing, without the prospect of moving up to "more profitable" economic activities? Or the related worry that raw-material exports expose countries to economic instability? These concerns miss a crucial point: natural resources represent potential wealth; without the resources, developing nations would be even poorer. Many developed nations, including the United States, have prospered from renewable natural resources, as long as the land, labor, and capital required to exploit it have a higher rate of return than alternative uses of these financial, human, and land resources. If a resource is non-renewable, then the key task is to draw it down at a rate and in a manner that will provide the greatest investment potential to make the rest of the economy grow sustainably.

Chile is an excellent case in point. Through the 1980s, Chile's economy was still highly reliant on copper production for foreign exchange and government revenues. Copper constituted more than 50 percent of Chile's exports in 1976 and more than 40 percent all through the 1980s. Payments from the state copper company to the central government accounted for one-fifth of government revenues as late as 1991. However, copper wealth, combined with relatively good economic policies, has fueled strong economic growth and a diversification of the economy. Some of the diversification has involved other natural-resource-based sectors, such as fruit, timber, and wines, for which the Chilean economy is well suited, as indicated by the profitability of producing these commodities for domestic and international sales. Some of the diversification has been in manufacturing and the expansion of the service sector. Yet the Chilean government has avoided forcing the economy away from natural resources; the choice of economic activity has largely been left to the market signals of profitability. To be sure, historically Chile's copper (and before that, its nitrates) exposed the country to economic booms and busts, as the world prices for these materials have fluctuated during this century. However, there is no question that Chile has been better off than, say, Paraguay, which has far less natural-resource wealth, or Bolivia, whose gold and silver were depleted early on. Moreover, over the past two decades Chile has learned how to smooth out the impacts of changes in raw-material export prices. When Chilean copper prices are high, the additional revenues go into a stabilization fund that is available to offset lower government revenues when world copper prices are low. As a consequence, Chile has done a good job of managing both the resource and the proceeds from its export sale. No one in Chile is arguing that the nation should turn its back on the copper wealth, which still accounts for roughly 40 percent of export earnings.

A final complaint is the more subtle worry that natural-resource export booms can damage other economic sectors. An export boom generally increases the value of the local currency, making it more difficult for the nation's other exports to find markets.[5] In addition, the flood of export earnings can lead to inflation and rising demand for imported goods that displace domestically produced goods. Yet here again the culprit is not the export boom itself, but its faulty management and poor macroeconomic policies. Governments can support the sectors with long-term "postboom" potentials and keep portions of the windfall profits out of the local economy in order to smooth out disposable income. The problem of more valuable local currencies is real, but many governments have kept their currencies overvalued beyond the effects of the export boom and could do much more to rein in their currency values through general monetary policies.[6]

Finally, the stakes involved in natural-resource management go well beyond the economy to critical environmental considerations, particularly for renewable resources. More and more crucial links have been discovered between natural resources and the increasingly fragile world environment. Renewable resources have two faces: as raw materials and as elements of ecological systems. Trees are not only potential timber; they are also stores of carbon, nesting places for birds, and anchors for the soil. In some cases, natural resources are best left intact.

The Range of Faulty Resource Exploitation

My most fundamental premise is that poor resource practices are caused by government policies. To support this premise, I must show that government policies can induce or even force poor resource exploitation and that the damage done by these policies is significant. To determine how resource exploitation goes wrong, we obviously have to identify the types of exploitation problems. This is a big task, attempted in some depth in chapter 2. For now, some simple distinctions will give a better idea of the range of natural-resource policy failures.

Problems can occur in resource development, extraction, processing, or the use of the proceeds from resource exploitation. For resource development—the increase in the stock and availability of resources—the financial resources may be inadequate or excessive. Thus, large sums of money have been wasted on foolish petroleum and mineral exploration (e.g., Peruvian exploration in the Amazon is examined in some detail in this study). On the other hand, several state oil companies, most prominently those of Mexico and Venezuela, have been undercapitalized to the point of being unable to increase oil production and sales when world prices were unusually high. In addition, the wrong resource bases may have been developed. For example, in some cases land best suited for forest has been converted into pasture, or reforestation has been undertaken with unsuitable tree species. Resource development may also be ineffective and inefficient. Mexico's irrigation system has been particularly inefficient; most of the dams built in Sri Lanka's massive Mahaweli Dam scheme were structurally defective and therefore much less capable of providing the intended levels of irrigation and electricity.[7]

For resource extraction, the value of the resource can be squandered by extracting and selling it at the wrong times (e.g., when the prices are too low) or by extracting it with excessive losses (e.g., pumping oil out too rapidly leaves more in the ground; reckless timber harvesting can cause great damage to other trees). These are essentially conservation issues, assessed in terms of both getting the greatest economic value out of the resource endowment and preserving ecosystems.

For resource processing, inefficiencies can come about from both excessive costs (e.g., the huge energy costs of aluminum smelting, especially in old smelters) and loss of material (e.g., cutting timber in crude sawmills). In many instances, resource processing should not even be undertaken in particular countries, given their lack of comparative advantage and the inefficiency of their facilities.

Finally, for the use of resource proceeds, the problems arise when the resource exploiters fail to convert the natural-resource wealth into efficient investments and worthwhile consumption for the society. Squandering oil revenues on high-prestige but money-losing operations such as inefficient steel factories or helicopter fleets has been depressingly common. Investing forestry wealth into inefficient and unsustainable wood-processing industries has been equally common.

How Resource Policies Cause Faulty Resource Exploitation

What causes these problems? I will show in chapter 2 that the most immediate causes that induce poor resource exploitation by private exploiters are

- mispricing of the inputs and products of resource exploitation;
- poor information;
- vague property rights; and
- monopoly arrangements.

For state agencies involved in resource exploitation, these causes are also relevant, but so too are

- direct commands to over- or underexploit the resource base;
- under- or overcapitalization of the state agency;
- wasteful spending by state agencies that are not held accountable for the waste; and
- poor investment decisions by the state agencies.

Remarkably, these policy failures are strikingly common across the diverse types of natural resources. Beginning with the forestry sector, most governments have underpriced timber on public lands, ignoring the dictum that the government must "devise administrable instruments that enable the government-as-owner to appropriate as large a rent share as is practical" (Gillis 1988a, 85). The result has been reckless and excessive timber harvesting. In this book I will examine such cases in Brazil, Cameroon, Costa Rica, Honduras, Indonesia, and Malaysia. Excessive logging spurred by the failure of the government to charge the appropriate stumpage fee does have beneficiaries — typically the large-scale, commercial loggers — but the policy does avoidable damage to forests. The damage is avoidable in the sense that even if government officials are bent on indulging these beneficiaries, this could be done without destroying the natural-resource endowment.

In the face of deforestation, many governments have adopted so-called reforestation programs. In some cases these schemes actually result in deforestation because of overpricing of reforestation subsidies. In Indonesia the so-called reforestation fund turned out to be a slush fund for highly questionable investments outside the forestry sector, with virtually no contribution to reforestation; it has actually encouraged a wasteful form of logging (Gillis 1988a, 61–62).

Another clearly unsound forestry policy found in many developing countries is the banning of raw-log exports, which can be viewed as an extreme measure to reduce the price of timber for domestic buyers. The rationalization is typically that the country's economy would benefit by stimulating a "downstream" industry of sawmills, plywood factories, and furniture manufacturing. A wood-products industry based on a captured domestic timber supply is vulnerable to both inefficiency and supply shortages of raw timber. Log-export bans in many other countries have had similarly poor consequences.

In the oil sector, governments have also underpriced the basic resource by failing to charge royalties for state companies' access to the oil deposits. In addition, state enterprises entrusted with petroleum production and export have suffered from a combination of undercapitalization and poor investment of oil proceeds. R. M. Auty (1990) found that all eight oil-exporting countries included in his study had quite disappointing experiences with resource-based industrialization. The oil companies themselves often absorb large portions of the oil wealth through their exorbitant wages, salaries, bonuses, and plush facilities. For their part, governments intent on spending oil revenues instead of raising taxes, and worried that state enterprises will capture the oil surplus for their workers and managers, have often raided state oil companies' investment funds. This provokes the state companies to hide their capital, often in low-yielding investments, thus weakening the companies' capacity to increase production when world prices are high. Even the relatively competent Venezuelan state oil company PDVSA has had limited capitalization for oil exploration and production within Venezuela, thus limiting Venezuela's ability to sell oil when world oil prices are high, and has invested in very expensive and controversial refining and marketing ventures overseas. Other state oil companies, in Indonesia, Mexico, Nigeria, and Peru, have had similar — and usually worse — performance in investment choices and inefficiency.

Artificially low domestic prices of petroleum products, most importantly gasoline, diesel, and kerosene, have also undermined the growth potential of oil-rich nations. Excessive consumption of these products wastes petroleum that could be exported to earn foreign exchange. Making matters worse, subsidized energy encourages inefficient, energy-squandering industries and even encourages air pollution by reducing the incentives to conserve fuel and replace old vehicles.

In the minerals sector, similar problems of misinvestment abound, reflecting battles between the enterprise and the government rather than sound economic or employment strategies. State mining enterprises are often highly inefficient and sometimes exploit unproductive deposits. I will explore how these actions produce the perverse outcome of reducing national wealth through resource exploitation. State enterprises in mineral exploitation are also often constrained by the same limitations on their production and capitalization plans as on state oil companies. Even the enormous and technically competent Chilean National Copper Corporation (Codelco) has been hemmed in by government restrictions on its investment budget and even on the deposits it has been allowed to exploit.

Mineral processing has often extended into uneconomical activities because government officials have tried to promote regional development, income transfers, and prestige of heavy industry. Many iron ore and aluminum ventures were launched in the cheap-energy era and have been kept alive only through costly subsidies. The enormous Brazilian state mining conglomerate CVRD has remained "profitable" only through a 30 percent subsidy on fuel oil provided by other state enterprises and special tax-treatment subsidies for its operations in economically depressed areas.

If we focus on agricultural and grazing land as a resource, it is easy to identify serious problems of overuse and inadequate efforts to reduce soil erosion (Blaikie 1985). Insecure property rights on what should be communal or private lands encourage overexploitation by rich and poor alike. The overgrazing of cattle has denuded hills and valleys wherever governments have undercharged for grazing fees on public lands.

Water resources have suffered disastrously from underpricing. Virtually free irrigation water has led to massive depletion of aquifers, rivers, and lakes, from Mexico to Central Asia. The Aral Sea, once crucial for the nations of Central Asia, has been depleted by three-fourths of its 1960 volume to irrigate cotton fields and other agricultural ventures that would not be the least bit profitable were it not for the failure of the government to impose water charges. In addition, squandering fiscal resources on large dams has been the result of both underpricing (i.e., the demand for water is very high when recipients know that they do not have to pay for either the construction or the operations of the major irrigation system) and investment decisions made with little regard for the rate of return. Indeed, governments often favor expensive "major irrigation" over minor irrigation despite the greater efficiency that ponds, wells, and tanks often hold over dams and canals (Ascher and Healy 1990). Farmers who receive cheap water certainly benefit, but the overall economy suffers more.

What do these examples demonstrate? First, they show that governments frequently violate fundamental principles of sound natural-resource policy. Second, there is no shortage of cases in which the overall costs to society exceed the benefits for particular individuals or groups; in many cases the government does have the financial capacity to compensate those who would lose the benefits of unsound resource exploitation.

Are Natural-Resource Policy Failures Significant?

Demonstrating that natural resources remain important for developing countries, and that policies can induce poor resource practices, still does not establish that unsound resource policies in fact do account for significant damage. We know that there is rampant waste of forests, marshes, soil, oil, minerals, water, wildlife, and fish, but that does not tell us to what degree unsound policies are to blame. Many other factors might be involved: greed or desperation by private actors with access to natural resources, poor private choices in converting land uses, bad luck in developing and extracting resources that subsequently suffer price collapses, or unanticipated ecosystem collapses following the extraction of a particular resource. Many observers, including government officials and conservation activists, have condemned local people for slash-and-burn agriculture, excessive hunting and overfishing, destructive mining, overgrazing, and so on. Even if government officials wish to stop these behaviors, they may not have the capacity or the legal standing to do so. It is therefore possible that natural resources can be squandered without policy failures.

Yet there is ample evidence that resource policy failures cost governments and societies hundreds of millions of dollars. A World Resources Institute study by Mark Kosmo (1987, 34) examined energy pricing in the mid-1980s, which was the heyday of the cheap-energy industrialization strategy. Kosmo showed that unwarranted energy subsidies cost the Chinese government more than $15 billion annually, the Mexican government $5 billion, the Nigerian government $4 billion, the Egyptian government $3 billion, and the Venezuelan government nearly $2 billion. If the governments had recovered the costs of providing energy, they could have saved themselves and their economies the trouble of bringing in revenues through higher taxes or inflationary spending. Furthermore, because low energy prices encourage greater energy consumption, the oil-exporting countries will run out of oil earlier than they otherwise would have. Today Nigeria and Mexico are much closer to becoming net oil importers than if domestic gasoline and diesel prices had been allowed to reach market levels.

In the oil-rich countries, state enterprises dominate the oil sectors. Because these enterprises are formally creatures of their central governments, their practices must all be considered as government policies. Therefore, governments are ultimately responsible for their own state oil enterprises often being notoriously inefficient and corrupt and squandering their earnings on gold-plated operations, excess employees, and unprofitable investments.

For the forestry sector, the combination of appropriating forest lands from traditional small-scale forest users, and then underpricing the timber extracted by commercial loggers, has contributed greatly to deforestation and forest degradation that have cut off economic opportunities. Cheap timber, whether because of low royalties or the government's failure to prevent illegal logging, encourages far more cutting than is appropriate for society's welfare. In addition, many governments have adopted misguided policies of trying to strengthen wood-products industries by banning the export of raw timber, with the effect of forcing many timber companies into timber processing with inefficient sawmills and factories. This has led to enormous waste of timber, which in many instances could have been exported more profitably in its raw form. It has also led to collapses in the wood-processing operations when forest depletion strangled the supply to the mills and factories. For many countries, especially in Southeast Asia and West Africa, the timber boom that could have been extended into the twenty-first century is already over or nearly so. In Thailand, for example, a complete ban on timber cutting was imposed in 1989, after the government discovered how rapidly deforestation had progressed. From the early 1980s to the early 1990s, Thailand lost nearly 14 percent of its forest and woodland, Cambodia and Laos 11 percent, and the Philippines 9 percent (World Resources Institute 1996, 217). The economic impact is much greater than these figures indicate, because the most valuable trees are usually the first to be cut, leaving other areas still classified as forests, but with far less economic potential or capacity to maintain the ecological systems. Severe shortages of timber have already occurred in Indonesia's Sumatra, where investments in the wood-processing industry have been very high. Many logging companies that have been leaving Southeast Asia and West Africa are now moving to Central Africa, where the risk of excessive deforestation and wildlife habitat destruction has risen rapidly. In all these cases, governments face declining opportunities for export earnings and employment.

The deterioration of irrigation systems is also caused primarily by policy failures: a combination of overbuilding major irrigation systems (dams and canals) and underpricing water and electricity produced by these systems. In countries like Mexico, Sri Lanka, and the Central Asian republics, the deterioration of major irrigation systems has contributed greatly to agricultural decline and government deficits.[8]

Agricultural deterioration generally occurs at the hands of farmers rather than the government directly. When farmers neglect soils and terracing, it is often because governments fail to guarantee that the farmers can benefit from their own hard work and investments. When farmers choose inappropriate crops or livestock, or overuse fertilizers, pesticides, and water, it is often because they were induced to do so through unwise government subsidies for unproductive agricultural ventures. When farmers abandon their land, it often reflects the collapse of ventures despite the subsidies or the impact of heavy taxes on agricultural activities.

A country-by-country assessment also demonstrates how costly natural-resource policy failures can be. The following examples relate to the cases examined in this book:

- In Costa Rica, low royalties and very lax enforcement of forest regulations, combined with government incentives to convert forests into pasture, contributed strongly to renewable resource losses in the 1970s and 1980s. During this period, the total losses amounted to more than $4 billion (in a country with a population of only 3.3 million people), reducing the GDP growth by 1.5 to 2.0 percentage points a year, or roughly 25–30 percent of Costa Rica's potential economic growth (Solórzano et al. 1991, 4–5).
- Indonesia's forestry policies cost the economy more than $400 million in 1981–82, when the government banned the export of raw logs. The 1979 export earnings level was not restored until the late 1980s (Gillis 1988a, 95–97; Schwarz 1989, 86). The private sector has retained as much as $1.2 billion a year of timber value that should have gone to the central treasury;[9] some considerable but unknown proportion of this windfall was removed from the Indonesian economy as the private loggers diversified their holdings internationally.
- In Malaysia, a 1994 audit of the Sabah state forestry organization revealed that more than $1 billion was missing from its accounts (*New Straits Times* 1996b).
- In Honduras, the state forestry enterprise's wood-processing ventures left it with debts of $240 million by the late 1980s, with virtually no effective capacity to process timber (Pickles 1989, 42–43).
- In Brazil, the government's subsidies for converting Amazonian forest lands into ranches, amounting to $700 million, were practically a total loss, not to speak of the 4 million deforested hectares (Mahar 1989, 16; Binswanger 1991, 828).
- In Ghana, government taxation during the 1970s and early 1980s reduced the production of cocoa, Ghana's most important export crop and source of government revenues, to one-fifth of its mid-1960s level (Pratt 1990, 128).
- In Nigeria, a 1992 World Bank–UN Development Programme study assessed the economic and financial losses from poor investments, inappro-

priate domestic pricing, and corruption in the oil sector at $2.5 billion per year (*Newswatch* 1993, 27). Oil subsidies were costing the Nigerian treasury $1.9 billion annually in the early 1990s (ESMAP 1993, xix). Oil smuggling alone cost the country revenues of roughly $1 billion a year in the mid-1980s (*Oil Daily* 1984, 10).

- Indonesia's state oil company, through reckless investments both within and outside the oil sector, ran up a foreign debt of $10.5 billion in the mid-1970s, which exceeded the government's own debt by more than $2 billion and virtually bankrupted the government.

- In Peru, by the late 1970s the state oil company was bankrupt after pursuing highly questionable Amazonian explorations, leaving the government to refinance a foreign debt of nearly $1 billion. The very costly Amazonian oil pipeline proceeded even though foreign investors rejected it as a losing proposition.

- In Venezuela, highly controversial overseas investments amounting to more than $1 billion during the 1980s were undertaken by the state oil company, in reaction to government efforts to raid its investment fund. A very low domestic gasoline price not only denies the government $2 billion in revenues annually but also perpetuates an aging vehicle fleet that worsens Venezuela's air pollution.

- In Mexico, as much as 85 percent of the contracts of the state oil company in the 1980s were awarded illegally without competitive bidding (Ramírez 1981). One estimate of the discrepancies within the enterprise's own oil-sales accounts was more than $3.5 billion for 1980 alone. Despite earlier predictions that the state company would help to reduce Mexico's foreign debt, its own debt reached $25 billion by the end of 1982 (Guzman 1988a, 396–97), strongly contributing to Mexico's financial collapse. At roughly the same time, one error in neglecting to lower Mexico's international oil price cost the country $1 billion in forgone oil sales (Teichman 188, 108).

- In Chile, the decision made in the 1980s to ban the state copper company from exploiting new deposits within its own holdings, in favor of multinational exploitation, may have cost the Chilean economy more than $300 million annually from the mid-1980s through the year 2000 (Tironi and Grupo de Minería CED 1985, 198).

- The Indian government has kept a copper-mining operation going despite uneconomical ore grades, spending more than $40 million a year in wages and salaries to produce copper at nearly twice the world price. Even though the state copper enterprise was the third largest money-losing public enterprise in India by 1980, the government made it "profitable" by charging higher copper prices for both imported and domestic copper, with major distortions to the Indian economy.

- The Nigerian steel facility at Ajaokuta absorbed over $3 billion beginning in the early 1980s and yet had not reached full production by the early 1990s (Auty 1990, 188–89; 232–33).

THE PUZZLES

This widespread abuse of natural resources in developing countries poses many perplexing riddles. The first and most obvious question is why governments are so cavalier about how natural resources are developed and extracted, even though the prosperity and growth of many nations still depend on sound resource exploitation. In many cases these problems jeopardize what is clearly the nation's major opportunity to climb into higher levels of prosperity.

The second puzzle is why governments often sacrifice their own earnings by adopting resource policies and practices that provoke wasteful resource exploitation and divert money from their central treasuries. Much has been made of the money-grabbing tendencies of governments. Indeed, some theories assume that government officials can best be understood by assuming that their top priority is to maximize the revenues that can be extracted from the economy. And yet governments chronically ignore the first principle of resource economics for public lands, namely, that they should charge the users the full value of the resources they extract, lest the users overexploit "cheap" resources. It is rare for governments to try to collect as much as half of the value of the resources taken by others from public lands.

The third puzzle is why state organizations involved in resource exploitation tend to be so complex in structure and operation. For example, the Peruvian state mining enterprise Centromin was a part owner of the mixed state-and-private mining company Mineroperú. Mineroperú, in turn, was a part owner of Centromin (Gallegos 1985, 43–44). The organization chart of Peru's state mining sector looked more like a puzzle maze than a coherent corporate structure, and profit accounting was virtually arbitrary. Such complicated state enterprise arrangements greatly compromise transparency and accountability. Government officials lose control over the very institutions they depend on for huge fiscal resources. What functions does this very costly and seemingly gratuitous complexity serve?

A fourth and closely related puzzle is why state enterprises in the natural-resources sector have been permitted so much autonomy — often gained informally through the lack of transparency and accountability — from the government agencies that have formal control. In Mexico, Nigeria, and Venezuela, for example, the state oil company has been regarded as "the state within the state." In Chile and Zambia, the same is said of the state copper company. At various times either these enterprises operated with considerable autonomy from the government, despite the government's formal control, or else the government has had to strangle the enterprise's profit-making activities in order to reassert government control.

The fifth, and related, puzzle is why, despite the high autonomy that state resource enterprises have often enjoyed, many governments have kept their own state enterprises severely undercapitalized. It would seem that governments should be intent on keeping key state resource industries primed to increase production to take advantage of sudden increases in world prices. This is particularly true in the oil and mining sectors, where major price fluctuations are not uncommon.[10] Yet even as they squander money on excess labor and investments of their own proceeds outside of the oil and mining sectors, many state oil and mining companies lack the investment budgets that would permit them to operate effectively within the oil or mining sectors, especially to increase production in response to high export prices. Some, like Mexico's notorious oil company PEMEX, have been saddled with enormous foreign debts while still lacking sufficient capital.

The sixth puzzle relates to the tendency of governments to ignore highly relevant understandings from natural and social sciences regarding resource exploitation and its consequences. If knowledge is power, it is striking how often governments, seemingly willfully, ignore scientific knowledge. For example, Indonesian logging rules ignore the insight that Indonesia's most important tree species regenerate better when they are not thinned through selective logging. Similarly, for many years, agronomists and human ecologists have noted that shifting cultivation (also known as "swidden agriculture" or "slash-and-burn" agriculture) can be sustainable, as long as local people retain sufficient range to allow cultivated areas to regenerate before the next round of cultivation. As we will see, this knowledge has been ignored by governments in Brazil, Indonesia, and Malaysia, at great cost to the welfare of the small-scale agriculturalists who practice shifting cultivation.

How can we solve these puzzles? The most superficial level of explanation is that the natural-resource exploiters are to blame. The diagnosis is that commercial loggers cut too many trees; forest peoples burn them to make way for unsustainable agriculture; farmers waste water; fishermen overfish; state workers in mines and oil fields are lazy or incompetent. Policies based on this naive diagnosis are typically both punitive and counterproductive. Vast forest areas have been wrenched away from local people by governments claiming that they were protecting the forests from local people's irresponsibility. Fishing grounds have been declared off limits; hunting has been banned even in areas where local people depend on it heavily for their protein. In many developing countries, the victims of these "protective" policies are among the poorest, eking out their living in the forests, on the rivers, or scratching minerals from the ground. Governments regularly browbeat or coerce farmers, loggers, hunters, miners, oil workers, rubber tappers, fishers, and other resource users to comply with regulations, work harder, extract less or to get them to stay away from lands that their families had used for generations.

A deeper diagnosis recognizes that government policies are flawed, and that these policies encourage or even drive resource exploiters into unsustainable resource exploitation. But the conventional wisdom that is usually associated with this diagnosis is simply that unsound natural-resource policies and practices grow out of the greed or incompetence of the government and state officials who oversee both private and public resource exploitation.

However, the most basic insight of the cases reviewed in this book is that to understand the failures within the natural-resource sector, we have to look at government strategies directed to problems and objectives far beyond the natural-resource sector.

Consider the fact that the Indonesian state aircraft industry is financed through the Forestry Ministry's reforestation fund, collected from commercial logging operations. These payments by commercial loggers, which were never refunded for actual reforestation, would not have been possible were it not for the excessively low royalties that the loggers paid to the government. These low royalties, as we will see, have been a major cause of excessive logging in Indonesia. Yet what resource expert would think, as a matter of principle, that the problem lies in the financing of an aerospace industry?

The Theory

For the sake of clarity, my general theory to account for governments' faulty natural-resource policies is presented here as a series of simple propositions, with accompanying definitions and commentaries.

Motives

1. High-level government and state officials may have different economic objectives. These include

- promoting particular development projects;
- distributing or redistributing economic benefits, either to broad population groups or to specific individuals or families; and
- enhancing the overall level of central treasury financial resources.

Commentary. Note that I am not proposing that "governments have objectives," because governments are not actors; they consist of many people and institutions, often with conflicting objectives. Indeed, an important premise of the theory is that many actions related to resource exploitation arise from the conflicts among government officials.

Note also that, as obvious as this proposition may seem to most readers, some approaches assume that adequate explanations and predictions can be based on the presumption that government officials have a single motive, such as attaining and staying in office or maximizing agency revenues. In addition to these economic motives, political ones must be added:

2. High-level government and state officials may have different political objectives. These include

- gaining greater control over the uses of financial resources, by
  - enhancing the standing and power of the particular ministry, agency, or state enterprise controlled by the particular officials;
- reducing the political costs of pursuing any of the objectives listed above; and
- gaining the cooperation of other private or public actors in pursuing any of the economic or political objectives.

Commentary. Gaining control over the uses of financial resources goes well beyond capturing these resources for the officials' own use. In other words, even if government officials are not interested in personal financial gain, they still may struggle mightily to be able to determine how government and state financial resources will be directed.

3. Officials within the same government will have some differences in objectives and priorities.

Commentary. Governments are not monolithic. Even governments dominated by a single political party will have officials with different outlooks and values. In addition, the division of labor within government — for example, transport ministries look after road-building, education ministries after schools and teachers — leads to different priorities among officials who otherwise would be like-minded. The transport minister has to make transportation his or her main priority. However, some governments are certainly more divided than others, and some allow for more cooperation and compromise among ministries and agencies.

Resources

4. The financial resources involved in natural-resource exploitation go well beyond natural-resource wealth. They include:

- central treasury funds — often devoted to subsidizing resource development;
- funds of resource extractors — often captured by the government through taxation or through the requirement that the output be purchased by the government at low prices, and often redirected to consumers or downstream producers by government price ceilings;
- funds of consumers — often captured by the government through high prices on state-produced resources;
- international loans — often borrowed by state resource enterprises; and
- grants from other governments, international organizations, and international nongovernmental organizations — often devoted to resource development and conservation.

Commentary. As important as natural-resource wealth is for many countries, resource exploitation taps into many additional sources of wealth. For example, in addition to the depreciation of Costa Rica's natural resources, a misguided program enacted in the 1980s gave tax credits to companies that replanted forest areas. As we will see in chapter 5, this reforestation-incentive program was a major failure. With very little reforestation resulting from this program, in effect it drew funds out of the central treasury to enrich the companies taking advantage of the incentives. During various points in Mexico's checkered history of oil production, the soundness of PEMEX's operations has been almost secondary to the issue of how much foreign capital the state company could borrow. For Cameroon, the national park initiative has been motivated as much to attract grants from international environmental organizations and conservation-minded foreign aid agencies as it has been to promote conservation per se.

The multiplicity of financial sources also makes the exploitation of natural resources much more complicated. Resource economists like to think that the main task is to get the highest return on resource development and extraction. However, the economic challenge is much broader: extracting the right amount of wealth from resource exploiters, setting output prices to encourage economic efficiency, using resource wealth wisely, borrowing off the resource endowment and using the loans efficiently for long-term economic growth, finding the best means of taxing (which may or may not involve taxing natural-resource outputs), and sometimes even putting foreign aid to best use.

Logic of Indirection

5. In some governments more than others, objectives and priorities are not resolved at the highest (e.g., cabinet and legislative) levels. Therefore, government and state officials often try to achieve their objectives through indirect measures, knowing that other officials would try to block direct measures.

Commentary. In short, disunity within government provokes efforts to circumvent the opposition of other government officials.

6. When high-level government officials wish to pursue objectives opposed by other officials, they will seek alternative means to finance the pursuit of these objectives.

7. Manipulations of the natural-resource exploitation process often provide opportunities for low-visibility financing of investments and income transfers.

Commentary. Natural-resource exploitation is typically carried out in areas far removed from major population centers, and it is very difficult for outsiders to have enough information to translate physical characteristics of resource exploitation into economic implications. For example, the value of timber cannot be easily calculated without detailed information on the species composition of particular forest stands, and the rates of timber harvesting are extremely difficult to determine by anyone outside of the logging company. Illegal logging is frequently difficult to monitor unless the government takes special measures. Mining and fishing production, and the value of their output, are also very difficult to gauge from afar. In Chile, for example, many government officials involved in mining policy were apparently unaware of the illegal development of a copper mining site by the government's own state copper company. These manipulations require a certain degree of ignorance on the part of other actors. Therefore, the information vacuum typical of natural-resource exploitation is very attractive. Compare the relative transparency of industrial policy, involving well-organized labor unions and owner groups continually scrutinizing wage levels, taxes, utility prices, and other factors.

8. Often the natural-resource exploitation process is particularly convenient for manipulation, because of the low political costs of distorting this process:

- the manipulations appear to be of low redistributive impact;
- the current losers from resource distortions are often the poor, with few political resources to exact money or revenge for the damages;
- the future losers are future generations, who are typically even less powerful than the poor; and

- some natural-resource manipulations appear, falsely, to be pro-development and pro-conservation.

Commentary. Natural-resource manipulation typically has lower political costs than distorting other economic activities. This is due in part to the low visibility already mentioned. Yet it is reinforced by the false presumption that natural-resource exploitation is not a matter of winners and losers. This is rooted in the image of natural-resource wealth springing from the earth without human loss or cost. For the benefits of resource exploitation to end up in the hands of particular groups therefore often lacks the cruel image of redistribution that other economic transfers create. This distinction is largely an illusion: one group's benefits from resource wealth certainly represent a forgone opportunity for other groups. Yet the enrichment of particular groups from the exploitation of natural resources, of uncertain value in a remote area of the country, is generally very different from the openly combative issues such as tax policy, central government spending, or wage policy.

The political costs are also low because the losers from poor resource exploitation are often economically marginal people who have little voice to protest the manipulations, as well as the future generations who will suffer the loss of resource wealth and healthy ecosystems. Sites of natural-resource exploitation (with the exception of conventional farming) tend to be geographically and economically marginal areas that have become the refuge for similarly marginal groups, often of minority ethnicity. In these areas, property or user rights tend to be poorly defined or have passed into state control. Therefore, protests against resource abuses are stymied by the legal weakness of such claims, in addition to the political marginality of the protesters. Similarly, insofar as the cause of future generations is weakly defended by today's political actors, resource depletion and other squandered opportunities entail lower political risk for officials than do policies that extract benefits from current generations.

The final reason why programmatic goals are often pursued through natural-resource manipulations is that the manipulations can often be passed off as healthy for the economy, the environment, and the society, despite their actual damage. Thus, reforestation programs often have great panache, and it is a rare politician who is willing to go on record as opposing reforestation, even though some reforestation programs have had disastrous consequences. By the same token, inefficient domestic resource processing has often been conveyed successfully as a great contribution to national economic development because processing "adds value" to products before they are exported. However, the mere fact that processed goods can be sold at a higher price than their raw materials does not make the processing profitable, let alone ensure an economic return as high as alternative activities. Poor resource policies dressed up as "green policies" or "value-added policies" have often allowed government officials to pursue ulterior motives while gaining political credit. While illegal or excessive resource extraction is typically done furtively, unsound resource development and processing are often done with great fanfare because of misconceptions of soundness.

9. Therefore, government officials are often willing to resort to unsound manipulations of the natural-resource exploitation process in order to finance objectives that would otherwise risk being blocked by other government officials or that could not be pursued directly without high political costs.

10. When government officials wish to distribute economic benefits with low accountability to those who do not benefit, they will seek low-visibility mechanisms. Government officials also seek low-visibility income-transfer mechanisms to reward specific allies outside of the government, in exchange for their cooperation in achieving the official's objectives.

Commentary. Programmatic income redistribution (i.e., income redistribution for its own sake) is frequently an objective of particular government officials, but it obviously runs the risk of opposition from groups that lose in the transfers. Therefore, redistribution through devious natural-resource exploitation holds out the hope that other officials and the losing groups will not be able to mobilize against these actions.

The other type of redistribution, designed to reward cooperative groups, is based on exchanges frequently termed "rent-seeking behavior."[11] Government officials provide opportunities for private-sector actors to gain excess profits (rents) by restricting competition or by simply giving away assets. In order to qualify for (and maintain) such rents, the private actors provide political support, money, or cooperation to the officials who determine who qualifies.

11. False claims about the impacts of resource-exploitation strategies, and unnecessary complexity, are among the tactics used to reduce transparency and therefore accountability.

Commentary. The means for reducing transparency and visibility are many, as one would expect for strategies that need to keep at least one step ahead of the efforts of others to understand what is going on. Government officials often invoke specious positive benefits to justify inappropriate resource policies. For example, a scheme to wrest logging rights from local, traditional forest users may be couched in conservationist rhetoric, even though certain government officials intend to hand out logging concessions soon thereafter. Or continued exploitation of unproductive mineral deposits may be defended in the name of national security through an argument that such production is essential for the country even if ample supplies could be stockpiled. Transparency is also reduced by making the financing and operations of resource exploitation so complex that the manipulations will be obscure to those who might oppose them.

12. Because of the general advantages of being able to direct financial flows to achieve the various policy objectives outlined above, government officials struggle among themselves, across different ministries, agencies and enterprises, to control these flows.

Commentary. The point here is that the general power of individual government officials and their units is determined in part by their control over allocating natural-resource wealth and the other financial flows involved in resource exploitation. In other words, quite apart from having different programmatic objectives, agencies struggle with one another for the discretionary power in and of itself.

Note that this is not the same as saying that officials wish to capture resource wealth for themselves. They may regard the power to assign resources to others as far more compelling than enriching themselves or their families and friends. While some government officials obviously do try to enrich themselves, in general the struggle over who controls the resource-related financial flows is an issue of power and the capacity to accomplish policy goals. It is, therefore, an aspect of *bureaucratic politics*, in which different government units compete for standing and influence by trying to wrest control over resource exploitation away from other government (or state) units.

Very often this struggle pits the central government's fiscal units — the ministries and agencies directly involved in the central budgetary process — against sectoral ministries and agencies (such as the Forestry Ministry or the Ministry of Transport) and decentralized agencies and enterprises (such as regional development authorities or state oil companies). Therefore, in many cases a crucial issue is whether the natural-resource wealth extracted from government-controlled lands or waters is channeled into the central treasury. Government policies and state control over natural-resource exploitation are often beyond the jurisdiction of the conventional budget authorities, although budget authorities often try to capture control. Therefore, if a government official or agency wishes to move financial resources around in ways that the officials of the Finance Ministry, the planning agency, and the budget office oppose, then the manipulation of natural-resource exploitation provides an alternative channel.

From the perspective of officials involved in the government's overall budget process, better investment and distributional decisions can be made at this highest and most central point. They often argue that only the central budget process can identify and pursue the most economically productive and socially worthwhile investments across the entire country. They typically see officials from specific sectoral ministries, decentralized agencies, and state enterprises as short-sighted in their preoccupations with their own activities. Officials from these sectoral and decentralized units counter that the financial ministries are often more politicized, making decisions on the basis of partisan calculations rather than societal welfare. Critics of central fiscal control also argue that the central government is further removed from the reality of the people and the specific conditions of particular localities. The officials of sectoral ministries, decentralized agencies, and state enterprises often resent the micro-managing that central budget authorities impose on their operations, as well as the "confiscation" of funds by the central treasury.

13. Officials of government and state natural-resource units will sometimes sacrifice sound practices in order to fend off the efforts of other units to gain control over their operations and the disposition of financial flows.

Commentary. This proposition clarifies that the intragovernmental struggle may trigger a whole series of defensive measures at the cost of unsound resource policies and practices. For example, a state oil or mining company that sees the Finance Ministry trying to capture the enterprise's investment fund may rush to put the money out of reach of the ministry by making hasty purchases of overseas assets.

14. In order to enhance their capacity to manipulate natural-resource exploitation for all the purposes listed above, government officials often appropriate resource-ownership and user rights from private or communal owners.

Commentary. Taking over control of natural resources not only signifies a redistribution of wealth from the former owners/users to the government's coffers, but also opens up these opportunities for maneuvering through natural-resource exploitation. Natural-resource confiscation is thus not just a matter of "protecting" the resources from the people; nor is it just a matter of government grasping. Sometimes it is a step toward playing the resource-manipulation game.

Perverse Strategies Emerging from These Dynamics

15. Therefore, government officials will sometimes induce and engage in unsound natural-resource exploitation strategically in order to pursue the following ends:

(Programmatic Strategies)

a. financing controversial development programs;
b. providing economic benefits for particular groups, areas or individuals;
c. capturing natural-resource rents for the central treasury;

(Political Strategies)

d. creating rent-seeking opportunities in order to gain private-actor cooperation in pursuing other objectives;
e. capturing and maintaining discretion over the financial flows involved in
   resource exploitation, at the expense of other government or state agencies;
   and
f. evading accountability through reliance on low-visibility resource maneuvers.

Commentary. These six strategies are the heart of our explanation for
why governments sacrifice the soundness of natural-resource exploitation
to pursue programmatic and political objectives. The strategies are often
deliberate, even if the negative consequences for natural resources are unintended or even unanticipated side effects. For example, a government
official may intentionally undercharge a particular group for access to resources on public lands, in order to benefit that group. In other cases,
resource policy failures may arise for other reasons, but still may further
one or more of the six strategies, and for that reason be allowed to persist.
For example, the charge for access to public-lands resources may start out
at the right level, but decline because of inflation without the relevant
government officials adjusting the royalties to the appropriate level. In
those cases, the *perpetuation* of the resource policy failure is a passive but
nonetheless important way of pursuing the strategy.

It is useful to note that the six strategies can be separated into *programmatic* strategies and *political* strategies. Government officials can manipulate
natural-resource exploitation to further their developmental, distributive,
and revenue-raising programs; they can also try to increase their political
power. Of course, the political strategies can enhance the officials' efforts to
pursue their favored programs, but they can also strengthen the officials'
overall power and political security.

Much of the analysis of subsequent chapters will explore how these
strategies are pursued and how they can be thwarted.

Why a Complicated Theory of Manipulation Is Necessary

The theory outlined above tries to connect political conditions, particularly intragovernmental political conditions, to financial maneuvers;

these financial maneuvers to resource policies that serve a multiplicity of possible strategies; and these policies to poor resources practices by both the state and private resource exploiters. Some might regard this model as unnecessarily complicated, for three reasons.

First, some observers have been struck by the importance of *political patronage* as an explanation for poor natural-resource policies. In particular, they see government actions that allow or permit the overexploitation of timber, oil, minerals, soils, and water as a straightforward way for a government to reward its politically powerful supporters (Blaikie 1985; Broad 1995; Hecht 1984; Hecht 1992; Ross 1996; Sanderson 1986; Teichman 1988; Utting 1993). Some observers regard the government's willingness to give resource rents benefits to powerful groups as a sign of weakness; the state is weak if it needs to curry favor by sacrificing sound resource exploitation to maintain its support (Broad 1995). Others view the capacity of government officials to hand out natural-resource-based economic benefits as an instrument that contributes to their power. Regardless of which diagnosis is drawn from observing the use of resource rents as political patronage, these interpretations typically pursue the question of why governments are willing or compelled to engage in this sort of exchange. Our approach does not dispute that political patronage is one of the motives of natural-resource giveaways: the rent-seeking strategy encompasses that motive. Rather, I argue that currying political support through patronage is only one of several rationales for granting privileges to private resource exploiters to abuse natural resources. I also note that many other mechanisms undermine natural-resource soundness beyond allowing private actors to overexploit natural resources, whether to provide political patronage or not. And, most importantly, I emphasize the importance of finding out why government officials find it necessary or convenient to exchange natural-resource rents for the support and cooperation of the privileged recipients. Gaining political support and cooperation is not just an end in itself. Thus, instead of defining the next question as "What conditions determine whether the government will sacrifice natural resources to enrich the politically powerful?" I believe that it is more useful to ask, "What motives, in addition to the obvious need to stay in power, are prompting government officials to exchange resource-based benefits for the cooperation of the recipients?" In short, because of the multiplicity of programmatic as well as political motives that drive resource manipulations, political patronage and the resulting cooperation are best viewed as means as well as ends.

Second, the theory may seem to be an overly elaborate way of explaining what can be much more simply dismissed as ignorance, incapacity, or incompetence. A common refrain, heard from officials from both developing and developed countries, is that poor countries often lack the information, expertise, and administrative capacity to manage natural resources effectively. However, these failings are quite unsatisfying as fundamental explanations, even though resource experts frequently presume that policymakers (particularly in developing countries) simply do not know any better, and therefore simply need to be educated. Ignorance and weak capacity are, to a significant degree, the *outcomes* of policy. As Michael Dove (1983) has pointed out very elegantly, ignorance may well be a strategy and a deliberate outcome of government policy designed to allow certain government officials to evade the criticism they might face if correct information and theory were accepted.[12] When we focus on the most important natural resources, involving millions or even billions of dollars of resource rent, it is rarely plausible that top government officials would not devote sufficient attention and expertise to understanding the implications of natural-resource policy options.

Similarly, it has become almost trite to point out that the administrative capacity to implement resource-use regulations is typically very weak in developing countries. The implicit recommendation is "institutional strengthening" — now part of many international and bilateral foreign assistance projects. Yet administrative weakness often grows out of *decisions* to underfund particular agencies, to assign substandard personnel to those agencies, and sometimes to burden these agencies with cumbersome bureaucratic requirements before they can take action. The classic example is the nearly worldwide tendency of governments to underbudget their forestry agencies, even as they publicly lament the high incidence of illegal logging as if it were an inevitable consequence of the inability of low-income countries to enforce forestry regulations. In short, we can view much of ignorance, incompetence, and administrative weakness as a policy failure rather than as an inevitable given.

The third, "simpler," explanation for natural-resource policy failures is the obsolescence of formerly sound policies in the face of contextual changes. Here, again, it is certainly true that good policies can become inappropriate. Once decision-making routines, job descriptions, and bureaucratic power have developed around a given policy, it may be more difficult to change that policy, and policymakers pursuing their individual and institutional interests may lack the incentive to alter their suboptimal practices. For example, a land-use policy that is optimal for a particular population density may not work at higher population densities. But then we must ask why no-longer-optimal policies are not promptly changed. The fundamental question remains: what motivates top government leaders to retain suboptimal policies, or to develop institutions that cannot easily adapt to changing conditions?

Finally, we are left with the broad explanation that sound natural-resource exploitation is often the victim of the pursuit of other objectives *through* resource exploitation. Government officials *choose* to distort the development, extraction, and processing of natural resources in order to do many things.

Unsound Resource Policies and "Policy Failures"

It is important to point out that when we talk about government policy failures, we are identifying failures of the government to serve the interests of the nation's people, current and future. Because we have no particular interest in keeping any given set of government leaders in power, we are far more concerned with policy failures with respect to society's welfare than with political failures of particular government leaders. Of course, we must recognize that many policy failures are political successes for the officials that commit them, and often the political success for these officials is why the flawed policies are adopted. We may admire the cleverness of certain government officials in strengthening their political positions through maneuvers that come at the expense of the soundness of resource exploitation, but nonetheless these maneuvers constitute policy failures.

There is an even more complicated issue in defining policy failures and unsound resource policy. What should we say when resources are not exploited most beneficially for the nation's people *in order that other laudable goals can be pursued?* For example, what if the only way to provide adequate income to a thoroughly deserving group of people, who otherwise would be destitute, were through wages earned from working in unproductive mines that should be shut down in terms of sound resource considerations? This is what India faces in the dilemma over whether to keep open the highly wasteful copper mines. What if financing a new industry really were in the nation's interest, and the only way the president could accomplish this in the face of wrongheaded legislative opposition is to siphon funds from resource exploitation in ways that lead to reckless exploitation? From the perspective of former President Suharto in Indonesia, the aircraft industry was a highly laudable goal, and if it took manipulating forest royalties to do it, then it was worth it. Are these actions policy failures?

The key to resolving this paradox is to understand that *in principle*, any of these programmatic objectives could be pursued without distorting the resource-exploitation process. John Stuart Mill (1848) pointed out that the productive process can and should be insulated from the inefficiencies of trying to accomplish distributional objectives by manipulating production. Government spending, rather than manipulations of the productive process, can accomplish distributive objectives. Natural-resource exploitation is certainly part of the production process to which Mill was referring. And we can extend his dictum beyond the distributive objectives to include all the other objectives reviewed in this chapter. In principle, the government can impose conventional taxes that do not distort resource exploitation, and use the revenues from these taxes to pursue a host of ends, from income redistribution to financing high-prestige industries or buying a copper stockpile for national security. However, this is quite different from saying that in the existing political and institutional context, the goal would be accomplished through the taxing-and-spending (i.e., conventional budgetary) means.

This means that if a political leader must resort to unsound natural-resource policies and practices in order to accomplish a socially desirable objective, then the institutional structure is flawed. A better institutional structure would permit the pursuit of that objective without the resource distortion. For example, if Indian copper mines are kept open because providing income for mineworker families is the societally correct thing to do, and yet the Indian parliament cannot agree to pension off copper workers, then the failure is in India's governance structure, rather than in the actions of any particular official.

CONCLUSION AND PREVIEW

This introduction has tried to show that sound natural-resource exploitation is still crucial for many developing countries and that government policy failures are responsible for huge losses in many of these nations. Rather than assuming that resource policy failures can be dismissed as the outgrowths of greed or ignorance, the chapter presents a theory to account for why government officials would resort to distorting the natural-resource exploitation process to pursue other programmatic economic and political objectives.

To elaborate this diagnosis and to explore possible reforms, I first develop a systematic assessment of natural-resource policy failures. Chapter 2 identifies twelve broad categories of natural-resource policy failures and traces out how these policy failures can further the six strategies outlined in this chapter. Chapter 3 looks in depth at the case of oil and timber exploitation in Indonesia, where natural resources have been manipulated in such extreme fashion to promote particular development programs that the dynamics stand out very clearly. Chapter 4 reviews the many mechanisms involved in manipulating resource extraction in order to finance development agendas, and elaborates on specific cases in which development agendas are particularly prominent in determining government action. Chapters 5 and 6 undertake parallel analyses for the mechanisms and illustrative cases for the strategies of endowing economic benefits and capturing revenues for the central treasury, respectively. For these three chapters, many policy failures will emerge, but some cases also hold lessons of reform. The strategies of creating rent-seeking opportunities, capturing control over relevant financial and natural-resource flows, and evading accountability occur in so many cases that these dynamics are also analyzed in chapters 3–6. Chapter 7 summarizes the case patterns, reviews the utility of the theory for accounting for policy failures, and offers recommendations for changing institutions and processes to reduce the incidence of natural-resource policy failures.

Anatomy of Resource Policy Failures and Their Linkages to Programmatic Strategies

INTRODUCTION

Throughout the first chapter I referred to sound natural-resource practices and equated "policy failures" with societally unsound practices. That presumes that reasonable, well-informed people could agree on what practices of resource exploitation are best ("optimal") for society. Without a sense of best practice, we can hardly define optimal policies and distinguish them from policy failures. Therefore, this chapter begins with a framework for determining the forms and rates of optimal natural-resource exploitation. By identifying good policies, this framework can help identify categories of bad policy. As table 2.1 demonstrates, the variety of policy failures is remarkable.

With one exception, I define best practice in terms of efficiency rather than distributional equity. Distributional equity is extraordinarily important, but we cannot reach technical agreement on the best distribution; distribution is a matter of values. No two resource economists or resource managers would necessarily agree on whether a given distribution of proceeds from, say, timber harvesting is optimal from a distributional perspective. Equally important, we should exclude distribution from defining best resource practices. In principle, achieving the best distribution (however one may wish to define it) should be pursued outside the production process.

The exception is that we insist that a resource practice should not lead to lower societal well-being for future generations. This tenet of sustainable development is a compelling distributional demand that largely avoids the arbitrariness of choosing the specific division of benefits within today's population. While I would not dare to specify the optimal income distribution for Chile today and label certain resource practices as sound or unsound on that basis, I am willing to hold that society (including those not yet born or not yet eligible to vote) is better off without a decline in living standards.[1]

Defining Efficiency

How should we think about the maximization of societal welfare? Distributional issues aside, total societal welfare is maximized when resource exploitation is subject to *dynamic efficiency*. Tietenberg (1992, 30) straightforwardly defines dynamic efficiency this way: "An allocation of resources across n time periods is dynamically efficient if it maximizes the present value of net benefits that could be received from all the possible ways of allocating those resources over the n periods."

Two clarifications are necessary for understanding this principle. First, the "resources" include financial capital, labor, and other resources besides natural resources. The wisdom of investing money, effort, and land into developing and extracting natural resources, compared to their alternative uses, is as relevant as the wisdom of creating or extracting a particular natural-resource unit at a particular time.

Second, the present value of the net benefits is crucial because we must adjust the valuation of benefits and costs occurring at different times. Generally a benefit coming earlier is valued more than one coming later, because of both impatience and the opportunity to invest current savings for greater value in the future.

The "Marginalist" Principle

Economic theory tells us that, at any point in time, efficient resource exploitation occurs when society's benefit from the last (marginal) resource unit exploited equals its societal cost. (This assumes that more profitable resource units will be developed and extracted before less profitable units.) This principle is based on the idea that any unit of resource — if it deserves to be exploited at all — should be developed according to a particular time table and extracted at a particular moment. The timing depends on the costs of developing the resource and its changing value up to the point that it is extracted and sold. A resource may gain in value because the market price of that commodity simply rises over time, because extraction becomes more efficient, or, for renewable resources, because of the physical growth of the resource. The best timing also depends on the value of leaving certain resources intact to gain from the benefits of the positive spillover effects that they provide, such as a forest's contribution to reducing soil

Table 2.1 Policy Failure Categories and Variations

Policy Failure Category	Instrument or Circumstance	Example	Outcomes
Underpriced costs to the resource exploiter	Market-ignoring cost ceiling	Below-market fertilizer price	Overexploitation
	Neglect of negative effects	Lack of charges or regulation of pollution	Overexploitation
	Oversubsidizing for positive externalities	Ranching subsidies; excessive tax credits for reforestation	Overexploitation
Underpriced resource outputs	Price ceilings on privately produced resource outputs	Food price ceilings	Underexploitation
	Price ceilings on state-produced resource outputs	Low gasoline prices	Overexploitation
	Restriction on sales opportunities	Mandatory, low-price government purchases; raw-log export ban	Underexploitation
	Neglect of charging for negative externalities	Neglect of gasoline pollution taxes	Overexploitation
Overpriced costs to the resource exploiter	Overcharging for government-provided inputs	High fertilizer prices from state monopoly	Underexploitation
	Overcharging for negative externalities	Excessive reforestation fees; bans on resource exploitation	Underexploitation
	Undersubsidization for positive externalities	Failure to subsidize appropriate reforestation efforts	Underexploitation
Overpriced resource outputs	Government purchase of privately produced output at high prices	High farmgate prices paid by state agencies; high latex prices paid by state agencies	Overexploitation; neglect of other resource opportunities
	Government sets high output prices: low demand sensitivity to price	High copper prices (in India); high staple food prices	Overexploitation
	Government sets high output prices: high demand sensitivity to price	High nonstaple food prices	Underexploitation
	Excessive negative externality charge	Excessive "reforestation tax" on wood products	Underexploitation
Failure to ensure competition	Granting or allowing private monopoly: domestically oriented production	Dairy-products markets dominated by large or exclusively licensed dairies	Underexploitation; inefficient exploitation

(continued)

Table 2.1 *(continued)*

Policy Failure Category	*Instrument or Circumstance*	*Example*	*Outcomes*
	Granting or allowing private monopoly: export-oriented production	Noncompetitive logging concessions on public lands	Overexploitation; inefficient exploitation
	Granting state monopoly	State oil companies	Inefficient exploitation
Suppression or failure to provide adequate information	Supression of information	Secrecy regarding logging concessionaire performance	Overexploitation; excessive negative externalities
	Neglect of information gathering and dissemination	Lack of information regarding future timber prices	Over- or underexploitation (likely overextraction and underdevelopment)
Weakening or inadequate protection of property rights	Government restrictions or denial of pre-existing resource-user rights	Goverment confiscation ("gazetting") of forest lands	Hasty overextraction; underdevelopment
	Government neglect of property rights enforcement	Forests open to exploitation by anyone	Hasty overextraction; underdevelopment
Excessive policy instability	Frequent resource policy changes	Frequent changes in forestry regulations	Hasty overextraction; underdevelopment
Inappropriate government orders to state resource exploiter	Directives to state resource enterprises	Directives for greater oil production; directives for less mineral production	Depends on direction of distortion
Undercapitalization of state resource efforts	Failure to approve adequate budgets	Low investment budgets for state oil companies	Underexploitation; wasteful exploitation; inadequate concern for negative externalities
	Excessive taxation of state resource enterprises	Taxing state oil companies into indebtedness	Same
	Allowing or forcing state resource enterprises to invest outside of the core sector	Requiring state oil companies to divert capital into steel manufacturing	Same
Government directives for inappropriate investments	Directives to invest within the resource sector	Overbuilding of oil or mining infrastructure despite nonrenewable nature of the endowments	Over- or underexploitation of various aspects of resource exploitation; wasteful exploitation
Failure to hold state resource exploiters accountable	Inadequate monitoring and accounting systems	Impenetrable state company accounts	Wasteful exploitation; under- or overexploitation

erosion and providing animal habitat. Therefore, this perspective can yield both the extent of resource exploitation and its timing.

Note that even conservationists should condemn both over- and underexploitation. We can define underexploitation as resource development and extraction that falls short of fulfilling society's potential for gains, taking into account all considerations of benefits and costs. If a low level of resource extraction is indeed in society's interest, perhaps because it permits the intact resource stock to provide environmental services, or because extraction requires great economic or environmental costs, then low extraction is optimal; underextraction would be even lower.

Why should a natural resource be exploited in any given time period just up to the point that the benefits of the last unit should equal its cost? Costs include not only the direct and obvious costs of exploiting the resource but also the lost opportunities that developing and extracting it would foreclose. These opportunity costs include the economic benefits that alternative uses of capital, effort, and the land itself could have produced. They also include the environmental benefits from leaving the resources intact rather than extracting them. Thus, the marginalist principle simply means that a given resource should be developed only if its net benefits are greater than the benefits arising from alternative uses, and we should extract each resource unit when its net benefit is greatest. Less exploitation in a given time period leaves worthwhile resources unexploited (i.e., the exploiters fail to exploit resources whose net benefits are greatest at that moment). Conversely, more exploitation would be wasteful because the costs of developing and extracting the additional resource units, plus the forgone future opportunities to gain from the resources, are greater than the benefits provided by these units.

Conditions of Efficient Resource Exploitation

The crucial question for this chapter is, thus, How can government policies encourage natural-resource exploiters to achieve dynamic efficiency? The answer is based on five conditions.

1. *The free market will set input and output prices such that private and societal interests will converge, under conditions of perfect information, competition, and secure property rights.* This is, of course, Adam Smith's classic principle of the "hidden hand." The market prices of the inputs needed by resource exploiters will reflect the direct societal costs of providing the labor, money, and raw materials required for their production. For example, the free-market price of fertilizer would reflect the costs of the raw nitrate or

phosphate inputs, the investment in building the fertilizer factory, the labor costs and other costs of operating the factory, and competitive profits for the factory owners and distributors. Similarly, allowing resource exploiters to set output prices on a market basis encourages them to extract the volume that purchasers want at a price that reflects the direct costs (which prices include the exploiters' normal competitive profit). In other words, the competitive output price leads to the production of resource units that purchasers judge to be worth the price they have to pay for them.

This principle has two obvious limitations. First, the conditions of competition, perfect information, and secure property rights may not hold. Second, some societal costs and benefits go beyond the direct costs and benefits impinging on the resource exploiter. Therefore, two additional principles are necessary to address the functioning of the market.

2. The government must take actions to ensure competition, good information, and secure property rights, as long as these actions are not more societally costly than the additional net benefits they provide. This principle recognizes that one class of market failures arises when the market itself does not create the conditions of competition, perfect information, and secure property rights.

Competition discourages input providers from raising their prices, which decreases demand and thus the number of resource units developed and extracted to below the socially optimal level. Competition also discourages resource exploiters from raising output prices, which would also lead to fewer units produced and sold.[2]

Efficient resource exploitation also requires that the exploiters know what actions will maximize their gains. Of course, future prices are always somewhat uncertain, as are unforeseen costs and the yields from alternative investments. It is also true that information has its costs; obviously the reduction of uncertainty can be taken too far if the spending on information exceeds the benefits that the information provides. Yet the inability to reduce this uncertainty when information is not prohibitively costly can leave resource exploiters ignorant about what resources to develop, how rapidly to exploit them, and at what cost. Therefore, lack of information is a market failure, justifying government action to provide more accurate information so that resource exploiters can make better choices.

When property rights are insecure, resource exploiters will not consider future benefits adequately, because of their uncertainties about whether they can obtain these benefits. Many regard the protection of property rights as the most fundamental responsibility of government.

Finally, it is worth distinguishing a special case of poor information that arises when government policies are unstable and unpredictable. Policy unpredictability casts doubt that resource exploitation will pay off. Perhaps today's input costs and output prices are attractive, but policy changes may dramatically change the situation in the future.

3. *The government must take actions to make private resource exploiters bear the indirect costs to society and reward private resource exploiters for providing benefits to society.* This principle addresses the fact that many "spillover effects" (commonly called "externalities"), whether positive or negative, do not directly affect the resource exploiter unless the government takes measures to make the exploiters feel the whole range of consequences of resource exploitation. The resource exploiters have to take into account this environmental damage; government can impose these costs onto the resource exploiter through "pollution charges."[3] Unless the total costs borne by the resource exploiter reflect these damages, the resource exploiter will overexploit the resource units that yield private profits despite high net societal costs.

Conversely, transfers or subsidies from the government to the resource exploiter can encourage positive externalities. Typically, these positive effects emerge from renewable-resource development (i.e., increasing the resource stock), such as tree planting, by enhancing the landscape. Positive externalities may also come from resource extraction that provides economic benefits such as hard currency earnings from export (e.g., exporting agricultural products, minerals, and oil). If inducements to engage in resource exploitation for the sake of positive externalities are lacking, then the resource exploiter would not develop or extract up to the last societally beneficial unit; resources would be underexploited.

4. *Government must ensure that state resource exploiters are kept accountable for the quality of their resource management and the damages they cause.* A special form of "externality" also occurs in state resource exploitation. State resource managers may also ignore societal impacts when they do their own "private" calculations of financial, political, professional, or institutional benefits; that is, state resource managers may not internalize the social consequences. If state managers can escape accountability, they can pursue their own interests even when these interests do not coincide with those of society.[4]

5. *Government must ensure that directives to state resource exploiters call for appropriate rates and methods of resource exploitation.* While state resource exploiters may be quite sensitive to the market forces addressed by the principles outlined above, often they also exploit resources under direct orders from higher government authorities. Whereas the first three principles concern government policies that influence resource exploiters' behavior, the government can affect the rate and manner of state resource

exploitation more directly, simply by issuing directives to the government agencies or state enterprises. Therefore, beyond the sensitivity that state resource exploiters may have to inappropriate costs and prices, they may also be forced into improper resource exploitation by government fiat. Governments often order state entities to extract resources too rapidly or without adequate spending to limit environmental damage, in order to provide immediate revenues.

Categories of Resource Policy Failures

Twelve broad categories of resource policy failures become apparent from considering the five principles discussed above. These categories hold many variations, a fact that is very important for appreciating the flexibility with which government officials can manipulate resource exploitation. Nevertheless, it is striking that so many variants of resource policy failure are violations of the simple pricing, property rights, and accountability principles that define economically sound resource exploitation.

1. *Government may cause or permit the costs to resource exploiters to be underpriced.* The concept of underpricing is perhaps the most obvious insight into why natural resources are overexploited, because cheap inputs mean greater eagerness to exploit beyond the point of responsible resource stewardship. Yet first we must develop a careful definition of input-cost underpricing, so that cases can be definitively identified. I start with the concept of optimal net costs. To be optimal, these costs must reflect

- the direct costs at market prices;
- the indirect costs of external damage (negative externalities); and
- reductions in costs to stimulate exploitation if there are positive externalities worth the costs of the incentives.

The term *net* is important: the preferred outcome is the maximum benefit less the costs. Thus, underpricing occurs when the input costs are below this optimal net cost.

On occasion, government may underprice an input because it sets the price without accurately gauging the actual costs of providing it. Sometimes inputs such as energy are produced and priced in very complicated ways that make it difficult to determine what the hidden costs of production may be. But much more spectacularly, in many instances the government simply gives away the most obvious input, the natural resource itself. Government-created irrigation systems often bring water to farmers at no cost; the water is deemed to come from God and therefore requires no payment. Similarly, the failure to prevent illegal logging (when such prevention is economically feasible) typically means that no royalties are collected. The situation is scarcely better when the government charges an obviously inadequate fee for access to the natural resource under government control; then the resource exploiter can even claim that he or she is paying for the resource. Commercial loggers often deny that they get a windfall by logging on public lands, but very low logging royalties — the most common state of affairs throughout the developing world — mean that the loggers are underpaying.

An even more extreme situation holds for most state resource exploiters, particularly in the oil and mining sectors. They usually pay no royalties at all, on the grounds that they are creatures of the government and will eventually pay dividends as well as taxes. Yet the key question is not whether these enterprises will pay something to the government, but rather whether they have incentives to overexploit the resource and operate wastefully. As long as the raw-resource input is underpriced, the state resource managers are prone to regard it as a free or cheap good, to be used in excess as long as it appears profitable for the enterprise.

An equally common and pernicious reason for underpricing inputs is the government's failure to charge adequately for negative externalities. Government should treat negative externalities as another cost to the resource exploiter, to compensate society for the damage or depletion caused by resource exploitation. If not, government inaction encourages excessive and reckless exploitation. For example, loggers charged only for the trees removed from public lands and not for trees damaged by this removal will harvest more timber than is optimal, given that some of the harvesting creates more damage than benefits. It is useful to note that these last two sources of underpricing occur through weak enforcement. Governments reduce effective costs by not imposing costs.

A less common source of input underpricing occurs when the government oversubsidizes resource exploitation for presumed positive effects. In other words, the resource exploiter gets a subsidy, sometimes even a direct cash bonus, for developing or extracting a resource. The government may argue that the society benefits from that resource exploitation; for example, governments of several Latin American countries (most notably in Brazil) have claimed that ranching provides societal goods, ranging from foreign exchange from exports to improving the nutrition of domestic consumers. Yet it has been quite clear that many ranches have been launched where ranching made little sense, just to cash in on the subsidies. By the same token, subsidies for reforestation have sometimes resulted in the wrong trees being planted in the wrong areas (for example, in areas already covered with natural forest). This has been the case in Costa Rica. Of course, tree planting may be a very laudable effort, but when the bonus significantly exceeds the true societal benefit, tree-planting schemes can be highly counterproductive.

All of these forms of input underpricing provoke resource exploiters to overexploit. Because of the attractiveness of exploiting this resource, they may underexploit other resources requiring their money and effort. Therefore, land-use decisions will be distorted. Often the resource exploiters will also be less cost-conscious because of the lower apparent costs of using inputs.

2. *Government may cause or permit the underpricing of resource outputs.* Looking at the output side, we see an even more complicated pattern. First, underpricing of output prices (e.g., lumber, rubber, gasoline, food) may occur through government-imposed price ceilings on resource outputs, a measure often adopted to increase the purchasing power of consumers. Second, underpricing may occur through government restrictions on how an output can be sold; for example, a ban on a product's export will reduce its demand and thereby its market price below what that could have been. This is the widely seen consequence of bans on the export of raw logs. Third, when governments require that resource exploiters sell all or part of their produce to a government or state agency, the price is often below the free-market price. Finally, the government's neglect to charge for negative externalities through product taxes may also result in underpricing resource outputs.

Output underpricing produces different kinds of distortions, depending on whether the resource exploiter is private or public and who bears the cost of underpricing. If the resource exploiters are private (and therefore profit-driven), government-imposed limits on the output price will drive exploiters out of production, leading to underexploitation. This is the all-too-common result of price ceilings on food, which in many countries have driven farmers away from food production (Pinstrup-Andersen 1988; Timmer 1991; Bautista and Valdez 1993).

However, if the output is underpriced because the government failed to charge for negative externalities, then the resource exploiters can still profit from selling units that are not societally worthwhile, given the damage that they cause. The result is overexploitation and unchecked environmental damage. Grazing lands become eroded and livestock wastes pollute rivers in those countries where consumers pay little for cheap meat because they do not pay to restore the land or to cover health costs due to water pollution.

Government often limits the output prices of state resource exploiters, for example, gasoline prices charged by state oil companies. If the state enterprise is unwilling or unable to cut production to maximize profits, then the increased demand for cheaper outputs will lead to overexploitation to meet the demand. This is why low prices for gasoline, diesel oil, heating fuels, and other fuel oils cause overproduction of oil and financial losses in refinery operations. The same holds when negative externalities are ignored: if the government does not charge exploiters or output purchasers for the damage that exploitation causes, there will be overconsumption and overexploitation.

3. *Government may cause or permit the costs to resource exploiters to be overpriced.* Overpricing is also defined in relation to the optimal net costs. Governments often overcharge for inputs when they are the sole or major suppliers. For example, governments often monopolize the sale of fertilizer, or even claim to own all trees. Or, by claiming control over land itself, governments may overcharge for the very access to the resources.

Governments may also exaggerate the charges invoked to prevent or reduce negative externalities. For example, forest users may be charged "reforestation fees" in excess of the actual damage from extraction. The ultimate charge is to ban exploitation altogether (the cost, then, is the penalty suffered if caught violating the ban), which is sometimes imposed even though some resource exploitation is justified.

Conversely, the costs facing a resource exploiter may inhibit worthwhile exploitation because the government fails to provide an adequate incentive. Consider a case in which reforestation would be good for the society even if tree-planting is a bit too costly for the forest user. Without the reforestation bonus, reforestation would remain privately unattractive because its costs are too high.

The overpricing of exploitation costs discourages both resource development and extraction, simply by making fewer resource units profitable from the exploiter's perspective. Underexploitation includes not only underextraction — which conservationists often applaud — but also underdevelopment. Without adequate incentives to plant trees for their eventual harvests, few are likely to plant trees at all.

4. *Government may cause or permit overpricing of resource outputs.* Again, the overpricing of resource outputs is more complicated than distorting the cost of inputs. If resource exploitation is in private hands, the government may set high output prices through its own purchases. For example, government agencies sometimes buy agricultural produce or forest products (such as rubber) at above-market prices, in order to supplement the incomes of the sellers. The resource exploiters are then likely to overexploit

the resources. This is one reason why Brazilian rubber trees have sometimes been overtapped.

Alternatively, the government may set higher output prices that private purchasers must pay. The impact of this policy depends on how sensitive the demand for the product is to its price (that is, the price elasticity of demand). If the demand does not decline very much despite higher prices (e.g., for necessities such as food and critical industrial products with few substitutes), then the higher revenues going to resource exploiters will encourage them to overexploit the resource. If the demand is highly sensitive to the price, then overpricing is likely to have the long-term effect of reducing demand and thereby undershooting optimal resource extraction.

Finally, the government may overprice outputs produced by private resource exploiters by overcharging for negative externalities through a consumer tax (also called a "pollution charge"). Excessive charges will discourage the demand for societally worthwhile resource output, the resource exploiters will get no windfall, and the demand for the output will be dampened by its high price. Clearly the resource exploitation will be less than optimal. In many countries, pollution charges, whether levied on the producer or on the consumer as pollution taxes, are simply a pretext for taxation, imposed without regard to either the match between the charge and the damage or the likelihood that the charge will reduce the damage.

The overpricing of state-produced outputs may also reduce demand, thereby leading to underexploitation. However, if demand remains high despite high prices, the state resource exploiters may be encouraged to overexploit the resource. For example, the near-doubling of the domestic price of copper in India allowed the state copper company to produce far more copper than is sensible given India's very poor ore grades.

5. *Government may fail to ensure competition.* Under either private or state resource control, overpricing of outputs targeted largely for the domestic market may occur because the government permits or encourages restrictions on competition. These restrictions enable the resource exploiter to charge more; the higher price will dampen demand and total production, although the producer would have a higher profit. Thus, the granting of monopoly privileges, or the failure to break up monopolies, would lead to overpricing and underexploitation. When the output is largely exported, it is unlikely that restriction to one or just a few producers within the country would have much impact on the world price or decisions to underexploit. Instead, government failure to ensure competition is likely to create uncertainty for resource exploiters about their long-term capacity to hold onto monopoly privileges. Therefore, they are prone to exploiting

resources at a recklessly high rate because of fears that their special privileges will be withdrawn. Over time, this leads to overexploitation. Finally, a resource exploiter operating without the pressure of competition is less likely to be cost-conscious, resulting in inefficient exploitation. This holds for private monopolies, but even more so for state monopolies. These state monopolies are typically insensitive to price signals because their performance cannot be compared to private or state competitors operating in the same environment.

6. *Government may suppress or fail to provide adequate information.* Governments often deliberately suppress information concerning resource exploitation under government sponsorship or control. This permits excessive extraction and excessive negative externalities to go unnoticed and unpunished.

The more generic lack of information due to governments' neglect of information gathering and dissemination will cause resource exploiters to choose the wrong resources, the wrong timing, or the wrong resource-exploitation techniques, depending on the nature of their ignorance. The consequences may be either under- or overexploitation, depending on the biases caused by faulty information. However, insofar as resource exploiters know that ignorance puts them at risk of making blunders in long-term resource development and extraction plans, they tend to extract resources quickly wherever immediate profits appear. Therefore, there may be a greater tendency toward immediate overextraction and inadequate resource development. Ignorance will also provoke wasteful exploitation due to lack of knowledge of true input costs or output prices.

7. *Government may weaken or neglect property rights.* Governments have frequently restricted or denied the pre-existing user rights of private or communal resource exploiters. Yet in practice, the original resource-exploiting groups, or others, still have the opportunity to extract the resources — even if the government regards this extraction as illegal. Lacking any expectation that they will be able to count on long-term benefits from the resource endowment, the resource exploiters are likely to try to extract the resources quickly while they can, but they have little incentive to invest in developing the resource stock for future extraction. The obvious result is hasty overextraction and underdevelopment.

Similarly, when the government fails to fulfill its role of enforcing property rights, the risk that outsiders will be able to extract the resources also provokes hasty extraction and disinterest in long-term development of the resource stock. This is the well-known problem of "open-access" resources. Sometimes resource exploiters attempt to enforce their exclusive access by threatening or attacking encroachers. Because this has its own

Why Governments Waste Natural Resources

costs, it also leads to underdevelopment of resource stocks. When violence does occur, the prospects for long-term success appear even dimmer, reinforcing both the tendency to hasty extraction and the disinterest in resource development.

8. *Government may indulge in excessive policy instability.* Governments often need to change policies in the face of inadequacies of past policies, changing conditions, and new objectives. Yet some governments change policies because they see political advantages to "reformism" for its own sake. This creates serious problems in shortening the time horizons of resource exploiters. In adding uncertainty concerning future conditions, excessive policy instability provokes both inefficient and hasty extraction and inadequate resource development. This is reinforced by the threat that policy instability poses to the security of property rights. Because excessive policy changes reduce the exploiter's confidence that developing, extracting, and selling the resource will be both possible and profitable, policy instability is a threat to both information and property rights.

9. *Government may direct state resource exploiters to develop or extract resources inappropriately.* Rather than distorting resource exploiters' incentives, governments may simply demand that state agencies engage in over- or underexploitation of any given resource. The government may also set the prices of state-produced outputs too high or too low.

10. *Government may undercapitalize state resource exploitation.* Undercapitalization of state resource exploitation (i.e., keeping the state investment level below its appropriate level) is worth identifying as a policy failure in its own right. Undercapitalization can come about through the government's unwillingness to approve adequate investment budgets, its excessive taxation of state operations, or its failure to prevent state firms from diverting funds away from needed investments. Undercapitalization is so important because of the timing issue in resource exploitation. While it may seem that an available resource (such as a mineral deposit or a forest) is simply waiting for exploitation, the capacity to exploit it at a particular moment in time is often pivotal for taking advantage of high prices. The societal benefit from extracting and selling a resource when its price is high can make an enormous difference for the many resources with greatly fluctuating world prices, such as copper or oil.

Contrary to the common view that a state resource enterprise will simply do less damage if it has less budget for resource extraction, threadbare state resource operations are often incapable of developing and extracting natural resources with adequate efficiency or environmental care. Sloppy logging, oil-well blowouts, and mining disasters are more likely when state resource enterprises have to make do with minimal budgets.

11. *Government may direct state resource exploiters to make inappropriate investments both within and outside the resource-exploitation process.* In addition to the government's control over the level of state-sector investments, it may require or encourage state resource exploiters to invest in inappropriate activities or to use the proceeds of resource exploitation in wasteful ways. Poor investment of resource earnings often takes the form of unwise intrasectoral expansion (i.e., doing more of the same) or vertical diversification (i.e., adding activities that provide inputs to the existing resource exploitation or that use the outputs of this exploitation). For example, poor intrasectoral expansion of oil production means expanding exploration and production where it is not justified. Poor vertical diversification may involve overly expensive local development of seismographic equipment, which could be purchased more cheaply from abroad, or a money-losing petrochemical industry "downstream" of oil production.

Sometimes diversification involves investments beyond the resource sector altogether, into areas where the state venture has little expertise or experience. While this problem may seem beyond the issue of natural-resource exploitation, three reasons make it highly relevant. First, the primary reason for resource extraction is to convert the natural-resource endowment into other forms of wealth for society. Therefore, if state resource managers are responsible for wasting the earnings of resource exploitation, it is important to understand why this happens. Second, a wasteful use of earnings can easily distort the resource-exploitation process itself. For example, when a state resource enterprise is losing money on activities beyond the resource sector, the enterprise managers may feel compelled to speed up resource exploitation in order to cover these losses. A quite striking example comes from the history of Indonesia's state oil company, which in the 1960s and 1970s increased oil production in order to finance a huge steel factory and an airline, both economically shaky. Third, government officials and state resource managers often use proceeds unwisely as part of a strategy to improve their positions in the struggle to control the resource exploitation process. Thus, the waste of resource earnings is often a cost of unsound arrangements within the state sector that provoke poor investments. For example, state oil companies often "park" large sums of money in low-return overseas investments in order to keep the funds away from other officials.

12. *Government may fail to keep state resource managers accountable.* The lack of accountability is a very broad problem that can lead to poor investments, inappropriate exploitation rates, and rampant inefficiency if state managers are permitted to pursue personal, professional, or agency objectives at the expense of sound resource practices. Lack of accountability

occurs when responsible government officials fail to require transparent accounts, permitting state resource managers to manipulate their investments and operations with minimal visibility. An even more blatant accountability failure occurs when government officials collude with state resource exploiters to engage in low-visibility maneuvers, such as laundering payments to oil-worker unions or financing projects indirectly with the earnings from resource exploitation.

How Resource-Manipulation Strategies Give Rise to Policy Failures

We are now prepared to link the strategies identified in the first chapter to the policy failures defined above. My point is to show how these strategies can account for resource policy failures, because the failures either are instruments of these strategies or result from the strategies.

Recall that government officials frequently resort to six strategies of manipulating natural-resource exploitation:

1. financing controversial development programs;
2. providing economic benefits for particular groups, areas, or individuals;
3. capturing natural-resource rents for the central treasury;
4. creating rent-seeking opportunities in order to gain private-actor cooperation in pursuing other objectives;
5. capturing and maintaining discretion over the financial flows involved in resource exploitation, at the expense of other government or state agencies; and
6. evading accountability through reliance on low-visibility resource maneuvers.

Financing Development Programs

Imagine a government official bent on promoting a development program despite opposition from within his or her own government. Furthermore, the development program has some potential to embarrass the official because some of its elements do not appear to be very sound economically. Nonetheless, for reasons of politics, ideology, or even long-term vision, the official is determined to implement the strategy even if this has to come at the expense of sound natural-resource management.

Also imagine that the program is directly linked with natural-resource exploitation. For example, it may involve a wood-products industry in tandem with logging, or a petrochemical industry linked to oil production. It may focus on developments such as energy-intensive industry or high-yield agriculture that use natural-resource inputs, such as energy or water. Or it may simply be a program for developing economic activities in the region where particular natural resources are exploited.

The most direct approach would be to manipulate the resource's input and output prices to make the promoted activities more profitable. By the same logic, government officials could try to turn resource exploiters away from different development options by manipulating prices to make them more expensive. For example, officials frequently try to influence the production and use of one type of fuel (e.g., kerosene) over another (e.g., fuelwood) by making the production of the former more profitable than the latter. Or they try to make one fuel more affordable to consumers than the other. The most straightforward way to make a fuel both more profitable and more affordable is to subsidize its inputs, so that the sale price could be lower.

Officials can also manipulate the costs of inputs and outputs to stimulate particular phases in the production and processing of natural resources. Underpricing the inputs for the next stage of the process will make that next stage more profitable, at least in the short run. The most prominent example is the frequently disastrous strategy of trying to stimulate a wood-products industry by forcing loggers to sell timber domestically at low prices, which has led to the temporary profitability of inefficient industries dependent on an endangered timber supply.

Pricing failures can also finance development programs in a broader though less direct way. When resource exploiters are left with greater surpluses owing to government policy, they may be willing to invest part of that surplus in accord with the development-strategy preferences of government officials, or even at the direction of the government officials responsible for the exploiters' good economic fortune. Therefore, a wide range of development programs can be financed by creating a pricing-based surplus for economic actors who either are interested themselves in particular development programs or are beholden to government officials who can direct the investment of part of the surplus.

State-sector failures can also promote development programs. Excessive exploitation obviously expands the current operations but also will promote, at least in the short run, the downstream industries. For example, high levels of forest exploitation by state forestry enterprises in Honduras and Liberia expanded the entire forestry sector — until dwindling stocks of marketable timber called for a new strategy. Output underpricing has the same effect on downstream industrial promotion, by providing the downstream firms — whether state or private — cheaper inputs for their own operations. In the 1980s the Liberian state forestry companies, faced with the ban on exporting raw logs, ended up selling them cheaply to the — temporarily — burgeoning sawmills and other wood-products processors. Similarly, inexpensive gasoline, diesel, and fuel oils in oil-exporting countries like Mexico, Nigeria, and Venezuela have been a key component of industrial strategies based on cheap energy.

Inadequate exploitation and undercapitalization are common consequences of draining too many financial resources out of the state enterprise in order to finance extrasectoral development. For example, the severe undercapitalization and production declines of the Mexican state oil company after the 1978 fiscal reform were due, in part, to the government's policy of overtaxing the company to finance the government's overall industrial expansion strategy. The surpluses captured by state enterprises by overpricing outputs with little price elasticity of demand can also be diverted to finance development programs. Overspending on inputs may also subsidize the industries that provide these inputs. For example, many state oil companies are required to rely on expensive and sometimes inefficient domestic suppliers and contractors, as a means of stimulating upstream development. The Peruvian state oil company at one time was required to rely on army helicopters for Amazonian oil exploration, a costly and bizarre form of subsidy for the army's materiel program.

The strategy of using state resource exploitation to promote development programs often culminates in unsound investments within and outside the resource sector, even if these policy failures are not instruments of the strategy. This is because programs financed through state-sector laundering are usually not subjected to the scrutiny performed on programs financed through the conventional budget process. The indirectness of such promotion also contributes to the lack of transparency, oversight, or sanctions, leaving state managers unaccountable.

Economic Benefit Strategy

Now imagine that the government official is committed to transferring economic benefits to particular segments of the population and is willing to sacrifice the soundness of natural-resource management to do so. Of course, the same logic that holds for manipulating natural resources to stimulate development programs can be used to transfer economic benefits, in that the stimulated economic activities will have workers and owners to benefit from their expansion. More directly, though, the pricing manipulations again appear as straightforward instruments, because they can enrich anyone put in a position to buy cheap or sell dear. For example, cattle ranchers can be enriched either by being allowed to pay too little for the right to graze on government land (their input cost) or by price floors on the sale of beef (their output price). Conversely, more expensive inputs provide benefits for those at earlier stages in the resource-exploitation process; cheaper output prices benefit producers or consumers further down the chain of production. Thus, low food prices benefit urban dwellers, at least until the agricultural sector collapses and they have to buy imports. Similarly, low timber prices — sometimes effected by banning log exports — have enriched wood processors in Indonesia, Liberia, and many other countries.

If the government official wants to avoid blatant pricing manipulations, he or she can resort to a more subtle tactic, weak enforcement, which has very similar implications as underpricing inputs. Weak enforcement allows resource exploiters to benefit by permitting them to exploit more resources, or to exploit resources without costly observance of regulatory limits. Half-hearted forestry regulation in Brazil, Costa Rica, Indonesia, Malaysia, and a host of other countries permits loggers to encroach into protected areas, cut undersized trees, and evade royalty payments. Similarly, weak enforcement allows cheap resource extraction and processing when pollution regulations go unenforced. The failure of governments to impose pollution charges for pesticide or fertilizer runoff, or for smog-producing oil refining, are obvious examples.

A government official can also redistribute wealth by overcharging for alleged negative externalities, by penalizing exploitation with such severe penalties (e.g., huge fines, confiscation, or risk of imprisonment). Taken to this extreme, invoking environmental protection can strip the original exploiters of their resource-use rights and often gives the government the opportunity to assign these rights to favored others. This is exemplified by the pattern of putting forest land and pastureland into state-controlled reserves as a prelude to reassigning the land to other users. For example, large tracts of the Petén region of Guatemala have been declared as reserves, putting an end to much of the small-scale agriculture and forestry by local people and low-income migrants, but huge ranches for the politically powerful, especially high military officers, have been consolidated.

The neglect or suppression of information can also transfer economic benefits by minimizing information about rule violations, allowing resource exploiters to cut costs in defiance of explicit rules. Similarly, vague property rights permit certain government officials to shift the benefits of resource exploitation from one group to another. The migration of Hispanized people into the Andean highlands was abetted by the failure of the governments of Colombia, Venezuela, and Ecuador to recognize the customary rights of the indigenous Amerindian peoples, giving the migrants the opportunity to lay claim to productive lands.

State-practice policy failures may also serve the redistributive strategy. Excessive exploitation and output underpricing provide immediate benefits at the expense of future generations, with the benefits shared by today's resource exploiters and by consumers enjoying lower current prices. The most striking case is the overproduction and underpricing of gasoline and other hydrocarbon products by state oil companies; in Nigeria and Venezuela, gasoline prices have been one-tenth to one-fifth the optimal prices.

The government official may wish to direct benefits to the state resource exploiters, who are often well organized politically. For this motive, unsound investments in resource exploitation will benefit — at least in the short run — the state employees in the new ventures and others upstream or downstream to them. State investments in low-grade mining ventures, as in Hindustan Copper Limited's current operations, have clear distributive benefits. Similarly, the diversion of resource profits into unsound extra-sectoral ventures will benefit the owners and workers related to these ventures, and possibly many other residents in their region. High costs of state operations often reflect overemployment, excessive wages and bonuses, ostentatious facilities, excessive employee or community services, excessive payments to favored suppliers, or expensive operations in relatively unproductive locations for the benefit of nearby populations. The combination of excess labor and high wages can result in the complete capture of potential profits by labor, as in the case of Chile's nationalized copper sector in the early 1970s. Similarly, many state oil companies maintain excess labor, provide luxurious headquarters facilities, and have been implicated in permitting contractors to overcharge. They build movie theaters and supermarkets for neighboring communities beyond what government authorities provide comparable communities, and with higher costs that reflect the enterprises' lack of expertise in the provision of community services.

Finally, the economic-benefit motive frequently induces government officials to obscure the operations of the state actors. When the official views the redistribution as politically risky, he or she may try to reduce its visibility. However, what is less visible to the public and to political opponents is often also less visible to the same government official. Therefore, the lack of accountability of state actions is a frequent outcome of such distributive strategies.

Capturing Revenues for the Central Treasury

Imagine that the government official is intent on drawing more revenue into the treasury, without risking the political costs of increasing obvious taxes. Pricing failures can serve as revenue-raising instruments when the government or state enterprises are directly involved in buying and selling. Most commonly, if the government controls the purchase of natural-resource outputs from private exploiters, a purchase price below the market-price level would provide the government with a greater spread between its purchase price and the price at which it resells the output. Thus, marketing boards, whether directed for reselling to the domestic market or for export, provide an opportunity for government to buy cheap and sell dear.

Governments also capture producer and consumer surpluses by overcharging for inputs necessary for resource exploitation, such as fertilizer for agricultural production or electricity for refining. The government may impose a fee for access to resources that the exploiters had enjoyed previously without having to pay for access. The extreme case is confiscation of resource access, giving the government the opportunity to exploit the resource directly or to sell the access rights to other exploiters. Any encroachment on user rights, whether through government charges or outright confiscation, may increase the insecurity over property rights and thereby induce shorter time horizons, reluctance to pursue resource development, and more reckless, hasty resource extraction.

The central budget can also be enriched by overcharging for alleged negative externalities. When imposing reforestation fees, governments often invoke the need to redress the damage to the forest caused by logging or other activities, but sometimes (as in the Indonesian case examined in the next chapter) the funds remain with the government rather than going to reforestation efforts.

Suppression of information to resource exploiters and consumers can abet the government's maneuvers to capture greater producer and consumer surpluses from resource exploitation. For example, government input suppliers have an incentive to suppress information on what their inputs would cost in a free-market context, just as marketing boards have an incentive to hide the fact that they may be reselling at a high profit.

Creating Rent-Seeking Opportunities

Imagine further that the government official is interested in benefiting not so much a large segment of the population, but rather a set of specific economic or political actors whose support or cooperation is particularly valued. Government measures that indulge specific producers or consumers can create rent-seeking opportunities. The government can ration these privileges so that the recipient either benefits directly from the assignment of an asset at low or zero cost (e.g., a land giveaway) or has an advantage over potential competitors in the same sphere of economic activity.[5] Obviously, restricted competition is the core to the strategy of creating rent-seeking opportunities. Yet there are many other instruments. Awarding licenses and charging low royalties for the exploitation of government-controlled natural resources, such as public timber stands, is a widespread practice. So, too, is providing cheap inputs, such as credit at below-market rates for the establishment of ranches, for selected recipients.

In like vein, government can reward targeted resource exploiters by selectively failing to charge them for creating negative externalities, or by overrewarding them for creating positive externalities. This latter strategy is particularly clever, because it gives the policy an aura of environmental concern. For example, the value of the tax credits for reforestation offered by Costa Rican governments in the 1980s was in some cases well in excess of the reforestation efforts required to qualify for the program, but the governments were able to seem to pursue conservation while providing benefits for those able to obtain licenses.

The rent-creation strategy reduces the security of property rights by raising the risk that resource access and competitive use will be stripped away to indulge other resource exploiters. For example, where logging concessions are seen as political rewards, the current concession holders have to worry that their privileges may be withdrawn if other potential exploiters gain the favor of the current government or its successors.

Because of the potential political embarrassment to the government of indulging particular individuals or firms over others, rent-creating government officials often try to suppress information about rent-seeking arrangements, actual costs, and actual benefits. This suppression of information also exacerbates the problem of low accountability of government and state officials involved in resource exploitation.

Capturing and Controlling the Surplus

Next consider the government official who tries to capture control over resource flows, whether to use this control to enhance his or her agency or to engage in the strategies described above. If the official can establish authority to set input or output prices, then under- or overpricing will direct the flow of benefits. The common debate over whether price controls and subsidies are legitimate is often a reflection of the struggle over who has the power to control the flow of financial and natural-resource wealth. Vague property rights also often emerge from efforts to capture discretion, as officials find that recognizing or denying the property rights of particular private actors can control the benefits from resource exploitation.

Control struggles within the government also account for uncertainty about the jurisdictions of different agencies and the rules that actually apply to a given resource. For example, the land reform agencies and forestry agencies in Brazil, Costa Rica, Honduras, and Indonesia operate with different land-use classification schemes that leave doubt as to which activities in forestry and agriculture are legal or illegal.

The government official may also try to exert control over resource flows by accumulating and distributing natural-resource wealth within a state enterprise. Overpricing state-produced outputs will allow the government or the state to capture consumer surpluses, while underpricing of state-produced outputs allows the price-setter to control the benefit of the consumers. The government official who can dictate the state enterprise's production rates, investment budget (magnitude, content, or both), output pricing, operational plans, or use of proceeds has gained control over the natural-resource surplus and possibly treasury and consumer surpluses as well. The failure to minimize costs, in turning spending toward state employees and contractors, gives discretion to those who control operational spending and wish either to indulge these beneficiaries or to promote the activities where the overspending is targeted. Excessive exploitation by state resource enterprises provides the government officials controlling state enterprise spending with greater natural-resource rents than they otherwise would have in the short run.

However, the struggle for control is not confined to government officials: the state resource managers may also manipulate prices and investments so that they can gain or maintain control. State managers sometimes decapitalize their own core production in order to move their assets into holdings (e.g., overseas operations) that are less vulnerable to capture by the government. Thus, part of the motivation for Venezuela's state oil company PDVSA to invest in controversial overseas ventures in the mid-1980s was to remove its remaining investment fund from the risk of appropriation from the central treasury. To prevent state officials from capturing the surplus, government officials often overtax and undercapitalize the state enterprise. Hence unsound investment portfolios can also emerge from the struggle between government agencies and state enterprises. This can easily extend into inappropriate use of proceeds beyond the resource sector, as either the state enterprise officials try to hide their surpluses or government officials pull the surpluses into sectors they control.

Finally, strategies to capture and maintain control over the surpluses often entail the kind of complexity and laundering that reduces the accountability of state managers. Just as redistributive strategies often require nontransparency to minimize the political costs of providing benefits via the resource exploitation process, the general manipulation of resource-related surpluses often requires state managers to operate beyond accountability. Ironically, in some instances the government officials' clever use of state enterprise operations as an off-budget fund creates such complicated and untraceable financial accounts that the government officials lose control.

Evading Accountability

Imagine that the official is preoccupied with finding the path of least political cost in pursuing any of the strategies already examined. Any policy that minimizes awareness of the policy itself or of its consequences, or that obscures the responsibility for such policies, has potential for government officials who wish to pursue initiatives with reduced accountability. Generally this means avoiding the most overt approach of paying for these initiatives directly from the central budget. Often it means avoiding the blatant act of confiscating land, output, or money without a seemingly lofty goal such as protecting the environment or enhancing national security. Therefore, it is not surprising that government officials often resort to pricing manipulations rather than direct taxation and spending to pursue those strategies. Price distortions are often complicated enough to obscure which activities are subsidized or penalized. Oversubsidization for activities involving positive externalities, and overcharging for activities involving negative externalities, can mask other motives by invoking environmental or conservationist appeals. Similarly, government directives to manipulate state-produced output prices can pursue developmental and distributive objectives without direct governmental accountability. For example, the Nigerian government sometimes attributes responsibility for gasoline and diesel price increases to the Nigerian National Petroleum Corporation to deflect responsibility for unpopular price hikes.

More broadly, poor information allows the government to manipulate resource exploitation to provide economic rewards with minimal transparency. Under- or overpricing may not be revealed as such in an information-poor environment. Poor information also facilitates the financing of development programs through the resource exploitation process, again by making such financing less obvious to those who would oppose these strategies. For government officials who do have relevant information, suppression of this information to other agencies or to the public gives the information holders a power advantage in the struggle to control related surpluses.

Vague rights often directly serve the evasion of accountability, by obscuring government responsibility for who benefits from resource exploitation. Many forests and fishing grounds are ostensibly under government or community control, but in practice other actors have access to their resources without wide publicity. The domination of landholdings in Guatemala's Petén region by military officers was obscured by ambiguous titling and inconsistent property laws. The armed forces even prohibited the dissemination of maps of the area, invoking far-fetched claims of national security.

Manipulating state exploitation rates is also less visible than direct spending from the central budget as a means of indulging beneficiaries or financing development programs. Excessive state enterprise production may have the same economic stimulation impact as money-supply expansion or fiscal budget expansion but is more removed from direct government responsibility. In Mexico in the mid-1970s, for example, oil production expansion was viewed by many government leaders as a crucial impetus for economic expansion at a time when money expansion or higher federal spending would have been heavily criticized. Similarly, undercapitalization and the consequent underproduction may be used as low-visibility techniques to drain the company of financial resources that the government can use for various programmatic purposes without raising taxes. If the undercapitalization is accompanied by international borrowing plus confiscatory taxes on the state enterprise that borrows the funds (as in the case of Mexico's state oil company after 1978), then the government can even borrow internationally without suffering any political embarrassment of raising official direct borrowing.

The evasion of accountability, for unsound investments within the sector or the inappropriate use of proceeds beyond the sector, is also aided by the fact that state enterprise budgets and operations are removed from the typically more transparent central budget process. If a government leader wants something financed that would entail political embarrassment if done openly, the state enterprise with large resource revenues is often a conveniently invisible fund. Poor investments both within and outside the resource sector also grow out of efforts to evade accountability, insofar as these efforts induce governments to allow or force state enterprises into complex, secretive, and unmonitored activities that undermine the oversight and analytic filters that would otherwise weed out poor investments.

Because the evasion of accountability often entails the accumulation of a large fund kept in the state resource enterprise or government agency, the resulting lack of a tight budget for the enterprise or agency often permits excessive spending. For example, the so-called reforestation fund of the Indonesian Forestry Ministry has been used as an off-budget fund by top Indonesian government leaders, but it has also allowed the Forestry Ministry to operate with a degree of extravagance. The forest-based Sabah Foundation in Malaysia has also funded such extravagance. Similarly the huge state oil companies that provided much of the off-budget financing in Mexico and Nigeria during certain periods took advantage of the presence of poorly monitored funds to spend excessively on operations, salaries, and perquisites.

Finally, the arrangements through which government officials evade their own accountability—complexity, laundering, misleading accounting, and so on—ironically make the state officials operating in these arrangements less accountable to the government. In their own efforts to evade accountability, government officials often make state officials less accountable.

Conclusions

This chapter attempts to show that natural-resource policy failures can be readily identified through simple models of economic optimization and government-state relations. The concepts of price distortions, externalities, property rights insecurity, uncertainty, direct state mis-exploitation, and nonaccountability can produce any of the policy failures that one encounters in surveying natural-resource management. We see that under- and overpricing are not only outcomes but are also easy and tempting instruments for government officials. We also see that several government policies and practices provoke hasty and reckless resource exploitation by increasing the uncertainty of future returns. We recognize that governments can mis-exploit natural resources directly through state practices or by allowing state entities to deviate from sound resource management to pursue their own objectives.

Just as important, these policy failures can be straightforwardly linked to the strategies of pursuing other objectives through natural-resource manipulations. This chapter demonstrates the possibility that the adoption of these strategies can create the whole gamut of resource policy failures.

However, this logical possibility does not demonstrate that these objectives, and the institutional factors presented in the first chapter, actually cause the resource policy failures encountered in developing countries. This can be demonstrated only by examining specific cases with enough depth to provide an understanding of possible motivations and strategic choices. Therefore, the next four chapters examine such cases. After looking at the Indonesian oil and timber cases in considerable depth in chapter 3, I devote a chapter to exploring each of the programmatic motivations: development financing, economic benefit, and revenue raising. In each, I elaborate on the linkages sketched in this chapter and take up several cases to illustrate how the strategies culminate in policy failures. Where relevant, I also examine the reforms that have brought better resource management.

CHAPTER 3

Oil and Timber Abuses to Fund Off-Budget Development Programs in Indonesia

I begin with the cases of Indonesia's oil and timber because they so clearly illustrate the complexity of natural-resource policy failures. The abuse of natural resources in Indonesia under President Suharto (1965–98) has generally been cast as a simple matter of power and patronage. We will see that these abuses reflect deeper and much more surprising circumstances. First, the motive of certain government officials (including Indonesia's president) has been as much to pursue particular development strategies as to maximize political power or wealth. Second, the abuse occurred because of disunity within the Indonesian government. Certain government agencies and officials opposed using government funds to undertake these development strategies. They could have, at a minimum, heightened tensions within the government and possibly embarrassed the president if he tried to pursue these strategies through the most direct government channels. To avoid this clash, the president created mechanisms to pursue these development objectives outside the central budget, diverting natural-resource rents gained from government-controlled oil and timber, providing a convenient and low-visibility source of "off budget" financing. Unfortunately, these maneuvers have severely abused the natural-resource base.

This explanation holds for both the Indonesian oil sector in the 1960s and early 1970s and the forest sector beginning in the mid-1970s and persisting today. Oil rents that would normally have gone to the central treasury were diverted through the operations of the state oil company Pertamina, which served as the president's off-budget "development agency" for many projects that key agencies such as the Finance Ministry and the national planning agency, BAPPENAS, would not support. Furthermore, the price of gasoline, kerosene, and other oil products had been set artificially low to promote oil-dependent industries. Since the mid-1970s, forest rents have been diverted to private loggers by undercharging for forest concessions and royalties. To reciprocate, these private loggers have applied part of their profits to development projects that President Suharto signaled as his priorities. Within the state, the Forestry Ministry also assisted in diverting forest rents to finance the rapid and highly controversial development of Indonesia's Outer Islands. A more recent maneuver involved the Forestry Ministry's diversion of money in a "reforestation fund" to help finance the state aircraft industry. All these mechanisms allowed the president to evade accountability for pursuing development initiatives that are potentially embarrassing from an orthodox, neoclassical economic perspective.

How do these maneuvers detract from sustainable resource exploitation? First, by undercharging for concession privileges and royalties, these manipulations encourage overexploitation—the obvious result of cheap access. This problem was severe for both the state oil company and the private loggers. Undercharging in the forestry case also led to reckless exploitation—the result of exploiters' uncertainty that their privileges will be available indefinitely. Second, underpricing of outputs, first oil products and later logs, caused uneconomical domestic resource consumption. Petroleum-processing and wood-processing industries have been both inefficient and vulnerable to future scarcity.

THE OIL SECTOR

Indonesia's state oil company, Pertamina, emerged in 1968 in the same fashion as did many other state oil companies: combining pre-existing state oil enterprises with the larger operations taken over from international oil companies. In Pertamina's case, a 1963 agreement with Shell, Standard Oil of California, Texaco, Standard Oil of New Jersey, and Mobil greatly expanded the holdings of small state producing companies. The multinational oil companies received long-term contractor arrangements in exchange. Some pre-existing state operations had been in the downstream activities of oil transport and gas stations. Pertamina thus became a vertically integrated company with exclusive formal control over exploration, production, refining, and domestic marketing. However, because Pertamina was short on expertise in nearly all aspects of the oil business,[1] it continued to rely on international oil companies for many services. Pertamina's own exploration and production operations (i.e., apart from international contractors) actually produced only 10 percent of Indonesia's oil output in the 1970s and 1980s and just 3 percent in the first half of the 1990s.

One novel aspect of the pre-1968 arrangement was that several small state operations were directly and formally controlled by the armed forces. Permina and Nglobo Oil Mining (later called Permigan) were established in the 1950s under military control when the army began the post–World War II, post-independence reconstruction of the devastated oilfields. It was widely understood and accepted that oil exploitation by these state enterprises was a source of revenues for the armed forces.

Moreover, the charismatic head of Permina, General Ibnu Sutowo, became the head of the new Pertamina. Thus, the heritage of Pertamina was a set of practices dedicated to augmenting the revenues of the armed forces and an instinct to keep the operations and financing secretive. This was a moderate problem when military-controlled oil operations were of modest dimensions, but by 1974 Pertamina's revenues, in the wake of the OPEC price increase, were US$4.2 billion — one-sixth of Indonesia's gross domestic product (Schwarz 1994, 54). At the same time, Pertamina's international debt exceeded that of the Indonesian government.

As a wholly government-owned enterprise with enormous domestic and international revenues, Pertamina was an overwhelming temptation for political leaders to direct toward political, distributional, and developmental objectives beyond its mandate as an oil company. The key political challenges for the government of President Suharto were to maintain the unity, strength, and support of the Indonesian military, to keep riot-prone populations and business groups content with a growing economy, and to counter the forces of separatism and Communist insurgency. All the while, the Indonesian government was trying to cultivate sources of foreign assistance, including the United States and other developed countries, as well as multilateral agencies such as the International Monetary Fund. An openly defense-heavy national budget would have looked very bad; international borrowing beyond agreed limits would have looked even worse.

The armed forces had controlled the centrifugal forces of the culturally and ethnically fragmented country, but these same armed forces had toppled Suharto's predecessor General Sukarno. They were also struggling to contain a Communist opposition, several separatist movements, bloody interethnic conflicts, periodic food riots, and other challenges to order and security. Adding to the potential for disintegration was the fact that regional commanders often had enough power to pose the threat of warlordism. The armed forces' demands for financial resources were enormous. As Hamish McDonald notes,

> The size of the military budget in particular had long been a delicate problem since it was proving less and less adequate to cover real needs. By the time Suharto took power it was an accepted fact that the armed forces had their own independent sources of funds. Suharto's need to unify the military vastly increased the demand. A basic strategy was to make soldiers rely as much as

possible on Defence headquarters, rather than their regional commander, for their new uniforms, improved housing, pay and meal supplements. There were about half a million men in uniform to keep happy. Added to this were 1.7 million civilian employees (according to a special census taken in 1974 to see just how many were on the payroll, the first time a total had been determined), forming a comparatively small percentage of the population but in absolute numbers an enormous burden on Indonesia's revenue base. (1981, 115)

Thus, as a way to finance the armed forces without the visibility of central government spending, a huge but unknown portion of Pertamina revenues went to the military. This persisted even after the military-controlled oil companies were brought into the single company structure.

More broadly, Pertamina was the public-works patronage agency and the few-questions-asked development agency when the Finance Ministry, the planning agency BAPPENAS, and the international lenders were insisting on austerity. Pertamina built hospitals, schools, and roads that served many people and purposes beyond the oil sector. In 1970 a presidential "Commission of Four" appointed to examine general charges of corruption in government criticized Pertamina for, among other things, "making unauthorized donations" (McDonald 1981, 124).

The development strategy pursued directly through Pertamina operations was a remarkably broad industrialization and infrastructure expansion, unfettered by government oversight or careful analysis of profitability (Bresnan 1993, 168–71; 182–83). Some of Pertamina's expansions were clearly connected to the oil business, although a state oil company could have easily forgone investments like two US$1 billion liquified natural gas facilities and a 3-million-ton tanker fleet requiring a US$3.3 billion investment. Some were downstream petroleum-reliant industries, most prominently in petrochemicals and fertilizer. However, other investments were hardly connected to the oil sector: a chain of hotels, rice estates, automobile distributorships, insurance, telecommunications, and the Pelita airline, which boasted the largest helicopter fleet in Southeast Asia. Pertamina even financed and created an entire industrial center on Batam Island (McDonald 1981, 157).

One project in particular epitomized the "nationalists' " agenda: Krakatau Steel. This was a project to revitalize and expand the Soviet-built steel-making facility that suspended production in 1965, facing severe problems of old technology, lack of nearby ore and energy sources, and shortage of skilled labor. None of the economic analyses showed that the original project, or any modification at that site, was worth undertaking, but the steel industry was the quintessential emblem of modernization and industrial prestige. Sutowo quadrupled the targeted output of Krakatau and invested US$2.5 billion for new construction, including a pipeline to bring natural gas from 130 miles away (McDonald 1981, 157). Pertamina made these investments without formal authorization by the government.

President Suharto allowed Pertamina to undertake these tasks not only because of General Sutowo's personal dynamism and close relationship with the president but also because Pertamina's access to investment capital was greater than any other institution short of the government treasury. The treasury was guarded by formidable "technocrats" who had the potential — through their technical expertise and international connections — to embarrass the president about questionable development ventures if he tried to pursue them through the conventional budget process. These technocrats were influential even when Suharto wished to pursue development projects that ran counter to their vision of Indonesia's development. R. M. Auty notes that

> the Indonesian civil service, which had been so faction-ridden as to be almost incapable of action under Sukarno, became more effective under Suharto. Even though rent-seeking flourished and political fiefdoms persisted at local and national levels (in both the public and private sectors, notably in industry), a bureaucratic pluralism existed . . . Able technocrats retained sufficient independence from the military to prevent key development ministries (Finance, Mines and Energy, Industry, and Public Works) from being wholly dominated by considerations of patronage. Although the balance of power shifted between two polarized technocratic factions, one comprising sectoral, statist nationalists and the other pragmatic, market-oriented technocrats . . . the latter faction was effectively used during the two oil booms to realign the economy periodically to real external constraints. (1990, 116)

Pertamina's access to capital obviously rested on oil revenues, but the company also had access to huge foreign loans that could be directed to spending targets chosen jointly by President Suharto and General Sutowo. The billions of dollars of loans to Pertamina were ostensibly for petroleum exploration, production, refining, and distribution, but both revenues and borrowed capital were also directed to other ends.

Pertamina's capacity to serve these functions clearly rested on the company's lack of transparency. The 1970 presidential Commission of Four complained about Pertamina's opaque accounting, lack of government oversight, and failure to relinquish funds ostensibly collected for the government (McDonald 1981, 124, 154). It is significant that the Indonesian government never officially released the Commission of Four reports; public knowledge of them came only through leaks to the press (McDonald 1981, 125). McDonald put it bluntly: "Suharto needed Ibnu Sutowo to get things done ... to provide funds for a threadbare army, to wean troops away from regional commanders, and to carry out essential political patronage. Ibnu Sutowo provided access to a vast, invisible system of taxation and expenditure that would be difficult to justify to the public if added to the official budget" (1981, 151).

McDonald's assessment makes it clear that Pertamina's capacity to operate without transparency was largely dependent on the support of the president. Pertamina's clashes with government agencies over the control of oil revenues were highlighted by the controversy over the type of relationship the company should maintain with international oil companies. In 1966 General Sutowo, as both head of Pertamina's predecessor Permina and the government's Director General for Oil and Gas, signed production-sharing contracts over the objections of his formal superior, Minister of Mines Slamet Bratanata. In early 1967 Bratanata retaliated by offering leases that negated Sutowo's contracts, despite President Suharto's support for Sutowo. Suharto responded by removing Permina from the ministry's control, and by October he had removed Bratanata from the cabinet. Similarly, in 1973 President Suharto fended off attacks on Pertamina's international borrowing by asserting that Sutowo had been entrusted to find his own financing (McDonald 1981, 151–55).

The Fall of Pertamina

Pertamina's downfall came not from the questionable spending of its own revenues but from its international borrowing. Like Mexico's PEMEX (examined in chapter 6), Pertamina secured its own credit ceiling with the international banks, beyond that of the Indonesian government. By 1975 Pertamina's foreign debt was US$10.5 billion, compared to the government's foreign debt of US$8 billion. Given the enormous range of Pertamina activities, obviously not all of this borrowed capital would go into the development of the oil sector. Pertamina was, in effect, borrowing for a broad range of programs and projects that President Suharto, if not the Indonesian Finance Ministry, was eager to fund off-budget. For its part, the Finance Ministry had to cope with the overall problem of declining hard-currency reserves.

In 1972 the Finance Ministry negotiated an agreement with the International Monetary Fund (IMF) that put a ceiling on the government's medium-term (one-to-fifteen-year) loans, backed by a government decree requiring the Finance Ministry to approve all medium-term borrowing by state enterprises or government agencies. Pertamina was reprimanded for borrowing more than US$350 million in 1972 without permission, but government oversight was not appreciably improved (McDonald 1981, 154–55).

Apparently Pertamina then chose to respect the medium-term borrowing limits enforced by the Finance Ministry. Yet by 1973, Pertamina found ways to borrow massively without violating the then-publicized prohibition on unauthorized medium-term borrowing. Taking advantage of the growing supply of short-term loans available because of greater international liquidity, Pertamina increased its short-term exposure, while also taking out long-term loans that also did not require Finance Ministry approval.

By 1975 Pertamina's debt included US$1.5 billion in short-term loans that the company could not cover after falling world oil prices sharply reduced Pertamina's revenues. Pertamina's capital was tied up in long-term projects like Krakatau Steel and the natural gas projects. International banks, learning more about Pertamina's precarious position, took advantage of cross-default contract provisions that permitted them to call in their loans.

The Indonesian government was forced to take over Pertamina's debt obligations, cancel or postpone many Pertamina-controlled projects, and suffer from severely reduced international borrowing for the rest of the decade. This was no isolated event of a state-enterprise bankruptcy; given the size of Pertamina's total debt, the entire nation's creditworthiness was on the line. The central bank had to renegotiate its own loans to secure hard currency needed to meet Pertamina's repayment obligations.

Pertamina had to reduce its total debt burden by selling tankers, canceling tanker leases, and postponing the petrochemical and industrial complex on Batam Island. Pertamina also had to cut back Krakatau Steel to its original targeted output, now under the direction of a BAPPENAS official. Other sell-offs and cancellations largely dismantled Pertamina as a multisectoral conglomerate. The government managed to obtain new medium-term financing to cover the short-term obligations, with the support of the U.S. government and other industrial nations. McDonald (1981, 164) reported that Indonesia's international borrowing up to 1980 was only half of what it would have been if Pertamina had not gone bankrupt.

The Structural Changes of the Aftermath

By early 1976 the government dismissed Ibnu Sutowo (although "with honor"), and Pertamina was placed under the direction of the former budget director of the Finance Ministry, Major-General Piet Haryono. By 1976 the government had made the following reforms:

1. Bank Indonesia (the central bank) assumed all Pertamina debts;
2. Bank Indonesia, acting for the Finance Ministry, had to negotiate and sign all Pertamina loans;
3. Bank Indonesia became the recipient of all Pertamina revenues and supervised this special account;
4. Non-oil projects were either canceled or transferred to other government units, and the company was expressly forbidden to operate beyond the oil and gas sector;[2] and
5. Bank Indonesia tightened up on its supervision of Pertamina financial records (Royaards and Hui 1977, 37).

In addition, international auditors (the firm of Arthur Young & Associates, later Price Waterhouse) were brought in to restructure Pertamina's books. Finally, and of much broader importance, all government agencies and state enterprises were required to submit their financial and investment plans to a tripartite committee of officials from Bank Indonesia, the Finance Ministry, and BAPPENAS. This committee had to preapprove all loans for government agencies and state enterprises (Royaards and Hui 1977, 42). In short, the central budgetary authorities won — for the time being.

A modified oversight arrangement for Pertamina capped these reforms. The Board of Commissioners was strengthened. Pertamina was now to be governed by the Board of Commissioners chaired by the Minister of Mines, with the Finance Minister as vice chair. Other members were the Minister State Secretariat, the State Secretary for Research and Technology, and the head of the planning agency BAPPENAS. Informally, the cabinet ministers of mines, finance, communications, and planning — all prominent "technocrats" — took control of straightening out the oil and gas sector (Rutledge 1976, 26). Combined with greatly improved (but still not ideal) financial and operational transparency, this collective oversight dramatically reduced the capacity of any intragovernmental actor to use the company to circumvent the policy preferences and jurisdictions of other agencies. Although Pertamina was not dominated by the technocrats, whatever ulterior motives Pertamina might pursue had to be thoroughly vetted and approved by this broad range of government agencies. Certainly the visibility of Pertamina operations through this oversight made all involved agencies aware of the company's operations.

This structure also forced the involved agencies to seek agreement on how Pertamina's operations should be conducted and its revenues spent:

Pertamina is no longer the self-willed prestige state within a state that it once was . . . All major policy decisions on hydrocarbon investment, production and pricing appear to be taken by the government primarily in the form of the Minister of Mines and Energy and the country's president. However, the National Development Planning Agency (BAPPENAS) and key ministers such as the Coordinating Minister for Industry and Trade . . . play important roles in major policy decisions. The interlocking directorships and chairmen of the various bodies involved in energy matters should allow a reasonable consensus to be developed. (Barnes 1995, 154)

This is not to say that Pertamina was tamed overnight. Company accounting remained inadequate, if better than in the pre-1975 era. The *Economist* (1981) reported in mid-1981 that "since Pertamina crashed six years ago, the accounting firm, Price Waterhouse, has been struggling to audit the company's books. Every year it has said it would have the books ready for public inspection, and every year it has had to postpone the unveiling." Nevertheless, the periodic efforts to clean up the records and root out corruption made inroads, inasmuch as Pertamina was no longer able to dismiss these efforts as it was prior to 1975. Most important, Pertamina ceased to be the prime vehicle of off-budget wheeling and dealing. Philip Barnes, in an otherwise quite critical assessment of the Indonesian oil sector, summarizes the strides made in reforming Pertamina:

By 1979, much of the non-oil business had been dismantled and the company had largely, although not wholly, reverted to its statutory role as an oil and gas enterprise. Pertamina is still allowed to involve itself in some outside interests in support of its oil and gas business but such activities now seem to be kept within reasonable bounds. Oil and gas revenues are channeled to central government to finance development plans and there is a suitable level of auditing. (1995, 151–52)

Of course, as long as Indonesia continued to export oil in large quantities, the revenues were available to the government. Pertamina remained a "cash cow," but the bulk of the cash was distributed through the central budget process.

However, in one area Pertamina remained outside the grasp of those government officials who wished to wrest more of the oil rents from the enterprise. Pertamina remained, and indeed grew, as a patronage employer. The 1979–81 second oil boom prompted Pertamina to add employees despite the shedding of direct exploration responsibilities; by the mid-1980s, Pertamina had fifty-four thousand employees in addition to twenty-four thousand contractor employees in exploration and production (Auty 1990, 145).

It is important to point out what Pertamina has done well. It has done a solid job in overseeing the rate and pricing of oil production destined for export. The continued reliance on international oil companies for exploration and production ensured that market considerations would remain important in decisions on exploration rates, production rates, sales volumes, and export pricing, within the parameters permitted under OPEC. Compared with PEMEX and PDVSA, the major producers in Mexico and Venezuela, respectively, Pertamina's role in "upstream" oil production has essentially been to negotiate contracts and collect royalties from the international companies. Pertamina has performed this function well, through continual pressure on the companies to accept lower shares of the oil they produce.[3] More than one hundred different companies and consortia bid on Indonesian oil contracts, allowing Pertamina to select attractive bids and to pace exploration according to the government's need for income and the company's assessment of the likelihood of major oil finds in the blocks put up for bid. While some Indonesians have complained that the production-sharing contracts have been more generous than those of the Middle Eastern oil giants, this reflects the greater risks of finding profitable oil fields in Indonesia, and the more difficult production conditions in the forests, swamps, and offshore locations where Indonesian oil is found. Because the international oil companies have been interested in Indonesian exploration and production only when market conditions have been appropriate, Indonesia has avoided squandering financial resources on politically motivated exploration (as in Peru). It has also avoided the consequences of state enterprise undercapitalization (as in Mexico and Venezuela).

However, one weakness in Pertamina's relations to the international oil company contractors has been the requirement that the contractors provide social and community services in the regions of oil exploitation. While this serves the political function of giving the appearance that the government has squeezed the international companies to provide even more than their royalty payments, it places the responsibility for planning and undertaking community and social services (such as health clinics, town paving, and even entertainment) in the hands of international oil companies, who are no better in these spheres than Pertamina oil geologists were to run hotels. In addition, providing these services in specific oil-producing areas often entails inequitable benefits compared with other areas.

In terms of the advisability and efficiency of downstream investments, Pertamina's performance also seems reasonable. Large-scale projects such as refineries and liquid gas facilities have typically been joint ventures. Therefore, the private-sector partner scrutinizes each project for profitability. Often the projects have required international borrowing, which brings in the scrutiny and approval of the oversight ministries, the central bank (Bank Indonesia), and the planning agency, as well as the international bank. Some corrupt practices in local contracting have been reported, but the overall soundness of Pertamina downstream projects has been vastly improved compared with the days of Krakatau Steel.

Domestic Pricing Problems

During the 1970s, the government heavily subsidized the domestic prices of Indonesian petroleum products. This led to overconsumption, lost opportunities for oil export, and the development of industries vulnerable to future energy-price increases. For a country likely to be a net oil importer early in the twenty-first century, this last risk was much more serious than for countries like Venezuela and Mexico with much greater potential reserves. From 1975 to 1980, domestic consumption of primary petroleum products grew by an annual rate of more than 9 percent, compared with a GDP growth rate of 7 percent. In 1980 the government set up the National Energy Coordinating Board with the principal objective of reducing domestic oil consumption (Barnes 1995, 82). In particular, the huge subsidies for kerosene, initially rationalized as support for low-income households to cover their energy needs, led to the inappropriate use of kerosene for transportation, heating, and other nonhousehold purposes. As late as 1987, kerosene accounted for more than a quarter of Indonesia's domestic petroleum consumption, a figure far too high given Indonesia's biomass potential (Barnes 1995, 87–90). The subsidy also led to smuggling, as some individuals bought cheap kerosene in order to sell it abroad at a markup.

The policy of low domestic petroleum product prices that prevailed in the 1970s was propelled as much by a cheap-energy industrialization strategy as it was to mollify a mobilized consumer population. The nationalists favored inexpensive energy for industry and transport, while the expansionary climate made it difficult for the government to insist on the discipline of keeping domestic prices in line with rising production costs. Yet the core of the strategy of oil-led industrialization was to maintain petroleum exports as the chief source of foreign exchange to finance domestic industrial and infrastructure growth.

Liberalization came once there was a strong demonstration of how onerous the costs of underpricing were for this core strategy. The 1982 economic crunch that reduced Indonesia's GDP growth from nearly 8 to only 2 percent coincided with a 25 percent production decline of crude. Even though world oil prices remained very high, declining government revenues were so alarming that the technocrats could press for increased domestic petroleum product prices as the obvious way to make more crude available for export. Higher prices would reduce the domestic demand for crude, leaving a larger portion of Pertamina's share of crude production for export. Barnes (1995, 23) notes that "diminished oil production reduced government revenues and strained the policy of using production-sharing crude for subsidized sales of petroleum products to the domestic market. As a result subsidies were cut in 1982–83 and domestic fuel prices increased by 60 to 75 percent."

The liberalization also reflected changed views on the entitlement nature of energy. As long as Indonesian oil seemed limitless, cheap oil-based energy was widely regarded as a gift of God. The decline in oil production was a very sobering reminder of the finite nature of the nation's oil reserves.

Then, too, the economic crisis put the technocrats into a stronger position to determine economic policy. One of the technocrats' main concerns was the adequacy of central government revenues, which they controlled through their dominance in the Finance Ministry and the planning agency BAPPENAS. However, there was a broadening consensus that energy prices ought to be liberalized. Price subsidies failed to serve the development objectives held dear by the nationalists, because higher domestic consumption reduced the oil exports that were supposed to be the engine of ambitious expansion plans. It was then just a matter of finding the path of price increases that would keep public dissatisfaction within tolerable bounds.

The result of cutting the subsidies has been a lower increase in the growth of domestic oil consumption. In the 1990s overall petroleum product growth has been approximately 8 percent per year. Reductions in subsidies for kerosene reduced the growth in kerosene demand from 10 to 5 percent by the 1990s (Barnes 1995, 87). The overall pace of energy consumption is not as low as the energy conservation planners would like and not much lower than the rates of the 1970s. Yet, coming at a time of rapid economic growth (GDP growth of 7–8 percent until the 1998 crash) and expansion of the transportation fleet, such growth in petroleum consumption is not a reckless outcome.

Analysis of Root Problems

The 1975 bankruptcy, and the poor investments that it revealed, provide important insights into the relationship between fiscal arrangements and financial profligacy. One root of Pertamina's 1975 debacle, and indeed Pertamina's lack of discipline since its inception, was that the company so easily held onto the oil resource rent. Pertamina, like so many other state oil companies, paid royalties that were not based on the full oil rents that should be captured at the outset by the resource owner (i.e., the government rather than the state enterprise). This underpricing was itself a policy failure that induced overexploitation, but it had the additional perverse effect of leaving Pertamina with huge windfall profits when world oil prices were high. Even if Pertamina had not been guilty of failing to turn over all of the revenues owed to the treasury, as the Commission of Four alleged, it would still have had enormous surplus to allocate, especially in boom years like 1974.

Yet this underpricing is particularly problematic when combined with minimal transparency and high willingness of top government officials to allow or even demand extrasectoral investments by the state enterprise. From the outset, Pertamina was conceived as a conglomerate and rewarded for behaving as such. Barnes (1995, 151) puts it well when he says that Pertamina "ran itself as a kind of national development corporation for Indonesia" (we will see that in later years the Forestry Ministry played a comparable role). Pertamina's 1968 articles of incorporation, and the 1971 law specifying its monopoly over oil-related operations, did not limit Pertamina to the oil sector, and indeed the idea that Pertamina was a far-flung conglomerate akin to the multinational corporations was a source of pride for many Indonesians.

However, this conception of a rent-capturing state enterprise as a diversified conglomerate violated a basic principle of public finance that the government's resources ought to be allocated centrally to increase the likelihood that the most worthwhile projects and programs will be chosen across the entire economy. Pertamina publications in general stress that all of its ventures have been chosen with the expectation of profitability, but the company has never been in the position to be able to judge whether its investment possibilities have been as great as other possibilities available to the government. Moreover, the technical capability of oil company executives to select and manage non-oil-related ventures was clearly problematic. Thus, the reforms that Pertamina has undergone have increased its managerial efficiency as well as its investment efficiency, simply by reducing the scope of the company to the sector in which it has a fighting chance to operate with solid professional judgment.

The Forestry Sector

The forestry sector was largely untouched while Pertamina was the main agent of off-budget government spending. Dipterocarp forests blanketed Sumatra, East and West Kalimantan on Borneo, and Irian Jaya. Modest farming and plantations were emerging on Sumatra, and local peoples engaged in even more modest shifting cultivation on Kalimantan and Irian Jaya, yet forest clearing was essentially limited to the few logging concessions that the government began issuing in the late 1960s in the wake of the Foreign Investment Law of 1967 and the Domestic Investment Law of 1968. In 1970 the sixty-four concession areas covered less than 8 million hectares, a tiny fraction of the vast expanse of these islands.

Yet in the 1970s and 1980s, the concession areas increased vastly in number and size, and legal and illegal logging exploded. Of course, not all deforestation was due to logging; slash-and-burn agriculture, as well as conversion of natural forest to plantations and to sedentary agriculture, was also important. Yet even the slash-and-burn agriculture could be partially traced to logging, as logging roads opened the path for slash-and-burn cultivators to move farther into the interior.

The serious impacts of overlogging on the forests have been documented elsewhere.[4] Here it is necessary only to point out that beyond the impact on the forests and ecosystems, the forest-products industry, propped up by cheap but shrinking inputs, is both inefficient and vulnerable to supply shortages. The proceeds from forestry exploitation have been squandered in unwise investments both within and outside the forestry and wood-products subsectors.

The government policies responsible for these problems are not hard to find: huge, unmonitorable concessions; harvesting regulations that permit high-grading and high damage to nonharvested trees; inadequate royalties that also encourage high-grading; a reforestation fee-and-refund system that rarely provides refunds or stimulates reforestation; a ban on log exports that has shrunk the market for Indonesian timber, costing hundreds of millions of dollars in lost exports and exacerbating the inefficiency of wood-products industry; land classifications that contribute to poor land uses; and an ineffective plantation-subsidy program.[5]

At first glance, it seems that the same basic pattern of cheap forest concessions and underregulation existed to benefit the politically powerful during the entire period from the late 1960s to the present. This has prompted some observers (e.g., Broad 1995) to characterize the entire period as a uniform and static arrangement. In fact, there have been critical changes over time that reveal important changes in the logic and political motives of these policies.

The groundwork for these policies was laid before timber rents became important. In the late 1960s the Suharto government appropriated 90 percent of all forest land, thereby centralizing government control over forest resources, negating traditional property rights. This set the scene for a massive forest concession system and eliminated obstacles for foreign firms to operate forest concessions.

Royalties and taxes on timber harvesting were kept low, amounting in total to only one-quarter of the stumpage value during the 1967–75 period and declining to less than 10 percent by 1985–86. Domestic and foreign timber companies responded enthusiastically; from 1967 to 1973 timber exports more than doubled every year. By 1973 Indonesia was the world's largest tropical timber exporter. Foreign investment in the forest sector boomed, with Japanese, Korean, Philippine, Malaysian, and U.S. timber companies investing heavily in roads and equipment, although the demand for round-log exports kept investment in local processing (e.g., sawmills) quite low. The multinationals were making respectable profits based on rather large investments, but the major rent beneficiaries were top military leaders who had been granted concessions and the Indonesian Chinese loggers brought in to provide the expertise and operational capability in partnerships with these officers. As in Malaysian Sarawak (Hurst 1990, 105; Stesser 1991, 62–63), the politically powerful rent recipients could largely sit back and have others exploit their forest concessions for a split of the proceeds. In Sarawak this has been the powerful civilian *bumiputra* Sarawakians; in Indonesia it was the armed forces.

Yet, beginning in 1979, the government moved to tax and then ban all round-log exports by 1985.[6] This ban seems to fly in the face of political logic, inasmuch as it dealt a blow to the economic fortunes of the presumably politically powerful military concessionaires. This policy also destroyed millions of dollars of timber value by forcing Indonesian timber into highly inefficient, value-reducing domestic production. The forestry sector as a whole suffered, as would be expected of any constraint imposed on the predominant activity — in this case raw log export — chosen by the concessionaires to maximize their returns. In 1980 the Indonesian government also began the exclusion of foreign firms as concessionaires, expanded to a full ban by 1984. Some joint ventures with Indonesian firms remained viable, but clearly the multinational companies, formerly encouraged, were to all extents and purposes removed from logging. This made it much more difficult for the forestry sector to take advantage of the multinationals' technological and potential environmental expertise. Theories of the insidious power of the multinational corporation certainly fall flat in accounting for this turnabout.

In 1980 the government also established a reforestation fund under the control of the Forestry Ministry. Initially represented as an environmental measure, this fund collected a fee on the volume of declared timber harvested. In theory, it was to be refunded to concessionaires who reforested, but because the refund would be far less than the costs of reforesting, virtually none of the fund was ever devoted to reforestation. Thus, the reforestation charge amounted to a royalty; however, it was retained by the Forestry Ministry rather than sent to the central treasury as a charge on extracting the nation's timber wealth.

Tighter Regulation and the Growing Centrality of the Indonesian Chinese

Around 1987 the government began to tighten up — selectively — on logging regulation, while launching several well-publicized "reforms" to increase the timber royalties. While it is true that some fines and threatened license cancellations were reversed, others were enforced, and a number of logging firms lost their concessions (Ross 1996, ch. 5). This was certainly an odd way to treat the concessionaires if they indeed had, as Robin Broad (1995, 331) puts it, "captured" forest policy away from the government.

The political logic of this pattern is not obvious. To be sure, favoring the military has a straightforward explanation. As a relatively minor military figure who emerged from the chaos of the end of the Sukarno regime, General Suharto needed — but could not take for granted — strong backing from the armed forces leadership. In a brilliant financial maneuver, Suharto set up "foundations" (yayasans) that would provide for very generous financial benefits for the armed forces and retired military personnel, particularly those of highest rank — as long as Suharto remained in office as president.[7] But why not also favor the mainstream civilian pribumi political elite, as was done in Sarawak, to share with the military in exploiting the underpriced concessions? Instead, Suharto looked favorably upon joint ventures between military officers, both active and retired, and the Indonesian-Chinese business community, despite the Indonesian Chinese's lack of independent political power. We may speculate that Suharto may have perceived the pribumi business sector as believing that it was entitled to preferential treatment, rather than believing that such treatment would have been an indulgence provided by the president. The pribumi elite may have been both a threat to Suharto, if it could have pursued an alliance with other contenders for political leadership, and nonessential to Suharto if he could count on military support and undercut the economic power of the pribumi business elite. In cutting them out of most of the rent-seeking opportunities in the oil and forestry sectors, Suharto neutralized much of the power of this group that had possessed the potential for independent political power. Instead, he brought in the Indonesian Chinese, a much more dependent group.

Why the ethnic Chinese? This is the most intriguing and most important question in understanding the political economy of Indonesian forestry policy. It is not enough just to say that a collaboration between the ethnic Chinese and the Indonesian armed forces, including General Suharto, dates back to the 1950s.[8] This historical fact does not explain why the relationship was established or retained, nor whether the rationales for maintaining it were even connected with the original motivations. There is, indeed, one consideration that makes the ethnic Chinese seem like a poor choice as the recipients of vast timber rents: they were so politically beholden to the government, and in particular to General Suharto, that directing lucrative rent-seeking opportunities to them might seem like a waste of a resource. Certainly if their political support were the only factor, then billions of dollars worth of timber rents, on top of the fortunes they have been amassing through other business ventures, would have been unnecessary. Clearly the simplest rent-seeking model — the exchange of economic rents for the political support of the recipients — is inadequate to explain Suharto's choice of the ethnic Chinese.

However, if we look at the economic behavior of the ethnic-Chinese logging entrepreneurs, we see rather clear evidence that they reciprocate for their receipt of benefits, at the expense of their private profit maximization, in the choice of some of the business ventures they undertake. For example:

- The current industrial plantation strategy has put pressure on loggers to develop plantations even though some are unprofitable (Haughton, Teter, and Stern 1992, 7);
- Some vertically integrated wood-products companies have undertaken clearly money-losing activities, including particle-board manufacture that has positive environmental symbolism but negative rates of return.[9]
- Logging firms have a formal obligation to provide community development assistance to the populations near or within the concession areas. While this obligation is vague, ad hoc, and poorly monitored, the Forestry Ministry does have considerable influence over whether and how the obligation will be met. Therefore, the very fact that the obligation is discretionary gives the Forestry Ministry the opportunity to direct the "community development" in ways that conform with particular development strategies, for example, electrification or road building. Again, by placing the financing of such development projects on the shoulders of the private sector, the Forestry

Ministry can pursue these projects without having to subject them to the evaluation and approval processes of the central budget authorities.

- In 1990–91 Prajogo Pangestu and the head of another major Chinese group, Liem Sioe Liong, reportedly covered US$420 million in foreign-exchange losses of the Bank Duta, which is largely owned by foundations connected with President Suharto (Schwarz and Friedland 1992, 42). The same source reports that Prajogo paid for the Taman Mini theme park monorail at the behest of the president's wife, financed a biography of Suharto, and accepted the president's children Trihatmodjo and Rukmana into joint partnerships.

Other projects of questionable societal value have been undertaken by ethnic-Chinese Indonesians with the help of President Suharto against the policy preferences of the technocrats. For example, establishing a world-scale, wholly Indonesian-owned petrochemical industry has been a major attraction for the nationalists. One enormous Indonesian-owned petro-chemical venture, the US$1.8 billion Chandra Asri olefins complex, had already begun construction by 1991, when an interministerial coordinat-ing group addressing Indonesia's increased foreign debt called for a slow-down on large development projects entailing significant foreign borrow-ing until 1995 and even set up a loan-coordinating group (labeled "Team 39") that had to approve the foreign borrowing of all state-related in-vestments in infrastructure and petrochemicals (Schwarz and Friedland 1992, 46). Chandra Asri was deemed to fall under the Team 39 restrictions because it was "state related" in the dual sense that it was designed to use naphtha inputs from the state oil company Pertamina and had borrowed heavily from the state-owned Bank Bumi Daya (Schwarz and Friedland 1992, 46). However, although *pribumi* businessmen initially seemed to be slated to control the private-sector component of this venture, President Suharto intervened to make Prajogo Pangestu and Liem Soie Liong the major private partners (Suharto's son Bambang was also involved). By or-chestrating pressure from multinational oil companies, international banks, and even the Japanese Ministry of International Trade and Industry, their two conglomerates succeeded in gaining an exemption from the investment freeze. Once the project was underway, the Suharto administration made it privately profitable, despite its highly questionable societal value, by shield-ing Chandra Asri outputs with import tariffs. In short, the Indonesian Chinese provided the private-sector economic and political link, allowing President Suharto to avoid becoming beholden to *pribumi* business elites, while continuing with the project despite objections from within the government. The rewards for the Indonesian Chinese reflect their usefulness to the presidency not only for their business expertise, international connections, and pre-existing business links with the armed forces, but also for their lack of status as an independent political force. Of course, the resentment of the Chinese on the part of the *pribumi* rose as a consequence, increasing Chinese marginality without the protection of Suharto even more, and thus increasing their dependence on Suharto.

The log-export prohibition raises the second puzzle, inasmuch as there seems to be an inconsistency in the political logic of imposing the export ban on the same actors who were increasingly privileged by underpriced timber royalties. One explanation is that the military no longer rated the patronage they had been receiving before. By 1980 President Suharto had reorganized the armed forces, which became much less of a threat to his control (Crouch 1988). The simple business of contracting for the extraction and sale of logs was no longer the reward for military support; patronage now would go to those who could master the much more complex business of making a profit from manufacturing and marketing. The survivors were the firms that were adept enough to combine their access to logging concessions with their own sawmill, plywood facilities, and export connections. Many military officers had to sell out, moving the control of the forestry industry more firmly into the hands of the Indonesian Chinese. Second, the establishment of a wood-products industry fit into a broader strategy of industrializing the Indonesian economy despite the questionable efficiency and profitability of these developments. The "nationalist" position in the Indonesian economic debate had—and still has—considerable ideological appeal and, when pursued, has meant considerable economic benefits for some interests. There is no inconsistency in regarding the development of a wood-products industry as both a concession to nationalist economic sentiment and a strategic end in itself. Whatever combination of explanations holds, it is notable that President Suharto could afford to pursue this development strategy even though it meant withdrawing some of the benefits to presumably politically powerful groups.

One might ask whether this post-1987 policy regime truly represented a new strategy. After all, royalty rates remained low, and regulation remained sporadic.[10] It has still been easy for privileged private loggers to make huge fortunes from the nation's forest wealth through the underpricing of state timber and selective enforcement. However, two differences were crucial. First, the concessionaires ran a risk of losing their concessions to a degree unknown in the earlier period. Violations of forestry regulations could result in heavy fines, the withdrawal of concession rights, and other negative sanctions. In short, timber concessionaires became vulnerable to regulation that could be applied selectively by the Forestry Ministry in alliance with the presidency.

Second, the continual (if somewhat superficial) efforts at forestry policy reform not only represented a degree of responsiveness to pressure from environmental groups and international agencies such as the World Bank but also put the concessionaires on notice that their collective performance had to satisfy government objectives sufficiently to keep the reformers from wiping out the rent opportunities altogether. Thus, both individual and collective vulnerability were introduced; the consequence was that concessionaires had to work for their privileges. A consequence of the pressure for reform coming from the Finance Ministry, BAPPENAS, the U.S. Agency for International Development, and the World Bank was the loggers' greater dependence on the president's protection. Discretionary enforcement and partial reform posed additional risks to the already politically vulnerable Indonesian Chinese — risks that the military beneficiaries of forest rents did not have to face in the earlier period.

Thus, the new strategy that ousted the multinationals and pushed the military out of the forestry sector did not eliminate rent-seeking opportunities; it shifted the beneficiaries and the terms. Initially the government offered forest rents in exchange for political support from the clearly powerful military; it became an exchange of forest rents for cooperation by the Indonesian Chinese in financing development projects and other off-budget initiatives. The Indonesian Chinese began as subsidiary actors in a political arrangement, involved for their business expertise; they became the linchpin of a much more complicated economic and fiscal arrangement.

The important role that President Suharto entrusted to the Indonesian Chinese makes it easy to understand how the "capture" interpretation arises. Many observers pointed to Mohamad (Bob) Hasan, a long-standing confidante of President Suharto, as more influential in forestry policy than the Forestry Minister. Despite his adopted name, Mohamad Hasan is Indonesian Chinese. As the head of the plywood manufacturers association Apkindo (the Indonesian Wood Panel Association), virtually a cartel, he has wielded great power over the wood-processing industry, and over the logging industry as well. Many forestry officials have resented this penetration of a private actor into government decision making and the general blurring of institutional and private-public boundaries (Schwarz 1989, 86).

Yet the key to understanding the power of Mohamad Hasan is to appreciate that it was derived from, and wholly dependent on, the power of the president. Individuals such as Mohamad Hasan "penetrated" or "captured" the state only as agents of the presidency, just as the penetration of

Suharto's family members into so many private-sector ventures represented the private sector's success in linking their fortunes directly to those of the president's family. The crucial question is whether Mohamad Hasan, or the other immensely successful Indonesian Chinese entrepreneurs, could have acted against the interests of the presidency. Thus far there is no evidence that they could or would have had any incentive to do so.

Intragovernmental Rent Capture

The "reforestation fund" demonstrates the same theme of off-budget development financing, but through the state sector rather than the private sector. The fund, financed by a charge on logging ostensibly to be refunded to loggers willing to reforest their concession areas, was set at a level that effectively discouraged any such reforestation. The fund, estimated at around US$800 million, has had no external controls or monitoring on its disposition of the money.[11] There was much speculation that the funds were used to finance the campaigns of Suharto's political party, Golkar. But more important for our arguments, the retention of the reforestation fee by the Forestry Ministry has served an internal bureaucratic-alliance purpose of providing the Forestry Ministry with an incentive to cooperate with the presidency in development activities that seem very strange for a forestry ministry, given that the concession practices and agricultural conversion policies have essentially liquidated the Indonesian forests. Yet, in addition to maintaining jurisdiction over forest-designated areas even if they are not forested, the Forestry Ministry oversees — to be sure, in partnership with the presidency — an enormous portion of Indonesia's territory: the three-fourths that is formally designated as forest, whether or not trees stand on this land. Therefore, the Forestry Ministry has had major (although not uncontested) jurisdiction over much of the on-site operations of the *transmigrasi* resettlements on the Outer Islands. As Pertamina was the "quick and dirty" development agency of the late 1960s and early 1970s, the Forestry Ministry assumed this role after the Pertamina financial collapse (Ascher 1993a, 11–12). In the late 1980s the reforestation funds were directed to the concern over diminishing timber supplies. The Forestry Ministry offered 0 percent interest loans, plus government equity participation, for the establishment of plantations ("timber estates" in Indonesian parlance).[12] The World Bank estimated the subsidy at US$425 per hectare (World Bank 1990, 14). The claimants were largely already established, vertically integrated timber companies.

The policy was criticized by the technocrats for the short subsidy period, limited to three years, and for the high likelihood that the same concessionaires benefiting from the government's low timber-rent capture would be subsidized yet again in their plantation initiatives.[13] The lack of subsidy beyond the third year encouraged the planting of inexpensive species and minimal maintenance, leading to stands of little value at harvest time. As prohibitions against foreign ownership of concessions effectively deter the largest multinational timber companies, the provision of sufficient capital and technology for successful plantations is very much in question (Gillis 1988a, 75). The low timber-rent capture from the concession areas still makes the logging of natural forests more economically attractive to the forestry industry. Independent estimates showed the plantations as having negative net present values (Haughton et al. 1992, 10). Because these projects were largely privately unprofitable, there was an incentive to capture the benefits of the 0 percent interest loans by diverting the funds to other projects and then walking away from the plantations, because even successful production would be difficult to sell in light of the low prices of logs from natural forests. Finally, the initiative ignored the fact that most plantations in lowland humid tropics around the world have failed. The real issue at the heart of the technocrat versus nationalist debate was whether to subsidize the downstream wood-products industry.

Finally, in late 1994 it was revealed that President Suharto had directed the Forestry Ministry to make a US$174 million interest-free loan to the state aircraft industry IPTN for the development of the new N-250 (*Jakarta Post* 1994). The aerospace industry had been regarded by the technocrats within the government as a wasteful, money-losing prospect that could not be justified on economic grounds. The nationalists, on the other hand, saw it as an important symbol of Indonesia's international industrial prestige and potential in high technology. It is interesting, however, that the intragovernmental clash over whether the Forestry Ministry's loan was appropriate was not what brought the issue to light; it was the angered reaction of Indonesian environmental groups. For these groups, the use of the reforestation fund for aircraft development certainly symbolized the end of any hope or pretense that the reforestation fund would be used for reforestation, even though the more skeptical environmentalists and analysts had much earlier doubts. The environmental groups filed suit against the government for this diversion; the courts ultimately refused to hear the case on the grounds that it was beyond their jurisdiction.

The environmental call to arms over the diversion of the reforestation funds to the state aircraft industry was a fascinating reframing of a clash over development strategy — another subsidized nationalist initiative with a questionable economic rate of return — into an apparent conflict between development and environment. In fact, there was never any environmental impact of the reforestation fee, because it had never been seriously applied to reforestation. The real issue was how the rent captured by the Forestry Ministry, rather than the treasury, would be directed. It was clearly directed to investments that the conventional budget authorities did not support. If the rent had been captured from the loggers and moved directly to the treasury, it would have been more under the control of the technocrats and certainly more transparent in terms of which projects were economically unviable without subsidization. In short, in the reforestation fund, President Suharto had found another off-budget vehicle for pursuing projects that would be difficult or at least awkward to undertake through the conventional budget process.

CONCLUSIONS

The Indonesian forestry case is a clear demonstration of suboptimal forest policies and practices that can be linked to the off-budget pursuit of development strategies ranging from downstream wood products to aerospace. To be sure, this motive was commingled with other motives such as political campaign finance and personal aggrandizement. Yet the fact that President Suharto allowed and directed forestry rents to flow into investments in support of the so-called nationalist economic development strategy, specifically when liberalizing, free-market officials tended to dominate "on-budget" fiscal and monetary policy, is the clearest demonstration of this dynamic that has emerged from the examination of a large number of cases.[14]

My argument runs counter to the conventional view that President Suharto was all-powerful and obsessed with enriching himself and his family to the maximum extent possible, but it also rejects the view that the natural-resource exploiters "captured" a "weak state." The first view presumes that the machinations with forestry concessions were simply means to enrich Suharto relatives who were so often in partnership with the Indonesian Chinese logging conglomerates. To some observers who (quite correctly) noted that the logging had typically been unsustainable and environmentally damaging, the government's actions (granting logging concessions to these entrepreneurs, nonenforcement of forestry regulations, and the involvement of Suharto's relatives in the conglomerates) seemed like overt nose-thumbing by a president who did not care about impressions. This interpretation presumed that the spectacle of abuse apparent to the expert observer who has access to the *Far Eastern Economic Review* was as apparent to the Indonesian public. In truth, the machinations in the forestry sector were, for many years, only murkily perceived by the public and even by rather knowledgeable Indonesians. The pursuit of development objectives through the manipulation of natural-resource exploitation was less transparent than the obvious alternative of pursuing them through direct government expenditures through the central budget.

The mechanism of "laundering" timber rents through the private loggers was rather distinctive because in most other countries this laundering is conducted through state actors. This distinction has led some observers to diagnose the Indonesian situation as "state capture" by presumably powerful private groups, such as the Indonesian Chinese. The state-capture view is put perhaps most extremely by Robin Broad, who argues that in both Indonesia and the Philippines

> [the forestry] sector molds the state and influences the policy-making environment . . . The political influence of those who gain economically from the exploitation of rainforest resources . . . is used to thwart proposals both for broader-based development and for environmental reform. (1995, 321–22)
>
> The abundance of natural resources has catalyzed interactions further entwining the state with privileged groups. That state finds itself without relative autonomy to pursue policies that do not reflect the short-term interests of the exploiters; parts of the state are not just politicized but are "captured." Such a state is not what has been called a "strong state" or a "developmental state" — that is, one able to formulate and implement policies independently of powerful groups. (1995, 331)

Broad's analysis ignores three crucial facts. First, the Indonesian Chinese logging entrepreneurs have had very little independent political power; indeed, they were selected as successful rent-seekers precisely because of their limited independent political power. In exchange for their privileged position, they were obliged to help the president. A more independently powerful group might have been able to regard its privileged economic access as simply its due.

Second, the Indonesian Chinese were unable to use the profits from logging in a profit-maximizing way. The crucial fact is that hundreds of millions of dollars worth of timber rents were destroyed by the imposition of the log-export ban, and the domestic logging concessionaires could otherwise have captured much of this value. The need for vertical integration was forced upon the domestic logging companies, often at considerable loss to these companies. Further financial loss-leaders followed, in the classical mode of "rent dissipation" foreseen in the models of actors who, rather than controlling the state, have to compete for its favors (Tollison 1982).

Third, the Indonesian presidency (if not the entire government or state) was quite capable of pursuing a long-term development policy; it just happened to be a mixed nationalist and neoclassical strategy that was obviously not to Broad's liking, but it was a strategy nonetheless, and the Indonesian Chinese were instrumental in furthering this strategy.

From this perspective, the state was not so much weak as it was divided; the nationalist-technocrat divide made the game of resource-rent diversion necessary if these divisions were to be kept relatively quiet. To assert that the Indonesian state was weak because it had to keep these divisions from becoming overt would also be misguided, inasmuch as the Suharto government was able to keep them quiet, and pursue a mix of nationalist and technocrat-approved projects, at minimal political cost.

Several intriguing interpretive questions remain. Why was it that President Suharto, certainly very powerful if not omnipotent, went to such lengths and sacrificed the soundness of the natural-resource exploitation? Many governments use off-budget slush funds; why rely on one that sacrifices gains from such an important industry? Could not the serious inefficiencies in the nation's second-largest foreign-exchange-earning industry have been avoided if Suharto had pursued these development projects through other means, including straightforward budget allocations over the objections of the Finance Ministry, BAPPENAS, and other agencies?

One reason, surely, is that there was an enormous premium on the appearance of consensus, as part of the *Pancasila* ideology. But why was the reduction or avoidance of apparent disunity within the government preferable to the scandals that the circumvention of the conventional fiscal authorities occasionally precipitated? Was it simply the case that in Indonesian political culture, the credibility of governance depended more on running the government smoothly than on running it without scandal?

Whatever the answers to these questions, appreciating the richness of the motivations and circumstances that led to unsound natural-resource policies and practices allows us to raise and explore the following pragmatic issues:

1. Under what circumstances would government oversight of the exploitation of a particular natural resource prevent some government agencies from sacrificing the soundness of resource exploitation in order to circumvent the influence of other agencies? For example, would the interministerial oversight that seems to work well for the oil sector also work for the forestry sector? Would ecosystem management reduce the incentive for agencies like the Forestry Ministry to adopt unsound policies that under

current arrangements cost such agencies little in terms of their institutional interests? What would happen if the Forestry Ministry could maintain jurisdiction only over areas that are actually forested?

2. At what level of visibility and notoriety of resource abuses would the top government leaders find that the political costs exceed the benefits of hiding intragovernmental disunity? Some of the reactions to the criticisms of local groups and the international community in both the oil and forestry sectors indicate that avoiding such notoriety has been a relevant motive for some modicum of reform. In other words, how important is transparency, and how can it be combined with other actions (such as conditionalities) to reform natural-resource practices?

Chapter 4

Development Programs through Natural-Resource Abuses

Introduction

The stories of Indonesian oil and timber yield strong lessons. Government officials launched development initiatives at the expense of sound natural-resource policy and practices, compelled by internal conflicts over development strategies, although officials rarely acknowledged these conflicts. Often various officials took advantage of poor information to reduce the political costs of resource abuse. Yet, on occasion, revelations made these mis-exploitations too costly to pursue. Multiple oversight, by government agencies with different development agendas, have reduced the feasibility of diverting natural-resource rents to go around bureaucratic rivals, as shown by post-1975 Indonesian oil exploitation.

This chapter is also about resource abuse for the sake of financing development programs. It reveals that government officials have pursued many development programs at the expense of sound natural-resource exploitation; Indonesia is no fluke. Yet the political logic in these cases differs from that of Indonesia. Some differences must exist, because President Suharto did not have to pay as much attention as most political leaders must to currying political favor. Yet many cases of natural-resource abuse for the sake of pursuing development programs do occur in countries with politically weaker governments. Is the entire political equation different? If so, do the resource abuses also reflect intragovernmental division, as in the Indonesian case?

Types of Resource-Based Development Programs and Their Distortions

Governments pursue a wide variety of development programs at the expense of the soundness of natural-resource policies and practices. Our

Table 4.1 Development Programs: Types, Cases, and Instruments

Development Objective	Variant	Cases	Specific Policy Instruments
Industrialization	Downstream processing	Indonesia, Ivory Coast, Liberia	Timber underpricing to promote the wood-products industry
		Honduras	State-enterprise retention of timber rents to finance the wood-products industry
		Nigeria, Venezuela	State-enterprise retention of oil rents to finance the refining and petro-chemical industry
	Upstream diversification	Mexico, Venezuela	Banning multinational participation to promote domestic expansion in oil exploration and production
	Energy-intensive industrialization	Mexico, Nigeria, Venezuela	Underpricing of domestic oil and gas products to promote industrialization through cheap energy inputs
Agricultural expansion	Agricultural extensification	India, Mexico	Subsidization of irrigation
		Brazil, Egypt	Land giveaways
	Agricultural intensification	Brazil, Costa Rica	Subsidization of agricultural inputs (credit, fertilizer, pesticides, seeds, equipment)
Regional development	Private expansion	Brazil	Amazonian ranching subsidies
	State expansion	Peru	Amazonian oil exploration
		India	Mining in "backward" areas

case studies reveal five types of programs. Some types overlap, but the distinctions are important. These cases represent both the motives for manipulating resource development and extraction and the policy failures that emerge.

Industrialization through Downstream Processing

The logic of "downstream industrialization," also called "downstream diversification" or "forward integration," represents a straightforward, if often misguided, rationale for distorting the prices of natural-resource outputs. Minerals economist Marian Radetzki (1977) points out that selling metals such as steel, copper, and aluminum, rather than raw ores, is alluring because it promises to improve the producing country's bargaining position in international markets. It may limit the multinational corporations' power to manipulate transfer pricing to avoid taxes and royalties and reduce the risk of declining world ore prices, by allowing domestic processors to take advantage of cheap ores. Downstream processing can also open new long-term economic growth possibilities through diversification. Diversification often entails appealing to the "infant industry" logic: a new industry may be weak today, but with proper nurturing it can become a major source of true profits, employment, and national pride in the long run. Another argument for downstream diversification is that it ensures markets for raw materials through the fail-safe, direct approach of creating the domestic production that will use the nation's raw-material output. This argument is often reinforced by grim predictions of faltering markets for the nation's raw material exports, while bolstering enthusiasm for the market prospects of finished-goods exports. Similar arguments have been made for wood-products processing: the allure of exporting higher priced plywood and furniture rather than simple logs, the prospect of employing workers in mills and factories, and the desire to escape the imagined collusion of timber importers in developed countries to keep prices low.

Still, the chronic problem for downstream industrialization is very low productivity and net economic losses, although the latter are often masked by government subsidies. Auty (1990, ch. 9, esp. 194–96) evaluated the downstream industrialization efforts of eight oil-producing countries and found that all performed "well below expectations." Because of problems of low growth, increasing debt, and stagnant sectoral structure, these downstream efforts "placed the main burden of post-boom adjustment on the non-hydrocarbons tradeables sector" (Auty 1990, 196). Summarizing the experience of more than a dozen timber exporters, Gillis and Repetto (1988, 405) note that "many ambitious forest-based industrialization programs have been based on wishful thinking." Nevertheless, government officials often cater to the widespread perception that a sound development requires capturing every opportunity to add value to domestically produced natural resources. This perception may stem from the misconception that "value added" means productivity and profits, whereas it simply means that a larger proportion of costs and price markups are incurred domestically. This does not mean that the processing is efficient or provides a high rate of return for the capital invested. For hard minerals, Radetzki (1977, 330) points out that "since the costs of metal smelting and refining are unrelated to the mineral-exporting country's rich natural endowments, there are no obvious reasons to presume that these processing activities would render high levels of profit. Unlike the mining ventures, mineral processing activities are not self-evidently attractive in terms of the national goals pursued by the country." Moreover, downstream diversification is not terribly effective for countering cycles, as world-market fluctuations affect the demand for processed materials along with raw materials. The international markets for finished products such as steel and copper wire hold harsh prospects for finished exports as they do for raw exports. Even the employment benefits are highly questionable. Mineral processing is often even more capital-intensive than mining itself (Radetzki 1977, 330); other investments are likely to provide far more jobs.

Similar logic holds in the wood-products industry. Several industrial countries have such sophisticated equipment that timber-producing developing countries must either invest heavily for comparable equipment or suffer from large losses in wood stock. As Gillis (1988a, 91) puts it for Indonesia, "As long as plywood recovery rates remain low, most of the 140-odd plymills will swallow timber rents as surely as black holes do nearby celestial bodies." In Indonesia in the mid-1980s, plywood exports worth $109 per cubic meter of processed logs cost $133; a cubic meter of logs that could be exported for $100 produced only $89 in sawn timber from the local sawmills, and a $20 loss in export taxes. For the Ivory Coast, Gillis (1998b, 340) calculated that processing high-value woods such as *acajou* or *iroku* in the mid-1980s cost the Ivorian government $43 to $52 in foregone export taxes in order to add $19 to $25 of value added to the Ivorian economy.

Any temporary success of downstream industrialization typically comes from government subsidies. Even with the subsidies, the sustainability of the industry itself is often problematic. Nonrenewable resource supplies eventually decline, and even theoretically renewable resources (such as timber) suffer supply shortages when processing industries consume inputs voraciously because of subsidies.

Nevertheless, invoking "value added" in an economic-nationalist vein can generate political backing even if the argument is patently absurd in the particular case. It is not simply that the value-added and infant-industry arguments hold sway; it is also that the severity of the economic losses is usually difficult to detect or prove.

However, the questionable wisdom of downstream raw-materials processing is not the main interest here: it is the distortions to the resource exploitation process that occur to promote downstream processing. To approach this question, we must first identify the major strategies that governments employ to promote downstream industrialization at the expense of the soundness of natural-resource exploitation.

1. Depressing raw-material input prices promotes downstream industrialization by reducing its costs. Sometimes the government directs its state enterprises to sell their raw output below the prices that they could

otherwise obtain, or the government may regulate private price-setting. Government officials often require state oil enterprises to sell crude oil cheaply to refineries. If the state oil sector is vertically integrated, the enterprise is required to sell the gasoline, kerosene, heating oil, and other petroleum products at low prices to domestic industries.[1] The state oil companies explored in this book—in Mexico, Nigeria, Peru, and Venezuela—suffer under these burdens. In other cases, the government manipulates output prices less directly.

A less direct but common approach is to prohibit or discourage exportation, which reduces total demand and thus domestic prices. In addition to Indonesia, Gillis (1988b) documents various log-export restrictions and taxes in Gabon, Ghana, the Ivory Coast, and Liberia. Log-export bans have long existed in Brazil, Ecuador, and Malaysia (with the exception of Sarawak State). Despite the apparent growing awareness of the liabilities of such a policy, similar bans were introduced in Vanuato in 1993 and Papua New Guinea in 1994.

2. Forcing state enterprises to produce more than is optimal from a business perspective also induces lower raw-materials costs. This strategy also ensures at least temporarily greater supply for the expansion of domestic processing.

3. Providing subsidized loans for downstream processing induces domestic investors to establish processing operations that otherwise would not be privately profitable. In Ghana, for example, the state Timber Marketing Board provided interest-free loans to sawmill and plywood operations in the late 1960s and early 1970s (Gillis 1988b, 339).

4. Permitting or requiring state raw-materials-producing enterprises to retain the resource rents for investment in the downstream industry will stimulate downstream industrialization even if profitability is low. In the oil sector, downstream processing has been subsidized by allowing state enterprises, such as Venezuela's PDVSA and Nigeria's NNPC, to retain oil royalties rather than surrender them to the government as a private oil company would. This strategy often appeals to the expansionist impulses of state managers who seek greater budgets and discretion for their enterprises. For example, the Honduran state enterprise COHDEFOR launched a disastrous wood-processing subsidiary, Corfino, in the 1980s.

Resource Policy Failures from Downstream Industrialization

Low raw-material prices induce overuse of these materials. At the same time, low raw-material pricing discourages resource development. Low output prices reduce the incentives to explore and develop mineral or petroleum deposits, to plant and nurture forests, to keep soils rich, and so on. The combined effect is diminished supply that may lead to insufficient inputs to sustain the new downstream industry. Investment in the processing sector, strangled by the diminishing supply, adds to the economic costs.

When state enterprises are required to overproduce, the resource distortion is the exploitation of resource endowments that are not truly profitable from an economic perspective. In addition, the tactic of banning or restricting raw-material exports has the perverse effect of inducing vertical integration by firms that may not be equipped to do so effectively; that is, the raw-material producers can recoup their losses if they enter into processing as well, as was the case for the timber companies operating in Indonesia. In Ghana many small and inefficient wood-processing industries were attracted by the subsidized loans and other artificial incentives (Gillis 1988b, 339), despite the fact that Ghana was bound to suffer from supply shortages.

The distortions caused by subsidies to downstream processing also encourage overconsumption of raw materials. Just as cheap raw-material inputs induce greater resource use, any other reduction in the costs of resource processing, including low capital costs, will encourage higher production and higher resource consumption. For potentially renewable resources such as timber, the rush to consume the raw resource while the subsidy lasts often provokes serious resource depletion. The West African cases cited above are similar in this respect to the Indonesian pattern.

The participation of state enterprises in downstream processing raises two more problems. First, state managers from a raw-material-extracting company may not have the expertise in processing operations. The skills required to manage a sawmill, or an oil refinery, differ from those required to manage a forest or drill for oil, despite the fact that the terms *forestry sector* or *petroleum sector* imply a strong connection between "upstream" and "downstream" activities. Managerial and technical inefficiency is a common consequence of the downstream diversification of a state enterprise. Second, when state enterprise managers want to expand their budgets rather than maximize profits, production and resource consumption will be elevated even higher.

Industrialization through Upstream Expansion

If the government wishes to stimulate technology development, equipment production, and "upstream" resource development activities such as oil exploration or forest plantations, it can do so by

- subsidizing investment in these activities;
- leaving state resource exploiters with large surpluses to engage in these activities;
- forcing "downstream" resource extractors and processors to purchase these inputs domestically; and
- nationalizing foreign firms that show flagging interest in investing in these activities.

Some of the rationales for upstream industrialization are the same as for downstream industrialization: deepening economic growth, gaining greater national control over the entire resource exploitation and its profits, and diversifying into activities for which the country ostensibly has experience and expertise. In addition, upstream industrialization often has the allure of high technology. Finally, upstream industrialization and the maintenance or expansion of raw-material supply that it implies is attractive for ensuring continued inputs for already-established downstream production.

Subsidies

The most direct and perhaps most common approach to encouraging upstream industry is to subsidize these activities through a mix of tax incentives, cheap credit, land giveaways, and low royalties for access to land. For example, plantation forestry has been encouraged through tax credits and permissive rules for claiming open-access land in Brazil (Browder 1988, 267; Schneider 1995) and Costa Rica (Lutz and Daly 1990), and by tax credits, cheap leases, and subsidized credit in the Philippines (Boado 1988, 180). Tax holidays and cheap leases of government land have been common as an incentive for mineral exploration.

Forced Domestic Purchases

Guaranteeing a market for domestic producers will permit them to increase prices and their profits to maintain or expand resource development efforts. For example, when the Indian government wanted to keep up unprofitable domestic copper exploitation, it directed the armed forces to purchase copper from the state enterprise Hindustan Copper Limited, despite the high prices necessitated by low ore grades. Similarly, the Brazilian state oil company Petrobras has monopolized domestic petroleum product sales, using part of the profits to finance Brazil's oil areas with marginal prospects.

Surpluses for State Enterprises

While conventional fiscal policy theory calls for state enterprises to surrender both resource rents and profits to the central treasury, governments sometimes allow state enterprises to retain surplus revenues in order to finance upstream investments. Venezuela's state oil company PDVSA was left with a large investment fund prior to 1983, to be used in part to expand its research and development facilities as well as its exploration capacity (Brossard 1993).

Nationalization

Although it obviously has had many other motivations, the nationalization of foreign-owned "upstream" resource exploitation — oil and mining exploration and production, timber-lands development, and harvesting — can also be considered a strategy for strengthening upstream industry. One of the main preoccupations of governments during the period prior to the wave of nationalizations in the 1970s and 1980s was that multinational resource companies reduced their investments and production, whether because they found exploration and production to be too risky or insufficiently profitable, or because they wanted to "punish" governments for clamping down on the companies' profits or discretion.[2] Thus, in many cases in which oil or mining production had historically been very important and the government feared the decline of the industry, governments took over the oil or mining sectors to avert investment declines as well as to gain political support, reduce resource-rent losses, and gain control over major off-budget financing instruments. The nationalization debates regarding Chilean copper and Venezuelan oil, for example, were replete with arguments that only government control could guarantee that mineral and oil production, respectively, could be maintained (Grupo de Minería del CED 1985; Moran 1974; Coronel 1983; Martínez 1989; Randall 1987). Another aspect of upstream industrialization implied by nationalization is that the state resource firm is more likely to develop or contract domestically produced technology. Multinational firms are likely to seek technology (e.g., seismographic equipment) from whatever sources around the world that provide the best quality and prices; the nationalized firm can be directed to purchase from local suppliers, or to establish its own technology-development operations. Thus, oil exploration technology R&D was financed in Mexico by excluding foreign oil companies from engaging in exploration and allowing the state oil company PEMEX to retain large surpluses prior to 1978.

Resource Policy Failures from the Pursuit of Upstream Expansion

Upstream expansion that has to be "forced" by nonmarket pricing distortions promotes resource development and extraction that is unproductive from the perspective of the economy as a whole. Beyond that, the specific strategies for promoting upstream expansion have peculiar problems. The subsidies for resource development set up a situation of perverse incentives for the resource developers who try to take advantage of the subsidies. While the resource development per se is likely to be unprofitable — or else the subsidy would not be necessary to encourage resource development — the difficulties of enforcing true compliance to the terms for receiving the subsidies often lead to reneging on the part of the resource developers. In Costa Rica, for example, many firms taking advantage of reforestation tax credits failed to choose appropriate tree species to plant or to nurture the young trees long enough to ensure their survival (Lutz and Daly 1990).

The granting of surplus retention to state resource enterprises places them at the same risk of going beyond their true sectoral expertise as does downstream industrialization. Moreover, surplus retention on the part of state enterprises frequently comes to be regretted by the government; in trying to retake the surplus, the government may trigger a strategy of hasty investment on the part of the state enterprise in order to keep the surplus away from the government. In chapter 6 I will examine the case of Venezuela's state oil company PDVSA to explore this pattern in detail.

Forced domestic purchases raise the prices of domestically processed downstream products, making these products noncompetitive internationally. One reason why India has failed as an exporter of metal-based manufactured goods is the high price of copper and steel.

Nationalization creates several problems, beginning with the same question of expertise. There are also serious dangers for a developing country to invest large sums of money on risky resource development efforts. Multinational oil and mining companies, with high capital levels and exploration risks diversified across many countries, are better positioned to take these risks. Single governments, particularly of low-income countries, can ill afford to subject their peoples to the risk of losing billions of dollars on questionable exploration and production. This risk is exacerbated by the fact that governments worried about ensuring future raw-material supplies have often intervened precisely because the experts of multinational firms had concluded that further resource development was unpromising.

Energy-Intensive Industrialization

Industrialization has been promoted in many oil-rich countries by keeping the prices of domestic oil products low. This has occurred in Mexico, Nigeria, Peru, Venezuela, and other oil-exporting countries with significant non-oil economies. Heavy overdevelopment of hydroelectric power by the state, and underpricing of the electricity produced, is a similar strategy of industrial promotion in many countries. Colombia in particular has had extremely high hydroelectric costs that, in not being transferred to electricity users, have stimulated energy-intensive industries but also excessive electricity use and production expenses.

By making energy inputs cheap, this strategy obviously leads to rapid depletion of domestic energy supplies, as well as to the development of industries that are highly vulnerable to this very depletion. Moreover, the elevated consumption of exportable energy resources such as oil or coal denies the country of foreign exchange earnings, often exacerbated by smuggling. In Nigeria, for example, petroleum smuggling has been so prominent that the military governments have executed accused smugglers; the armed forces itself has been implicated. Finally, the most perverse impact of the low prices of polluting energy resources is that the increased domestic consumption increases air pollution, both directly through greater energy consumption and indirectly through the retention of older, less fuel-efficient vehicles and machinery.

Agricultural Development

The expansion of agriculture has been stimulated by excessive investment in public works such as dams and irrigation networks in Mexico, India, and many other countries. While some irrigation projects have added immensely to agricultural productivity, others provide expensive water to areas with little additional agricultural potential, as indicated by the inability of these projects to recover their costs from the farmers receiving the water. Cheap inputs of credit, fertilizer, seed, and pesticides constitute another common set of price distortions to stimulate agricultural production. Land giveaways without appropriate charges for the land's intrinsic resource rent are also employed as agricultural promotion policies. This has occurred in Egypt's notorious policy of giving agricultural land to college graduates even if they lack agricultural experience and training, and in the Brazilian land giveaways in the Amazon.

These approaches of excessive infrastructure investment and underpricing of state-provided resources have the same effects as when employed in the development strategies already reviewed. Free or cheap inputs encourage overuse. In the case of agriculture, this becomes an issue of suboptimal land use. Agricultural promotion that overrides the intrinsic physical and economic considerations of optimal land use has been the root of much of the land conversion that has transformed forests into agroplantations and ranches that are sustainable only with the continuation of the subsidies. Estate crops such as tea, cocoa, palm oil, and rubber have been planted all over Asia and Africa to the detriment of pre-existing forests; annual crops such as rice have also been introduced on forest lands when encouraged by cheap inputs. In Latin America the more typical pattern has been clearing forest and other uncultivated areas for cattle, especially in Brazil, Colombia, and Costa Rica, based on generous and economically indefensible subsidies.

Regional Development

Governments promote the development of particular regions out of a mix of motivations ranging from distributional concerns to geopolitical strategy. "Backward areas" sometimes get special attention out of concerns for poverty alleviation or worries over migration; politically pivotal areas also frequently get special attention. Border areas, particularly at sparsely populated frontiers, are often subject to government efforts to stimulate migration through economic opportunities. The same holds for nonborder areas where the government's political control is tenuous.

Private Expansion

Efforts to stimulate the economic growth of particular regions through private-sector expansion have been encouraged by much the same menu of cheap inputs, land giveaways, and lax regulation that permits inexpensive resource extraction. Just as Costa Rica's decentralization policies gave land away outside of the central valley of San José, Brazil's land giveaways and cattle-ranching subsidies in the 1980s were part of a regional development strategy of Amazonian settlement.

State Expansion

Directing state enterprises to operate in a particular region despite adverse economic indications is another common approach to developing the region. The Peruvian government's counter to Brazilian Amazonian expansion in the 1970s and 1980s was to require the state oil company

PetroPerú to undertake large-scale and expensive exploration in the Amazon despite indications of low prospectivity. In the mineral sector, the development of several "backward" districts in India has been promoted by continuing money-losing copper mines; this is as much a regional strategy as it is an income-distribution strategy.

The subsidies that promote regional development lead to suboptimal land uses as well as to the waste of the subsidies themselves on economically nonviable projects. The forced state exploitation constitutes overuse of the resources involved, because resource exploitation would have been less if the state enterprise had to choose its exploitation strategy on the basis of its true profitability.

Explaining Reliance on Resource-Distorting Pursuit of Development Strategies

Thus far this chapter has identified numerous strategies for pursuing industrialization, agricultural expansion, and regional development and an even broader array of specific policies that pursue these strategies through the distortion of natural-resource development and extraction. While none of the cases cited has thus far been examined in any detail, the ease of finding cases involving resource distortions demonstrates the prevalence of the tendency to sacrifice the soundness of natural-resource policies for the sake of these initiatives.

If these sacrifices were unavoidable for the pursuit of the development strategies, we might say that the explanation is simple: the objective is important enough for policymakers to tolerate the costs of poor natural-resource exploitation. However, I will now demonstrate that the soundness of natural-resource exploitation need not be sacrificed in order to pursue the development objectives of these strategies.

Regarding industrial promotion, the government can stimulate investment through a host of general measures to reduce the cost and increase the supply of capital, provide tax incentives for industrial investment, adjust exchange rates to make industrial exports more competitive internationally, and so on. This is not to say that all of these measures are optimal from an economic efficiency perspective, inasmuch as some of these measures introduce their own distortions. However, it is generally the case that industrial expansion can be unleashed simply by removing existing distortions such as credit restrictions, overvalued exchange rates, and existing subsidies that draw capital away from intrinsically attractive industrial investments.

If some government officials have the specific objective of promoting downstream processing of natural resources, for whatever political, economic, or social reasons, this can be pursued with less resource-exploitation distortion than the measures frequently applied. Making credit available to downstream processors, assisting in the development of export markets, or undervaluing the domestic currency will stimulate demand for raw materials. While artificially stimulated demand may lead to overproduction of the raw resources, at least it avoids the problem of discouraging resource development through depressed raw-material prices. We can conclude that much if not all of the resource exploitation distortions that occur in the pursuit of downstream industrialization could be avoided even if this objective is still pursued.

Similarly, upstream expansion can be promoted through cheap credit or other subsidies to the upstream investors in areas such as resource-exploitation technology and development without distorting later stages of resource exploitation. Moreover, if the government is concerned about increasing upstream exploration and production, it is easier and less distorting to change the terms of entry for multinational firms, to calibrate the inducements to perform at targeted levels of exploration or production, than to risk the nation's capital or to rely on suspect domestic expertise by moving state enterprises into these upstream activities.

Basing industrial expansion on cheap energy is a resource-pricing distortion in and of itself. Yet its objective of encouraging industry through inexpensive inputs can be pursued in ways that have little impact on the soundness of resource policy. The same industries that have benefited by artificially cheap energy inputs could be subsidized through tax credits, cheap credit, government-funded research and development, and so on.

The same logic holds for agricultural promotion: aside from the economic distortion that is intrinsic in government promotion of a particular sector of the economy, it is possible to pursue this promotion through measures that do not distort natural-resource exploitation. In many countries, agriculture can be promoted most dramatically and straightforwardly by simply removing the biases that exist against agriculture in favor of industrial growth, such as price ceilings on staples and credit regulations that favor industrial investors (Pinstrup-Andersen 1988; Timmer 1991).

Regarding regional development, although any effort to increase population or economic activity in a particular area will increase the pressure on the natural-resource endowment, many measures to promote regional development are less damaging than the land giveaways, underpriced raw-material outputs, reckless exploration, and subsidized resource extraction that our examples have revealed. Investments in physical and human-resource infrastructure are superior to the direct distortions of resource exploitation. Backward regions can often be helped immensely if only the government were to eliminate the pre-existing policy distortions that favor more advanced regions.[3] Of equal importance is that one of the most prevalent purposes for regional development, channeling benefits to particular groups, can be addressed directly through central treasury transfers to these groups. Thus, if the Indian government wants to maintain the incomes of families in the depleted mining areas of Rajastan and Madhya Pradesh, it can simply allocate funds for this purpose without creating distortions in land use or unsustainable mineral exploitation, as occurred in the case of Hindustan Copper Limited taken up in chapter 5.

The question then becomes: Why pursue development objectives of industrialization, agricultural expansion, or regional development through measures that create gratuitous damage to the natural-resource endowment? If industrial, agricultural, or regional expansion can be justified by economic argument (for example, one can make a superficial comparative advantage argument in favor of a cheap energy strategy, or argue that a particular region will take off economically if only it can be prompted by subsidized development), why not do so through the central budget? Do other cases show the same combination of circumvention of intragovernmental opposition and evasion of accountability that has been so prominent in the Indonesian case? While some support of development strategies that distort natural-resource exploitation do involve direct central-treasury expenditures (major irrigation expansion, government subsidies of agricultural inputs, and centrally funded purchases of raw inputs at high prices), many cases also involve the maneuvers seen in the Indonesian case. Five cases are considered in this chapter. To find parallels in the timber sector, I will contrast the very straightforward case of political exchange of logging concessions in the Malaysian state of Sarawak with the much more convoluted case of its neighboring state of Sabah. We will find similar downstream wood-products industrialization occurring in Honduras and a highly explicit regional development strategy in Brazil. In the oil sector, I will review Peruvian oil exploration in the Amazon, an odd twin to the Brazilian regional strategy.

Cases of Development Strategy Financing through Resource Abuses

Malaysian Forests: Rent-seeking in Sarawak and Sabah

The complexity and subtlety of the Indonesian forestry case are best highlighted in the comparisons with the neighboring Malaysian states of

Sarawak and Sabah in East Malaysia (Malaysian Borneo). Satellite photographs offer striking visual proof that as bad as the deforestation has been in Indonesia's Bornean provinces of East and West Kalimantan, the Malaysian states have done even more damage.

In particular, Sarawak has been widely condemned for reckless overharvesting, caused by the classic combination of low stumpage fees and tolerance of illegal harvesting. Commercial logging is crucial to this predominantly rural and nonindustrialized state, and yet the rates of deforestation prior to 1990 led the International Tropical Timber Organization to predict the full depletion of primary forests by 2001 if Sarawak did not reduce log production. The ITTO study estimated that 9.2 million cubic meters of timber was the maximum sustainable production, yet the rate in 1991 was 19.4 million cubic meters and as late as 1994 was still over 16 million (Bruenig 1993, 259). Some experts argue that maximum sustainable production is even lower than the ITTO estimate (Wakker 1993, 221).

The situation in Sabah is more complicated. The state apparatus captures an impressive portion of the timber rent through appropriately high royalties on legal logging. However, illegal logging is rampant (Tsuruoka 1991), preventing the royalty fees from deterring loggers from cutting trees that have inadequate economic value. Just as important, the peculiar agency that oversees most state forest exploitation has long been implicated in reckless logging, inefficient downstream processing, and waste of timber proceeds, traceable to its lack of accountability both in its timber operations and in the deployment of its proceeds. Although Sabah has less than half the forest area than Sarawak, in the mid-1980s Sabah was losing more forest on an absolute basis than Sarawak (59,000 hectares vs. 41,000 hectares) (Hurst 1989, 84). In the 1980s Sabah was losing roughly 2 percent of production forests each year, four times the sustainable level (Adlin 1988, 21).

Political Exchange in Sarawak

Forestry policy in Sarawak poses the same political economy riddle as in Indonesia's Outer Islands, but with a much simpler answer.[4] Why would a government forgo an excellent opportunity to collect revenues, particularly when full rent collection would actually make resource exploitation sounder by discouraging loggers from removing more trees than is economically warranted? The value of the timber concessions awarded by the mid-1980s has been estimated as high as M$30 billion (Means 1991, 169), equivalent to US$12 billion. Therefore, with even moderate levels of rent capture, the capabilities of the state would have been far greater. The question is even more perplexing for Sarawak because timber rents are the main source of income for the state government, constituting between one-quarter and one-half of the Sarawak state government's revenues; they could be much higher. The fiscal arrangement with the Federation of Malaysia gives the state governments control over timber, in exchange for giving most of the control over petroleum — and its proceeds — to the central government.

Gaining a concession in Sarawak has been a straightforward bonanza. The timber boom got under way with very low total taxes (in 1981 and 1982, timber taxes were only 18 percent of export value, compared to nearly 37 percent in Sabah and nearly 28 percent in Indonesia) (Gillis 1988b, 148). Because of the existence of logging firms willing to buy the harvesting rights and bear all responsibilities and costs of harvesting and marketing the timber, the concessionaire who receives the political gift of a concession can realize a profit with no effort or risk. Raj Kumar (1986, 85) notes that "more often than not, politically influential *bumiputra*, most of them relatively well-off, have the best opportunities for securing harvesting rights."[5] As in Indonesia, the logging companies are largely run by ethnic Chinese, who make up roughly 30 percent of Sarawak's population (Means 1991, 165). A 1990 article in the *Economist* (1990, 23) reported a typical arrangement involving a subcontractor's payment of M$75 to the concessionaire for one ton of timber worth M$800; the subcontractor would pay the taxes of M$13–M$28, as well as the harvesting and transportation costs. Yet even the subcontractors do not have to demonstrate competence in forestry. Kumar (1986, 97) and King (1993, 242) provide evidence that the subcontractors are often short on capital and incentive to engage in long-term forest management.

Unlike Indonesia and the neighboring Malaysian state of Sabah, there is no evidence that Sarawak's timber rents have been channeled off-budget into development projects by either state or private actors. Timber processing is encouraged by a tax discount, at times amounting to 50 percent, and a 10 percent export tax on logs (Miranda et al. 1992, 293). Yet the absence of an outright ban on log exports, or confiscatory log-export taxes, has kept the export of logs, particularly to Japan, as the most lucrative activity for the forest sector. The state's forest-industrialization agency, the Sarawak Timber Industry Development Corporation (STIDC), has mercifully been kept at a low level of financing and intervention in timber markets, thus avoiding the timber-rent destruction that has plagued Indonesia, Honduras, and many other countries with heavy-handed forest-products industrialization programs.

Thus, in lieu of the elaborate transfers focusing on forest-industry development, the forestry transactions in Sarawak seem to be much more straightforward: receipt of concessions for political support. Gordon Means writes that

> lucrative timber licenses which were issued by the state government became an important instrument of political power jealously controlled by the Chief Minister. Since the licenses were worth many millions of ringgit, they could be distributed to reward political supporters and be used to build a stable coalition at the state level, often including those politicians who claimed to represent the interests of interior native peoples. (1991, 165)

Why is the diversion of timber rents so straightforwardly dedicated to currying political support? Means (1991, 166) explains that the failure of any party or coalition to be confident of its longevity in government was due to the "continuous competition between parties for shifting and transient supporters as well as endemic internal factional struggles for power within all major parties." Although the Sarawak Barisan Nasional (National Front) coalition of various parties has enjoyed dominance of Sarawak's parliament, it has comprised parties of changing strength and influence, depending on how many members of the various ethnic groups can be won over to particular coalition members. Thus, the multi-ethnic composition of Sarawak's political parties, while incomplete, has precluded any party from dominating by having the permanent support of the majority ethnic group. While the so-called Dayak non-Malay indigenous communities constituted just under 44 percent of the population, as of 1980 they have been wooed by several parties and have been fractured by tribal and factional divisions (Means 1991, 165–66). This political pluralism may be healthy for Sarawak's democracy, but it has prevented government leaders from being able to count on sufficient political support without tending continually to economic payoffs of one sort or another (King 1993, 236).

A strikingly overt example of the political use of logging concessions was provided in 1987, when an open conflict between two top-level political figures stripped away the usual opacity of concession awards. That year the Chief Minister Abdul Taib Mahmud tried to establish himself as the leader of the PBB Party over his uncle Abdul Rahman Ya'akub (who had previously also served as chief minister before the federal government tapped him to serve as governor). According to Means (1991, 168), Taib handed out patronage, including logging concessions, often against the advice of his uncle, using the state's discretion over forestry to defy Rahman Ya'akub. Ya'akub convened a group of twenty-eight state council members to form a rival political group and to demand Taib's resignation. Taib promptly revoked twenty-five timber concessions of members of the group, spanning roughly three million acres and worth an estimated M$22.5 billion. Ya'akub retaliated by claiming that Taib had previously assigned nearly four million acres to family members, including his wives, through "front companies designed to disguise the beneficiaries (Means 1991, 171; Stesser 191, 62). Other reports of high government officials and their relatives holding forest concessions abound (Stesser 1991, 62–64; Pura 1990, 124).

The 1987 episode highlights the blatant connection between concessions and political support. It also reveals the fragility and lack of harmony within the Sarawak governing elite, quite unlike Indonesia's *pancasila*. Without judging whether this lack of harmony is good or bad for Sarawak, it is clear that public officials with the power to grant timber concessions cannot afford to manipulate the timber rents for more ambitious development purposes.

The distributional impacts of the cheap forest concessions largely disadvantage the indigenous non-Malay groups (Iban, Bidayuh, and other tribal peoples sometimes termed Dayaks) who inhabit the hinterlands where forest extraction is a major component of subsistence livelihood and whose forest access is increasingly limited.

The Dayaks lose out in another, more indirect way. Echoing the distributional politics on the Malaysian mainland, where the "indigenous" Malays have successfully asserted their claims to greater economic benefits at the expense of the wealthier Chinese minority, the Dayaks have been pressing their claims as the low-income indigenous peoples of Sarawak. Given the numerical strength of the Dayaks and their potential to swing electoral victory from one party or coalition to another, the governments of Sarawak have, at least rhetorically, embraced the priority of uplifting the Dayaks economically. Yet the neglect of timber rent capture restricts the potential for benefits accruing to the Dayaks. Instead, timber rents have flowed to the Malays, Melanaus,[6] and Chinese: the Sarawak Malays and Melanaus are the most likely to receive concessions, and, as mentioned above, the Sarawak Chinese are the most likely to serve as logging contractors. These groups share the timber rents that bypass the conventional budget process and reduce its capacity to provide greater benefits for the lower-income populations.

While the hinterland Dayaks complain bitterly of the encroachment by commercial logging, some government officials and logging interests denounce the Dayaks' shifting cultivation as a more serious source of deforestation. This is a common controversy in tropical countries where small farmers and commercial logging vie for user rights. As we have seen in the

Indonesian case, in Malaysia the debate is characteristically muddled by extremely poor data, vague definitions concerning what constitutes forest land and what constitutes deforestation, and seemingly willful blindness on both sides to the fact that commercial forest exploitation and shifting culti-vation are intimately intertwined. Logging roads attract shifting cultivators into areas that had previously been inaccessible, and it is striking that the official statistics on deforestation caused by logging and shifting cultivation reveal, in any careful analysis, a strong bias toward underestimating the impact of commercial logging and exaggerating the impact of shifting cul-tivation. This is because most officially sanctioned commercial logging claims to undertake selective cutting; regardless of how much collateral damage is done to other trees, the land remains officially "in forest." In contrast, the clearance of forest cover from shifting cultivation, particularly if it is prohibited or discouraged by the government, is often counted as full deforestation, even when some or all of the land had earlier been under cultivation. Michael Dove (1983), referring primarily to the Indonesian case, points out how convenient it is for governments to blame shifting cultivation rather than the forestry concessions that they award. In the Malaysian case, John Walton reports that

James Wong, Minister for the Environment, claims that shifting cultivation causes more destruction to the environment than logging, and results in irre-versible damage to the ecosystem. He claims logging, however, does not cause serious environmental problems and that logged over areas will return to nor-mal after five years . . .

The above view is challenged by the Malaysian environmental group Sa-habat Alam Malaysia (SAM), which claims that in the 1963–85 period 2.8 million hectares, or 28,217 square kilometers of primary forest were logged, this being equal to 30 percent of the total forest area of Sarawak . . . SAM also claims that the large-scale hill-logging operations in Sarawak are already caus-ing floods, siltation of rivers and reduced aquatic and wildlife populations.

According to Dr. S. C. Chin, an ethnobotanist at the University of Malay-sia, a family of shifting cultivators clears and plants an average of five acres per annum or a total of 180,000 acres for the whole of Sarawak, given the current estimate of 36,000 shifting cultivator households. Moreover, of this total only 5 percent or 9,000 acres may come from primary forest, the rest will be from agricultural land that has already been fallowed. Chin therefore suggests that the frequently alleged claim of shifting cultivation destroying 100,000–150,000 acres of forest each year is completely misleading. If Chin's estimate of 9,000 acres (3,600 hectares) is correct it represents only a fraction of the 270,000 hectares logged by the timber industry in 1985. (1990, 136–37)

A quite minor form of distribution to the Dayaks via control over timber was instituted in 1971, with the establishment of the Sarawak Foundation to promote education and "Malaysian consciousness, national unity and national loyalty amongst the peoples in Sarawak," working largely through scholarships. The foundation was given control over a "Timber Cess Fund," established in 1963 ostensibly to benefit hill peoples through revenues from a small tax on hillside timber harvest, and the government reserved some forest land for the foundation. Along with private contributions, these funds permitted the Sarawak Foundation to report that in its first three years it spent just under US$3 million (Searle 1983, 134). The Sarawak Foundation was heavily criticized for its partisan nature, inasmuch as the trustees and administration of the foundation were all appointed by the chief minister from among his own ruling coalition members and civil servants and out of concern that it was a device for imposing mainstream Malay culture onto Dayak (and in particular Iban) youth (Searle 1983, 134–35).

Sabah: Strongmen and Laundering

Just east of Sarawak is Malaysia's other Bornean state, Sabah. The similarities in population, resource endowment of oil and timber, and geopolitical circumstances make it all the more illuminating that the institutional modes of forest exploitation have been quite different. In contrast to Sarawak's straightforward rent-seeking as political support-gathering, Sabah has experienced machinations reminiscent of Suharto's Indonesia, although in Sabah's case through a quasi-public institution called the Sabah Foundation, rather than through the private loggers or the Forestry Ministry. The catastrophe for the forests has been similar for Sarawak and Sabah, although the paths have been quite different.

Recall that Sarawak has the so-called Sarawak Foundation, founded in 1971. Five years earlier, the state government had established the Sabah Foundation, chaired by a powerful politician named Tun Mustapha Harun. Tun Mustapha then won the 1967 election to become the chief minister. For the next nine years he dominated Sabah politics much more thoroughly than any politician has ever dominated politics in Sarawak. The Sabah Foundation has dominated Sabah forestry to a degree that dwarfs the operations of the Sarawak Foundation. Like the Sarawak Foundation, the Sabah Foundation was established to improve educational attainment of the people of the state. In 1970 the Sabah Foundation was given a broader mandate to promote the social and economic advancement of Sabah peoples and a 100-year lease for over 855,000 hectares of virgin forest—out of Sabah's total land area of 7.4 million hectares. Over time the foundation was able to secure more land from the state; by 1989 its holdings spanned 1.07 million hectares (Burgess 1989; Miranda et al. 1992, 287). Moreover, in contrast to the many undercapitalized state enterprises reviewed in other parts of this book, the Sabah Foundation has withheld royalty payments to the state government, sometimes for years. The leniency of the Sabah State government has thus permitted the Sabah Foundation to deploy not only the concessionaire's share but also more of the timber rent.

Tun Mustapha used the proceeds of the Sabah Foundation to enrich his political associates and win electoral support. The scholarships and monetary distributions were consistently scheduled just before elections; the beneficiaries were overtly "rewarded" for their political backing (Means 1991, 42; Ross-Larson 1976, 131–40). Prior to the 1974 election, Tun Mustapha had the Sabah Foundation issue M$60 timber shares to every adult citizen (Means 1991, 42). This political patronage cemented his political position so firmly that until he ran afoul of the federal government in 1974, over the disposition of Sabah's newfound oil wealth and his extraordinarily ostentatious lifestyle, he ruled with unchallenged authority.

Tun Mustapha's hold over Sabah far exceeded the power of any political leaders in Sarawak. Crouch observes that

> only in Sabah during the rule of Tun Mustapha (from 1967 to 1975) were violations of democratic practices so flagrant that elections lost their meaning. When Sabah participated for the first time in a national election in 1969, opposition candidates managed to file nominations in only six of the sixteen constituencies, the rest being disqualified for one reason or another. In 1974 only one opposition candidate succeeded in being nominated. The leaders of an opposition party were said to have been bribed to abandon their challenge while supporters of another party, the peninsula-based Pekemas, were physically intimidated by Mustapha's men. (1996, 63)

To a large degree, Tun Mustapha's political control — until near the end — approached that of Suharto in Indonesia, although obviously on a different level of state rather than nation. This may explain why the deployment of the timber rents, as in the Indonesian case, did not adhere to the short-term political currying of favor seen in Sarawak. Through the Sabah Foundation, Tun Mustapha pursued both distributional and development objectives. The former included more than micro-instances of rewarding rent-seekers with contracts; it included wholesale cash distributions to all Sabah citizens and permanent residents over age twenty-one in 1971, 1973, and 1974.

After Tun Mustapha was forced to resign in late 1975 under strong pressure from the central government, the Sabah State government transformed the foundation from a private entity into a statutory body under the direct authority of the state government, indeed, "an integral and important development agency of the Government" (Hepburn 1979, 400). If the new government of Sabah thought that these changes would bring the foundation under leash, they soon discovered the advantage of allowing it wide latitude. Although it became a formal creature of the government, it never ceased to operate apart from the state bureaucracy. While the chief minister presided over the Sabah Foundation board of directors, most of the investment and other business decisions were taken by the foundation's investment arm, the Innoprise Corporation, with its own board of directors.[7] Innoprise, in turn, has dozens of subsidiaries, many of them joint ventures and stock companies, operating with very little oversight or interference by the state administration or legislature. The Sabah Foundation remained an extraordinarily flexible instrument for a host of developmental and distributional objectives. It invested in sawmills, paper mills, wood-based chemicals, shipping, investment banks, reforestation projects, university and community-college development, furniture manufacturing, tourism, and real estate (the thirty-two-floor Sabah Foundation headquarters also houses the offices of key state government leaders, including the chief minister). The foundation continued its cash payments, still closely tied to election campaigns, in 1978, 1979, 1980, 1981, 1985, and 1990, the last payment being RM200 (equivalent to US$75 — similar to previous "dividends") (New Straits Times 1996b). This amount was certainly not trivial, given that per capita income was less than US$1,000. The Sabah Foundation has sponsored everything from golf tournaments to workshops on lead poisoning.

In the post–Tun Mustapha era, Sabah was governed for a decade by the multi-ethnic Berjaya Party, which was also more authoritarian than the norm for Malaysia[8] but received support from the federal government by virtue of its membership in the National Front (Barisan Nasional) that has ruled the federation since independence. Its long tenure reflected the dominance that federal support, patronage, and a hampered political opposition had created. Like Tun Mustapha, the Berjaya Party administration, under Chief Minister Harris Salleh, continued to allow the Sabah Foundation to pursue its development agenda. This is not to say that the foundation was freed from the task of favoring politically pivotal groups and individuals,[9] but the Berjaya administration was able to meet patronage requirements without having to yield forest concession rights outright to the politically powerful.

In 1985 some Berjaya dissidents formed a new party, the Parti Bersatu Sabah (PBS), which attracted a strong and enduring base of non-Muslim Kadazans (the largest, predominantly Christian, ethnic group in Sabah) and the Chinese and won the state elections handily despite the opposition of the national government. The PBS stayed in power until 1994, when its internal defections under pressure from the federal government allowed for the victory of the Kuala Lumpur–backed United Malays National Organisation (UMNO) coalition. Under Dr. Jeffrey Kitingan, brother of the Chief Minister Joseph Pairin Kitingan, the Sabah Foundation continued to serve as the chief development agency for the state, with little monitoring or control by the central state apparatus.

Thus, Sabah has had three strong regimes, each lasting nearly a decade and enjoying considerable confidence during most of its tenure that its multi-ethnic coalition arrangement was solid. Therefore, Sabah seems closest to the Indonesian forestry case, in which the immediate political security of the chief executive permitted timber rents to be devoted to financing development projects rather than to be either collected by the central treasury or dissipated to politically powerful rent-seekers. In contrast, the "continuous competition between parties for shifting and transient supporters" in Sarawak, as mentioned earlier, led to greater turnover and little confidence that government control over long periods could be taken for granted (Crouch 1996, 52–53, 79).

It is important to note that the Sabah government and the Sabah Foundation did two things right, resisting strong pressures to do otherwise. First, in spite of many announcements that a log-export ban was in the offing, Sabah continued to permit the export of round logs, although there was both international pressure (e.g., from the Philippine government) and advice from misguided "development specialists" to fall into the value-added trap. With Sabah lacking efficient sawmills or other endowments that could have provided a rationale for nurturing a downstream wood-products processing industry, the Sabah government desisted from forcing all log production into local processing, although the Sabah Foundation has invested in downstream processing, with generally disappointing results. Second, in setting royalty rates and arranging harvesting contracts with private loggers, the Sabah government and the foundation have captured much of the timber rent. Gillis (1988b) calculated that the government of Sabah captured an astonishing 81 percent of legally harvested timber rents during the period 1979–82. While this figure clearly cannot take into account the sizeable volume of illegal harvesting, it is still remarkably higher than the rents captured in Sarawak or Indonesia. This rent capture reflects the strong incentive of the Sabah government to use the foundation to steer forest revenues into projects that served the developmental and political objectives of the Sabah government, without the participation of the legislature and the conventional executive fiscal apparatus.

However, the use of these revenues in wasteful downstream wood-products industries and nontimber ventures severely diminishes the advantages of having a state entity that guards its rent-capturing capacity only to misinvest its proceeds. For example, in the mid-1980s one of the foundation's shipping companies was closed down after running a US$3 million loss per year since 1971, and timber-processing installations that absorbed at least US$24 million in the mid-1980s should have cost no more than US$4 million (Hurst 1989, 109). In 1993 eight of the foundation's subsidiary companies were moneylosers (Bingkasan and Bangkuai 1995). A 1994 Price Waterhouse audit found huge losses stemming from timber transactions (*New Straits Times* 1996b). Not surprisingly, the Sabah Foundation's lack of transparency in its operations has also provoked many accusations of corruption. Malaysia's Prime Minister Mahathir Mohamad claimed in 1994 that the Price Waterhouse audit revealed that more than $1 billion was missing from Sabah Foundation accounts.

The same lack of accountability that has allowed the Sabah State political leadership to use timber rents without the constraints imposed by budgetary discipline or legislative controversy renders the Sabah Foundation beyond the control of the government. The Sabah Foundation's investment arm, Innoprise, has operated more than a dozen subsidiaries. Although the Sabah Foundation is technically a part of government, the spending decisions of the subsidiaries are three steps removed from government decision makers outside of the foundation. In 1994 the incoming Sabah State Chief Minister Datuk Salleh Tun Said demanded a restructuring of the Sabah Foundation's organization in order to impose more control over Innoprise. According to the chief minister, it was not enough that he chaired the foundation's board of trustees; he insisted that he and other government officials sit on the Innoprise board of directors as well (Bangkuai 1995).

The End of the Sabah Foundation's Autonomy?

The efforts since 1994 to rein in the Sabah Foundation reveal the Sabah State executive's priority to control the foundation but still maintain the foundation's jurisdiction over timber rents. This is reflected by both the reforms of the foundation's governance and the efforts to privatize timber holdings. For the nine-year period before the victory of the UMNO in the 1994 state elections, the Sabah government had been under the control of the PBS (United Sabah Party), a party long at odds with the UMNO-dominated federal government. The PBS was led by Chief Minister Joseph Pairin Kitingan, whose brother, Jeffrey Kitingan, was the head of the Sabah Foundation. A politician in his own right, Jeffrey Kitingan objected vehemently to the federal government's capture of Sabah oil wealth. In 1991 the federal government detained Jeffrey Kitingan for thirty-one months under the Internal Security Act; he was accused of plotting the secession of Sabah from the Malaysian Federation. The Sabah Chief Minister launched a wide investigation of the Sabah Foundation, fired Jeffrey Kitingan under charges of massive corruption (later dropped after he defected from his brother's party), and sought to revise the Sabah Foundation charter and structure to increase its accountability.

The major privatization initiative to date has been the overture by the private North Borneo Timber Corporation (NBT) in the mid-1990s to buy Sabah Foundation timber holdings. This initiative had the enthusiastic support of the critics of the Sabah Foundation, who believed that the privatization would bring in capital to spur Sabah's economic growth, which had fallen badly behind the rest of Malaysia, and increase the transparency of the timber business. Yet instead of a cash payment to the foundation by NBT, the Sabah state government allowed the Sabah Foundation to fashion an asset-for-stock swap that gave the foundation a 60 percent controlling interest in NBT (*New Straits Times* 1996c, 23; *Business Times* 1995).

The Absence of Central Government Control

One may well wonder why the squandering of Malaysia's timber wealth to serve the political and financial interests of state-level politicians and cronies would be tolerated by the Malaysian national government. Timber rents are a major portion of the wealth generated in East Malaysia, in both Sarawak and Sabah, and yet the central government's policies and actions play a very small role. The reason goes back to 1975, when the central government wanted to have the state oil company Petronas control the exploitation and revenues of the oil recently found in Malaysia, particularly in East Malaysia. The deal struck with both Sabah and Sarawak stipulated that Petronas, the central government's state oil company, would exploit the oil deposits, while timber exploitation would be controlled by the state governments (Walton 1990, 136–38). The federal government thereby avoided the grave risk of putting all decisions concerning the redistribution of natural-resource wealth into its own hands — the fundamental issue that tore apart Nigeria and culminated in the Biafran War. However, the federal government's abandonment of forest policy left Sabah's and Sarawak's forests in the hands of state-level officials with little compunction against simple rent-seeking and off-budget excesses.

Honduras: The Statist Variant on the Indonesian Forestry Theme

The Honduran Forestry Development Corporation (COHDEFOR) is a strange hybrid of forestry agency and state enterprise. It demonstrates that some of the same policy failures that the Indonesian government committed through the private loggers can emerge from direct state action. The corporation has intervened to develop a downstream wood-products industry through state control rather than regulation of the private sector. After a period of go-for-broke logging, which along with agricultural conversion resulted in the loss of one-quarter of the nation's forested area,[10] it has been rather successful and efficient in developing and harvesting the pine forests of eastern Honduras. Yet it has been a disaster in terms of conserving the biologically rich broadleaf forests and in fulfilling its mandate to address poverty alleviation among populations living in and near the forests. Most relevant for this chapter is that COHDEFOR failed dramatically in the promotion of downstream forest-products processing. The result has been that the proceeds from pine exports, which provided the bulk of COHDEFOR's budget and could have been a major source of earnings for either the original property owners or the central government, have been squandered. COHDEFOR is thus a prime example of the folly of forced downstream diversification, and of a state entity given far too many tasks. The forests also suffered from the heated competition between COHDEFOR and the land reform agency to exploit forest lands.

Background

In 1974, a pauperized Honduran military government established COHDEFOR as a state enterprise that could go much further in extracting forest resources than the predecessor government agency within the Ministry of Natural Resources. COHDEFOR received virtually no central government budget but rather was required to support itself from timber sales, the export of sawn timber, commissions from intervening between local residents (often indigenous groups) and commercial loggers, and grants from foreign donors. The bulk of COHDEFOR's revenues would come from its monopoly on the export of sawn wood, with which COHDEFOR sought to capture both the timber rents and the value added. Despite the usual calls for conservation, the decree law stated that COHDEFOR would not only "undertake the optimal exploitation of forest resources on which the country depends, assure their protection, improvement, conservation and increase," but also "generate funds for the financing of state programs to accelerate the nation's process of economic and social development" (República de Honduras 1974).

The potential for COHDEFOR to capture timber rents was enormous. At its creation COHDEFOR was given formal control over all trees in Honduras. The state's confiscation of Honduras's most important natural resource, aside from land itself, was part of a broader, strongly reformist program by a radicalized military government. The 1974 fifteen-year National Development Plan also encompassed confiscation of "inadequately utilized" private lands for land reform. As in Costa Rica and Brazil, finding an outlet for land hunger competed with the land-use initiatives that involved commercial logging and large-scale ranching.

There was stiff opposition within the military as well as the civilian business sector. The more traditionally minded military had not been purged, and the Honduran business sector was deeply skeptical of the reform package put forth by the government of General Oswaldo López Arellano that came to power in 1972. The land reform, as well as strong government intervention in the economy, was so threatening to the more conservative military officers that López Arellano was deposed in 1975. Nevertheless, the more conservative military successors did not reverse COHDEFOR's control over all forests despite the ideological shift. It was clear that COHDEFOR expanded state power considerably and was not to be relinquished easily.

COHDEFOR's Power

Technically, all would-be loggers would have to obtain concession rights from COHDEFOR, and timber exports had to go through COHDEFOR as the sole purchaser and exporter of timber and lumber. In practice, the government chose to recognize some forest-use rights of indigenous people but often sent in COHDEFOR to mediate conflicts between timber companies and local residents, particularly the indigenous groups with recognized user rights. In these cases COHDEFOR set the stumpage rates and took a cut for itself. As the sole exporter, COHDEFOR had the power of a marketing board to set the prices for exported logs cut by commercial loggers and community groups. By setting these prices low in relation to world timber prices, COHDEFOR stimulated domestic private wood processing as well as its own downstream operations (Miranda et al. 1992, 283).

COHDEFOR also took over the management of the Olancho Forest Reserve, established in the most densely forested area of Honduras in 1966. With a total area of nearly 1.5 million hectares, making it Central America's largest protected area, the Olancho Reserve had 129,500 hectares of pine forest and 187,500 hectares of broadleaf forest. Numerous indigenous groups and settlers had been extracting resources from the Olancho area at relatively low levels; the protected area status made much of their extractive activity illegal. Under COHDEFOR management, concessions for logging the pine forests of Olancho increased dramatically, while little effort was made to protect the broadleaf forests. In the early 1980s the Corporación Forestal Industrial de Olancho (Corfino) was set up under COHDEFOR control to construct and operate a huge sawmill for Olancho timber. The sawmill, opened in 1983, had the capacity to produce 182,000 cubic meters of sawn timber per year, three times the country's previous capacity. Prior to launching the project, its cost was estimated at $57 million, but infrastructure costs left out of the rate of return analysis, such as road construction and port facilities, tripled the actual cost (Helsingin Sanomat 1984). Two other unprecedentedly large mills were built by COHDEFOR in Yoro and Siguatepeque. To supply the Yoro mill, the large timber company Yodeco was nationalized and accounted for nearly half of the pine harvests of this formerly heavily forested area (Utting 1993, 142).

The Timber Supply Crisis and the Inefficiency of the Wood-Products Industry

Yet by the mid-1980s the sawmills' appetites for timber, slash-and-burn cultivation, clearing for agriculture and resettlement, and deliberately set forest fires had created a serious supply crisis. As fast as COHDEFOR was arranging for the commercial logging of pine forests, the National Agrarian Institute (INA), Honduras's land reform agency, was trying to secure land for an increasingly aggressive peasant movement. The more conservative governments of the post-1975 period declared the commercial plantations (bananas, coffee, sugar, and citrus fruit) as off-limits for land reform; the forest lands, though of dubious long-term agricultural potential, therefore became the target of much of the land reform efforts. The INA-COHDEFOR conflict thus was quite similar to the scramble in Costa Rica involving the government land reform and forestry agencies. It is true that the relatively well-organized Honduran peasants would have challenged the ownership of rural lands with or without the support of the INA, and indeed several land invasions occurred without the compliance of any government agency (Morris 1984, 96–100). Yet the INA's efforts were significant and competed directly with COHDEFOR's claims of jurisdiction over forest lands. The forest fires were a grim reminder of the power of local people to undermine a resource base when their rights to it had been abrogated. Utting (1993, 152, 157) reports that many of the forest fires in Honduran protected reserves were set by local inhabitants as revenge for the restrictions on their user rights.

The resulting forest degradation led to the supply shortage just as the enormous sawmills were scaling up to full production. As early as 1979, total export volume fell by one-quarter from 1974 levels and then fell to just over half that level by 1988 (Miranda et al. 1992, 283). Yet it is also true that even without the deforestation to that point, the overly ambitious wood-products industry would have put enormous strain on domestic timber supply. For example, logging so depleted the Yoro Department that Yodeco, even as a state enterprise, began to encroach into the Olancho concession areas assigned to other companies (Utting 1993, 142). Moreover, the inefficiency of the new installations both exacerbated the supply problem (even in the late 1980s more than two-thirds of operating sawmills used circular saws, which waste 45 percent of the wood compared to 15 percent for band saws) and rendered Honduran wood exports less competitive (Pickles 1989, 43). The privately held sawmills were also inefficient; the logging companies' preference for domestic processing was artificially stimulated by the low prices COHDEFOR offered for logs destined for export.

Partly because of its abysmal financial performance, and partly because of the victory of a more economically liberal government, COHDEFOR began to lose its power in 1985, when it lost its export monopoly. Yodeco was reprivatized in 1986. In the late 1980s the COHDEFOR sawmills in Yoro and Siguatepeque were sold at a loss of roughly $20 million. The Olancho paper mill was operating at a fraction of its capacity. With virtually nothing to show for its efforts, COHDEFOR's debts constituted $240 million (Pickles 1989). In contrast to many countries where downstream processing cannot be definitively assessed because of the complexity of long-term impacts on the economy, the quick collapse of COHDEFOR's downstream investments at huge losses makes it clear that the wood-products strategy was misconceived and implemented in obvious excess. From the perspective of the international organizations that were trying to bring Honduras through the structural adjustment process, COHDEFOR became a prime target for elimination or reform.[11]

Sustainable Harvesting at Last

Perhaps the only positive outcomes of COHDEFOR's control were rent capture and eventually a sustainable rate of pine-forest harvesting. Because COHDEFOR had a strong interest in utilizing the proceeds from timber harvesting, the agency captured a respectable proportion of the stumpage value of the timber. This kept the logging companies from receiving excessive rents (Synnott 1989, 87) and reduced the desperate and reckless harvesting observed in other countries, such as Indonesia, Malaysia (excluding Sabah), and Costa Rica, where timber royalties have been small fractions of the full stumpage value. Determining what constitutes a sustainable harvest rate is, of course, fraught with difficulty, because estimating the regeneration cycle of relevant tree species in particular conditions is inevitably uncertain. Nonetheless, Honduran and international forestry experts were essentially in accord with the judgment that a sustainable rate of harvesting was reached by the late 1980s, albeit on a smaller forest base than what was available in the mid-1970s. This result is at first consideration especially surprising in light of the direct connection between timber harvests and COHDEFOR's budget. At some point in the mid- to late 1980s, COHDEFOR officials and mainline staff came to realize that the existence of their agency, their jobs, and their pensions depended on the existence of marketable timber.

Lessons

Several aspects of the COHDEFOR case may seem quite puzzling at first. If the intervention of the state came initially because of concern over reckless logging, why did the state agency then engage in even less sustainable harvesting and provoke other sources of deforestation? If COHDEFOR's powers overstepped the appropriate role of a state agency, which was the view of most post-1975 officials, why did successive governments resist the many calls to reprivatize the timber industry? It was not until 1985 that the government reprivatized the export of timber, and even then COHDEFOR long thereafter maintained the right to grant concessions.

Part of the answer is that at least some Honduran government officials recognized that capturing the timber rent would enable the government to finance development objectives without raising taxes, while at the same time being able to invoke conservation. Second, in greatly reducing the economic decision-making power of the private timber and sawmill companies, the Honduran government gained control over a crucial sector, even if it could not or would not pay for control mechanisms that would be effective in keeping deforestation within tolerable bounds. One could well imagine COHDEFOR capturing huge timber rents and some producer surplus on behalf of the Honduran government, if COHDEFOR had simply collected royalties on auctioned concessions and production, or if it had simply controlled exportation (in effect, as a marketing board). Yet by making itself a timber processor as well as owner and tax collector, COHDEFOR exposed the Honduran timber industry to the gross inefficiencies of its own processing complex — the same form of rent destruction that Indonesia experienced when log exports were banned.

Finally, many of the downstream projects undertaken by COHDEFOR and its affiliated enterprises were driven by the government's desire to secure capital and foreign exchange through loans from international lending institutions, in particular the Inter-American Development Bank and the World Bank. We will see in chapter 6 that this dynamic is not unique to Honduras; the Mexican oil company PEMEX borrowed at a far greater magnitude to secure borrowed capital. However, in that case the government wrested much of the capital away from PEMEX. In the COHDEFOR case, the difference was that rather than borrow from private banks, whose predominant concern is the timely payment of interest and principal, COHDEFOR borrowed from official international agencies that quite naturally insisted that the capital be devoted to the projects for which they were lent. Therefore, a closer parallel is Sri Lanka's grandiose Mahaweli Dam Scheme, which secured largely bilateral loans and grants in the 1970s for a massive but poorly thought-out irrigation system (Ascher and Healy 1990, 95–111). Honduras's grandiose projects of the mid-1980s, sometimes entailing single loans of over $100,000,000, brought in capital at quite significant magnitudes for a small economy of 4,500,000 million people with a per capita income of $600. The international financial institutions were in a difficult bind: their officials wanted to be proactive in the important forestry sector, stay involved in the dialogue over forestry policy and practices in Honduras, and transfer capital to the limping economy. COHDEFOR projects seemed to fit all of these needs, but hindsight shows that they were based on false optimism about the supply of timber and the potential efficiency of wood processing in the Honduran economy.

Brazil: Land Giveaways, Geopolitics, and Populating the Amazon

The resource policy failures in the Brazilian Amazon are distinctive as failures in the time path of resource extraction, with hasty and reckless exploitation caused by intragovernmental struggles over Amazonian development strategies. Browder (1988, 247) estimates that as of the mid-1980s, the value of industrial round logs in the Brazilian Amazon was US$1.7 trillion. The greatest societal value of the Amazon forest would lie in gradual extraction of valuable hardwoods, facilitated by government policies to encourage the marketing of more than the handful of species currently used in significant volumes (Browder 1988, 249–50), and the environmental and habitat services provided by the intact forest.[12] Yet with the establishment of the Superintendency for the Development of the Amazon (SUDAM) in the mid-1960s, the Brazilian government opened the region to accelerating deforestation and unwise land conversion, with very little return from marketing (as opposed to burning) the trees. Cattle ranching and small-holder agriculture, in that order, have been the major causes of deforestation, with little effort at either timber extraction or conservation despite formal requirements to keep land forested (Ascher and Healy 1990, 82–89). The actual exploitation has been predominantly in private hands and has involved wholesale clearing more than deliberate logging of commercial timber.[13] Gasques and Yakimoto (1986) and Ronald Schneider (1995) document the remarkable phenomenon of large areas cleared and then completely abandoned (up to 30 percent in the mid-1980s for SUDAM-sponsored projects), as the holders of recent government-provided deeds found that much of the potential production on Amazonian lands outstripped the effective demand for their output and that the government was unwilling or unable to enforce their land claims. The fact of abandonment is itself an indication of the initial haste of these land exploitations. Different government agencies vied with one another to provide subsidies for the kind of Amazonian development under their jurisdiction. Subsidized credit and tax benefits made the resource development of the Amazon, ostensibly to agricultural land and pasture in place of "low-value" forest, into a prime rent-seeking opportunity from the mid-1960s into the 1980s. Resource management thus proceeded as if the private resource rent of a typical piece of Amazonian land was minimal; its value was not so much in the trees or in the soils, which are generally poor for agriculture and even for livestock, as in the opportunities to receive government largesse (Hecht 1992, 11).

Background

Under successive military governments from 1964 through the early 1980s, the general commitment to populate the Amazon was abiding and deep. Far from being a simple matter of greed for frontier resources, it was propelled by a vision of manifest destiny, geopolitical assertion, defense against leftist insurrection, and a vehicle for unifying the Brazilian people. The philosophy of the Brazilian military's most prominent intellectual, General Golbery do Couto e Silva, is well summarized by Hecht and Cockburn:

> Golbery outlined a coherent philosophy of action. To have any long-term resonance, policies had to be set in the geopolitical realities of Brazil. With its clusters of population clinging to the coastline from Porto Alegre to Belem, Brazil had ignored the "vast hinterlands waiting and hoping to be aroused to life and to fulfill their historic destiny" . . . this destiny was the consummation of Vargas's "March to the West." Such a march would kindle the population to a sense of national purpose, and achieve the all-important occupation of empty hinterland and unguarded frontier, exploiting unused resources . . .
>
> Geopolitics is the lode star which orients goals and policy. In the Brazilian case, the developed South would serve as the "maneuvering platform" through which geopolitical consolidation of the Northeast, Central West and Amazonia would occur. Such geopolitics, formulated as "grand strategy" were matched with "total war" against internal and external subversion: the cold war optic. Indeed the national security of Brazil demanded the complete integration of economic and military strategy and space, since rapid economic development was mandatory for neutralizing political challenges from the left . . .
>
> Golbery was extremely concrete in his three-phased program in which the Amazon was to play a central part. The first phase was to strengthen integration between the Northeast and the South, and at the same time close off such possible corridors for guerrilla subversion as the valleys of the Tocantins, the Araguaia, and the Sao Francisco which could funnel insurgency to the "central platform" and the south. The second phase was to redirect colonization in Brazil's southern frontiers to the Northwest (what are today the states of Rondonia and Acre), launching this advance on the Northwest from the "central platform," the area of southern Mato Grosso and Goias which was "the real heart of the country," and simultaneously integrating this central platform with the politically and economically developed regions to the east and south. The final phase . . . was to "advance from a forward base, developed in the Central-West and co-ordinated with an east-west progression following the bed of the great river, to protect certain frontier points and inundate the Amazon forest with civilization. (1989, 102–3)

Despite the consensus among the military that the Amazon should be rapidly developed, Amazonian development policy was subject to fierce disagreement and even bloodshed regarding the specific approach to populating and developing the region. While each era had an identifying label or slogan associated with its program that gives a misleading impression of coherence, the internal bureaucratic battles over the nature of Amazonian development and its beneficiaries continue even now. "Operation Amazonia," begun in 1965, emphasized large-scale cattle ranching, largely organized by SUDAM. The 1970–74 "National Integration Program" emphasized colonization by low-income migrants from the Northeast and other impoverished areas, in large part through the development of the TransAmazon Highway. The 1975–79 "Program for Amazonian Development" reemphasized the role of large-scale private entrepreneurs to oversee a more orderly development and to reduce the incidence of deforestation and subsistence agriculture on inappropriate soils. Hecht (1984, 380) points out that this was "a charge that could just as easily have been made against ranching enterprise."

The central disagreement over Amazonian colonization and development strategy hinged on the balance between large- and small-scale resource exploitation: relatively extensive cattle ranching versus family farms,[14] São Paulo capital (albeit heavily subsidized by the government) versus spontaneous and officially sponsored migration. SUDAM and the Interior Ministry pushed a large-scale commercial development approach by assigning land rights to entrepreneurs (represented through the Association of Amazonian Entrepreneurs), sometimes for the same land that the land reform agency INCRA claimed was under its jurisdiction. Hecht (1992, 12) points out that medium-scale ranchers were also encouraged by SUDAM, weakening the interpretation that SUDAM was simply catering to the economically and politically powerful São Paulo elite.

The rents realized from the Brazilian Amazonian forests have been disappointing for several reasons. As timber lands, their economic yield in the context of the world timber prices of the 1970s and 1980s would have been low because of biological factors such as the enormous diversity of tree species (many of which have no established commercial markets, whether because of their rarity or the government's failure to promote and standardize their sale for lumber or pulp) and the low density of marketable trees compared to Southeast Asian exporters. Since the early 1970s there had been a ban on raw-log exports (lifted in the mid-1980s), which discouraged logging because of the exclusion of demand from overseas sawmills and the weak sawmill capacity in Brazil. The government tried, if ineffectively, to promote downstream processing through tax holidays, reflecting its preference for channeling the rents to the processing industry (Gillis 1992, 166). This practice is still in effect in Brazil despite its elimination in many other countries where these subsidies have been recognized as short-sighted.

Browder (1988, 248) points out that Brazil has nearly one-third of the world's hardwoods but accounts for only one-tenth of hardwood exports. Logging has been growing in the Amazon, increasing fourfold from 1975 to 1985 (Mahar 1989, 9), and some selective cutting of highly valuable trees is often the first step in land clearing. Yet timber harvesting is of minor impact compared to the huge number of trees of low commercial value that are burned. The Brazilian deforestation story has much less to do with commercial logging than does Indonesian deforestation.

As pasture for cattle ranching, the Amazonian forests converted for that purpose have been disappointing because of the biological unsuitability of many land parcels and the distance from markets. Schneider (1995) argues that clearing for ranching has been motivated by the expectation that enough population would eventually move into the Amazon to make cattle marketing profitable; until that happens, the ranch titles and ranching development are mechanisms for holding onto the future opportunity to profit from improved market conditions. Ranch abandonment reflects the fact that often the costs of maintaining the holdings (including fending off low-income encroachers without government policing) have exceeded the expected benefits of holding the land.[15]

Similarly, the agricultural potential of the Amazon is quite limited, partly for the now well-known fact that forest soils are often very poor for annual crops, and the same problem of distance from markets that has plagued the cattle ranchers. Here again the diagnosis suggests that among other problems, the conversion of Amazonian forest lands was premature from an economic perspective.

Interagency Scramble

The land reform agency INCRA, abetted by the zeal of the National Department for Roads and Highways (DNER) for building highways into the Amazon, was able to reorient Amazonian development policy to focus on low-income settlers during the early 1970s (Bunker 1985, 100–120; Hecht 1992, 378–79). Yet INCRA was not able to demonstrate that low-income settlers could contribute to the sustainable economic development of the Amazon. Even more than the large- and medium-scale ranchers, the low-income migrants from the South and the Northeast were seduced into migrating without awareness of the poor soils and lack of infrastructure at the settlement sites, and they lacked knowledge of appropriate farming techniques. The technical Agency for Research in Agriculture and Cattle Ranching (EMBRAPA) was responsible for providing soil and hydrologic information, but its studies were sparse and in any event largely ignored by INCRA in assigning land to settlers (Fearnside 1985, 229–34). As the settler policies sputtered, the advocates of corporate, large-scale development gained the upper hand. Pompermayer (1979) documents how the interior minister in the late 1970s succeeded in transferring land originally assigned to INCRA so that it ended up in the hands of large-scale ranching entrepreneurs. Yet land concentration was also propelled by the unsustainability of many of the small-scale farms and the fact that cheaper credit available to larger-scale ranchers allowed them to purchase land from small farmers at a price that was attractive to the small farmers — given their higher operating costs — and still permit the more heavily subsidized large-scale ranchers to operate profitably.

INCRA had another run at steering the focus of Amazonian development to the low-income settlers in the early 1980s when it secured World Bank financing for the so-called Polonoroeste project, again in alliance with the DNER (Fearnside 1985, 246; Ascher and Healy 1990, 82–89). Through the Polonoroeste project the Amazonian road system was expanded further into Rondonia and Mato Grasso, and twelve thousand families a year were allocated one hundred hectares of land, along with credit and technical assistance. Fifty hectares of each holding were to be kept in their forested state; the other fifty could be exploited by the farmer. It turned out that in many cases, the fifty exploitable hectares required too much capital and labor to develop profitably, and the farmers opted for felling as many trees as possible on all one hundred hectares and selling their land to ranchers or speculators in order to capture an immediate windfall (Ascher and Healy 1990, 87). The regulations that in theory would have controlled deforestation by small-scale farmers were particularly weak, because of the severe lack of enforcement capacity by underfunded agencies such as the Institute for the Defense of the Forest (IBDF), which had the responsibility to regulate forest clearing and logging, and the National Indian Foundation (FUNAI), responsible for defending indigenous property rights from incursions by settlers and ranchers. Then, too, Brazilian law still recognized clearing ("effective use") as a basis for a land claim. Settlers thus had the option to abuse the land for which they had received formal title and subsidies, abandon that land, and claim another parcel to repeat the process.

The weakness of FUNAI reveals the redistributive implication of the Amazonian development strategy. Numerous indigenous groups were forced from the lands where they had exercised customary user rights for generations. This de facto appropriation was rationalized in various ways by government officials, ranging from the argument that the more remote areas of the Amazon were "almost empty," to the patronizing view that government must still bring development and civilization to the local populations (Hecht and Cockburn 1989, ch. 7). In this respect, the two-step transfer of land, from indigenous use to formal state control to control by newcomers, has been justified on the same grounds as the appropriation reviewed in the Cameroon case of chapter 6.

The intragovernmental disagreement over Amazonian development strategies offers an additional explanation for the excessively rapid and ill-considered resource exploitation in the region. It may seem that the haste of Amazonian development was simply a manifestation of the military government's desire to strengthen Brazil's Amazonian presence, spur overall growth, and relieve population pressures in other regions. Undoubtedly these motives were relevant, but the disorderliness and waste of Amazonian development would seem quite uncharacteristic of a military government, especially one that was clearly more powerful than any other nation with Amazonian claims. The additional factor was that the intragovernmental clashes, and the failure of the Brazilian leadership to resolve these clashes through compromise or declaration of a winner regarding formal jurisdiction, made the Amazon an "open access" area for government agencies. That is, just as areas with no clear property or user rights are labeled as "open access" and private actors are observed not only to tend to overexploit open access resources but also to exploit them hastily in order to take advantage of their possibly temporary opportunities to do so, so too the lack of clear jurisdiction in the Amazon made it open to public agencies' hasty efforts to pursue their objectives while they still had the opportunity.

More importantly, however, the low private economic value of Amazonian land (aside from its public goods value) reflected the fact that for the ranchers it was merely a prop for the real rent-seeking game, using land holding to qualify for fiscal rents: grants and subsidized government credit, tax credits, and the opportunity to sell the land in the future. Sometimes tax credits were equivalent to up to 75 percent of the investment costs in Amazonian projects such as cattle ranches (Browder 1988, 257); to attract corporate groups to establish ranches, even grants of up to 75 percent of ranch development costs were awarded by SUDAM (Hecht 1992, 12). However, it would be a mistake to interpret the land giveaways as simply politically motivated transfers to the wealthy São Paulo elite. It is true that from the rancher's or farmer's perspective, the land giveaways were more a pretext for rent-seeking extraction than efficient conversion to sustainable agriculture.[16] The natural-resource endowment (i.e., the trees, the biodiversity, the ecosystem as a whole) essentially got in the way of the most convenient form of obtaining subsidies. Yet the explanation that the government was simply currying favor with its strongest political supporters only goes so far, because of the subsidized stimulation of small- and medium-scale farming and ranching and because the infrastructure clearly intended to provide a population safety valve for the low-income populations from other Brazilian regions.

Aftermath of the Rush to the Amazon

By the late 1980s, the problems of both small- and large-scale operations in the Amazon led to a rethinking of the wisdom of government land giveaways and subsidies to production. Ranching subsidies were eliminated in mid-1987. In the same year, the World Bank suspended the bulk of its highway construction support for the Amazon, largely because of environmental concerns. Of course, the problem of economically unproductive deforestation of the Amazon has not disappeared. Hecht (1992, 12, 23) points out that the large population already attracted to the Amazon without a sustainable basis for maintaining their crop or livestock production has been a chronic source of continued and indeed increasing deforestation. The provision of the 1988 constitution that prohibits the expropriation of cleared land has made land clearing even more attractive for pursuing rents through land clearing and later sale. Moreover, the greater awareness that productive land in the Amazon is limited has led to innumerable conflicts between ranchers and low-income settlers.

The final question is how much was accomplished in pursuing the goal of Amazonian development, and at what costs. First, it must be acknowledged that the Brazilian Amazon has become more populated. General Golbery's vision of "flooding the Amazon with civilization" has been fulfilled at least to the degree that the broad Amazon region[17] achieved a population of roughly 12 million as of the mid-1980s, and nearly 18 million in 1991, compared to only 8 million in 1970 (Wood and Wilson 1984; IBGE 1992).

The costs, however, are very sobering. Binswanger (1991, 828) estimates that the tax credits for livestock ventures may have caused as much as 4 million hectares of deforestation. Mahar (1989, 16) concludes that the bulk of the $700 million of fiscal subsidies paid to ranchers was a total loss, inasmuch as only ninety-two livestock operations had received certificates of completion by the late 1980s, and surveys of productivity indicated that many ranches, if producing anything at all, were yielding small fractions of their projected returns. The afforestation efforts, ostensibly intended to offset forest destruction, also had steep fiscal costs but resulted in little if any improvement (Binswanger 1991, 828).

Peru: Occupying the Amazon through Oil

After enormous investments in oil exploration in the 1970s, Peru's oil sector has been virtually stagnant since the early 1980s. The state oil company, PetroPerú, narrowly averted bankruptcy in 1979 and the late 1980s and is currently being dismantled in a drawn-out privatization. Although the limited international oil company exploration in Peru paid off with several significant discoveries, international oil companies have largely shied away from Peru, and yet, despite the country's not inconsiderable oil potential, PetroPerú has been severely undercapitalized. This undercapitalization, itself a policy failure, arose from a combination of unnecessarily risky investments of state capital in Amazonian exploration, and later from a chronic unwillingness on the part of the Peruvian government to keep domestic fuel prices at levels that could have financed PetroPerú and husbanded Peru's dwindling oil reserves. Thus, the story of Peru's oil highlights the costs of pursuing development strategies through unsound resource exploitation. First, it shows that an Amazonian regional development strategy can be mounted not only through land giveaways and cattle-ranching subsidies as in the Brazilian case but also through the manipulation of oil exploration. Second, Peru has been one among many nations that have tried to mount a cheap-energy industrial strategy by underpricing petroleum outputs.

The period since oil nationalization in 1968 has seen two distinctive phases with very different policy failures.[18] From the early 1970s through 1979, state resources were recklessly invested in Amazonian exploration. In addition, low domestic fuel prices, which exacerbated the severe undercapitalization of PetroPerú, arose from a combination of commitment to a cheap-energy development strategy and political concern over potential dissatisfaction with high fuel prices. From 1979 through the 1980s, reckless investment was transformed into overcaution, and although domestic fuel prices were brought into line for a short time, underpricing of the government's oil-in-ground reduced the incentives for PetroPerú to keep costs low. When the government allowed real fuel prices to decline in the 1980s, the company became even less willing or capable of developing Peru's oil potential. In sum, PetroPerú has been paradoxically both underfunded and high-cost, a result of the near irrelevance of the company's own actions on whether it produces a profit or a loss.

Background

Oil exploration became a strategic instrument for the Peruvian government when the leftist-nationalist military government of General Juan Velasco Alvarado expropriated the International Petroleum Corporation operations in 1968. This Standard Oil of New Jersey affiliate had been by far the largest producer, refiner, and retailer in the Peruvian oil sector. While other foreign oil firms were permitted to operate in Peru, the new state enterprise PetroPerú immediately dominated and, like several other state oil companies such as Nigeria's NNPC (reviewed in chapter 5), insisted on joint venture arrangements in Amazonian exploration, rather than allowing foreign firms to bear the full financial risk of exploration. From 1970 through 1976 PetroPerú spent nearly $400 million on exploration and production (Campodónico 1986, 172). This was puzzling because the Peruvian government had adopted the production-sharing contract approach pioneered by Indonesia, which could have allowed the state enterprise and the government to avoid risking national capital altogether because the contracting company (generally a major international oil company) would cover costs of exploration and production in return for a prespecified share of oil produced (Campodónico 1986, 78–86; Hunt 1975, 335–36).

The Velasco government directed PetroPerú to develop Amazonian oil resources before the international firms regarded the region as sufficiently attractive to invest in the pipeline necessary to bring discovered oil to the coast. After 1973, however, higher world oil prices and supply concerns induced Japanese investments in the oil pipeline, but the Peruvian government insisted on owning, constructing, and operating the project. The pipeline suffered numerous delays because of poor execution and lack of financing from the Peruvian government, and operation was delayed until 1978 (Gieseke 1991, 4). By 1984 the government had sunk $830 million into the pipeline and its infrastructure (Campodónico 1986, 173). In the meantime, exploration proved disappointing; discoveries in the range of 50 to 100 million barrels were far below the 200 to 500 million barrel fields that had been anticipated. While the international companies had their disappointments (all but Occidental relinquished their exploration areas) and moved on to other countries, PetroPerú, which had been granted large tracts for its oil exploration and development, lost heavily in its initial burst of exploration and lacked the capital to proceed with further exploration or oil-field development (Gieseke 1991, 4). By the mid-1980s, PetroPerú found itself with operational responsibility over roughly one-third of the country's proven reserves, with inadequate technical or manpower capabilities (Mayorga Alba 1987, 75, 105–11).

How can we account for Peru's strategy of exposing PetroPerú (and national capital) to such risks when multinational oil companies were disposed (and encouraged by easy terms) to invest their money? Without a doubt, nationalism played some role in the decision to involve PetroPerú so heavily. Yet by the mid-1970s the Peruvian military government had become more conservative than it was in 1968. When world oil prices shot up, the government openly courted foreign oil companies, which were offered quite generous terms to explore in the Amazon (Gieseke 1991, 3). The arrangement was a 50–50 split of produced oil, with the state oil company also covering the bulk of the tax obligations of the international companies. The strategic importance of developing the Amazon was thus reflected by the willingness to bring in foreign firms, the generous terms they were offered, and the government's insistence on being an equity partner at the risk of national capital.

A pivotal consideration was that the armed forces itself could use PetroPerú as an instrument for both the military and the economic fortification of the Amazon. Without such a motive, the decision to rely on foreign oil companies and risk Peruvian capital would be truly baffling. Government capital not only increased the total exploration effort but also gave the government, through PetroPerú, more say in the selection of areas subject to exploration. Some of these areas were chosen because of the geopolitical advantages of siting settlements rather than because of their prospectivity. In addition, PetroPerú was required to hire Peruvian military helicopters, at very high costs, to transport exploration teams. The operational control over the oil pipeline similarly allowed the military and the government to choose the specific route and to keep pipeline construction crews in strategic locations.

Internal Division and Circumvention

Velasco was under great pressure, because of both the military's populist ideology and considerations of political support, to mobilize the urban population. To court their support required that the government address urban unemployment, inflation, and decaying infrastructure, not only in Lima, where political disruption was always a serious risk, but also in the smaller cities and towns suffering from the favored treatment of the Lima area in pricing and the provision of public services. At the same time, the Velasco government was publicly committed to improving rural conditions and mobilizing small farmers, the latter through government-sponsored peasant leagues. Land reform was thus also an expensive item on the government's agenda.

This very cluttered agenda, revealing the desire and need of the "Revolutionary Government of the Armed Forces" to maintain a populist base, left little room for an Amazonian adventure. A straightforward military expansion in the Amazon, or fiscal financing of Amazonian incentives to match those of Brazil, would have incurred the strong opposition of the technocrats within the government, particularly those in the Finance Ministry.[19] This was so even though the top government officials during the military government period were active officers of the armed forces.[20] The divisiveness extended from the armed forces itself to the government. Cleaves and Pease García point out that

the October 1968 coup was promoted by a nucleus of officers close to Velasco that collaborated in the planning and execution of the overthrow of Belaúnde. This nucleus was not a full-fledged government faithfully representing the three service branches, but a team of like-minded army officers who surrounded the president and gradually moved into important jobs in the government.

It soon became apparent, however, that there was no substantive agreement among military officers about the policies the government would undertake. The summit of power was heterogeneous, and most of its members had been weaned on the militant anticommunism of the 1950s; these officers were prepared to be the protectors of the established order and not the promoters of social change . . . Some members of the armed forces wished to mend fences with the oligarchy and the IPC; others were intransigent about ending their dominant role in the economy. Some military men wished to promote industrial development through a strong state, and others were more attracted to a liberal economic model. (1983, 227)

Moreover, the justifying myth of the Revolution was the new definition of national defense rooted in economic development and national reconciliation of all classes but the oligarchy.[21] The armed forces proclaimed a mission beyond its own aggrandizement; this was not just another self-interested military looking for bigger budgets and military adventure. To have financed the armed forces' expansion directly through the central budget would have endangered the Revolution's legitimacy both within and outside the armed forces.

Domestic Fuel Pricing and Decapitalization

Despite the increase in the world oil price, the military government required PetroPerú to sell gasoline and other fuels domestically at very low prices, throughout nearly all of the 1970s. Without the huge export revenues to help offset production and marketing losses for the domestic market, PetroPerú incurred enormous losses by the mid-1970s. In 1977 PetroPerú's losses accounted for half of the government's budget deficit (Gieseke 1991, 5). Of course, the state enterprise's deficit was a virtually artificial outcome of governmental decisions on tax and royalty charges (e.g., PetroPerú, like many state oil companies, has never been charged for the oil-in-ground as a resource rent should be charged, and yet it has been subject to a series of taxes that do not correspond to the taxation of other state or private entities). Nevertheless, PetroPerú's deficit status made its pleas for a greater operating budget less plausible than they would have been if the company had shown a paper profit. The government decided that PetroPerú needed to be self-sufficient in financing its operating budget but would continue to finance its exploration (Gieseke 1991, 6).

Faced with this resistance from the government, in 1977 PetroPerú tried to resort to the smoke and mirrors that other state enterprises have used to circumvent partial government restrictions on financing. PetroPerú tried to relabel operating expenses as "current investments" (*inversiones corrientes*), covering expenses normally placed within the operating budget such as equipment maintenance.[22] Although PetroPerú tried to obfuscate the purposes of the funds, in part through hiding the analysis within reams of computer printouts, the Peruvian government saw through this. By 1979 the government refused to make any cash transfers to PetroPerú, a policy that was maintained thereafter even when many other parameters changed (Gieseke 1991, 6). In a sense, the fiscal expectations for PetroPerú's capitalization became rigidified, even though the government frequently changed PetroPerú's revenue prospects by manipulating the domestic fuel prices.

When civilian government under former president Belaúnde was reinstated in 1980, PetroPerú's fortunes changed because the pipeline had finally come on line, in time for the 1979 world oil price rise, and the new government raised domestic fuel prices to close to international levels. Contrary to the conventional view that democratic governments find it much more difficult than military governments to eliminate fuel and transportation subsidies, the Belaúnde government raised the gasoline price to the equivalent of US$1.20 per gallon in consultation with the International Monetary Fund. Moreover, it also instituted automatic price adjustments to keep up with inflation (Gieseke 1991, 7). Behind this enlightened change, however, was the fact that the central treasury could no longer rely on PetroPerú to absorb the costs of the fuel subsidies. By 1979 PetroPerú was bankrupt. It had to ask the government to refinance nearly $1 billion in foreign debt and could not service its loans to the Japanese lenders for the pipeline without resorting to Peruvian government funds. Only under this circumstance, in which the central treasury had to cover PetroPerú's deficit directly, did the government consent to raise domestic fuel prices.

This policy of internal-level prices for domestic fuels put a partial brake on Peru's rising domestic oil consumption and put PetroPerú into a better position to take advantage of the high world oil prices that prevailed in the early 1980s, when PetroPerú oil revenues contributed nearly 30 percent of foreign currency earnings and nearly 40 percent of government revenues through gasoline taxation (Gieseke 1991, 7–8).

This arrangement collapsed when the Alan García administration succumbed to threats of disruption if the fuel prices were raised to keep up with inflation. Through the mid- and late-1980s, meager revenues from domestic fuel sales, and high taxation, kept PetroPerú poor and in disrepute (Pascó-Font Quevedo and Briceño Lira 1992, 15).

The Significance of Undercapitalization

While PetroPerú officials could bemoan the company's lack of capital to pursue its objectives, this in and of itself does not constitute a policy failure. After all, one could easily conceive of a Peru without a state oil company at all, where a government agency, perhaps an appendage of the Finance Ministry, simply collects appropriate royalties from private oil exploiters. Or, if for reasons of pride or politics, Peru needs a state oil company, it could be like the reformed Pertamina in Indonesia: a royalty collector rather than a major operating company. Under either of these scenarios, international oil companies would more fully set the pace of exploration and eventually production, based on their expectations of prospectivity as well as their assessment of whether the concession contracts provide great enough payoffs to offset the risks of failure to discover sufficiently rich oil fields. Nor would it be correct to say that the risk of national capital in oil exploration is a policy failure, if foreign firms are unwilling to take the risk. It may be that national capital does not have realistic opportunities for rates of return as high as those that draw the foreign firms away from Peru (even if the Peruvian government were to offer the most attractive contract terms), or that the side benefits of higher oil production, such as foreign currency earnings and development of technical skills, make the full returns to the nation greater than any return Peruvian oil exploration could provide the foreign firms. Radetzki (1985) argues that these gains may even offset the generally lower efficiency of state enterprises compared to multinational enterprises.

Yet, although it cannot be said a priori that either low or high capitalization of PetroPerú would constitute a policy failure, the act of denying it the revenues of domestic-market-price fuel sales, while leaving the company the crucial task of financing oil exploration and production in the wake of the disinterest of international companies, is a clear policy failure. This is so first because of the poor exploitation practices that the threadbare company has undertaken (e.g., lack of maintenance capability led to serious leakages in refineries and the Amazonian pipeline) and the suboptimality of its resource development pace. The rate of exploration certainly deviated from the optimal rate as determined by full (i.e., market) returns on the investment. Why should—or could—PetroPerú embark on exploration and production at the level that the opportunity to earn market revenues would dictate, when the company was losing money on every barrel produced and refined for the domestic market? PetroPerú's lack of financing also made it incapable of boosting production rapidly when world prices were high, and of inducing international oil companies to expand their exploration programs, knowing that heavy PetroPerú involvement could hamper the efficiency of exploration and add political constraints on exploration decisions.[23] By 1988 PetroPerú was losing US$1 million a day. In 1989, with PetroPerú bankrupt, the government forced the banking system to acquire national bonds worth nearly US$106 million, 25 percent of the minimum cash requirement of each bank, to prevent PetroPerú from defaulting on foreign loans. The government also decreed that the treasury had to buy PetroPerú's total foreign currency debt and that the state would assume PetroPerú's US$20 million worth of accumulated internal debt (*Latin American Weekly Report* 1989).

In the 1990s PetroPerú has been undergoing a drawn-out privatization. In 1991 it lost its monopoly over refining, distribution, and marketing. Ironically, the resistance to this liberalization was not fierce on the part of PetroPerú, because price ceilings had made these activities very unattractive financially for the state enterprise. In the mid-1990s, PetroPerú's holdings were gradually put up for sale. Thirty years of state control has culminated in close to a return to the status quo ante, but with Peru's oil prospects much diminished.

Mexican Water

I end this chapter with a case that helps make the transition from focusing on development-financing motives to the motive of distribution. The case of irrigation in Mexico is striking in how intertwined these motives can be.

Problems and Policy Failures

The problems of rural water management in Mexico entail the common combination of water depletion, overinvestment in large-scale irrigation, and the deterioration of the irrigation system. The result of water underpricing has been overdepletion of rivers, lakes, and aquifers, as well as soil damage — water logging and salinity — from the overuse of water that often occurs when farmers pay only a small portion of the costs. Gorriz, Subramanian, and Simas (1995) report that the levels of aquifers in the Central and North regions have been dropping at three meters per year. Some aquifers have been so depleted that they have been invaded by salt water, rendering them permanently useless for irrigation. Agriculture has been unnecessarily vulnerable to water supply shortages that arise because of groundwater depletion or drought. Since at least the late 1950s, Mexico has faced the deterioration of the existing irrigation system, which was built without taking into consideration the capacity of water users to pay, and was later undercapitalized and of very low conveyance efficiency. Gorriz et al. (1995, 3) observe that the 30 percent overall conveyance efficiency of the overall irrigation system, a result of its "major disrepair" by the early 1990s, required nearly twice as much water to irrigate the same area as in Arizona and California, where the conveyance efficiencies were from 50 to 60 percent. The inefficiency of the dam-and-canal system obviously put greater demands on other sources of irrigation, including pump irrigation, provoking greater depletion of aquifers. In Mexico's Pacific Northwest, beginning in the 1970s, the depletion of aquifers supplying pump irrigation, and the depletion of the reservoirs on the Fuerte, Mayo, and Yaqui rivers, forced farmers away from lucrative soybean cultivation (Sanderson 1986, 176).

For decades these problems, dating back to the 1930s, were overshadowed by what seemed to be an astounding growth of the irrigation system and an "agricultural growth miracle." P. Lamartine Yates (1981, 47) judged the national irrigation system "among the finest investments which the Mexican government has ever made." Yet as progress in agriculture faltered, and the irrigation system deteriorated, the financial management of this system came under increasing criticism. Miguel Wionczek posed the crucial puzzle for the immediate post–World War II period — which holds equally for much of Mexico's experience with irrigation in this century:

> It is difficult to explain the reluctance that the federal government demonstrated toward periodically revising the water charges . . . The value of the land and the harvests was increasing very rapidly, not only in the extensive districts of the North and Northwest, but also in the smaller projects in other regions of the country.
>
> The vast majority of the users of irrigation services could have paid considerably higher charges for water, without this having a significant impact on total costs and profits, since the . . . costs represented a very small proportion — around 1 percent — of the costs of production. It is very likely that if there had been an adjustment in water charges, combined with rational norms regulating its use, the result would have been a more efficient utilization of water resources and no increment in the price levels of agricultural products.
>
> The continuous subsidies that the federal government granted to put its irrigation plans into effect — such as the policy of concentrating on gigantic projects without allocating sufficient funds to undertake the secondary works and complete small-scale irrigation works in the frontier areas of the irrigation districts — considerably limited the optimal use of land and water resources and imposed a heavy burden on the Finance Ministry. (1982, 403–4)

Wionczek recognized that water underpricing was the policy failure at the root of these problems. For many years, the government continued to subsidize the irrigation system despite periodic and largely unsuccessful or short-lived efforts to increase user charges. In the 1960s, and again in the 1980s, the operating and maintenance expenditures needed to keep the system from rapid deterioration were simply not forthcoming, because of the scarcity of irrigation funds and, in the 1980s, because the government had been sharply rebuffed by farmers in its efforts to increase user charges. Whereas the initial policy failure was that the government subsidized an irrigation system for which the farmers should have been paying, during the 1960–65 period and throughout the 1980s the policy failure was that no one was paying enough to keep the investment viable. In addition, from the fiscal perspective, governments incurred unnecessary costs by overinvesting in large-scale irrigation when smaller-scale water sources would have been sufficient and failed to cover their own costs by charging the farmers. Indeed, there is evidence that the entire system is overextended, both in terms of the capacity of water users to pay (the best indication of the economic soundness of the investments) and the availability of water. Profound institutional reforms in the 1990s, however, have reversed the policy failure and have begun the slow process of revitalizing the irrigation system.

The problems that have plagued Mexico's water are well recognized by water supply officials and experts, both within Mexico and in virtually every other country with significant investment in irrigation. "Cost recovery," through payments by water users, has long been the mantra of irrigation experts sensitive to the economic aspects of irrigation finance and water-use behavior. The Mexican case is illuminating because it provides some insight into why governments would deliberately overspend, forgo opportunities to collect revenues, and later run the risk of agricultural collapse. In Mexico, as in other countries that have expensive, large-scale irrigation systems and have undercharged for water uses, these actions cannot be easily dismissed as simply benefits for a favored agricultural sector. Agriculture in Mexico has generally suffered vis-à-vis industry in the redistribution of resources by the government. Yet government overspending in water could have been reduced in order to allow for more productive investments and expenditures in rural credit, agriculture research, and extension.

The reasons for the overextension and the initial underpricing are largely to be found in the contested pursuit of agricultural development strategies, complicated by a regional-development strategy favoring northern states, but also with strong influences from distributional considerations that concentrated the irrigation benefits to regionally and sectorally differentiated types of farmers over time. The reasons why efforts to redress the underpricing problem took so long to take effect also illuminate the importance of distributional considerations and intragovernmental conflicts.

Background

The federal government's astounding emphasis on subsidized, large-scale irrigation as its primary contribution to agricultural development can be traced to the pursuit of competing agricultural development strategies for which cheap water was a tool of both sides. The Mexican Revolution, which began in 1910 and extended long into the 1920s, brought agricultural productivity to a dangerously low level, and the pre-existing irrigation system was virtually destroyed. The "champion of Mexican irrigation," President Plutarco Elías Calles (formally president from 1924 to 1928; informally clearly the head of the regime until 1934),[24] faced ferocious disagreements within the "Revolutionary Family" over how the Revolution should be consolidated, particularly with respect to the treatment of agriculture. Calles and his followers believed that essential productivity gains could be achieved only through agricultural modernization implemented by larger-scale farmers,[25] who in theory could afford to pay for irrigation. The financing of the irrigation expansion was to be from the sale of newly irrigated lands and from water charges collected from the new water users, who were expected, by virtue of the productivity gains that irrigation would bring, to become a new agrarian middle class (Wionczek 1982, 396). Through the National Irrigation Commission (Comisíon Nacional de Irrigación or CNI), established in 1926, Calles launched ambitious irrigation projects and established irrigation districts to administer water allocation, sell the irrigated government land, and impose water charges. Yet although the original concept of the post-Revolution irrigation was that it would be self-financing and would greatly expand the ranks of prosperous farmers who could afford to pay, the farmers on irrigated lands were never called upon to cover the investment costs of the irrigation system. There was never a market test of whether a particular irrigation expansion was an efficient allocation of either investment capital or water.

In terms of regional distribution, the northern states of Baja California, Sonora, Sinaloa, and Tamaulipas were strongly targeted. They ultimately received nearly half of the irrigation investment up to 1960. This concentration was strongly influenced by President Calles's geopolitical strategy of developing—and gaining the political support of—the northern tier of Mexican states, which had historically been the hotbed of opposition to government.[26] Calles distributed much of the irrigated land to co-opt enemies and consolidate fragile political alliances, creating a new class of well-to-do farmers out of political bosses to fill the vacuum of the large landowners who had dominated in the pre-Revolution North (Wionczek 1982, 396, 400–401). Through this arrangement the new landowners benefited from their privilege to buy the land, frequently at very attractive prices, but the irrigation districts were collecting a large proportion of the costs of operations and maintenance. One may well question the equity of this outcome, but from a water conservation perspective at least the incentives for excessive extraction of water from the system were held in check.

Even before the Calles era, some Mexican land had already been distributed to formerly landless families, typically organized into communal groupings called *ejidos*. Most *ejidos* were barely capitalized and hardly had the financial resources to acquire new land or pay for irrigation. Some members of the sprawling and ideologically diverse Revolutionary Family believed that to maintain the egalitarian principles of the Revolution, the restoration of Mexico's devastated agricultural sector had to concentrate on increasing the productivity of the *ejidos* and small farms. Lázaro Cárdenas, who became president in 1934, restored the primacy of the *ejido*-based, redistributive agricultural policy.[27] Wionczek (1982, 397) reports that while *ejidos* controlled only 15 percent of arable land within irrigation districts in 1930, by 1940 they controlled almost 60 percent of irrigated lands. Cárdenas took the control of setting water prices away from the CNI and placed it in the hands of his followers in the Banco Nacional de Crédito Agrícola (Wionczek 1982, 403). With the introduction of the "ability to pay" criterion, cheap water became an explicit subsidy, ostensibly for low-income *ejiditarios* and small-scale farmers, but in fact for all farmers. The specific imposition of water charges was essentially left to the individual district manager of each of the irrigation districts and the local political leaders (Greenberg 1970, 16). It would have been extraordinarily difficult to deny the larger-scale farmers the low water rates going to the others. Although the CNI suppressed its official statistics on deficits during the Cárdenas period, Tamayo (1946, 263) provides overall figures for 1936–43 that imply that only 43 percent of operating costs were covered by water-use charges.

In the 1940s irrigation became the overwhelmingly dominant target for public investment in agriculture. From 1941 through 1945, twice as much agricultural land received irrigation than in the previous fifteen years (Wionczek 1982, 398). Indeed, irrigation construction became entrenched as the agricultural investment strategy from a fiscal perspective. In 1940, 80 percent of total public agricultural investment went into irrigation; in 1945, 1955, and 1965 it exceeded 90 percent. In the early 1970s the National Water Plan Commission made an influential analysis of the irrigation system, previously underexamined in terms of its overall impacts on water supply, and determined that it was essential to shift from expanding the system to maintaining it physically and managing the water efficiently. Yet in 1970 the proportion of public investment in irrigation again exceeded 90 percent. In 1975 and 1980 the proportions dropped back and yet were still 76 and 59 percent, respectively.[28]

The subsidization policy was similarly entrenched. Roughly the same level of subsidization — leaving farmers to pay only 45 percent of operating costs — persisted from the beginning of the post–World War II period through 1959.[29] However, in the last three years of this period, revenues slipped even lower than before, to only 30 percent by 1959, while the government's overall fiscal difficulties led to a decline in irrigation investment (Orive Alba 1960, 216). The crisis in irrigation finance provoked a highly critical assessment by the CNI's successor, the Ministry of Water Resources (Secretaría de Recursos Hidráulicos or SRH), and motivated the ministry to develop the first long-term plan for Mexican irrigation. The 1960 Twenty-five-Year Water Resources Plan criticized both the concentration of irrigated land in the hands of large-scale farmers and the low cost recovery. The SRH emphasized that 10 percent of the cultivable land had suffered from severely reduced productivity because of the deterioration of the irrigation system. The SRH analysis "insisted that once the irrigation users began to pay for the services they received from the State, the development of the long-term program would conform perfectly with the financial possibilities of the federal government" (Wionczek 1982, 406).

It may seem odd that the SRH would criticize irrigation performance under its own management. Yet the ministry was witnessing its fiscal emasculation, and the growing dominance of large-scale farmers, a phenomenon over which the SRH had almost no control, was also reducing the ministry's capacity to become financially secure, insofar as these farmers could resist water charge increases. The resurgence of large farms despite the formal commitment to *ejido* development reflected economic dynamics that were very difficult to reverse through policy. It is almost an economic truism that when a scarce input is provided, economic actors with greater resources will be able to increase their productivity more than those with lesser resources. It appears that the export-oriented, more heavily capitalized farmers gradually found ways to capture more of the benefits of subsidized irrigation. In many areas large-scale farmers were able to assume control, openly or not, of communal lands within irrigated areas. It is also likely that the irrigation systems feeding lower-productivity *ejidal* lands and small-scale farms were subject to greater deterioration, because of the lack of a productivity rationale for their maintenance.

The Water Resources Ministry officials may have expected that their critique would put an end to subsidizing the rich farms. For a while, with the support of the Finance Ministry, the Water Resources Ministry was able to reduce the subsidy; from 1960 to 1965 the user charges rose steadily to over 65 percent of operating costs and rose to 70 percent for 1969–71. However, Schramm and Gonzales (1977, 21) show that for the 1960–65 period, this was due to a decline in operating expenditures rather than an increase in charges, in all likelihood contributing to the deterioration of the system. The proposal to set aside a substantial fund for smaller-scale systems, which would have targeted smaller farms, was rejected. From 1966 to 1971, expenditures again grew, with corresponding increases in water charges, but in 1972 and 1973 the expenditures went up dramatically without corresponding increases in water charges (Schramm and Gonzales 1977, 21).

Although the relative level of the subsidy declined during the 1960–71 period, the concentration of benefits to wealthier farmers actually increased, because of both the continuing process of land consolidation and a major policy reorientation in favor of promoting modern commercial agriculture at the expense of traditional subsistence agriculture.[30] In short, the government acknowledged that larger-scale farms were, and should be, favored; yet instead of eliminating the subsidies on the grounds that irrigation beneficiaries could pay, the government simply included the water subsidies as part of the general effort to promote agriculture. The SRH succeeded in 1967, under the Díaz Ordaz administration, to implement a program for smaller-scale irrigation,[31] but this also entailed water subsidies.

By then the long-term pattern had become entrenched: administrations committed to improving the plight of low-income farmers tried to direct irrigation benefits to the *ejidos* and small farmers and permitted low water charges to be part of the support package; administrations committed to promoting export-oriented, large-scale agriculture directed or allowed irrigation to go to large-scale farms and also permitted low water charges as a component of this promotion. During each period when one or the other approach prevailed, its champions took excessive advantage of the opportunity by giving away water that would not have been, even at full user charges, a terribly significant cost to either small- or large-scale farmers but was clearly a major factor in the inability of the irrigation authorities to keep up the maintenance of the system. Neither approach took into account the long-term impacts on the irrigation system as a whole.

Subsidization during the Uncertain 1970s and 1980s

This pattern was exacerbated in the 1970s and 1980s by rising inflation, faltering of the agricultural sector, fiscal profligacy, and the declining legitimacy of the PRI. In 1972–73, with rising inflation and a presidential election nearing, irrigation spending increased, and cost recovery again declined to below 45 percent of total operating, maintenance, and rehabilitation costs (Schramm and Gonzales 1977, 19). The difference between expenditures and charges typically increased during periods of high inflation, because the water charges were revised periodically rather than continuously, thus allowing inflation to erode the real value of the charges while the irrigation authorities had to spend in the face of actual cost increases. Then the Mexican oil boom began, and President José Lopéz Portillo vastly expanded the subsidies for Mexican agriculture, including water-cost subsidies (Sanderson 1986, 204).

To assess the implications of this policy, it is important to point out that Mexican officials were aware of the negative impact that an oil boom can have on other export commodities.[32] Subsidies for a sector hurt by an export boom can be justified if its comparative advantages can reemerge after the boom ends. This is especially true when the boom is due to the rise of a nonrenewable resource like oil or minerals. In such cases, vulnerable sectors may be sheltered from irretrievable deterioration, so that production can be resumed once the sector's output becomes internationally competitive again. Therefore, although subsidies are often the main culprits of economic policy failure, some subsidization of Mexican agriculture would not have constituted a policy failure. However, the inclusion of water-cost subsidies within the subsidy package was both unnecessary and costly in terms of the sustainability of water supplies. Because the agricultural sector continued to deteriorate, government overtures to reinstitute water charges were strongly resisted (Sanderson 1986, 95). The declining legitimacy of the PRI government completed the vicious circle: the government was particularly loathe to lose the political support of farmers who were increasingly less able to pay for water charges from a deteriorating irrigation system that—because of its deterioration—made it more expensive to bring the same quantum of water to the fields.

During the 1980s the subsidization and deterioration both worsened, to the point of only 15–25 percent recovery of operating costs (Cummings and Nercissiantz 1992, 743; Gorriz et al. 1995, 3). According to Sanderson (1986, 95), in 1981 the government tried to increase water charges but failed because of resistance from the farmers and the "lack of a constituency for such a change." It was essentially at that point that the ministry reduced its maintenance budgets, culminating in the severe damage to the physical structures that accounts for the abysmal conveyance efficiency mentioned earlier.

Reform through User Groups

By the end of the 1980s, the slow process of extending the liberalization reforms into all aspects of Mexico's economic and political management finally came to the irrigation system. The government could have tried to address the issue of water underpricing by simply raising the rates or developing a formula to raise the rates as irrigation costs rise. However, this would have left the pricing issue vulnerable to the same political pressures and strategic manipulation as before. The far more clever strategy was to transfer irrigation districts over to user groups, who gained a large degree of control just as they had to take on more responsibility for financing water costs. Thus, this initiative dovetailed conveniently with the prevailing preoccupation of increasing stakeholders' participation in decision making, while it certainly did not highlight the fact that water users would have to cover a greater proportion of the costs.

The progress in transferring water districts to water user organizations has been slow, because of the sage strategy of ensuring that training and financial accountability are in place before the transfer is effected. Yet by 1994, even though only 38 of the 80 districts had completed the transfer and 16 more were partially transferred, water users covered 80 percent of operations and maintenance costs, up from 57 percent in 1991 (Gorriz et al. 1995, 13).

The Mexican government has persisted with this strategy with perhaps surprising persistence over several administrations. It is no coincidence that these reforms occurred alongside of dramatic changes in the legal status of the *ejidos* that permitted *ejiditarios* to sell land and put it up as collateral. It thus appears that the commercialization (some would say dismantling) of *ejidos* and the chronic economic problems that have highlighted the need for greater agricultural efficiency have put an end to the agricultural policy struggle that motivated the misuse of water for so many decades.

Bias toward Major Irrigation and Large Scale

The lessons of Mexican water policy failures begin with the explanation for the heavy financial burden that the irrigation strategy has imposed upon all involved parties, which makes full cost recovery all the more difficult. The lack of full cost recovery is usually depicted as the core problem for irrigation system failures, implying that recognition and commitment by the government, and enlightened compliance by water users, would solve the problem. However, in many cases, including that of Mexico, the problem lies deeper: in the provision of a huge "major irrigation" system (i.e., dams and canals) that is too expensive regardless of the sources of financing. Adding to the problem is that in Mexico the largest-scale irrigation systems also have greater water losses than the smaller-scale systems (Gorriz et al. 1995, 3). Mexican administrations have favored major irrigation as opposed to minor irrigation (wells, tanks, ponds, etc.) despite some economic advantages of the latter[33] and favored large-scale major irrigation projects over smaller-scale ones. Leaving aside the distributional and poverty-alleviation considerations, major irrigation requires government involvement, and, if potential irrigation recipients are poor to begin with and skeptical about the actual benefits they will receive, the government has to pay at least the initial investment costs.[34] Once this precedent is set, it becomes very difficult to reverse.

The reasons why the Mexican governments, whether supporting large farms or *ejidos*, favored major irrigation can be found in the same short-sighted logic of favoring water subsidies. First, major irrigation gives the government more control over whether large farms or *ejidos* will be benefited. Minor irrigation can be promoted through credit and technical assistance, but at the end of the day the farmer still must undertake the work and risk of drilling a well or building a tank or pond. Second, by the same token the major irrigation project gives the government more political credit for providing irrigation, precisely because it does constitute a clear rent for the farmer. Because the dispute over whether the farmer ought to pay even for the operations and upkeep of the system diminishes the perception that the irrigation system as a whole does provide a rent, the efforts to raise water charges diminish the government's political credit. Third, major irrigation entails public works that provide highly visible employment opportunities and lucrative opportunities for contractors. In the Mexican case, the rise of Mexican nationals as major construction contractors can be found in the public works projects of the Calles era (Wionczek 1982, 396–97).

Finally, the political symbolism of irrigation expansion is crucial. The expansion of an irrigation system appears to be a clear instance of resource development, carrying at least a superficial connotation of husbanding resources, even though the expansion of an irrigation system is tantamount to an increase in resource extraction. However, it may well be the case that the blame for depleting water resources will be laid onto the water users, either for simple overuse or for their unwillingness to pay fully for the water so that the government can recover its operating costs if not its full costs of investment and operations. Furthermore, if an expensive irrigation system brings water to the farmer and there is an effort to establish the full costs of operating and maintaining the system, the problem will seem to be that of the farmer rather than of the overall scope of the system. Only by understanding the implications of an overextended, overly expensive system can one appreciate this problem.

Disagreement and the Blurring of Mandates

The heavy and multiple loading of rationales for irrigation helps explain why the economic and resource-sustainability considerations of the huge irrigation system did not play a greater role in the decisions on expanding the system and charging for the water. Low-cost water could easily be championed under the banner of helping the struggling *ejiditarios*; the fact that larger-scale farmers who could afford to pay were also benefiting was not so apparent. An expensive irrigation system was defended on the grounds of agricultural modernization, food self-sufficiency, national autonomy, poverty alleviation, and political stability.

The distributional implications were particularly misleading. Many of the debates, laws, and rules concerning the financing of Mexican irrigation have emphasized the criterion of "capacity to pay," implying that the principal distributional issue was the fate of the *ejiditarios* and other small-scale farmers within the irrigated areas. The "capacity to pay" mind-set gave a false impression that the subsidization of water use was a progressive measure in terms of income distribution. In reality, access to irrigation makes even small-scale farmers part of the "agricultural elite," with considerably higher incomes than farmers of comparable land holdings in nonirrigated areas, and the huge benefits captured by large-scale farms made the subsidies even more regressive.

Even before the Mexican Revolution, the highly respected development thinker Andrés Molina Enríquez observed that "generally it is assumed that every irrigation project provides the same benefits to society and can be developed in two distinct ways: through direct state investment in large-scale irrigation, or through state credit with which private owners, receiving relatively cheap money, could improve the quality of their lands."[35] One implication of this perception — which Molina Enríquez recognized as naive — was that irrigation decisions were not seen as being as significant in terms of distribution as they actually were. Another implication was that subsidization was largely taken for granted; the question was to whose direct benefit. Because the debate over agrarian policy was obsessed with the issue of whether low-income or large-scale farmers would be privileged, the implications of low water charges on the sustainability of the irrigation system were given scant attention.

The fact is that the Mexican leadership has had a peculiarly ambivalent policy toward agriculture in general, involving the dilemmas of whether land reform should be extended at the expense of efficient farming, which types of agriculture ought to be pursued, and whether food for urban populations should be kept cheap.

Barkin and Esteva (1981, 3–5) point to the simultaneous objectives of subsidizing Mexican urban workers — and hence Mexican industry — through inexpensive food, while also trying to stimulate agriculture through producer incentives. To make these goals compatible, the government believed that it had to intervene through subsidies. From the perspective of sustainable water use, it has been most unfortunate that cheap water has been one of these producer incentives. Moreover, the subsidies were a weapon wielded by many different Mexican leaders to further the particular form of agricultural strategy they preferred.

The Institutional Dimensions

Two institutional factors contributed to the failure of the Mexican government to maintain a balanced irrigation policy. First, the various agencies entrusted over the years with charging and collecting water-use fees were denied the institutional incentive to bring in these revenues. In the late 1930s and again in the mid-1940s, irrigation officials pushed for an irrigation fund that would collect and disburse user fees for the operations, maintenance, and rehabilitation of the system rather than collect for the central treasury and receive the annual disbursement for expenditures. Such a fund would have clarified and highlighted the financial need for servicing the irrigation system, the shortfall caused by insufficient payments, and the magnitude of any subsidy arising through the government's coverage of the deficit. The Secretary of Finance and Public Credit successfully resisted this effort. Wionczek observes that "on both occasions the Secretary of Finance and Public Credit frustrated this proposal in order to treat the income from water sales to agricultural users as taxes, with the objective to closely control the expenditures of the public works agencies in the sphere of water resources" (1982, 403, author's translation). While the finance officials won in the contest over who controlled the investment of any monies that might have been raised through user charges, the arrangement that persisted also meant that the irrigation authorities had little to gain, at least in the short run, by collecting greater fees, which would have been politically unpopular among their clientele in the farming sector. In other words, because the irrigation agency was not given discretion over spending for irrigation, it had little incentive or accountability with respect to collecting fees to finance the operations and maintenance of the system. Irrigation officials presumably understood that the government's commitment of funds for irrigation depended on high-level political and economic strategies, not on the efficiency of water-fee collection.

Indeed, during two periods the agencies assigned the task of setting water-user charges were completely separate from the irrigation authority. As mentioned above, from 1936 through 1943 the Banco Nacional de Crédito Agrícola set the prices, and, after the CNI had regained this prerogative in 1943–46, the function was given over to the Ministry of Agriculture for another five years (Wionczek 1982, 403). As weak as the irrigation authority's incentives were to charge for full cost recovery, the incentives for the agricultural credit bank and the agricultural ministry were even weaker. They were mandated to augment farmers' incomes and certainly would not suffer institutionally if the irrigation authority ran a deficit.

A second institutional problem helps to account for the overextension of the irrigation system. Except for a brief period in the mid-1980s, irrigation investment, although by far the most important fiscal commitment to agricultural development, was not carried out by the obvious agency that held the direct mandate to strengthen agriculture, namely, the Secretariat of Agriculture. It was only in the reform years of the early 1980s that the Secretariat of Water Resources was combined with the Ministry of Agriculture, such that the new Secretaría de Agricultura y Recursos Hidráulicos (SARH) could be held directly accountable for the contribution that its irrigation development, maintenance, and pricing would have on agricultural productivity. It is crucial to understand that the old SRH was, like the Brazilian Transport Ministry, "largely a construction-oriented agency" (Cummings and Nercissiantz 1992, 739). The SRH never had to face the question of how to maximize the overall productivity of agriculture and well-being of agricultural families through the most efficient allocation of all federal fiscal resources devoted to agriculture. Instead, the SRH leadership could be faithful to its mission by fighting the intragovernmental budget battles to secure as much funding as it could for expanding the capacity of the irrigation system. For its part, the Secretariat of Agriculture, insofar as it could regard the funding for the SRH as additional to its own funding, had an interest in supporting the expansion of the irrigation system, even if it would have allocated the SRH's funds differently if given the chance. However, in 1989 the irrigation authority was separated from the agriculture ministry through the formation of the National Water Commission (CNA). Once again the intragovernmental pressure for irrigation funds would come from an agency without responsibility for determining the optimal weight of irrigation investment within the overall portfolio of agricultural investment.

Conclusions

The cases reviewed in this chapter easily dispel any doubts about the penchant of government officials to resort to seemingly farfetched manipulations of natural-resource exploitation to finance development programs. The elaborate laundering seen in Indonesia is no fluke. The Sabah Foundation has shown comparable cleverness in transforming timber rents into off-budget investments and patronage. The Brazilian and Peruvian regional development initiatives gave rise to unusual if not bizarre machinations to bring people and capital to the Amazon. Mexico's agricultural strategy relied on water subsidies in both straightforward and devious ways. The cases show the wide variety of clever mechanisms, relying on both state and private intermediaries, to shift funds from many sources to development programs. By contrasting Malaysia's Sabah State with Sarawak State, we have been able to see the complexity that pursuing diverse development programs can bring to the arrangements for resource exploitation and the capture of financial flows.

We also find that in every case, an important rationale for resorting to unsound resource policies has been the desire by certain government officials to go around the opposition of other officials. Even for military governments, as in the Brazilian and Peruvian cases, intragovernmental opposition induced perverse policies: in the Brazilian case, the competition among agencies to give away land and subsidies; in the Peruvian case, the manipulations of PetroPerú.

Conceivably, good programs could be opposed by short-sighted rivals, and perhaps the only practical way to finance them would be through financial flows arising from unsound resource policies. However, it is striking that none of the policy distortions examined in this chapter were dedicated to development programs that outside observers would consider as sound. In these cases, the sacrifice of natural resources has been gratuitous, without the saving grace of promoting sound development. Yet in chapter 6 I will examine how the effort to finance necessary expansion of the Venezuelan oil sector prompted the executive to arrange an inappropriate formula for the state oil company, which ultimately led to unsound oil investments. Thus, it is certainly not impossible for bad resource policies to stem from efforts to finance good development programs; our cases simply hint that this tradeoff may be rather rare.

Chapter 5

Distribution through Resource Abuses

This chapter reviews natural-resource policies and practices that distribute or redistribute wealth at the expense of sound exploitation and asks why natural-resource exploitation is used as a vehicle of distributive policy despite these costs. As with the development strategies explored in the previous chapter, my argument is that disagreement within the government is the driving force behind the use of resource policies that provide economic benefits to particular groups. The inability to settle on a distributive strategy, and to pursue distributive objectives through other means, is a serious obstacle to sound resource exploitation. Distribution is the most nakedly political of our three programmatic strategies; Harold Lasswell (1936) defined politics as "who gets what, when, how." Key questions, then, are whether government officials rely on natural-resource manipulations to redistribute income because of the low transparency of resource exploitation, and whether they undertake additional efforts to blur the distributional patterns.

Mechanisms of Bestowing Economic Benefits through Resource Exploitation

We should recognize that nearly all faulty resource policies, and many sound ones, have income-distributive impacts. The policy instruments responsible for suboptimal resource practices result in transfers to and from

- the treasury,
- resource developers and exploiters (both owners and workers),
- downstream processors,
- producers,
- consumers,

- government officials,
- state managers and workers, and
- future generations.

Perhaps it is not surprising that faulty resource policies often slight future generations. Governments frequently deplete renewable resources too rapidly to capture future price appreciation or invest the proceeds effectively for the long term. The other transfers are typically less obvious. Tables 5.1 and 5.2 list these transfers.

These examples clarify that both resource development and resource

Table 5.1 Transfers Involving Private and Public Resource-Exploitation Institutions

Transfer	Instrument	Cases
Consumers to resource exploiters	Output price floor	Brazilian rubber
	Restrictions on alternative resources	Fuelwood bans; raise kerosene prices
Resource exploiters to consumers	Output price ceiling	Egyptian grains
	Raw output prohibition: round logs	Brazil, Indonesia, Liberia
Resource exploiters to particular communities	Services for local communities	Chilean and Indian copper; Indonesian forestry
Treasury to resource exploiters	Reforestation subsidies	Costa Rican and Philippine forestry
	Cheap government credit for resource developers	Brazilian and Costa Rican livestock subsidies
	Lax regulation of illegal (untaxed) resource extraction	Costa Rican forestry
Treasury to resource exploiters (workers)	High resource worker wages	Chilean copper (esp. 1970–73)
	Requirement of excessive workers	Chilean copper
Resource exploiters to treasury	Excessive royalties and/or taxes	Mexican oil (post-1978)
	Profit confiscation via dividends or forced loans to the government	Venezuelan oil (post-1982)
	Overvalued exchange rate for exported resource	Indonesian forestry
Consumers to resource exploiters and treasury	Tariffs on imported resource	Indian copper
Treasury and society to resource exploiters	Relaxation of environmental regualtions and charges	Brazilian forestry and Indonesian forestry; Mexican oil

Table 5.2 Transfers Involving State Resource-Exploitation Institutions

Transfer	Instrument	Cases
Resource exploiters to downstream processors	Forced sales to state downstream processors	Honduran forestry
Treasury to particular communities	State Extraction of uneconomical resources	Indian copper in early 1980s; Bolivian mines
	Social and development services for local communities	Chilean and Indian copper; Indonesian forestry
Resource exploiters to downstream processors	Forced sale to state downstream processors	Honduran forestry
Treasury to resource extractors	Low royalties on state resources; no royalties on state mineral or oil extraction	Chilean copper; Mexican oil
	Low royalties on state resources: low stumpage fees	Costa Rican forestry
Treasury to resource extractors and suppliers	Overspending by state resource exploiters	Chilean copper
Future generations to present generation	Taxation to extract international borrowing from state enterprises	Mexican oil
	Excessively rapid state extraction	Honduran forestry (until mid-1980s)

extraction provide opportunities for distributing income. One major distributional mechanism is the subsidization of resource development. Fiscal authorities provide these subsidies through tax credits, cheap loans financed by the central treasury, direct financing or grants of resource-development inputs (such as seedlings, fertilizer, or tools), low prices for state-provided inputs, and government-constructed projects such as major irrigation systems.

Subsidizing resource development (beyond the support necessary to encourage developments warranted because of their positive externalities) has two negative impacts on resource efficiency. The more obvious impact is to allow overly expensive resource developments to remain profitable. If efficiency is the ratio of output to input, then this is a clear source of lower efficiency. Second, subsidies for particular types of resource development promote land conversion to the subsidized types of development even if other land uses are intrinsically more productive. The conversion of forest land to pasture is a common outcome of subsidies for livestock raising.

Resource extraction serves the distributive motive when government fails to capture the resource rent from extraction of public resources. The government may also allow or require excessive and too rapid resource extraction, excessive wages or employment, or low output pricing that benefits the consumers of these outputs.

Tables 5.1 and 5.2 also clarify that income redistribution can emerge from many resource practices motivated by other objectives. It is a significant, if secondary, motive in cases reviewed in previous chapters. As we have seen, the Brazilian military's geopolitical strategy propelled the Amazonian expansion, as did the urgency of relieving population pressures in other regions of the country. Yet one of the main vehicles was the program of ranching subsidies that largely went to influential São Paulo business interests, who were enriched as a consequence. Similarly, the Mexican irrigation policy was part of a very broad agricultural-development strategy but nonetheless enriched the farmers who received inexpensive water. By the same token, Indonesian forestry policies and subsidies for the wood-products industry provided opportunities for enrichment for both owners and workers involved in this industry. If virtually any economic policy enriches some at the expense of others, a distributional consequence, and often a distributional motive, can be found.

Yet this chapter focuses on resource policies intended to redistribute income and wealth, rather than policies that have an incidental or secondary side effect of redistributing income and wealth. The cases driven by distributional considerations are fascinating because they reflect government actions that openly defy the principle of separating efficiency considerations from distributional ones. Why, as John Stuart Mill asked, should efficiency be sacrificed when there are mechanisms apart from the production process to enrich those whom the government wishes to favor?

The case of Costa Rican land and forestry reveals how willfully low levels of regulation and enforcement have indulged the existing population at the expense of future generations. At the same time, a reforestation scheme created rent-seeking opportunities that failed at reforestation despite high costs, and actually provoked the destruction of some natural forest.

I will examine two copper mining cases, Chile and India, that are curiously opposite. In Chile the early (1970–73) redistribution of copper earnings from the public coffers to state workers triggered decades of struggle over the enormous copper rents (Chile's premier foreign-currency earner), at times undercapitalizing the state enterprise and distorting its resource-exploitation strategy. In India the only legitimate rationale for operating mines in low ore-grade areas has been to maintain the wages of otherwise destitute miners. Even for this purpose, direct transfers to the families would be far more efficient in terms of both economics and the soundness of natural-resource exploitation.

The case of Nigerian oil reveals that the highly distorting policy of underpricing oil products serves several distributional purposes. It indulges high oil-consuming regions through low fuel prices, which in turn create opportunities for smuggling that benefit several groups, including factions within the military. The state oil company's very low transparency permits major redistributions without political accountability.

CASES OF DISTRIBUTION THROUGH NATURAL-RESOURCE ABUSES

Costa Rica: Forest Liquidation as a Transfer from Future to Current Generations

The case of Costa Rican deforestation during the 1980s reveals economic-stimulus policies directed at shoring up income levels, with the cost clearly borne by future generations. From the end of the 1970s through the early 1990s, Costa Rica faced declining economic prospects, as civil wars in neighboring countries choked off intraregional trade. In the face of internal and external pressures for austerity, Costa Rican governments resorted to indirect economic stimulation. Many of these policies were subsidies for rapid and unsustainable resource extraction. In addition to this problem, a distributional battle raged between a new agro-exporting group and lower-income farm families, each championed by different agencies within the Costa Rican government. The Costa Rican case is also a depressing example of conservationist rhetoric masking unsustainable policies. Costa Rica's strong conservationist reputation — very important for the crucial tourist industry — dictated that government policy appear to be pro-conservationist, when in fact Costa Rica suffered from a deforestation rate as high as any in Latin America. In addition, the cabinets were largely passive in the conflict over export promotion and land allocation to poor farmers. The government agencies siding with each position were free to try to grab and convert land, particularly forest land, in a hasty and reckless manner.

Background

In the 1980s, Costa Rican governments faced the dilemma of pursuing stabilization programs while also trying to cope with recession brought on by the decline in intraregional trade. The governments had to comply with stabilization and liberalization guidelines of the U.S. government, the International Monetary Fund, and the World Bank to qualify for crucial grants and loans. In the mid-1980s President Monge signed an IMF standby agreement and agreed to liberalization conditions required by the U.S. government's Caribbean Basin Initiative. Both bound the government to an aggressive export-promotion strategy. The strategy called for some liberalization, such as guarantees of foreign exchange at market prices, but it left open the possibility of subsidizing export-oriented activities. Brenes (1991, 292) notes that this exception to the overall antisubsidy thrust of the structural adjustment program (Programa de Ajuste Estructural I or PAE I) led to "the birth of the new and aggressive exporting group, as much in the agricultural-livestock sector as in the industrial sector, that today forms part of the privileged social class." President Oscar Arias, elected in 1988, signed another structural adjustment agreement (PAE II) with the World Bank to extend the efforts to reduce tariffs, existing subsidies, and currency overvaluation. This was the usual free-market liberalization package, but it included additional incentives for the agro-export sector. The new policy reduced subsidies for corn, rice, and bean consumption, even while the agro-export sector gained greater support from the state (Brenes 1991, 294). The distributional battle that emerged pitted the agro-export entrepreneurs, eager to avail themselves of the various subsidies, against the poor farmers and former plantation workers eager for resettlement and titles to new farms.

The Arias administration faced the additional challenge of reducing the financial role of the state, just when most policymakers recognized the need to reactivate the economy. Reducing the financial role of the state meant eliminating subsidies, including the state program of cheap credit (Brenes 1991, 295). While the state banks were recapitalized, the number of economically profitable ventures was still limited by the overall recession and the specter of continued unrest in the region. Most important, the range of traditional instruments that could be used to stimulate the economy was greatly reduced. Some of the excesses of forest exploitation can be laid to the almost desperate search for economic stimulus, even at the cost of the forestry sector.

Four aspects of forestry policy bring into question the vaunted conservationist reputation of Costa Rica: subsidies for cattle ranching (now eliminated), low prices for timber on state lands, poorly designed subsidies ostensibly for reforestation, and conflicting land classifications that unleashed hasty and reckless land clearing. The distributional clashes between the agro-exporters and the low-income farmers, as in Brazil, drew in government agencies that had their own incentives to rush to land conversions. These policies provoked deforestation through excessive commercial logging and unsustainable land conversion for pasture and cropping, in a country that already far exceeded the optimal conversion of forest lands into other land uses.[1] Like Brazil, the funds went largely from the central treasury to the resource exploiters, while the user rights went from the state to the private resource exploiters.

Cattle Ranching

Costa Rica's cattle ranching subsidies were similar to those in Brazil, but without the geopolitical motivation or regional-development rationale. In addition to the waste of financial resources, the damage to the natural-resource base was in the conversion of forest land to pastures with lower economic and environmental societal returns. When intrinsically profit-able on its own merits (i.e., without subsidies), cattle ranching may be the best use of a particular piece of land. Yet when ranching is financially unsustainable even with subsidies, it is clearly a misuse of land.

There are strong indications that the cattle-ranching promotion was a rent-creation device designed to increase the incomes of specific Costa Ricans. In the 1970s credit for ranching from the predominantly national-ized banking sector surpassed agricultural credit; by 1982 ranching ac-counted for 23 percent of all state credit (Lutz and Daly 1990, 16). Most important, much of this credit was never applied to serious ranching efforts. This is shown by the large number of loan defaults, reflecting the use of the credit for consumption rather than investment in cattle. By the end of 1985, livestock operations accounted for more than 70 percent of the delinquent loans. Delinquency rates for large ranchers and farmers were 63.1 percent, compared to 28.3 percent for small-scale ranchers (16–17).

In the face of these delinquencies, the president proposed a debt-rescheduling program, initially aimed at small and medium-sized produc-ers, as part of his agricultural reform initiative (Ley Fodea). Some members of Congress pressed for the interests of large ranchers, who eventually emerged as the major beneficiaries, receiving nearly half of the reschedul-ing credits provided by the Banco Nacional (Baltodano et al. 1988, 46–48). Fortunately, "Ley Fodea II" did not pass, partly because the World Bank objected that the program would violate the terms of Costa Rica's structural adjustment loan (Lutz and Daly 1990, 17).

Low Royalties

The stumpage prices charged loggers operating in public forest re-serves were remarkably low in the 1980s, amounting to 3 percent of the value of logs delivered to the mill (Abt Associates 1990, 69). The minimal field presence of the government forestry agency, the Dirección General Forestal (DGF), did little to prevent illegal logging; checkpoint inspection of logging trucks stopped only a small fraction of the illegal logs. The comprehensive Abt Associates survey of Costa Rican resource policies noted that "checkpoints have been unsuccessful for many . . . reasons, including bribery of officials. High officials have announced their intended actions in advance, ostensibly for political purposes. On one occasion, a leading newspaper carried an article that mentioned dates, times, and the area of the highway where checkpoints would be set up to deter transport of logs after dark" (68).

We can view the administrative weakness of the DGF as a de facto aspect of the excessive exploitation "strategy." Even without a conscious or planned strategy to underregulate the forests, the weak enforcement reduced the government's rent capture and provided a straightforward opportunity for rent-seeking.

For commercial loggers to undertake significant operations, they need to have sufficient effective control over the forest lands. In parts of Costa Rica where farmers had customary rights to harvest trees, and had done so on a small scale, the scope for large-scale, commercial logging was correspondingly limited. The 1986 Forestry Law severely tightened the documentary requirements for receiving harvesting permits in several areas in Costa Rica, including the requirement to have official land titles. Bruggerman and Salas Mandujano (1992) discovered that in the Barra del Colorado wildlife refuge, many farmers could harvest their trees only by contracting with commercial loggers with stronger resources and better government connections. Naturally, these commercial loggers gained financially from this situation.

Reforestation Incentive Schemes as Rent-seeking Opportunities

The rent-seeking opportunities were also extended into reforestation. The tree-planting incentive system that operated in Costa Rica from 1979 through the early 1990s was another vehicle for stimulating the economy. The government was wary about increasing the central budget because of heavy criticism by congressional opponents and international lenders such as the International Monetary Fund. However, by relying on tax credits rather than on budget appropriations, the reforestation scheme amounted to deficit spending outside of the central budget. In exchange for planting particular tree species, planters received certificates that yielded tax credits over a five-year period. The certificates were tradeable on the Costa Rican stock exchange.

The government claimed that the incentive program was designed to encourage plantation forestry to meet domestic timber demands and to restore forest cover. However, although the regulations did specify which tree species would qualify (fast-growing species, especially exotics such as gmelina and eucalyptus), they did not identify particular geographical areas where each species had to be planted to qualify for the benefit. Planters retained the option of reforesting with the cheapest species in areas where soil or climatic conditions were inappropriate for their long-term survival. Many companies with little or no experience in forestry took advantage of the incentives. There were many complaints that enterprises abused the program by planting inappropriate species and neglecting the postplanting care of the trees. In some cases, natural forests were actually cleared to make way for plantations. What little reforestation occurred certainly did not offset the societal costs of natural forest and biodiversity destruction. Therefore, many regarded this policy of permitting forest removal as the most serious failure of the reforestation incentives (González, Alpizar, and Muñoz 1987). In the face of these criticisms, the Arias administration transformed the reforestation incentive into a much sounder forest-retention program that provided modest payments to small-scale farmers to keep existing trees on their land. This is in keeping with the logic of encouraging positive externalities with just enough incentive to make them economically attractive, without providing such large rewards that the rent-seekers would be motivated to take advantage of the rewards in perverse ways.

Like the Brazilian and Costa Rican cattle-ranching subsidies, the reforestation subsidies amounted to fiscal transfers without economic justification from a societal perspective. While some Brazilian government leaders rationalized the Amazonian expansion in terms of national security and development, this aspect of Costa Rican rent-seeking was rationalized with the even more hypocritical rhetoric of conservation.

Ambiguous Land Regulation and "Open Access"

A final aspect of Costa Rican forestry policy reflects intragovernmental disagreement, again similar to the case in Brazil. Like Brazil, Costa Rica has long experienced pressure from land-hungry farmers, particularly when the national economy has been in recession. Like in Brazil, the land reform agency (Instituto de Desarrollo Agrario or IDA) took advantage of the absence of a predominant land classification system by designing its settlements without reference to any land-use classification. The forestry agency DGF had what was supposed to have been the definitive land classification system for determining which forest land ought to be kept as forest. However, no other government body was disposed to enforce the DGF's jurisdiction as forest guardian. Therefore, other agencies ignored DGF restrictions on the use of forest land as they targeted these lands for development. This enabled the IDA to establish farms on land that, according to other existing land classification schemes, should have been reserved for forest.[2] The failure to establish a definitive or dominant land-classification system was a convenient way for the Costa Rican government to avoid having to enforce land-use regulations. As in Brazil, forest land became "open access" among government agencies, with different agencies vying to establish effective control because formal jurisdiction was ambiguous.

Chile's Copper Rents

Chile's state copper enterprise, the Corporación Nacional del Cobre (Codelco), has been severely hampered by heavy-handed government controls despite its competence and honesty compared to other state mineral enterprises. Denied incentives to maximize its profits, Codelco has not adopted aggressive cost-containment measures. This has severely reduced Codelco's cost advantages over its U.S. and Canadian competitors.[3] Codelco has made some unwise investment decisions and has sometimes emphasized production expansion at the expense of long-term development, technological improvement, and environmental protection. The decisions by the Chilean government and Codelco on investment strategies and exploitation rates have sometimes neglected the appropriate criteria for calculating the optimal time path of resource extraction. At crucial points in its expansion of Chile's copper resources, Codelco was kept undercapitalized. Its costly maneuvers to pursue its investment agenda, despite hostility from certain Chilean agencies, also reduced the company's accountability. These problems have their origins in the distributional strategies of the Allende government as far back as the early 1970s.

Background

Codelco, the world's largest copper company, emerged from a rather typical nationalization effort.[4] Nationalization was fueled by the same concerns over capturing rents from the multinational companies and maintaining adequate investment and production levels that dominated Venezuela's oil nationalization reviewed in chapter 6. Chile's intense and prolonged debate over copper nationalization began when the foreign copper firms were still capturing resource rents, but by the late 1960s, when the nationalization was imminent, royalties and taxes on the multinationals had become quite effective in capturing the rents. Also like Venezuelan oil, foreign firms were reluctant to sink large investments into expanded production, because of adverse world prices and the increasing likelihood of nationalization.

One might therefore expect that the Chilean government would have given Codelco abundant capital and a free rein to revitalize the copper industry. Instead, the initial capture of copper rents by the mineworkers, following Allende's 1970 election victory, set the Finance Ministry against the company. The copper workers' victory actually reduced the government's rent capture compared to the pre-nationalization situation.

The "Chileanization of copper" was largely accomplished under the center-left government of Eduardo Frei (1964–70). After long government-company negotiations, the Chilean government bought controlling interests from the U.S. companies (Anaconda, Cerro, and Kennecott). The arrangement also gave the government the long-term option to buy out the foreign companies fully. In exchange for liberal above-book-value payments for the government shares, the U.S. companies agreed to find sources of investment (largely capital from international banks and Chilean sources) to expand both investment and production (Geller and Estevez 1972). The temporary joint ventures attracted enough investment to bring two huge new deposits on line (Andina and Exotica), while trying to limit wages to keep Chilean copper competitive. For decades, militant unions had secured wages in the copper sector far above those of any other significant blue-collar occupation. Because the mines had been foreign-owned, the various Chilean governments had often supported the mine workers union in its wage battles with the copper companies.

The unions strongly backed Frei's nationalization efforts, but they largely threw their support to the far-left Unidad Popular coalition in the pivotal 1970 presidential election. Indeed, the copper workers were among the most radical in Chile, and Allende's continual worry as president from November 1970 until his death in September 1973 was how to avoid being rejected by the far Left as well as by the Right and Center. The Allende government was fully radical on the copper issue, immediately nationalizing the remaining shares of the U.S. companies through a constitutional amendment and denying them the previously agreed-upon value of their assets. Allende claimed that the companies' prior "excess profits" were greater than the value of the mines.

The outlook for the copper industry under Allende was mixed. Just as Allende came to power, Andina and Exotica began production. Another favorable factor was the foreign reserve holdings of the government, which had prospered with the high world copper prices during the Frei years. On the negative side, Allende faced declining world copper prices and a domestic recession due to Frei's stabilization measures and the business sector's highly adverse reaction to Allende's victory. Reactivating the economy in a "Keynesian" combination of higher government spending, credit expansion, and wage increases therefore seemed both timely and politically appealing. Allende was trying to convince middle-income sectors, as well as his low-income supporters, that an economic recovery could benefit all but the "monopolists" (Ascher 1984: 240–48). The Allende economic planners had somehow convinced themselves that this could be done without severe inflationary consequences, because in expanding the "social property" sector the transfer of the surpluses previously going to foreign companies and the domestic economic elite would be devoted to expanding Chile's productive capacity faster than the demand for goods would be propelled by wage increases. Chilean economist Sergio Bitar noted that "the model assumed that profits from the Social Property Sector would compensate for the increase in public spending, thus reducing the inflationary impact of the deficit caused by reactivation and salary increases" (Bitar 1979, 106).

Under Allende the nationalized copper mines, which had been subsidiaries under the Cerro, Kennecott, and Anaconda managements, operated as separate "collective state societies" (Codelco 1989, 37; Allende 1985). The National Copper Corporation, the precursor to Codelco, was limited to the international marketing of the output of the five separate companies. As the newest entrants into the "social area," the enterprises shared the general outlook that it was time for manual workers to capture the wages they believed due them. This was inconsistent with the central government's expectation that copper revenues would fill the savings gap left by the flight of foreign and "monopolistic" capital. The companies' managers, facing strident wage demands and several work stoppages, made no significant effort to resist wage demands of the copper workers.

The copper workers captured nearly all of the resource rents. The budget office of the Ministry of Finance reported the figures in table 5.3 for the government's foreign currency revenues.[5] While low world copper prices and the decline in mine efficiency help to account for lower revenues in 1971–73 (Baklanoff 1983, 8–9), the clear beneficiary was the copper workforce, which had pushed up wages far ahead of inflation (Allende 1985).

The military installed the government of General Augusto Pinochet following the bloody overthrow of Allende in September 1973. The Pinochet government immediately recognized reclaiming the copper rents as urgent. There was no doubt that the military government could change wage structures drastically, but first it had to create adequate oversight to understand and control the complicated and easily hidden cost structure of the enormous mines. The government replaced the leadership of the

Table 5.3 Total Foreign Currency Revenues from
Copper, Government of Chile (US$)

Year	Revenues	Year	Revenues
1965	121.5	1972	25.7
1966	197.3	1973	19.2
1967	178.7	1974	190.6
1968	172.5	1975	176.5
1969	223.9	1976	351.9
1970	267.9	1977	353.2
1971	39.1	1978	316.4

state copper companies and asserted far more fiscal oversight, while banning work stoppages. The Finance Ministry increased its own oversight. In 1976, with the U.S. company claims to compensation resolved or close to resolution, the Pinochet government created another agency, the Chilean Copper Commission (Cochilco), to oversee the entire copper sector. The government reconstituted the Copper Corporation (now the National Copper Corporation of Chile) as the unified state enterprise in control of the major mining operations.

These measures managed to restore the flow of profits to the treasury, as early as 1974 (see table 5.3). The headquarters staff included many officials who had served in the Finance Ministry's oversight office before 1976, giving the Finance Ministry informal links to the headquarters office. Over the years, many close career and "team" ties have endured between the Finance Ministry and Codelco, especially within the Codelco finance office.

Yet the government was anything but content to allow Codelco to operate with any degree of autonomy. No less than six institutions assumed oversight responsibilities for various aspects of Codelco operations. First, the board of directors directs the enterprise. It was composed originally of the Minister of Mines (as chair), the Finance Minister, Codelco's executive president, three direct representatives (one of whom had to be a general or superior officer of the armed forces), a representative of the Confederation of Copper Workers, and a representative of the National Association of Copper Supervisors. Second, Cochilco is the monitoring agency for both large and small copper mining and processing, whether public or private. It is a watchdog agency and a policy-formulation agency, although its role in policy formulation has been small. Third, the Ministry of Mines sets general policies for the entire mining sector and is responsible for the central budget for mining infrastructure. Formally, Codelco operates under the "supervision" of the Mining Ministry, within Cochilco guidelines. Fourth, even though Codelco earns enormous revenues as Chile's largest exporter, the Ministry of Planning and Cooperation must review and approve Codelco's capital expenditures. Fifth, the Finance Ministry, in addition to its representation on the Codelco board of directors, elaborately monitors all Codelco financial transactions. Most important, the Finance Ministry approves the overall Codelco budget, including proposals for foreign borrowing. Finally, the president's office, though lacking formal oversight responsibilities, is highly influential in Codelco policy in many ways. The president appoints the Codelco executive president. Until 1989, the Pinochet administration chose, and regularly replaced, the top Codelco leadership to ensure loyalty to the president of the republic. Until the last year of the Pinochet administration, the Codelco executive president was an active military officer, rotated every two years. The president also selects from the nominations for board membership submitted by the copper workers' and copper supervisors' unions (República de Chile 1976; Codelco 1992).

Beyond these oversight structures, Codelco's operations were subject to three other very significant constraints:

- Codelco was authorized to exploit only those copper deposits that were operating or under development at the time of the company's incorporation in 1976. This policy was in force despite the fact that many other areas of Chile are highly prospective for copper. Indeed, Codelco was even prohibited from developing the deposits on land under its formal ownership.
- Codelco was largely prohibited from diversifying beyond copper mining and processing. The only exceptions to Codelco's narrow mandate to exploit existing copper deposits have been the Tocopilla power-generation facilities associated with Chuquicamata and a few, largely abortive, efforts to exploit byproducts, such as sulfuric acid production. New legislation may allow Codelco to participate in the development of new deposits, but for more than twenty years Codelco has been confined largely to copper production and sale, leaving exploration, new mine development, and other product development to the private sector.
- Codelco also has had very little discretion in the use of its surplus, as all profits must be transferred to the government annually. The operations and capital budgets can only proceed with the approval of the Finance Ministry and on occasion have been considerably less than what Codelco's management wanted.

Similarly, Codelco has little discretion and virtually no autonomy over foreign borrowing. This is the result of the Finance Ministry's effective authority to approve Codelco's capital budget, as well as the requirement to obtain specific permission to request loans from external sources.

On the other hand, Codelco has been relatively free of several forms of government intervention that have plagued the managements of state-owned natural-resource enterprises in many other developing countries. Codelco has been allowed considerable autonomy over operational decisions. Indeed, the Codelco central management, headquartered in Santiago, has afforded considerable operational discretion to all of the four major mine divisions, with the exception of the level of investment for expansion and some key aspects of labor policy. Codelco has also been allowed to sell its output with relatively little governmental interference. Copper marketing, along with finance the raison d'être of the Santiago headquarters, is conducted on an almost purely business basis, selling copper at world market prices without the geopolitical decisions of government playing any significant role (as sometimes occurs in other countries, particularly in the oil sector).

That Codelco has been highly restricted in its discretion over its overall level of expenditures, diversification, surplus retention, and the solicitation of external capital has generally kept the scope of Codelco operations within the capacity of the government to monitor and control the enterprise effectively. However, there are both costs and limitations to the effectiveness of control.

Costs of Heavy Constraints

The heavy constraints on Codelco limit the scope for dynamism and innovation on the part of its leadership, in addition to making the enterprise less attractive for the most dynamic managers. As described below, there is evidence that the government, for the sake of control, installed top Codelco management teams that were noted more for their loyalty than their competence in the copper business. In many respects, the Codelco headquarters behaves more like a ministry than a business enterprise. There is limited flexibility to respond to changing business conditions, and little opportunity for the expertise of the copper experts to prevail over the macro-economic considerations of the Finance Ministry officials even when copper development desperately needs greater investment. The surrender of all profits annually, in combination with the deafness of the Finance Ministry to Codelco appeals for timely investment authorization, has also stripped Codelco of any institutional incentive to rein in administrative and operational costs. On balance, however, it should be noted that Codelco's strict regimen has kept its performance far above that of the typical natural-resource parastatal.

The restraint on Codelco's authority to develop new deposits has had two types of costs. The more obvious cost has been the delay in opening up new mines with better ore grades and higher rates of return. For many years it was known that other deposits were even more promising than Codelco's existing mines, but with the restriction on Codelco and the fact that Chile was not ready politically to reprivatize the copper sector, these deposits were left undeveloped. It was not until the late 1980s that the enormously rich Escondida deposit was developed, and that was through a consortium of private companies as part of the government's initiative to reprivatize the copper sector without privatizing Codelco itself. In recognition of the costs of this constraint, the prohibition on Codelco to develop deposits within its own area has recently been relaxed.

The second cost has been some legerdemain on the part of Codelco to pursue its objective of exploiting high ore grades despite government restrictions. One very intriguing account, albeit difficult to confirm, is that in the late 1980s Codelco resorted to creative labeling and accounting in developing the "Las Pampas" copper deposit, near Chuquicamata. By relabeling the deposit "Chuquicamata Norte," and charging its development to Chuquicamata's operating costs, Codelco circumvented both its restrictions from exploiting deposits outside of its mandated area and Finance Ministry restrictions on its capital budget.

Limitations to Control: The Codelco Budget Confrontation of 1985–87

In the mid-1980s Codelco demonstrated that when a state resource-exploiting enterprise is pushed to the wall, it can temporarily evade the restrictions of fiscal authorities despite the remarkable degree of formal oversight. Codelco was in the midst of a crucial expansion of the Chuquicamata facility, the world's largest open-pit copper mine. Because the ore grades at a particular deposit generally decline over time (inasmuch as miners try to identify and extract the highest grade ores first), Chuquicamata's expansion was essential to keep Codelco's production costs down. The expansion was considered sound and important by all of the technical and economic analyses conducted within and outside Codelco; the long-term expansion plan was approved by the government in 1981, and the Finance Ministry approved the five-year investment program of 1984–88, which called for annual investments of nearly US$400 million.

However, in 1985, in the context of a commitment to the World Bank and the International Monetary Fund to curtail overall investment, the Finance Ministry imposed an annual investment ceiling for Codelco of US$300 million for both 1985 and 1986. This cutback threatened the expansion plans for Codelco's largest facility, Chuquicamata, and was seen by Codelco managers and disinterested observers as disastrous. With the apparent backing of the Ministry of Mines, Codelco proceeded to spend US$369 million in 1985 and US$378 million in 1986 (World Bank 1989, 24). To understand the episode, it is important to note that Chile's mounting foreign debt was a strong rationale for the Finance Ministry to try to maximize the hard currency that Codelco could transfer to the treasury; yet even analysts of the outside agencies pressing for investment restraint recognized that the 1985 investments were sound.[6] The situation in 1986 was different, in that some of the investments launched by Codelco in that year were for projects that had not been authorized by the Finance Ministry and the planning office. Moreover, it is important to note that the overrun in 1985 must have been apparent by 1986, and that Codelco was not literally locked into unbreakable foreign commitments to proceed at the higher investment level.[7] After the investment expenditures of 1986 had become known, Codelco was compelled to reduce 1987 investments very sharply, to less than $300 million, and the Codelco senior management team was dismissed, either because of the overruns per se or because of the perception that Codelco officials had deliberately obscured the company's investment activities. The cutback had very serious consequences for the Chuquicamata expansion, with delays of up to a year and a half in getting components on line, and for the coherence of the investment program subsequently. If the Codelco–Finance Ministry dispute had been resolved before the start-stop pattern of investment of 1985–87 had occurred, copper development would have been far more efficient and effective.

The episode shows, first, that the top Codelco management had enough influence, presumably with the president, to defy the Finance Ministry for two years. Although it is often said that the Codelco senior management is "in the orbit of the Finance Ministry," the institutional interests of the corporation clearly prevailed over the agenda of the Finance Ministry in Codelco decision making during this period. Yet ultimately the formal authority, intragovernmental political influence — or both — of the Finance Ministry outranked Codelco, and the critics of Codelco's actions were able to exact a high price for the corporation's attempt at autonomy. The most prevalent interpretation of the dismissal of the senior management team in 1987 (not just rotating the Codelco executive president, which was routine procedure) is that the Finance Ministry was punishing the senior management and trying to ensure greater compliance in the future.

This interpretation is borne out by the fact that the government then installed a management team with little experience in the copper sector and soon replaced that team with another of similarly limited experience. Although it is impossible to pin down the rationales definitively, this pattern is consistent with a tactic of reducing autonomy by selecting agents lacking the capability to manipulate the system to increase their autonomy and lacking prior loyalties to the corporation. The performance of both teams was judged unsatisfactory, as Codelco fell seriously behind in meeting its sales commitments. A highly experienced team was chosen in January 1989. This denouement has its own lessons: overseers may try to solve the loyalty problem by inserting managers who are less likely to adopt the institutional interests of the state enterprise, but if this requires dependence on managers without sufficient background in the relevant industry, it is likely to be a costly and short-lived strategy.

The 1985–86 budget clash demonstrates the motivation of the fiscal authorities to go beyond the limit of extracting surplus from the natural-resource sector; the budget approved by the Finance Ministry would have captured not only the resource rent but also the capitalization needed for reasonable resource development. Finance Ministry officials surely knew of the severity of the problems that the Codelco budget cutbacks would have caused.

Codelco Wages and Efficiency

Naturally the distributional conflicts over copper rents did not go away with the victory of the Finance Ministry. Since its inception through the end of military government in 1989, Codelco operated under a military-based, antipopulist regime that was, not surprisingly, opposed to labor militancy. Under Pinochet, strikes were banned at Chuquicamata on the grounds of its strategic importance; a few strikes at El Teniente in the 1981–83 period resulted in only small wage gains. The Confederation of Copper Workers' call for a national strike in 1983 led to the government's placing Chuquicamata and El Teniente under military control. There were no strikes between 1983 and 1989.

Nevertheless, the Confederation of Copper Workers endured, and, indeed, the Chilean government maintained a political sensitivity to the demands by the copper workers whose potential to launch very damaging strikes has always been well appreciated. The tensions over labor issues illustrate the difference in priorities between the government and Codelco, and the government's power over this key operational area. For the government, a work stoppage triggered by layoffs or wage disputes could have an enormous cost in lost revenues needed to maintain government spending commitments. Therefore, even under the Pinochet administration, the government was averse to labor confrontations; when such confrontations could not be avoided, the government intervened directly. In contrast, the

Codelco officials, whose performance has been evaluated to a large degree in terms of efficiency and productivity, have been more sensitive to long-term cost issues. While strikes and temporary production cuts would count against performance of the Codelco management, they would damage the corporation less than they would hamper the government's fiscal policy. Similarly, higher labor costs threaten Codelco's long-term efficiency more than they do the government's fiscal position, which can look to increasingly diversified exports and non-Codelco copper revenues as well as Codelco's own contributions.

Thus, the labor issue reflects a classic principal-agent problem: the enterprise does not have the same objectives or priorities as the government. Unsurprisingly, the government took the discretion for setting employment levels and wages out of Codelco's hands. Dealing with the Codelco workers is a matter of presidential and cabinet-level importance. Obviously, the accountability of Codelco with respect to labor efficiency is low, inasmuch as Codelco officials cannot be held responsible for factors beyond their control.

However, the government is still concerned with copper production costs. Therefore, it has used other means to reduce the wage bill without engaging in a head-to-head clash with the Confederation of Copper Workers. By opening up large-scale copper mining to other operators, while refusing to allow Codelco to expand, the government unleashed the expansion of the copper sector without increasing the workforce commanding Codelco-level wages and job security. For many job categories, Codelco employees receive twice the wage levels as their counterparts in the new, private mining operations. Thus, the diversification and privatization issues take on considerable significance with respect to the labor issue.

Codelco, sometimes on its own and sometimes through the Ministry of Mines, publicly expresses complaints about excess labor alongside of its complaints of being capital-starved. Of course, Codelco's complaints about excess labor also provides it an excuse for not reducing costs more dramatically. Yet high production costs threaten not only Codelco's performance and reputation but also its long-term security and survival in the scenario of further cost cutting by foreign competitors. And, since the labor costs do provide a rationale for expanding copper production outside of Codelco control, the enterprise's institutional interests also lie in finding a way to reduce labor costs despite the constraints imposed by the government. Consequently, Codelco has adopted its own strategy of circumventing the union's reach by contracting with third parties. Private companies provide approximately 17,000 workers for services to Codelco, compared with approximately 26,000 regular Codelco employees. These private companies are not bound by the same wage scale defended by the considerable power of the Confederation of Copper Workers, although they are now organized into their own union and are pressing for higher wages. The irony is that Codelco, to protect its long-term survival from adverse labor conditions, has had to undertake its own partial privatization.

Despite the dismissal of more than six hundred employees for militant or political actions, the clashes between labor and the Codelco-government management were considerably less frequent and less acute than one would have expected under these circumstances. The reasons lie not only in the Pinochet government's selective ban on strikes and the military control imposed in 1983 but also in the government's decision not to cut Codelco employment drastically. Furthermore, wages in the copper sector have remained quite high compared to other unionized activities in Chile. In short, the government reduced the incidence of work stoppages and other conflicts, keeping labor relations less acrimonious than they might have been, by forgoing opportunities to shed excess employment.

Moreover, the enforcement of work rules has not been very successful. The largest underground mine, El Teniente, had an absenteeism rate of just over 20 percent as of 1990, with the other Codelco mining divisions having absenteeism rates ranging from 5.5 to 8.5 percent, far above the national average of only 3 percent (Benitez 1990). This is the equivalent of three thousand additional employees required to provide the labor obtained if the absenteeism rate were at the national average.

The Costs of Crushing Codelco

In 1985 a distinguished team of Chilean economists, headed by Ernesto Tironi, undertook a very convincing technical analysis of the costs and benefits of major expansion of the Codelco holdings versus the encouragement of foreign private investment in the development of new deposits (Tironi and Grupo de Minería CED 1985). Without invoking ideological arguments concerning national control of production, Tironi found that Codelco expansion was far more economically attractive than the partial privatization of the copper sector that the government accomplished by inducing foreign capital to reenter. Under conservative price assumptions, a million dollars of investment would yield production valued at US$470 million over fifteen to twenty years by exploiting Codelco deposits (both potential and already operating), versus US$200 million by exploiting non-Codelco deposits. In terms of net income, a US$100 million investment in

Codelco expansion would yield US$22 million annually, while the same investment would yield only US$1.1 million for the non-Codelco deposits, largely because of the huge Codelco cost advantage (40 cents per pound vs. 70 cents). Codelco's advantages were richer deposits, pre-existing infrastructure, and economies of scale. Across the entire range of price and discount rate scenarios, the returns on capital were calculated as far superior for Codelco expansion (Tironi and Grupo Minería CED 1985, 196–97). The analysis also clarified that the advantage of attracting foreign capital to increase overall investment in Chile is illusory, because most of the capital raised by international mineral companies comes from international banks, mineral-consuming international companies, and equipment providers that would also extend credit to the national copper corporation. Second, foreign investment from any source counts against Chile's credit ceiling as determined largely by the international banks and official international institutions such as the IMF and World Bank. When Chile's foreign debt is near this limit, foreign investment attracted to mining is simply not additive to overall foreign investment.

Regardless of whether the Tironi analysis would have proved accurate in historical hindsight,[8] the judgment that Codelco expansion was a sounder economic approach would be very difficult to deny. Therefore, given the information then available, the government decision to forgo Codelco expansion in favor of encouraging foreign firms was a grave policy failure.

While the strategy had multiple motivations, including an ideological commitment to privatization, clearly certain government officials doubted that the government could secure its control over copper rents in the face of rent-capture efforts by both the Codelco management and the copper workers. Privatization in the copper sector and restriction of Codelco to its operating deposits meant both cutting down the state enterprise in relative size and cutting overall copper worker wages. Without forcing a confrontation over the wage discrepancy between Codelco workers and private-company workers, the government chose to phase out Codelco at enormous opportunity costs.

In the 1990s the government reversed at least part of this strategy. Codelco has been liberated from the constraint on exploiting previously undeveloped deposits within its own properties and has been able to pursue joint ventures with foreign firms. By the mid-1990s Codelco was developing multiyear investment-budget authorizations rather than the single-year authorizations that plagued its development in the 1980s. While these are welcome reforms, representing less animosity between fiscal authorities and the state company, they underscore the problems and costs of the earlier approach.

The Military's Cut

Finally, the most enduring legacy of the distributional struggle over Chile's copper rents is the earmark of 10 percent of Codelco's copper export revenues for direct transfer to the armed forces. This tax, established by a law passed during the Frei administration in the late 1960s, accounted for one-third of Codelco's tax obligations during the 1980s and even today causes problems for Codelco because of reported reluctance by neighboring countries to allow Codelco operations in their countries "due to the fact that the company finances the Defense Force."[9] The persistence of this earmark is a striking indication of the willingness of the Chilean presidency and congress to circumvent their own conventional budgetary process. Inasmuch as the law was enacted under a civilian government before the political dominance of the armed forces, it reflected a political convenience for the president, congress, and the armed forces to have an automatic appropriation rather than having to debate and justify the full military budget each year. Once the law was passed and came to be viewed as a fixture of Chilean political economy, executives and legislators were no longer held accountable for this component of military spending.

Hindustan Copper Limited: The Costs of Employment

The case of Hindustan Copper Limited (HCL) is relevant here because the decisions to continue HCL copper production have been motivated to maintain mineworkers' wages in the economically backward areas where copper mining has persisted despite depleted ores. Until the mid-1980s, Hindustan Copper Limited constituted a major drain on the central treasury's budget, because the state enterprise was a clear moneyloser in its mining and processing of copper ores. Copper ore grades in India are considerably poorer than in other countries such as Canada, Chile, the United States, and Zambia. Therefore, Indian copper production was a money-losing proposition as long as domestic copper, which has cost roughly US$2 a pound to produce, has had to compete with imported copper that could be purchased for roughly US$1 a pound or less.

Until 1987, imported copper could be purchased in India at world-market prices, which HCL essentially had to match, resulting in a huge financial loss for the state enterprise. In 1979–80 HCL was listed by the Bureau of State Enterprises as the third largest money-losing public enterprise in India.[10] Yet HCL was allowed to continue, defended by the rhetoric of the national security need for partial self-sufficiency (HCL provides roughly 30 percent of the country's copper needs), with its deficits covered by the central treasury. The redistribution from taxpayers to copper miners was obvious. India's copper mines are clustered in the states of Bihar, Maharashtra, and Madhya Pradesh, among India's poorest districts that are particularly lacking in alternatives for eking out a living. In 1988, 53 percent of the population of Bihar state was below the official poverty line, compared to 39 percent for India as a whole; and in Maharashtra and Madhya Pradesh the proportion was 44 and 43 percent, respectively (Government of India, Planning Commission 1993). Yet conditions in the mining regions within these states are even worse; agriculture is very poor, and large segments of the populations are marginal people (so-called tribals) who have never integrated into the mainstream economy. It is no coincidence that metallic ores are typically found in desolate regions: high concentrations of copper, iron, and other minerals render soil infertile for agriculture.

As we will see, however, copper pricing in India has also become an illuminating case of indirect taxation. Since the late 1980s, the Finance Ministry and HCL have found common cause in erecting a tariff barrier that taxes Indian industries and consumers for copper priced at twice the world price. HCL has benefited by the opportunity to raise its prices to match the heavily taxed imported copper, making HCL a "profitable" company overnight. The Finance Ministry collects the tariff on the roughly 70 percent of copper that India imports. HCL continues to exploit uneconomical deposits, thereby "justifying" the tariff under the banner of national defense, over the loud objections of the Ministry of Industry.

Rationales

From a purely economic perspective, there is no doubt that the Indian economy would be better off if the existing mines were closed and India imported all of its copper. Some HCL mines are so unproductive that no economic rationale is strong enough to justify them. The ICC complex lost roughly US$3 million in 1990–91 — a very significant magnitude in light of the fact that HCL's total profit was around US$20 million and the debt to the government was US$10 million.[11] There is even the possibility of developing shallow pit mines at ICC, at very little capital cost, to avoid forced dismissals of ICC workers. Yet the ICC mines continue to be operated, under the maxim that "You cannot close a mine in India." The well-worn argument that domestic production saves foreign exchange by reducing copper exports is very weak, because HCL mines rely heavily on importing their own equipment. In addition, the economic benefit of foreign exchange savings is greatly outweighed by the economic damage of producing copper at more than twice the world costs and keeping copper prices artificially high.

Two noneconomic arguments have been put forth to justify the continued operations of these mines and the subsidies that keep them operating. The initial official reason was that India's national security required at least partial self-sufficiency in copper production (Rao and Vaidyanath 1987, 27–28). The Indian Ministry of Defence is obligated to buy a large proportion of its copper from HCL. However, it is quite unclear that the domestic production of copper contributes significantly to India's "strategic self-reliance." The Defence Ministry did not request that India produce copper and in all likelihood would prefer that the additional expense of buying copper be devoted to buying materiel such as missiles or tanks. The scenarios of a protracted war that would persist long enough to exhaust copper stockpiles, or an effective blockade to keep copper and other strategic materials out of India, are hardly plausible.

The second reason is the primary focus of this chapter: the mines obviously employ wage earners. Although Indian mining wages are one-twentieth of those in the United States,[12] the vast majority of the miners do not have other earnings options that would come close to their incomes from mining. A government official concerned about the economic well-being of people in these districts may well assume that the only way to transfer income to them is through miners' wages. In theory, the government could transfer the equivalent of HCL's wages to these families and still save money by keeping the mines closed. This would fit nicely into John Stuart Mill's formula for attending to distributive justice without distorting productive activities. However, there is no particular reason to believe that India's parliament, or the state governments, were or are prepared to do this. After all, other households of these districts have dismally low incomes, and the governments have not been disposed to raise their incomes. In India the surrogate for income and the achievement of basic needs has become "employment"; therefore, the Labour Ministry has become the champion of the mining families that would have much lower incomes were it not for their unproductive jobs. Through its pressures to keep these jobs filled, the Labour Ministry undertakes a distributive role that should be handled through the central treasury, parliament, and the cabinet in setting income-transfer policies through the treasury. The failure of the system to make direct transfers leaves unproductive job creation as a second-best solution to the distribution problem, at the expense of the soundness of natural-resource exploitation.

However, the most important problem at these facilities is not a high wage bill per se. Salaries and wages accounted for just under 17 percent of costs for 1990–91, compared to 22 percent in Chile. The serious policy failure is that keeping workers employed has meant keeping open money-losing mines that require not only wage payments but also expensive equipment, fuel, interest payments, and so on. Because employment maintenance rather than self-reliance is the true driving force behind the continued operation of unprofitable mines at ICC, the labor issue affects the welfare losses of high copper prices in general.

Background

HCL was created in 1967 as a public sector enterprise to develop what the Indian government considered to be underexplored and underexploited copper deposits at Khetri and Kolihan in Rajasthan (henceforth referred to as Khetri). In this respect, the genesis of HCL was similar to that of nationalizations motivated by the desire to maintain upstream production, as in the cases of Chilean copper and Venezuelan oil. In addition, military conflicts with China in 1962 and Pakistan in 1965 had reinforced the argument for local production beyond the modest output of the private British-owned Indian Copper Corporation Limited (ICC) mines at Ghatsila in Bihar. At the time, India was importing the bulk of its copper, with imports of 78,000 metric tons in 1962 and 62,000 metric tons in 1965 despite considerable efforts at substituting other materials for copper. The Khetri development was given a high national security priority, although the deposits were of uncertain ore grade and magnitude. It is quite likely that many key decision makers expected the operations to be uneconomical. It turned out that the actual copper reserves confirmed in the late 1970s were only 40 percent of the reserve estimates that initially propelled the Khetri development (Rao and Vaidyanath 1987, 27–28).

While HCL was developing the plans for mining and processing at Khetri, the ICC was under criticism for high-grading its deposits in Bihar. This practice of working only the richest veins at the expense of long-term copper recovery was presumably economically rational for the private company. Yet this practice was unacceptable to the Indian government, which wanted to prolong the mines' operations and maximize their output. Therefore, in 1972 the ICC was nationalized and placed within HCL. Although operating the ICC mines without selectively exploiting the highest grades was recognized as a money-losing proposition, the government cited the rationales of increased domestic production and the conservation of copper that would be unrecoverable if high-grading continued.

Thus, in the 1970s HCL was operating a marginal mining facility at Ghatsila and rushing to develop the Khetri mines. With government loans,

HCL developed mining facilities at Khetri that were later discovered to be scaled beyond actual supply. Very costly mismatches in capacity emerged. Furthermore, the lack of indigenous experience led to serious technical missteps, and the mining workforce, in some of India's most economically backward areas, lacked technical skills and a disciplined work culture.

In the 1980s, HCL found itself saddled with low-productivity mines and extraordinarily high costs per ton of copper output. Since 1988 the HCL board has been calling for the shutdown of two of the ICC sites, with the support of the HCL top management. Yet the government, led by the Ministry of Labour, has rejected the proposal in order to maintain the four to five thousand jobs involved. The government expects that they will stay on the payroll until they retire, even though some mining operations have been scaled back or halted at certain facilities with the idled workers still drawing their salaries. The only permissible means of reducing the workforce, through attractive early retirement inducements and a hiring freeze, reduced employment from a high of 26,248 employees as of March 1984 to 24,159 as of March 1991.

The positive result of HCL's nonconfrontational labor policy has been the absence of work disruptions for more than a decade. Although the copper miners are associated with a dozen different unions, many with political party affiliations, neither wage conflicts nor layoffs have occurred to provoke strikes. The Congress Party–affiliated Indian National Metal Workers Federation is staunchly committed to higher productivity within the parameters of full employment. HCL pioneered a well-functioning "Joint Consultative Committee" in 1980, following labor-management confrontations that led to a general strike in HCL's facilities. The labor representatives are consulted across the entire range of company issues; confrontations have been reduced, but so too has the possibility that the management would act aggressively to reduce wages or excess labor even if the government were to permit these cost reductions.

Complicating this picture was the discovery of a very rich copper deposit at Malanjkhand in Maharashtra. Although the Malanjkhand operation currently produces roughly 22,000 MT of copper concentrates annually, based on estimated reserves of 58 million MT of ore, subsequent exploration led to a reestimation of the reserves to more than 800 million MT of ore at a 1 percent grade, most of which can be mined through open-pit operations. As early as 1986 it was recognized that an investment of Rs. 3,000,000,000 (equivalent at the time to approximately US$250 million) could bring a dramatically expanded Malanjkhand, with the potential to produce 100,000 MT of copper annually, on-stream within five years (Rao and Vaidyanath 1987, 94).

From Moneyloser to "Profitability":
The Shallowness of the Financial Profit Concept

As long as HCL was losing money, there was a chronic clash between HCL managers and the government. Contrary to the public image created by the government's annual railing against the "sick industries" among India's state enterprises, it was the government that required HCL to keep open the money-losing mines. Several HCL managing directors resigned after the government, particularly on the insistence of the Labour Ministry, rejected the recommendations of the HCL board to close marginal mines. It is not difficult to understand the frustration of HCL managers, who were continually castigated for the "inefficiency" implied by money-losing operations, while at the same time their efforts to reduce the losses were blocked by the government. For several years, HCL management had to put up with the parliamentary inquiries into why it was losing money, the ignominy of being an unprofitable company despite the widespread perception that resource companies ought to be able to convert natural resources into easy profits, and the lack of credibility to secure governmental or foreign financing to modernize or expand HCL operations.

The financial situation for HCL turned around in 1987, when after years of petitioning the government for a new formula the Ministry of Mines and the Finance Ministry embraced an HCL proposal (Rao and Vaidyanath 1987) to allow HCL to recover its costs through higher copper sales prices. The proposal's argument was that the prices of HCL's inputs had been rising far more rapidly than the price of copper; that comparable minerals such as steel, zinc, and coal had been permitted increases two to four times greater than copper; and that HCL's poor financial performance reflected costs beyond its control, such as higher energy costs, rather than HCL's failure as an enterprise (Rao and Vaidyanath 1987, 137–38). The proposal did not raise the question that any neoclassical economist would have raised: whether the high costs facing HCL really meant that the company should cease operations. Nor did it mention that the existence of price distortions in other metals prices was a very problematic justification for additional distortions in copper prices. Instead, the proposal argued that given the noneconomic tasks that HCL had to fulfill, the issue was how to encourage HCL to become as efficient as possible and to reward HCL for such efforts. Thus, the recommendation was to set the price of copper to ensure a target rate of return (12 percent was suggested by Rao and Vaidyanath) under assumptions of efficient rates of capacity utilization. In subsequent years, the price of copper should be adjusted to reflect HCL's input-cost increases, but only partially so as to put pressure on HCL to increase its efficiency and capacity utilization.[13]

This approach was opposed by both the Ministry of Industry and the Ministry of Commerce. The latter ministry did not want prices set by a state enterprise's costs; the Ministry of Industry did not want the price of yet another key industrial input to be raised dramatically. Because of their pressure, the government did not accept this direct "normative pricing" formula. Instead, the price set by the Ministry of Commerce's pricing committee, based on the price of imported copper plus customs duty and the handling costs of the state Minerals and Metals Trading Corporation (MMTC), remained the ceiling price for HCL copper.[14] However, the Finance Ministry had the control of import tariff levels. It constructed what was in effect a cost-plus treatment for HCL by ratcheting up the 1987 customs duty in the high-world-price context and making only marginal adjustments thereafter. In essence, the current rules of the game are that the customs duty will reflect the price target required of HCL to make a modest profit under current efficiency levels.

By becoming "profitable," HCL was upgraded from a *B* to an *A* category enterprise, in part because of the commonly held view that it has been performing solidly. One reward for HCL was less scrutiny — although government intervention is high for all Indian public enterprises compared to many other countries. The other reward was a memorandum of understanding with the Ministry of Mines that allowed HCL a higher ceiling on investments that the HCL board can authorize without governmental approval.

Intragovernmental Winners and Losers

The 1987 HCL pricing and financial arrangements changed copper exploitation from a drain on the central treasury to a gain, inasmuch as HCL no longer requires subventions, and tariffs on copper imports add to revenues. The Finance Ministry was able to justify revenue-generating protectionism despite growing hostility to nonliberal approaches. The treasury was able to capture consumer surplus through the high customs duties paid by MMTC (and, since 1989, by the large copper users granted import licenses), with an import duty as high as 140 percent. As of 1990, the duties totaled roughly US$180 million annually.[15] The Defence Ministry, one of the government entities required to buy HCL copper, lost some authority over its budget because it pays more for its copper, which constitutes roughly 12 percent of India's copper consumption (Rao and Vaidyanath 1987, 122). The Labour Ministry succeeded in reducing the visibility of HCL's losses and therefore the visibility of the problem of excess labor in the mines. The Ministry of Industry was the big loser from the 1987 arrangements, inasmuch as adding copper to the list of highly price-distorted industrial inputs hampered its efforts to liberalize the industrial sector. In this respect, the Hindustan Copper case inverts the outcome of the Indonesian oil and timber cases, in that the Indian development strategy of promoting more efficient industrial growth was sacrificed for another source of tax revenues.

Rent Capture without Resource Rents

It is worth examining the peculiar forms of rent capture that occur when domestic natural-resource rents are actually negative. The usual issue between governments and resource-exporting state enterprises is the control of the resource rents. In contrast, the issue of control over the surplus between the government of India and HCL focused much more on access to the rents embedded in contracts with the state enterprise and in the privilege to purchase scarce supplies. On at least two occasions, chief managing directors have resigned, reportedly because of their unwillingness to bend to pressures from the Ministry of Mines to assign contracts according to political or personal considerations. These pressures from specific government officials reflect the rents involved in HCL's outsourcing contracts for equipment, services, and construction of facilities. Thus, in the HCL case, the transfers have flowed from consumers to favored contractors, via the overpricing of resource outputs. Another source of rent capture comes from the private-sector opportunity for customs duty evasion. Numerous reports have accused private importers of bringing copper into India under customs declarations that evade the tariff (for example, fine copper has been brought in as scrap).

A closely related issue is the question of who captures the surplus generated from import duties established to preserve HCL's financial viability. MMTC, a state firm operating under the Ministry of Commerce, had, until recent liberalization measures, a monopoly on importing copper along with other metals. MMTC could have become a "cash cow" through buying cheap copper on the world market and selling it expensively in India. However, the government linked the MMTC sales price so tightly to the international price and the customs duty that the Indian treasury, rather than MMTC, captured the bulk of the surplus. MMTC was left with only the recovery of its costs and a commission on sales. This pricing system insulated MMTC from losses but also prevented MMTC from receiving windfall profits. In the late 1980s, HCL officials tried to secure permission to import copper directly, rather than going though the MMTC. Although by 1989 the Indian government allowed large private copper consumers to import directly, HCL was required to continue purchasing copper imports through MMTC. This policy precluded HCL from commingling imported and domestic stocks to capture some of the surplus created by the disparity between world-market and domestic prices. Overall, then, the Finance Ministry has kept both MMTC and HCL from directly capturing copper-import rents.

However, from another perspective, HCL captures import rents simply by operating at a societal loss. The total operating costs of HCL in fiscal 1990–91 were equivalent to roughly US$250 million, of which over US$40,000,000 went to wages and salaries for approximately twenty-five thousand employees. In light of the US$180 million in copper import taxes, this is a remarkably inefficient way to generate tax revenues.

Perverse Downstream Diversification

Beginning in the early 1980s, HCL tried to shore up its vulnerable position by entering into downstream industry by manufacturing wire cast rods at the Taloja facility. The novel aspect of this downstream diversification was that the wire cast rod facility was fed by imported rather than domestically produced copper. When this facility came on line in Maharashtra in 1990–91, it accounted for most of HCL's 30 percent increase in metal production and a 45 percent increase in rupee sales over the previous fiscal year (Hindustan Copper Limited 1991, 5). While the judgment of outside observers is that the Taloja facility operates smoothly and has a more disciplined work culture than other HCL facilities, nonetheless the Taloja development suffered serious delays, by some reports as much as seven years.

For a state enterprise with an intrinsically money-losing resource-extraction task, downstream activity offers HCL the possibility to move into production with positive returns that do not depend on possibly temporary tariff protection. Indeed, downstream diversification based on imported copper also allows HCL to hedge against reductions in either the world copper price or the customs duty, inasmuch as cheaper cathodes would increase Taloja's profits to offset the decline in HCL's domestic copper-production profits. However, this diversification strategy has a major risk arising from the foreign exchange reserve problem facing the Indian government: HCL could not be certain that it would have access to the hard currency to purchase imported copper. Yet even the processing component of HCL operations depended on the "artificial" economic environment created by the government, since customs duties on different forms of copper imports (e.g., concentrates) and the availability of foreign exchange make the difference between profitable and unprofitable processing. With consistent and low import tariffs on copper, Taloja would be unprofitable.[16] Because of the critical foreign exchange situation in early 1991, the government did not grant any supplementary licenses for the import of cathodes required for Taloja's production (Hindustan Copper Limited 1991, 6).

Even so, because HCL originated in the exploitation of commercially unattractive copper deposits, diversification into downstream processing has actually provided greater profitability. Perhaps HCL managers can be proud of their downstream accomplishments. Yet the essential question is why a state resource-extraction company should be involved at all in metal processing of imported inputs, especially under a government trying to encourage private-sector initiative. The state sector has ventured downstream not because of any benefit for the economy, but rather because state enterprise managers wanted to shore up the artificial and vulnerable solvency of HCL.

Lack of Cost-Saving Incentives

Although HCL stabilized its finances, the complacency of operating within a protected environment led to the neglect of cost-saving opportunities and the inability to close high-cost facilities or to launch a bold initiative to exploit lower-cost deposits. In becoming a "profitable" enterprise, HCL was liberated from the very intense scrutiny and intervention that prevailed when the company was on the list of "sick enterprises." Nonetheless, much of the top HCL management's energy remained devoted to responding to myriad government ministries and agencies on every facet of operations[17] and defending the boundary between the enterprise and the government, particularly from politicians' efforts to arrange contracts and appointments out of political considerations or personal favoritism. The fundamental problem of these arrangements is that the government, heavily interventionist even in regulating the Indian private sector, intervenes as owner of the state enterprises as well. As Iyer puts it, "The ownership role tends to slip into a managerial role; Ministries tend to function as if they were a kind of super-management on top of the Board of Directors. At the same time, the ownership role merges into the governmental role. Ministries tend to behave as 'Government' even when acting as owners: the authority of 'Government' seeps into all other roles" (1990, 49).

Thus, even beyond the huge inefficiency of keeping open money-losing mines, HCL has been sluggish in reacting to opportunities for cost containment. HCL ignored long-identified opportunities for energy conservation measures involving low-cost changes in processing or internally financed investments with extremely short payback periods. Savings of more than 10 percent of energy costs could have been effected almost immediately, and further energy conservation could have been pursued through modest investments with payback periods of less than a month. HCL's inventories have been extremely high, with no apparent justification. The sales of excess concentrates that could not be handled by existing smelting capacity have often been delayed pending approval of the relevant government agencies; HCL has had to borrow in order to maintain cash reserves that could have been covered by more timely sales. On some occasions, the state metals-importing company MMTC has continued to import copper when HCL has had a surplus. Similar sloppiness in the stock of supplies and spares has added to the problem.

Lack of Transparency Regarding True Profits and Rationales

The convoluted government-HCL arrangements (e.g., protectionism through customs duties rather than direct transfers; avoidance of any meaningful test of whether national security or foreign-exchange savings justify the current level of domestic production) disguise the costs of problematic policies. The lack of transparency as to whether domestic copper production is worth the economic costs is not a matter of being beyond scrutiny; if anything, HCL is still micro-managed by the government despite HCL's *A* rating.[18] Rather, the lack of transparency regarding the true costs of domestic copper production is a serious breach of responsibility because it does not permit the government to be held accountable for copper protectionism. The administered pricing system obscures the true returns on investments in the copper sector and distorts the input mix of copper users. The appeals to self-reliance and foreign-exchange savings have not been presented in any way that would clarify the costs of partial self-sufficiency, whether the current level of self-sufficiency is appropriate to any given definition of national security preparedness, or whether the implicit foreign exchange premium is reasonable. Since the governmental entities mandated to be concerned with the issues of national security and employment are not directly involved in establishing the price (and the Labor Ministry does not even bear any of the costs of the higher price), there is no mechanism currently operating to gauge these priorities on a "willingness to pay" basis.

Clarifying Priorities

The government's copper strategy of partial self-sufficiency began in a context of grave national security concern, at a time when state economic activity was more acceptable. Since then, the strategy has reflected the contradictions of an ill-defined degree of self-sufficiency, avoidance of labor shedding, and reluctance to allocate the required capital. The primary objective, with a clear consensus between the Ministry of Mines and HCL, is maximum production — within the constraints of budgeted expansions. This is shown in the extraordinary weight attributed to meeting production targets in the Memorandum of Understanding recently signed by the ministry and the company. This objective has clear tradeoffs with the affordability of copper for Indian industry.

The Indian government can pursue greater efficiency, reduced domestic prices, and a relevant degree of self-reliance in two ways. First, the government could define self-reliance in a more restricted manner that truly reflects compelling needs under reasonable security-crisis scenarios. By conventional reckoning within India, a cutoff of copper imports would threaten national security or the economy in general only if the defense industries and manufacture of electricity generation equipment were threatened. Yet these two end uses constitute less than 20 percent of the domestic demand for copper.[19] During the mid- to late 1980s, the self-reliance target was 50 percent (Rao and Vaidyanath 1987); since then it has been whatever HCL seems to be able to produce with all existing mines operating. A restricted definition would put it far lower: reducing domestic copper production to 20 percent would permit HCL to shut down the most marginal mines and reduce costs substantially.[20] Moreover, since the HCL copper price has a major impact on the price set for imported copper, the translation of reduced costs to lower domestic prices would reduce the price of all copper consumed in India. This strategy would entail greater copper imports, yet this is not a serious liability given the weakness of the foreign-exchange-savings argument in favor of import substitution of copper. With costs that are double the international average, the foreign exchange premium would have to be much higher than is reasonable to justify domestic production on economic grounds.

The best approach for gauging the importance and optimal degree of self-reliance is to rely on the Defense Ministry's judgment of the required level of copper self-reliance and its willingness to pay for more expensive domestically produced copper. This could be effected by decoupling the HCL price from the import price, allowing the Defense Ministry to negotiate directly with HCL on the price and volume of its HCL copper purchases, and subsidizing the purchase of the more expensive domestically produced copper by other state entities if the Defense Ministry believes that maintaining such a large domestic production capacity is truly a defense priority. If, however, the Defense Ministry determines that some of its copper needs ought to be secured from imports, this would reflect the ministry's judgment that preparedness is better served by economizing on its copper expenditures than by subsidizing domestic production.

The Failure to Finance Profitable Copper Exploitation

The second strategy would be to expand the only economically viable copper deposit, the Malanjkhand complex. Some knowledgeable observers and the HCL management have maintained that an expansion of the Malanjkhand facility, with an investment of US$250 million as of the mid-1980s, could have increased India's low-cost copper production dramatically. Coupled with the phaseout of the ICC's least efficient mines, a Malanjkhand expansion could bring HCL's overall costs down to world standards. HCL officials have maintained that the returns on this expansion would be very attractive, even taking into account the large investment requirements.[21] While the failure to proceed with ambitious expansion reflects sluggishness on the part of HCL to respond to strategic opportunities, blame can be laid largely to the government. The development at Malanjkhand has had an ironically inverted history in light of the experiences at the ICC and Khetri facilities. In those cases, the government has insisted on keeping unprofitable mines open; in the case of Malanjkhand, the government has refused to authorize the financing of an efficient mine expansion that would save considerable foreign exchange and avoid the economic distortions currently caused by the high price of copper in India. Yet the government of India would neither finance the Malanjkhand expansion nor permit HCL to seek foreign financing for the expansion. Either option would require the approval of the Finance Ministry. If HCL secured the financing from the government of India itself, the Finance Ministry would find another drain on the central treasury. The Finance Ministry rarely authorizes hard-currency borrowing by state enterprises that themselves do not or cannot earn hard currencies. Inasmuch as HCL would not be a significant exporter even if Malanjkhand were expanded, the Finance Ministry would not give HCL any priority in international borrowing. Perversely, the virtually automatic losses HCL incurred before 1987 tarnished its prospects as such a major investment even if the hard-currency issue were not at hand.

Nigerian Oil: Distribution via Price Distortion and Smuggling

The squandering of Nigerian oil, possibly the biggest tragedy of Africa's resource development, is the result of numerous major policy failures. Since the inception of the precursor state oil company in 1971, Nigerian oil policy and practices have been marked by severely underpriced domestic petroleum products, overproduction, bloated bureaucracy, corruption, opaque financial management, chaotic and almost continual administrative reshuffling, inefficient and unsustainable downstream development, and gratuitous risk taking in exploration and production. In 1992 a joint World Bank and UN Development Programme study estimated that the economic and financial costs to Nigeria from "misguided policies, inappropriate pricing, over-investments, neglect and all-pervasive corruption range around $2.5 billion per year" (*Newswatch* 1993, 27). For an economy exporting roughly $10 billion of petroleum a year, as the overwhelming source of foreign earnings, this is a staggering amount.

Some of these problems can be laid to the pursuit of a development strategy: the misguided approach of industrialization through cheap energy, as mentioned briefly in chapter 3. Yet greater insight can be gained by looking at Nigerian oil from a distributional perspective. Nigeria's industrial promotion could have been undertaken with far greater efficiency and sustainability by collecting full oil rents through the central or state treasuries and then providing investment financing for industrialization. Leaving aside the question of whether industrial promotion was itself folly for Nigeria, the decision to subsidize industry through a low-price policy that would rapidly deplete the country's oil reserves was a very dubious industrialization strategy. The eventual undercapitalization of the state company NNPC, as both oil producer and refiner, left Nigerian industry to the vagaries of highly unreliable fuel production. Some of the oil policy failures have held back the development policies. The involvement of NNPC as a joint partner in exploration and production and much of the laundering of NNPC financial flows, especially the apparently heavy flow of financial resources to the armed forces, indicate a distributional agenda in conflict with the industrialization strategy. Moreover, energy-intensive industrialization for a still predominantly rural country has itself been a thinly veiled distributional strategy, favoring urban dwellers and the industrial areas, though offset by very costly and largely ineffective industrial decentralization efforts. Industrial promotion has been a schizophrenic combination of policies that encouraged rapid urbanization through subsidies to the dominant Lagos industrial concentration and mega-projects dispersed to different areas to "appease regional rivalries" (Gelb 1988, 235). Most conspicuous was the disastrous Ajaokuta steel mill situated in a Yoruba area far from necessary inputs. First financed in the early 1980s, Ajaokuta absorbed over US$3 billion (Auty 1990, 188–89; 232–33) and is still struggling to achieve full production.

Background

Nigeria's oil is managed by a state enterprise that is structurally similar to Indonesia's Pertamina but has never undergone the thorough reform that restructured Pertamina in the mid-1970s. The Nigerian National Oil Corporation, subsequently reconstituted as the Nigerian National Petroleum Corporation (NNPC), was established in 1969, one year after Pertamina, basically to deal with international contractors rather than engage directly in exploration and production. Also like Pertamina, NNPC has been heavily involved in domestic refining, marketing, and petrochemical activities.

Despite Nigeria's relatively low per capita income in comparison with the other major oil-exporting countries we have examined, Nigeria has staked its national capital on risky oil exploration. Unlike Pertamina, NNPC has retained controlling shares (usually 60 percent) of equity in the local affiliate corporations of the international oil companies operating within Nigeria (Ikein 1990, 9–10; Ahmad Khan 1994, ch. 4). Therefore, with respect to roughly 90 percent of Nigerian crude production, NNPC is not simply a royalty collector but rather a joint venture partner.[22] As a consequence, NNPC and the Nigerian government have faced significantly greater risks because of involvement of NNPC capital in exploration and production. Ahmad Khan (1994, 71–72, 91–92) speculates that during the 1970s Nigerian policymakers were moving toward full nationalization of the oil sector, as in Mexico or Venezuela, with only the cost of nationalization and lack of managerial expertise as constraints, until it was realized in the 1980s that joint ventures entail avoidable financial risk. In 1993, the folly of undertaking this risk was explicitly acknowledged through a new policy of production-sharing arrangements that put the bulk of the risk on the international companies (Ahmad Khan 1994, 74). Thus, like Mexico and Venezuela, Nigeria has risked its national capital in upstream petroleum exploitation, but, like Indonesia, it has relied very heavily on operations managed by international companies (in Nigeria's case, roughly a dozen). We will see that the participation of international oil companies has probably mitigated against the possibility of the oil company itself absorbing even more of the oil rents, but the participation of NNPC as a partner instead of a royalty collector has increased its risk and the repercussions of its indebtedness.

Dimensions of Distributional Issues

The importance of distributional considerations for Nigeria has been obvious, given the legacy of the 1967–70 Biafran War and the continued ethnic tensions throughout Nigeria. The Biafran War was precipitated in large part by the conflict over how much agricultural, timber, mineral, and oil wealth of each region would be distributed to the others. When the Ibo's Eastern region was relatively poor compared to the agricultural-exporting Northern and Western regions, the latter regions insisted on federal budget allocations commensurate with each one's contribution; when the Eastern region's oil wealth emerged in the 1960s, the Northern and Western leaders secured greater allocations (Bienen 1985, 19–24; Gelb 1988, 223).

However, the tribal-regional divisions are greatly complicated by additional dimensions that have been taken into account in formulating oil policy. The most obvious dimension is the urban-rural distinction (Bienen 1985, 23–24), with oil policy strongly favoring urban dwellers. Agricultural interests, always divided by ethnicity and product differences across the country, have been weakly represented at the federal level and have had less capacity to threaten the disruption of the economy. With the oil wealth came the typical "Dutch disease" decline in agriculture, further reducing the economic basis for the agricultural sector's political power and lessening the impact of any threat on the part of the agricultural sector to withhold investment. Urban populations, in contrast, have been much more capable of making credible economic demands. However, largely because of the enormous oil-boom investments into infrastructure and education systems, which were rendered very inefficient by the haste with which they were made, little of Nigeria's oil wealth has resulted in higher real wages (Gelb 1988, 83, 255–56). This has put great pressure on the governments to keep fuel and food prices down, reinforced by urban riots whenever the government permitted price increases.

Surprisingly, there seems to be less preoccupation with the rent-capture potential of oil workers per se in Nigeria than in other major oil-exporting nations. In Nigeria occupational differentiation is less important in terms of political organization and economic demand making than regional and ethnic differentiation. Moreover, because Nigeria's industrial workers tend to remain within the network of extended family obligations (Adesina 1994, 61), incomes of oil workers are spread within their much broader family networks. Thus, the issue was not so much the wages going to the oil workers per se as it was the share of oil revenues transferred to the peoples of the main oil-producing area of the Niger delta, responsible for nearly all of Nigeria's on-shore oil production.[23] While the oil workers themselves have undoubtedly been well paid compared to other industrial workers in Nigeria, they are relatively few in number (fifteen thousand even before the efforts at streamlining), and the fact that Nigerian oil is produced via joint ventures with multinational corporations has imposed some discipline in both wages and intracompany corruption that precludes oil workers from receiving exorbitant benefits as have workers of the Mexican oil company PEMEX (see chapter 6).

The final distributional challenge for the Nigerian governments — which have been largely military governments since independence in 1960 — has been to secure financing for the armed forces. During the Biafran Civil War the armed forces increased twenty-fold, irretrievably losing many of the most highly qualified Ibo officers. Following the war, the military remained large, but its long-term financing through the formal budget was problematic. The military's claim on huge budget allocations was not bolstered by heroics in a war of independence or gallantry in the Biafran War, which was won largely through a blockade that forced the Ibos into submission (Bienen 1985, 52–54). Therefore, the armed forces have had to be concerned with maintaining the effective military budget without strong domestic legitimacy and, like the Indonesian military, against pressures from bilateral and multilateral donors and financial institutions to rein in military spending.

The armed forces have received financing via oil profits in three ways. Quite legitimately, the armed forces receive allocations from the central budget. While many would challenge the amount that the Nigerian military receives, there is little dispute over the fact that the budget for "defense" ought to be determined at the level of the cabinet and legislature, balanced holistically with other national priorities through the central budget. Second, the armed forces have received an unknown volume of off-budget allocations through "dedicated accounts," as described below. Third, the armed forces, or at least many military officers, have received a volume of financial resources through oil smuggling, the amount of which is even less clear. Smuggling plays a surprising role in adding pressure in favor of fuel underpricing, in that much of the rationale for smuggling disappears when fuels are marketed at international prices. The benefit that the military receives from oil smuggling is very important for understanding why even the military governments have tolerated low domestic fuel prices at the expense of both export potential and the environment (inasmuch as low gasoline, diesel, and heating fuel prices induce overuse and delay in replacing old equipment). Low domestic prices have allowed smugglers to benefit from greater profits in smuggling refined petroleum products into neighboring countries, sometimes at volumes amounting to at least 10 percent of domestic consumption (Lewis 1996, 90).

Domestic Price Subsidies

In the mid-1980s another serious policy failure emerged as the government was increasingly reluctant to keep petroleum-based fuel prices in line with inflation. Beginning in the 1970s, the government established an expectation that as citizens of an oil-rich country, Nigerians were entitled to cheap petroleum products. Up to the mid-1980s, the government, which sets all petroleum-based fuel prices on the retail level, left the price of gasoline at the pump constant for three to four years at a time. The nominal price increases masked a rather steady decline in the real price.[24]

Since 1978 every serious attempt to raise fuel prices has resulted in violent demonstrations involving organized labor (led by the Nigerian Labour Congress), students, and trade groups (Nuhu-Koko 1993, 3). Yet after 1986 the degree of price subsidization became and has remained very alarming, partly because of its magnitude, partly because the subsidies threatened Nigeria's compliance with IMF and World Bank conditionalities. Nigeria's subsidization of gasoline, diesel, and fuel oil has been even greater, by a factor of more than two, than Venezuela's (Ahmad Khan 1994, 128). The fuel subsidies have gone largely to urban consumers, yet because gasoline, diesel, and fuel oil prices often go below even their processing costs, the increasingly undercapitalized and problem-plagued NNPC refineries have often run short of output, leaving domestic fuel shortages that are as much a cause of public dissatisfaction as the fuel-price increases. It has been estimated that the fuel subsidies were costing the Nigerian treasury $1.9 billion each year in the early 1990s (ESMAP 1993, xix).

Why have repressive military governments allowed urban riots over fuel and transportation price increases? The riots have had a "stage-managed" air about them. For example, in the early 1990s the government ordered the replacement of its insignias with NNPC insignias on fuel vehicles and filling stations, announced that the NNPC had raised fuel prices, and invited the citizenry to protest at NNPC facilities. The magazine *West Africa* (1994, 1753) describes another comic-opera scene in October 1994:

On October 1, the national independence anniversary, Nigerians who were at pump stations with N3.25 for a litre of petrol were confounded — the price was without notice reviewed to N15 per litre. The government denied any price increase and within 24 hours Don Etibet, petroleum resources minister, said the increase was unauthorized; a denial taken with a pinch of salt by Nigerians. Nigerian National Petroleum Corporation (NNPC) is in charge of all domestically produced fuel and the oil companies whose only source is the NNPC could not have increased the price without NNPC authorizing it; NNPC in any case, could not have increased the price without authority from its non-executive head, in this case Etibet himself.

The willingness to suffer such a large loss reflects the importance of distributional considerations over the desire to maximize government revenues. It is, of course, relevant that by the mid-1980s Nigeria was subject to a series of austerity measures necessitated by the country's foreign debt and fiscal deficits. Whereas the oil boom had brought tremendous increases in spending on education and infrastructure (most of it benefiting urban dwellers), by the late 1980s direct government spending could not hope to be so impressive. This made any increase in fuel prices all the more intolerable to the relatively well-organized urban populations.

Yet another rationale for low domestic fuel prices is the interregional distributional issue. As mentioned above, the regional issue had been defined essentially in terms of the allocation of the federal government's budget; slighting the oil regions of the Niger delta, and the Eastern (Ibo) Region in general, had brought on Biafran secession and the civil war. So fixed was this definition of distribution that the siting of two of Nigeria's three major refinery complexes in Niger delta states (Delta State and River State) seems to have made almost no difference to the resentment of the peoples of this region. In effect, then, low fuel prices benefit the populations in the urban areas (largely Lagos), while at the same time the lower revenues for NNPC and the government have reduced the rents in contention in the battle over regional distribution of federal funds. If the government had captured the full oil rents through the central treasury, it would have had to face the full brunt of the question of regional distribution of resource wealth. The policy of allowing Nigerians all over the country to buy petroleum products at drastically reduced prices has had the effect of redistributing oil wealth to the non-oil regions without highlighting the direct budget-transfer issue.

However, the redistributive impact of the fuel subsidies has an additional wrinkle that makes the potency of the anti-price-rise riots easier to understand. First, it is important to point out that the smuggling is not a trivial activity (*Platt's Oilgram News* 1984). According to the *Oil Daily* (1984, 10), the 100,000 barrels a day of crude oil estimated to be lost to smuggling could have brought in extra revenue of US$1 billion a year. It is therefore deeply puzzling why the military governments have allowed such a drain from their own budgets, when an increase in fuel prices would not only have increased domestic revenues but also have reduced the smuggling.

The key is that the profits of smuggling depend on low domestic prices. If Nigerian petroleum products were at the same domestic price levels as those in Cameroon and other neighboring countries, the smuggling of Nigerian-refined gasoline, fuel oil, and diesel fuel would require riskier actions such as theft or diversion from the refinery rather than simple purchase and resale. Therefore, smugglers have a strong incentive to keep domestic petroleum product prices low. The question, then, is: Who are the smugglers? Periodically the military government prosecutes private citizens and a few foreigners for smuggling — a crime punishable by death. However, this is a misleading sideshow: the military itself is heavily involved in smuggling. Lewis concludes that

> petroleum smuggling was largely the province of senior military officers and a few civilian associates. Top officials sometimes arranged legal lifting contracts for companies in which they had an interest, but more typically they simply chartered tankers and covertly filled them at terminals of the National Petroleum Corporation. Hundreds of millions of dollars of revenue were foregone in this way. In addition the continued domestic subsidy on refined fuels, along with currency differentials, created an enormous gap in fuel prices with the CFA states. A lively illicit trade in Nigerian fuels, accounting for at least 10 percent of domestic consumption, flowed to regional neighbors. (1996, 90)

Similarly, Forrest (1995, 248) reports that in 1993 "the NNPC made unauthorised payments worth $64 million, ostensibly to fund a controversial project to store oil products in tankers anchored off Lagos to alleviate Nigeria's fuel shortages. The funds were made available through a company involved in smuggling fuel; this company was also closely linked to the military regime." Military control over petroleum export was open practice in Indonesia in the early years of Pertamina and the other state oil companies; in Nigeria the armed forces go to great lengths, and inflict considerable damage in terms of energy policy failure, to achieve the same result through hidden practices. This reflects, of course, the difference between the Nigerian military's lack of legitimacy and unity,[25] compared to the high standing of the Indonesian military in the post-independence period.

Lack of Transparency and Presidential Discretion

Corruption in NNPC has been a continual and highly publicized issue, but it is far more complicated than simple venality on the part of government officials. The level of oil-related corruption in Nigeria would be impossible if there were a modicum of transparency and accountability in NNPC and oil ministry accounts. One factor, strikingly reminiscent of the opacity of Indonesia's Pertamina (and Mexico's PEMEX, reviewed in chapter 6), is the flexibility that lack of transparency gives to the presidency. Forrest notes that

> large revenues did not pass into the federal budget to be shared but were held in various dedicated accounts. Decisions affecting the size of these funds and their use were often taken in the presidency and not in the ministry of finance. Quite apart from the fact that this practice tended to undermine the system of federal revenue allocation, the lack of accountability created fertile ground for rumour and suspicion of financial irregularity. (1995, 248)

What distinguishes Nigeria from Indonesia in terms of the presidency's control over oil rents diverted from the central treasury is that the dedicated accounts have been devoted to distributional rather than development initiatives.

A direct consequence of both the diversions and the low domestic fuel prices is that NNPC, like PEMEX in Mexico, has been chronically cash-starved and undercapitalized (Forrest 1995, 248). By the mid-1990s NNPC owed the major oil companies operating in Nigeria nearly US$1 billion, prompting threats of suspension of operations, pushing NNPC itself to call for renegotiating the joint-venture contracts, and dampening the enthusiasm of the multinationals to continue to explore in Nigeria (African Development Consulting Group 1996). Yet although NNPC is underfunded and in debt, it is important to note that this has come about because of the transfer of potential NNPC (and government) revenues to the consuming public, rather than because of the government's taxation of NNPC as in the PEMEX case.

The striking paradox of the Nigerian oil case is that a series of "strong man" military governments has done so little to attack the obvious problems of Nigerian oil policy. Yet the repressive nature of some of these regimes, along with the frequency of military coups even against military governments, is a sign of the disunity within the Nigerian state. Tom Forrest, one of the most astute observers of Nigerian politics, draws what might seem like an odd conclusion for a country long dominated by military governments:

> There are a number of reasons why, despite greater political and economic decentralisation, the centre has been weak and its capacity for government and economic management poorly developed. Among these are a lack of coherence or agreement among the political, military, and bureaucratic elites, political instability and a decline in the authority of state institutions.
>
> The political vacuum at the centre, which . . . existed at the time of decolonisation, was not filled by a coherent indigenous class or by a secure military-bureaucratic alliance. (1995, 250)

Thus, we see that in Nigeria, as in so many other cases in which natural resources are manipulated by particular government officials, some of the motivation for devious maneuvers comes from disunity and conflicting objectives within the state itself.

Conclusions about Resource Abuse Serving Distributional Objectives

The cases covered in this chapter demonstrate the prominence of distribution as a programmatic end. Political leaders may have an eye to their political support in choosing particular distributional strategies, but it is just as reasonable to view the distributional goals as the defining objectives of particular government leaders. Of course, greed and political pandering sometimes occur. The Sarawak forestry case, included in chapter 4 only to contrast it with that in Sabah, shows straightforward political favoritism. Costa Rica's unwise ranching subsidies and its reforestation scheme have been roundly criticized as vehicles of rent-seeking and political patronage to benefit key individuals and firms. Yet some cases clearly demonstrate that providing benefits to broad segments of the population, including the entire current population, can be as fundamental a motive as trying to curry political support. The Costa Rican policy of weak restrictions on forest conversion and logging reflects the broader motive of increasing economic opportunity and disposable income for Costa Ricans in general, albeit at the expense of future generations.

Consider India, where copper workers from so-called backward areas have received economic support through the operation of unproductive mines, even though neither the individuals nor their districts have particularly strong political resources. In Nigeria finding an appropriate regional distribution of economic benefits has been central to every administration's challenge — not just out of considerations of political support and survival, but because the regional balance defines the nature of Nigeria as a multi-ethnic nation. In Chile the key distributional question in the copper sector had long been how much of the vast copper wealth would remain with the politically powerful copper workers, an important part of the yet broader question of the economic rewards of organized labor. This was as central a programmatic issue for Chile as the regional distribution has been in Nigeria. The overarching point is that distribution is a crucial programmatic objective that cannot simply be understood as political maneuvering or economic self-aggrandizement by government officials.

The cases in this chapter also demonstrate the prominence of distributional maneuvers without any development strategy as motive or rationalization. Development strategies always have distributional impacts, but distribution may be pursued apart from development programs. Recall that at the beginning of this chapter I noted the risk that distributional policies will be viewed as nakedly political. Therefore, the distributional natural-resource abuses that cannot be dressed up as development strategies require other "cover" rationales. For example, Costa Rican land and subsidy manipulations have been more naked than Brazilian parallels, in that the Brazilians made opening up the Amazon the rationale. In lieu of a compelling development strategy, the Costa Rican officials responsible for the poorly designed reforestation program invoked a misleading conservation rationale. We see intricate evasions and obscuring of motives, nowhere more extreme than in the Nigerian oil sector, a theater of the absurd in which the government turns its state oil company into the scapegoat for government pricing decisions, and the military prosecutes oil smugglers even while oil smuggling is a major revenue source for military officers.

One sad implication is that distribution through natural-resource exploitation is extremely prone to corruption. The initial motivation may be distribution as programmatic objective, but the laundering of millions or even billions of dollars of resource rents and treasury funds creates enormous temptations for government officials and private citizens alike to divert these flows for rent-seeking and self-enrichment.

Another complication of distribution through natural-resource exploitation is that the battle over who ultimately gets the benefits is paralleled by an intragovernmental struggle over who controls the flow of benefits. Except for the strikingly simple Sarawak case of logging concessions for the powerful supporters of government leaders, distributional maneuvers pit government agency against government agency, and often state enterprises against the central budget authorities. These conflicts often become highly political and personal, sometimes leaving the agencies or enterprises in very poor shape to manage natural resources effectively. These intragovernmental battles over distribution leave long legacies of conflict. The conflict between Chile's copper company Codelco and the Finance Ministry took more than twenty years to subside to the point of allowing Codelco to exploit new deposits.

The cases here also provide insight into whether the distributional objectives sought through natural-resource abuses are both laudable and unattainable through more efficient available mechanisms. Let me first summarize the chief beneficiaries of the cases from this chapter and the Sarawak case from chapter 4:

- Costa Rica: large ranchers, firms benefiting from the reforestation subsidies, small farmers given land, commercial loggers — at the expense of income opportunities for future generations;
- Chile: organized, generally highly paid copper workers winning or losing over time in relation to copper rents otherwise captured by the central treasury — the inefficiency of measures designed to dominate the state copper company resulting in economic losses borne by all Chileans, especially future generations;
- India — economically marginal copper workers and low-income neighbors, some entrepreneurs involved in state enterprise contracting, state company functionaries — at the expense of all Indian consumers;
- Nigeria — urban dwellers, especially higher-income energy users in the non-oil regions, entrepreneurs involved in oil-sector corruption, certain military factions — at the expense of the oil regions and future generations that would have benefited from more orderly oil exploitation; and
- Sarawak — allies of government leadership — at the expense of low-income forest dwellers and future generations.

Only in the Indian copper case can one make a plausible argument that the distributional outcomes have come close to contributing to a more equitable society. Even in that case, it is just as easy to argue that millions of low-income Indians were held back from potential economic advancement by copper-pricing policies that distorted the entire Indian economy.

The cases also indicate that the pursuit of distribution has come at high costs that could have been avoided, or at least reduced, by addressing distribution through other means. In Costa Rica tax advantages did not have to come at the expense of land and forest. As mentioned in chapter 1, forestry losses in Costa Rica during the 1970s and 1980s exceeded US$4 billion, or more than US$1,000 per capita, and held back economic growth by 1.5 to 2.0 percentage points a year — 25 to 30 percent of Costa Rica's potential growth (Solorzano et al. 1991, 4–5). In Chile reining in Codelco may have cost the economy over US$270 million; surely other arrangements for preventing the company from holding onto the copper rents could have been developed without denying the company the opportunity to exploit Chile's most economical ore deposits. Sarawak's political patronage could have come from the central treasury rather than from logging concessions. The resulting deforestation has virtually nothing to show in terms of the economic capacity of the rent-seeking winners or the population as a whole, which has fallen behind the rest of Malaysia economically. Nigeria, the saddest case of all, has been denied the long-term benefits of impressive oil reserves, to face the twenty-first century with the prospect of becoming an oil importer.

Despite this depressing assessment, two positive aspects do stand out. First, conservationists can take heart that the evidence clearly fails to prove the case for sacrificing sound natural-resource exploitation to bring about more equitable societies. Opponents of resource misuses can point to the poor record of distributional accomplishments in those occasions when the government tries to invoke economic justice as a rationale for unsound resource policies.

Second, some reforms have succeeded in redressing the policy failures brought about for distributional motives. When the pretexts for distribution wear thin, government officials sometimes lose interest in maintaining the charade of bad policies that incur increasing political costs. In both Costa Rica and Brazil, the failures of rent-seeking-motivated programs to serve their stated goals — developing a viable cattle industry in both countries and reforestation in Costa Rica — prompted the governments to abandon the programs. In Chile the distributional battles between Codelco and the Finance Ministry finally ended when the combination of solid monitoring and the partial privatization of the copper sector convinced the fiscal authorities that it was safe to allow Codelco to regain the discretion necessary to operate as a dynamic enterprise.

CHAPTER 6

Raising Revenues through Resource Abuses

This chapter explores a dynamic that reverses the pattern seen in the Indonesian timber case. Recall that President Suharto managed to divert natural-resource rents away from the central treasury to finance development efforts that the conventional budget authorities opposed. Yet the central treasury is not always the loser: unsound natural-resource policies and practices often help the central treasury extract wealth that the government could not or would not extract through conventional taxation. Of course, not all rent capture by the treasury leads to resource distortions; the treasury should capture resource rents from government-controlled lands. If this is done through explicit and well-enforced royalties, the government can discourage overexploitation. However, other maneuvers to capture natural-resource rents do lead to suboptimal outcomes. I begin by outlining how and why these maneuvers arise, and then I explore several cases to understand the broader set of motivations and circumstances behind these maneuvers.

We have already seen several cases in which the central treasury eventually finds a way to extract financial resources from the activities of natural-resource development or extraction. The governments of Peru and Venezuela overtaxed their own state oil companies into severe under-capitalization (chapter 4). On occasion the Chilean Finance Ministry has starved the state copper corporation of investment funds so that the central treasury could have more cash on hand (chapter 5). In India the pricing formula that strengthened the state copper company's strong financial position also permitted the central treasury to collect very high import duties on copper (chapter 5). These distortions in pricing and undercapitalization may be every bit as serious as in those cases in which revenue raising was the initial motive. Yet the challenges of explaining why conventional fiscal authorities capture resource rents at the expense of sound resource exploitation are quite different. We can understand previously examined cases in terms of the struggle between the fiscal authorities and the officials who were striving to bypass them. The exception is the Indian case, in which the lack of domestic copper rents simply gave the government a handy pretext for imposing copper tariffs to "protect" the state copper company.

This chapter concentrates on cases more clearly driven by the motive of extracting resource rents. The cases reviewed here reflect the concern for funding the treasury without resorting to conventional taxation rather than winning intragovernmental struggles. Nevertheless, such struggles often emerge, as the maneuvers to raise revenues through resource exploitation undermine the finances of government agencies or state enterprises.

Mechanisms for Taxing through Natural-Resource Exploitation

Five basic types of maneuvers frequently occur.

1. The government infringes on the property rights of private or communal resource exploiters, bringing resource revenues to the state. The resulting policy failures begin with the likelihood that the private or communal resource exploiters who still have some access to natural resources will extract them hastily and recklessly, in anticipation of even less future opportunity to use them. Whether or not their own resources have been or will be subjected to government takeovers, these resource exploiters are likely to be more reluctant to invest in resource development. The fear of confiscation undermines the expectations that resource exploiters can eventually benefit from either resource development or deferring resource extraction. Even the concessionaires who gain access to resources previously controlled by others tend to engage in hasty resource extraction and to neglect resource development, because they too fear the reversal of their fortunes.

Second, resources under government control are typically more exposed to political pressures for rapid exploitation, whether by the state or by concessionaires. Moreover, government and state officials who design resource development and extraction typically have more tenuous commitment to sustainable development than do private or communal resource exploiters. When private or communal actors are reasonably certain that they can enjoy future benefits from resources under their control, they are more likely to focus on long-term sustainability. In contrast, long-term sustainability often has very limited direct impact on the standing and rewards of government and state officials.

2. State marketing boards "buy cheap and sell dear." In capturing producer surplus, marketing boards that underprice resource outputs discourage resource development. They may also hasten resource extraction by exploiters who need to maintain income streams from resource extraction.

3. Governments protect domestic resource production to justify high tariffs on imported raw or processed products. We see this in countries that produce some oil or minerals, such as Brazil (oil) and India (oil and copper).

4. Governments raise the prices of resource-based products sold by the state beyond market-determined levels. While this is not a direct distortion of domestic resource exploitation, it does have distorting effects on the extraction rates of substitute resources. For example, high prices of petroleum-based cooking and heating fuels induce greater use of charcoal and firewood, contributing to deforestation beyond what market-based prices would dictate.

5. Governments tax their own state resource-exploiting enterprises beyond the capture of the resource rent, sometimes saddling them with deficits that compel foreign borrowing. This maneuver may undercapitalize state resource enterprises such that they cannot develop resource endowments optimally or extract when prices are high. It may also provoke the state enterprises into reckless investment and resource exploitation to evade the extraction of their financial resources. Recall that both problems plagued the Peruvian and Venezuelan state oil companies when the governments sacrificed the companies' capacity for oil exploration in order to raise immediate revenues.

The logic of abusing natural resources to capture greater financial resources for the central treasury is in some respects parallel to the logic of the abuses designed to evade the central treasury. First, maneuvers involving financial laundering via the natural-resource exploitation process promise to avoid the high levels of public scrutiny that typify overt tax measures. The redistributive nature of overt taxes is all too apparent from the political calculus of the central government officials who wish to increase central budget resources; less direct mechanisms have the allure of capturing resources without the political costs that overt taxation typically incurs. Second, the victims of taxation through natural-resource abuse tend to be the politically weak: economically marginal people with customary natural-resource user rights and future generations.

I will now review each of the five instruments of taxation through natural-resource abuse and explore cases that reveal the conditions and political logic of each.

Confiscation of Private or Communal Property

Property rights are the most fundamental basis of economic power. Therefore, it is not surprising that the crudest form of resource rent capture is the confiscation of property rights, whether established initially through legal tenure or customary use. Governments openly seize property under many circumstances and pretexts. No less important, though, are the subtler forms of government restrictions of resource-use rights that enrich governments. Governments restrict the rights to develop resource endowments (for example, the planting of annual crops in areas declared as reserves). If this forces the former rights-holders to abandon the land, then others may pay the government for the privilege to exploit the land. Alternatively, the government may undertake exploitation directly, keeping all of the proceeds. "Property" is essentially a bundle of potential uses; therefore, these restrictions all amount to property confiscation to one degree or another.

From the government official's perspective, the question is how to confiscate or restrict property rights without undermining the entire property-rights regime and risk the government's political base. The cases reveal three strategies: (1) invoke seemingly high-principled causes to justify confiscation and restrictions, (2) limit the confiscation to the user rights of marginal populations, and (3) rely heavily on subtle and indirect measures.

High Principles for Low Purposes

The principles invoked to justify confiscation and user-right restrictions often and ironically include conservation and environmental rights. A very common motif entails the government's claim that local people are degrading an area through undisciplined resource extraction. Often ignorant of the true long-run impact of this resource extraction, the government agency designates the area as "gazetted," "protected," or "reserved." This designation places the land under the agency's jurisdiction and restricts the customary uses. Yet often the government eventually extracts the resources itself, perhaps through its state enterprises, or grants concessions to private actors. Recall that the Indonesian government consolidated its control over the Outer Islands' forests in the late 1960s, at the expense of local customary rights. This pattern occurs throughout Latin America (Cárdenas, Correa, and Gómez 1992) as well as in many Asian and African countries. It is also the norm for governments in developing countries to claim all subsoil rights, even where traditions of private mining had prevailed in earlier eras. Even when local people do not exploit the resource targeted for confiscation, the government may restrict other local user rights to ensure unimpeded access to the resource. Thus, local people are often cleared out to make way for strip mining, large-scale oil drilling, timber harvesting, and conversion to plantations.

The confiscation of resources from economically marginal users follows the straightforward logic of targeting the politically weak, who typically have less capacity to resist the restrictions of their user rights. However, effective resistance may be possible (see Peluso 1992 for examples); when certain resource users put up enough resistance to make confiscation costly for the government, the government may back down. Yet another rationale for targeting the economically marginal is the limited amount of resources that these exploiters can extract. Governments often invoke conservation to restrict the user rights of economically marginal populations. Yet the reality is that local people often have low extractive potential because of their low technologies of extraction and their limited consumption needs. The farmer with an axe, or the lone miner with a pick, will extract on a far smaller scale than the commercial logging or mining company. If the capture of large resource rents requires large-scale extraction, the government can increase its revenues by transferring resource extraction to commercial exploiters. The government can also share in the resource rents by collecting legal or illegal payments from commercial extractors in exchange for their newfound privileges.

The subtlety of confiscation often lies not only with invoking conservation but also in formalizing resource-exploitation rules. Because of the informal nature of most customary user rights, the government does not have to announce a naked confiscation. If the government simply requires formal documentation to establish user rights, economically marginal exploiters who cannot produce formal titles soon find their rights undermined.[1] This maneuver is prevalent even in open, democratic countries such as Costa Rica, as described in chapter 5.

Marketing Boards

By restricting users' rights to sell output to any buyer, the government can capture resource extractors' profits by manipulating the prices offered by government or state agencies. These agencies may sell to their customers for low prices, thus subsidizing these customers at the expense of the producers. However, for the treasury to capture resource rents, the strategy is to buy cheap and sell dear.

Government officials often pursue these maneuvers through marketing boards initially presented as protectors of either the raw-material producers or domestic consumers. As early as 1954, the economist Peter Bauer (1954, 321) predicted that governments would turn the marketing boards against the producers, to derive an easy source of government revenues. The boards' capacity to stabilize farmgate prices would therefore suffer. Initially, the agency placates producers with the promises of guaranteed price floors, smoother supply and price patterns, and the agency's potential to gain higher prices for exported products. The government often promises the consumers some protection from staple commodity shortages and price hikes; they frequently vilify private-sector "profiteers" to increase support for the state's intervention in marketing. Commodities such as rice, bread, and heating fuels are typically involved; the huge consumer expenditures for such necessities make them attractive for gaining revenues for the government. Therefore, many marketing boards have betrayed these promises. Here I enumerate some of the most blatant examples of marketing boards extracting surpluses from domestic sales and export sales.

During the Peronist era in Argentina (1946–55), the Argentine Institute for Trade Promotion consolidated the domestic purchase and international sales of grains and beef. Perón introduced the "institute" as a nationalist measure to offset the alleged monopsonist power of the beef and grain importers in Europe. The large-scale producers had controlled the earlier marketing boards, when the government price for grain was generally above the world price. Yet under Perón, the institute consistently underpriced its grain purchases; for wheat the government price was less than half the world price (Randall 1978, 101). Institute funds were rechanneled to the purchase of foreign transportation and communications companies (Randall 1978, 77) and to cheap government credit to Argentine industrialists (Ascher 1984, 54–56).

A second example can be found in Ethiopia, where after the so-called Socialist Revolution the military-led Revolutionary Government enacted a sweeping land reform that ended the widespread land tenancy in Ethiopia's southern region. The 1975 "Public Ownership of Rural Lands Proclamation" launched a massive land-titling process for peasants previously caught in land-tenancy arrangements with large landowners. Given the highly statist outlook of the government, it was not surprising that state agencies would play a major role in the agricultural sector. Yet just when the small-scale farmers increased their production, expecting to be able to clear bigger profits, the government required them to sell foodstuffs to the Agricultural Marketing Corporation (AMC). The AMC then resold the food to consumers. As Mengisteab notes,

> There is potential for the AMC's activities to generate revenues for the government since there are large differences between official procurement and retail prices . . . However, it is unlikely that substantial revenues can be generated in the near future as a result of the activities of the AMC, since less than 12 percent of agricultural output is marketed . . . Further, the AMC's activities are constrained by lack of adequate storage and transportation facilities; finally,

most of the marketing of agricultural output is still done by individual private traders, who pay the farmers considerably higher prices than the AMC . . . To the extent that the AMC is successful, however, the control of farm gate prices may become a disincentive to farmers to produce beyond their subsistence needs. (1990, 109)

This assessment makes the important point that farmers had the potential to reduce their marketable surplus or to sell to private traders. However, to reduce food costs for the urban population, which had been more important than the peasant population in supporting the "Revolutionary Government," the AMC was mandated to use increasingly coercive methods to secure its supply. The AMC began imposing mandatory quotas on the farmers and cooperatives. This effort led to a vicious cycle of farmers' resistance to supplying the AMC, greater AMC pressure on farmers, and farmers' reluctance to produce beyond their subsistence needs. This sad pattern, along with drought and transportation breakdowns, contributed to famine in Ethiopia.

As a final example, the Ghanaian Cocoa Marketing Board promised to stabilize the volatile cocoa market. Yet once the farmers realized they were losing income by selling to the marketing board, they cut back on cocoa production and smuggled much of Ghana's cocoa through neighboring countries. I review this case in detail in this chapter.

The most obvious economic impact of marketing boards that capture producer profits is to depress the incentives to develop and extract natural resources. Smuggling also denies the economy part of the economic rent, as well as the normal export taxes and profits taxes. If further processing is possible, the insertion of the government between raw-material production and processing will reduce the incentives for further production.

CASES OF REVENUE RAISING THROUGH NATURAL-RESOURCE ABUSES

Mexican Oil: From Distribution to Taxation

Recall that several state resource enterprises have evaded the constraints on central-budget financing by borrowing abroad. Indonesia's Pertamina did this to excess until 1975, as did Venezuela's CVG in the late 1970s. In both cases the borrowing capacity was strongly reinforced by the apparent creditworthiness associated with massive oil-exporting potential, and ultimately the borrowing required the central treasury to curtail other spending. In effect, the flow of transfers was from the central treasury to the state enterprises, their employees, and their business allies. In contrast, Mexico's state oil company, Petroleós Méxicanos (PEMEX), reveals an opposite pattern. Beginning in 1978, the Mexican government imposed such high taxes on PEMEX that it became a vehicle for central-government foreign borrowing at the expense of future Mexican generations. Like Venezuela's PDVSA and Peru's PetroPerú, PEMEX ended up undercapitalized and driven to investments motivated by the search for discretion rather than the soundness of the projects.

PEMEX's popular image has been remarkably negative: an incompetent, bloated rogue elephant beyond the control of the government. Although no one should underestimate PEMEX's problems, the enterprise has been as much victim as culprit. Its operations have been distorted by government schemes to provide cheap energy for domestic industry and to finance government deficits and government spending undertaken with very low transparency. Further distortions have come from the unwillingness or inability to keep oil workers from capturing excessive benefits from oil revenues.[2] The mechanisms used to channel some of these benefits have been as indirect—and nontransparent—as those of any state enterprise in the world. Yet the measures to tame PEMEX have made it even more vulnerable to government strategies to extract the company's financial resources, causing severe indebtedness that has compromised PEMEX's capabilities.

Background

The Mexican government has controlled oil exploitation since 1938 — by far the earliest expropriation and state oil management of any major oil-producing nation. Yet from the 1940s until the 1973 oil-price surge, very low domestic oil and gasoline prices kept PEMEX chronically undercapitalized. Despite vast oil reserves confirmed in the 1970s (fifth in the world in terms of proven reserves by 1980), PEMEX was ill-equipped financially and technically to explore and produce crude prior to 1975. Mexico was a net oil importer every year in the first half of the 1970s. Even in 1974, a year of great opportunity for oil exportation, Mexican imports of petroleum products exceeded exports by nearly US$300 million.

PEMEX's low capitalization came from the government's unwillingness to reduce consumption to finance economic growth. From the 1938 nationalization to the early 1970s, the government checked inflation, engineered a remarkably high and consistent economic growth rate (6 percent annually from 1940 to 1970), and rewarded key political constituencies without imposing high tax burdens. This magic had to have some costs: economic growth was subsidized by cheap hydrocarbon energy, and the economic structure was far more fragile than it appeared. The explicit policy was that domestic gasoline revenues would cover extraction and refining costs, without taking into account the value or replacement cost of the oil itself. Diesel and farm fuels such as tractor fuel were even more heavily subsidized, with the government invoking the poverty of their users as the rationale for below-cost prices. In the face of the generally mild inflation, the government's reluctance to raise energy prices to match increased operating expenses frequently left even gasoline prices significantly below the processing costs. PEMEX, of course, suffered from the low revenues, just as did PetroPerú after the Amazonian oil boomlet of the 1970s. In this respect, the pre-1974 Mexican oil policy fits easily into the category of an energy-intensive development strategy mounted at the expense of severely underpriced natural resources. Leaving aside diesel and farm-fuel subsidies, rationalized in (largely specious) redistributive terms, the low prices for industrial fuel uses constituted a subsidy to energy-using industries and consumers. This benefit could have been provided through other means that would not distort the demand and uses of oil-based energy.

The period of sustained high growth was based, in part, on a growing foreign debt and low tax effort. The Mexican treasury increasingly depended on high reserve requirements from the private banking system to prop up public expenditure (Teichman 1988, 38). Mexico's "tax effort," measured as the proportion of federal tax revenues and social security contributions as a proportion of gross domestic product, was only 9.9 percent in 1970, remarkably low by international standards.[3] Even so, this was a significant increase from the tax levels of the previous thirty years, reflecting tighter tax administration and increases in the income tax rates (Gil Díaz 1990, 254–55). Private-sector leaders were already grumbling about the higher tax burdens. The heavily statist policies of President Luís Echeverría (1970–76) increased the government's demand for revenues. This in turn increased the fears of the business sector, reinforced by the heated debate over whether to use the tax system to redistribute income. The business sector's unprecedentedly negative reaction toward Echeverría, including open disrespect, made it clear that sweeping tax reform would meet extraordinarily stiff opposition.

The other alternatives for financing economic growth were international borrowing and increased exports. Yet in Mexico's quite nationalistic climate, international borrowing was unpopular before the 1970s. Even the export of oil was considered in some circles (including some officials of

PEMEX itself) as a waste of the resource that would fuel Mexico's own industrial development (Teichman 1988, 59). Therefore, rather than borrow or tax in the conventional and transparent modes, the Mexican government underpriced domestic oil, thereby "borrowing" from the natural-resource endowment that otherwise would have been available for future generations. Such borrowing may have been sound if the returns on the financed activities had been high and the proceeds invested for future generations. However, in Mexico, economic growth achieved through a cheap energy policy wasted oil, created inefficient industries, and set the stage for the financial turmoil of the 1970s and 1980s. In this respect, the pre-1974 strategy also qualifies as a case of redistribution, essentially from future generations to the generations alive in the pre-1974 era. Oscar Guzman concludes that "the persistent deterioration in real petroleum product prices, which brought the oil industry to the verge of financial crisis on numerous occasions, leads one to suspect that income was being transferred to the consumer through the pricing system. PEMEX's cyclic productive and financial strangulation reinforces the notion of the oil industry's consumers' subsidy" (1988b, 414).

The unprecedented surge in world oil prices in 1973–74 changed PEMEX's situation dramatically. The huge but only recently confirmed oil reserves were suddenly highly attractive for export. To gear up for export, in 1973 the government granted large price increases to PEMEX for domestic petroleum products. In that same year, the government also liquidated PEMEX's debt of 3 billion pesos (equivalent to US$300 million), greatly improving the company's creditworthiness. PEMEX launched an ambitious expansion plan largely financed through foreign borrowing. By 1979 PEMEX was earning its income predominantly from export sales (56 percent compared with 15 percent in 1976). This reflected both the higher world oil prices and the declining real prices of domestic sales, which again had fallen prey to inflation (Guzman 1988a, 382, 389).

When President José López Portillo assumed power in 1976, a tax increase would have hampered his efforts to reassure the business sector, although his administration did undertake a tax reform focusing on a greater role for the value-added tax. Yet López Portillo faced many financial obligations inherited from Echeverría: a bloated state-enterprise sector requiring central financing of its deficits, high expectations of real wage increases, and growing social service obligations. After a short but effective period of austerity, López Portillo launched a dramatic increase in public spending — Francisco Gil Díaz (1990, 261) judged that by 1981, public spending had reached "dizzying heights."

PEMEX and the Expansionary Strategy

The oil boom gave López Portillo an obvious if short-sighted way to deal with the escalating demands for government spending. López Portillo launched PEMEX's remarkable transformation from reluctant exporter to Mexico's engine of growth by appointing his close colleague, Jorge Díaz Serrano, to head PEMEX in 1976. Díaz Serrano was an engineer and oil entrepreneur who had prospered from PEMEX contracts and excellent relations with the U.S. oil industry. In contrast to his predecessors' cautious estimates of Mexico's oil reserves, and their reluctance to boost production, Díaz Serrano published controversial estimates putting Mexico's oil reserves much higher than previously reported. He won acceptance of a plan to double oil production in six years, to 2.25 million barrels per day. At the same time he proposed to triple Mexico's petrochemical output (Teichman 1988, 60). In late 1979, with world oil prices rising again, he proposed that the 1982 production should be 4 million barrels per day.

Díaz Serrano argued, with some justification, that oil prices were rising but would not do so indefinitely; therefore, higher production was crucial for Mexico to take advantage of high-price windfalls while they were still available. In a famous statement, Díaz Serrano said that "petroleum is like tomatoes or pineapples. Either they are consumed or lost" (cited in Teichman 1988, 64; Teichman's translation). He recognized that financing PEMEX's expansion would require international financing, available from private international banks flush with petro-dollars and impressed with Mexico's newly unveiled oil potential. Díaz Serrano argued that increased revenues from higher oil exports could pay back the foreign debt needed to finance the expansion of the oil industry (61). He pressed for the government to strengthen its foreign exchange holdings (obviously not the same as spending all of the incoming foreign exchange), and to allow PEMEX to reinvest some of the oil earnings to maintain its productive capacity. López Portillo initially agreed. As Teichman observes, "originally the president's economic plan had called for three stages: the first using petroleum dollars to overcome the crisis [of foreign debt repayments], a second involving a period of consolidation, while the third stage was to be one of accelerated growth" (66). López Portillo and Díaz Serrano seemed to agree that Mexico could move to a new equilibrium of higher production and an improved, sustainable financial standing for PEMEX.

Contrary to these expectations, PEMEX's role as the new "lever for Mexico's development" encountered three huge problems. First, the opportunity to keep PEMEX's finances manageable was sacrificed for even greater and more rapid transfers for the central treasury's spending appetite. Second, PEMEX's own shortcomings in managing the enormous wealth passing through its hands undermined its claims for adequate capitalization. Third, the bureaucratic battles over jurisdictions triggered by PEMEX's newfound importance antagonized government officials in many other government agencies.

High Government Spending with PEMEX Compliance

The first problem was that, as Teichman (1988, 66) puts it, Mexico "skipped the second phase" of consolidation. Consolidation was supposed to entail, among other things, that "PEMEX was only to use external financing that could be balanced by income from foreign sales" (Guzman 1988a, 388). However, López Portillo opted to try for rapid economic growth through subsidies to many industries and greatly expanded social programs, financed through the oil wealth and greater foreign borrowing. Guzman (1988a, 397) notes that "early in the López Portillo administration the government decided that the country's social and economic development should be financed with the revenue from hydrocarbon exports." As table 6.1 indicates, whereas the federal government captured 59.4 percent of PEMEX profits in 1977, tax increases enacted in 1978 captured 92.6 percent of PEMEX profits by 1979 (390), a level maintained throughout the López Portillo administration.[4] Thus, the government did not finance PEMEX's expansion directly but rather unleashed PEMEX to borrow internationally at a much higher level.[5]

However, as with other state oil companies, the government calculated these profits without assessing the value of the oil-in-ground, which was owned by the government on behalf of the nation. PEMEX's "true profit" should have been calculated only after charging the company for the value of the oil. Moreover, PEMEX officials did not strongly oppose the capture of profits by the federal government (Guzman 1988a, 390); the key issue was how much of PEMEX's budget was allocated to operations and, most important, to expanding its capacity.

Until 1981, PEMEX's surrender of profit was not an impediment. Its investment budget was more than ample, and the profit taxes did not reduce spending for operations. PEMEX spending, by all accounts presided over by López Portillo and Díaz Serrano in close and cordial collaboration, had the classic characteristics of off-budget spending for developmental and distributional objectives.

One notorious example was the plan to develop the Chicontepec oil fields, despite dismal technical assessments of their potential and clear superiority of alternative deposits. Before López Portillo's administration,

Table 6.1 PEMEX Federal Tax Burden, 1975–1991

Year	Percentage of PEMEX Income Paid as Taxes	Percentage of Total Federal Taxes Paid by PEMEX
1975	21.7	—
1976	16.7	5.0[a]
1977	23.8	8.3
1978	28.1	9.6
1979	29.0	13.8
1980	43.1	24.0/22.9
1981	52.1	24.9/24.5
1982	31.0	29.9
1983	41.4	34.0
1984	45.9	32.9
1985	49.7	34.4
1986	48.1	38.5
1987	49.4	40.4
1988	43.4	31.2
1989	50.6	29.9
1990	51.0	28.3
1991	50.9	23.8

Source: First column (1), 1975–82: Instituto Nacional de Estadistica Geografica e Informatica and PEMEX, *La industria petrolera en Mexico,* 1986, table 5.15, p. 210; table 1.40, p. 25 for "impuestoas pagados por PEMEX"; 1991, table 4.7, p. 105; (2) 1983–89: *La industria petrolera en Mexico,* 1989; (3) 1990–91: *La industria petrolera en Mexico,* 1993. The first column reports the proportion of PEMEX sales transferred as federal taxes to the federal government. This is reported as "tax burden" (*carga tributaria*) in the 1983 *La industria petrolera en México,* p. 210. In subsequent volumes the tax burden was calculated quite differently to include the total taxes on petroleum products (exceeding the reported PEMEX tax payments to the treasury). For comparability over time, the figures here for 1983 and later are calculated from the PEMEX balance sheets reported in *La industria petrolera en Mexico,* 1991 and 1993, rather than taking the tax burden figures.
[a] Figures for 1976 through 1981 reported in Teichman (1988), appendix.
[b] Alternative figures for 1980–81 and figures for 1982–91 reported in *La industria petrolera en México,* 1986, 1991, and 1993.

PEMEX analysts rated Chicontepec at 7 billion probable barrels, with serious recovery problems posing higher costs and risks than other fields. Díaz Serrano implied that the potential was vastly greater—perhaps 100 billion barrels—although PEMEX later recanted and put forth a new estimate of less than 18 billion barrels. In fact, Chicontepec represented an opportunity to employ more than 23,000 workers for field development, to provide employment for 150,000 people, and to develop an urban area of 350,000 people (Grayson 1980, 72). PEMEX also expanded its already generous benefits for oil workers and their families, although oil workers were among the best-paid industrial workers in Mexico. PEMEX operated schools, hospitals, and commissaries for its workers and families. The flood of revenues allowed PEMEX executives to spend lavishly, both directly and through complicated transfers to the Petroleum Workers Union. PEMEX's accounting was extremely opaque. The subterfuges for retaining oil revenues ranged from paychecks for "ghost workers," to padded construction contracts for the powerful oil workers union, the Sindicato de Trabajadores Petroleros de la Republica Mexicana (STPRM). STPRM received half of PEMEX's contracts and was exacting a 5 percent charge on the salaries of contracted workers (Teichman 1988, 70). As much as 85 percent of PEMEX contracts were illegally awarded without competitive bidding (Ramírez 1981). Ultimately the charges of corruption during the Díaz Serrano years led to Díaz Serrano's imprisonment and the disgrace of López Portillo. One estimate published in the respected journal *Proceso* estimated the discrepancy within PEMEX's own accounts of oil sales at US$3.56 billion for 1980 alone (Mora 1982, 43).

The spending for nonproductive initiatives was on top of PEMEX's ambitious expansion. By 1980 PEMEX's expansion alone consumed over one-quarter of the federal investment budget and 45 percent of Mexico's imports. The 1977 Six-Year PEMEX Plan envisioned that PEMEX's debt in 1982 would be 40 percent lower than in 1976 (from US$2.5 to US$1.5 billion) and that PEMEX would generate a surplus of nearly 30 percent of its revenues. Instead, PEMEX accumulated a debt of US$25.2 billion by the end of 1982 (Guzman 1988a, 396–97).

This discrepancy between planned surplus and the actual deficit certainly added to Mexico's increasingly shaky financial situation, but it was largely due to the explicit strategy of using oil wealth for general economic stimulation and social services. The economic crisis that occurred in 1982 was not so much a PEMEX crisis as it was a crisis of general economic policy. The government's spending on industrial development, social programs, and PEMEX's own expansion led to inflation and declining foreign currency reserves. López Portillo's refusal to devalue the peso ate up more currency reserves, while making Mexico's other exports less and less competitive. Therefore, while PEMEX production rose, the Mexican economy and the government's finances became more fragile. Moreover, PEMEX's production capabilities expanded dramatically, if somewhat inefficiently. Production of crude oil increased by 23.1 percent per year from late 1979 through 1982. Guzman (1988a, 397) concludes that "there is no doubt that between 1977 and 1982 the Mexican oil industry's productive capacity underwent a kind of development that had never before been seen in its history; Mexico was one of the fastest-growing producer-exporter countries to emerge during the 1970s."

Intragovernmental Conflict

On the most contentious issue of how rapidly oil production and export would be allowed to grow, Díaz Serrano and PEMEX were dominant until 1980. PEMEX's proposal to boost production to 2.25 million barrels per day by 1980, rather than the original target year of 1982, was accepted by López Portillo. As world oil prices increased in 1979, Díaz Serrano proposed to increase production to 4 million barrels per day by 1982. This proposal provoked strong opposition from the so-called Economic Cabinet, consisting of the ministers of finance, commerce, natural resources and industrial development, budget and planning, and labor, as well as the director of the Central Bank and the chair of the Office of Economic Advisors to the President (Teichman 1988, 67). Their concerns were that higher production required greater investment, that greater export revenues would overheat the economy, and that the single-minded emphasis on oil was squeezing out attention to other sectors. In March 1980 López Portillo announced a 1982 ceiling of just over 2.5 million barrels per day, taken as a victory for the Economic Cabinet. Also in 1980, the Finance Ministry denied PEMEX nearly one-fifth of its authorized budget (106, 158).

Behind this policy conflict was a struggle over bureaucratic power and discretion over resources. Teichman observes that

> not surprisingly, PEMEX began to tread upon the jurisdictions of other government entities. PEMEX's role in international affairs expanded as its director general traveled to Europe and the United States negotiating credit and trade deals, sometimes accompanied by the Secretary of Finance. The revision of Article 27 of the Constitution which made petroleum a priority sector and made ejidal and communal lands subject to expropriation for petroleum exploitation, without the usual judicial proceedings, infringed upon the authority of the Secretary of Agriculture who had ultimate authority over ejidal lands. (1988, 67–68)

PEMEX Defeated

In the spring of 1981, before oil revenues could rise enough to offset the drain on foreign reserves, the world oil price began to decline. Ironically, Díaz Serrano was proven right about the temporary nature of oil price increases, but the turnaround came so early that PEMEX had not been able to offset its enormous capital expenditures. Export revenues in 1981 were only US$14.3 billion, rather than the US$20 billion that PEMEX and the Mexican government had expected (Guzman 1988a, 393). PEMEX's rivals seized on the eroding economic situation — and on Díaz Serrano's apparent defiance of the president's decisions on restricting the investments of petroleum expansion plans — to launch a campaign to oust Díaz Serrano.

Díaz Serrano faced an obvious problem of maintaining PEMEX's revenues in the face of what he knew would soon be lower prices. In May 1981 he announced that production in July 1981 would be at 2.9 million barrels per day (Teichman 1988, 105–7). Whether or not Díaz Serrano had the private approval of the president is not known, but the plan was clearly in violation of López Portillo's own public pronouncements. The Economic Cabinet denounced this act as disloyal to the president and to the government. When purchasers started to balk at PEMEX crude prices in the spring of 1981, Díaz Serrano had to respond either by dropping the price of Mexican crude or by falling even farther short of his production targets. He chose to reduce the price of crude by $4 per barrel. Claiming (probably fallaciously) that Díaz Serrano failed to consult with him, López Portillo dismissed Díaz Serrano in June 1981.

Almost immediately thereafter, the Minister of Natural Resources, José de Oteyza, who had been Díaz Serrano's archrival on the issue of the pace of oil production, instructed PEMEX to raise the crude price $2 a barrel. Some purchasers canceled their orders, and, since oil prices were still above $30 per barrel, PEMEX lost the revenues on roughly 800,000 barrels a day for more than a month until the price was dropped again in early August. This fiasco cost Mexico $1 billion (Guzman 1988a, 393; Teichman 1988, 108).

PEMEX Emasculated

The longer-term costs to Mexico and PEMEX are more complicated. Since PEMEX's bureaucratic defeat, the ministries and agencies involved in the conventional budget process have never allowed PEMEX to regain the opportunity to become as powerful as during the Díaz Serrano era. This has been accomplished largely by keeping PEMEX undercapitalized, rather than putting PEMEX operations and investments under interministerial management as in the Indonesian case (see chapter 3).

We have seen in the 1979–81 period (as well as in the Chilean copper case) that the surrender of state-enterprise profit to the government does not necessarily reduce the resources available to the enterprise; it depends on whether the company is authorized to spend and invest at the levels its executives believe are appropriate. Therefore, PEMEX's bureaucratic rivals concentrated on limiting its investment budget. From a high of $9.5 billion in 1981, the PEMEX investment budget was reduced to $2 billion in 1989, despite PEMEX officials' pleas for more adequate capitalization. A broad consensus exists among experts that PEMEX investments ought to be in the range of $4–6 billion annually,[6] and yet the investment rate has been between $2 and $3.5 billion annually from 1985 to 1996 (PEMEX, Memoria de Labores, various years).

Moreover, although PEMEX was often sent out to the international capital markets to try to secure loans, the tax regime (except immediately after Díaz Serrano's ouster) simply transferred much of the borrowed capital to the government. Over the course of the 1980s, PEMEX borrowed whenever and wherever it could, often hampered by the Mexican government's overall problems with high indebtedness. Occasionally the government improved PEMEX's capitalization in order to make the company more creditworthy. Yet the basic pattern was that PEMEX's investment budget was cut steadily through the remainder of the 1980s. Because of the Mexican government's low internal tax effort and great needs for hard currency, the temptation to raid PEMEX's potential investment capital was often irresistible, despite frequent statements by Mexican presidents that they understood the needs for greater investment. Guzman (1988a, 395) notes that PEMEX "was . . . responsible for one-third of the country's overall debt . . . By 1982 the rapid deterioration in PEMEX's financial situation had reduced its equity to a mere 25 percent of its total assets."

In the post-1982 era, when international banks had become leery about lending directly to the Mexican government, PEMEX still had some capacity to obtain loans beyond the levels each international bank had set for Mexico's "sovereign debt," as if PEMEX were a separate entity.[7] Like Pertamina a decade earlier, PEMEX resorted to short-term borrowing to maintain its meager operating and investment capital, but whereas Pertamina borrowed short-term to evade some of the controls on its adventurous investments, PEMEX was struggling to keep up its operations.

Costs of Undercapitalization

The fact that PEMEX did not receive the investment capital that its executives requested does not, in itself, mean that PEMEX has been undercapitalized from the perspective of the economy as a whole. Nor does the fact that PEMEX's proven reserves have declined: at current production rates, they would last fifty years. There are times when even disinvestment is justified by expectations of low prices or the depletion of a resource. Nevertheless, evidence of PEMEX's undercapitalization is widespread. A severe shortage of refinery capacity has held back the environmental program requiring unleaded gasoline and has prolonged the use of old, inefficient refineries (Werner 1993). Delays of up to five or six years have been common in the development of the petrochemical subsector, and inadequate petrochemical facilities have prompted PEMEX to try to dismantle its petrochemical branch (*Chemical Week* 1988; Werner 1993). A deteriorating oil transport system has led to both waste and serious environmental and safety problems (Smith 1992). PEMEX has imported large quantities of natural gas for want of transport facilities to move Mexico's own gas to the recipient areas. Throughout the 1980s Mexican presidents have chastised PEMEX for failing to meet exploration targets and yet have acknowledged the inadequacy of PEMEX investment funds.[8] For the 1992–97 period, the PEMEX investment plan, authorized by the government, was to be $20 billion, of which 40 percent was to be financed domestically (*Oil & Gas Journal* 1994, 21). However, PEMEX was only permitted roughly $500 million each year of domestic funds, and PEMEX has sometimes been unable to secure international loans (even at targets approved by the Finance Ministry) because of concerns over PEMEX's overall capitalization. When international disruptions have shrunk world oil supplies — for example, before and during the Gulf War — Mexico has not been very effective in increasing production to take advantage of higher world prices. Having remained outside of the Organization of Petroleum Exporting Countries, Mexico could take advantage of these opportunities for windfall profits, but supply rigidities have made this very difficult. When PEMEX attempts to pump oil very rapidly to take advantage of temporary increases in world prices, it runs the risk of reducing overall recovery from the wells involved.

PEMEX's chronic underfinancing reflects not only the bureaucratic-political rationales for keeping PEMEX on a tight leash but also the ease with which the Finance Ministry can drain PEMEX funds and limit its investment capital. As the *Latin American Energy Alert* (1996) observes,

> Another problem which often hampers public spending in the oil industry is that the Finance Ministry is often slow to release approved financing. Moreover, it often pressures Pemex to try to restrict spending when the government encounters cash crunches, a frequent occurrence. In most recent years, Pemex has spent considerably less than the amount of approved public spending, especially in areas such as maintenance and industrial safety.

Yet even into the early 1990s, the motive of capturing resources for the central treasury was combined with the motive of keeping PEMEX at bay. The distrust that the central government's "technocrats" had of PEMEX's corruption and inefficiency, particularly through the presidency of Miguel de la Madrid (1982–88) and the first four years of the presidency of Carlos Salinas (1988–92), remained an equally strong explanation.

Détente between the Fiscal Authorities and PEMEX?

In 1989, after officials of the STPRM threatened strikes and even hinted at sabotage, President Carlos Salinas had its notoriously corrupt leader, Joaquín Hernández Galicia, arrested along with other key union leaders. In 1992, in the wake of the Guadalajara gasoline explosion that killed two hundred people, for which PEMEX took full responsibility, President Salinas revamped the enterprise, installing more professional leadership, restructuring PEMEX into subsidiaries, and greatly increasing the requirements for reporting and monitoring (Grayson 1993). For the first time, officials outside of PEMEX — and the public — had specific information to assess the efficiency of particular refineries and petrochemical factories. Under new leadership, PEMEX saw the migration of many professionalized central government officials into the company's managerial ranks. This "colonization" of PEMEX has significantly reduced the gulf between PEMEX and the Economic Cabinet. Along with the greater transparency, PEMEX has been allowed moderately more flexibility in its financial operations. However, it is telling that even with its leadership on much better terms with the central budget authorities, the PEMEX investment budget was kept very low until 1997.[9] The motivation to capture oil wealth for the central treasury still has a powerful hold.

Domestic Prices

The tradition of low domestic prices of gasoline and other petroleum products dates back to the earliest years of PEMEX in the late 1930s, when the company was portrayed as the champion of the poor farmers and urban dwellers, always prepared to provide them cheap energy. This "entitlement" to cheap energy was reinforced by the long-standing notion that Mexican industry required cheap energy inputs as well. After a brief attempt to raise gasoline prices in the early 1970s, inflation drastically eroded the real price of domestic petroleum products. Nominal prices were held essentially constant from 1976 to 1980, despite moderately high inflation. By 1979 domestic petroleum product sales brought in $3.3 billion for products that would have sold for just over $20 billion at international prices (Baker 1981, 84). This subsidy of nearly 85 percent was a major factor impeding PEMEX's expansion and, for that matter, even the maintenance of its existing facilities.

However, in a remarkable turnaround, precisely during the oil boom years, the Mexican government succeeded in raising the real price of gasoline and other petroleum products close to international levels. Domestic prices have remained far closer to international prices than in other major oil-exporting countries such as Venezuela and Nigeria. The timing of price reform during times of an oil boom makes the reform all the more surprising; one might have imagined that when oil is most abundant the public would be most resistant to higher prices.

The Campaign to Rectify Domestic Fuel Prices

In 1973 PEMEX finances were so feeble that production bottlenecks necessitated greater imports. PEMEX officials argued that the oil infrastructure would crumble, oil exports would diminish, and oil imports would continue to rise unless the company could count on recouping more of its production costs for the domestic market. The López Portillo administration built strongly on this argument by emphasizing the link between PEMEX's total revenues, including its domestic sales, to its capacity to produce and sell even more oil abroad. In a break with the previous ideological commitment to preserving oil for Mexican development, the new argument was that Mexico needed the foreign exchange for development; therefore, wasteful domestic oil consumption of cheap petroleum products ought to be discouraged. In short, the government linked the potential success of the oil-led strategy to domestic policy reform. Because this oil-led strategy was already paying off for Mexicans through higher wages and expanded social programs, the price increases met with less hostility than they probably would have otherwise. Even so, these price increases were considerably below international levels; according to Guzman (1988b, 411), they were stop-gap and partial measures designed to offset the government's revenue declines rather than to solidify PEMEX's own financial situation. The extra revenues earned from higher prices were due to tax increases and therefore were absorbed by the government, not PEMEX. PEMEX was still running serious deficits from production targeted to the domestic market.

It was the administration of President Miguel de la Madrid that raised domestic prices of most products to cover production costs. The fiscal crisis that broke in 1982 enabled the government to embed the remedies for state enterprise deficits into the "Immediate Program for Economic Reorganization," the emergency program that de la Madrid announced upon assuming office in December 1982. Most of de la Madrid's economic team was already committed to free-market reform; the crisis that struck the still heavily subsidized Mexican economy increased the credibility of reform. Nevertheless, the official hydrocarbons policy still acknowledged that most domestic prices should be below international prices, so that the "economy could benefit from Mexico's competitive advantage as a hydrocarbon producer," and social priorities should be pursued by allowing fuels for lower-income groups to remain subsidized. Yet by adhering to the long-established principle that petroleum policy should serve populist goals, and maintaining that gasoline was a luxury good, the de la Madrid administration was able to implement a policy of pegging gasoline prices to prevailing international prices. The longer-term Six-Year National Development Plan (1983–88) consolidated these strides by instituting a crucial mechanism of automatic adjustments in fuel prices: quarterly revisions in gasoline prices and monthly revisions in industrial fuels (Guzman 1988b, 412–15).

This price reform puts PEMEX in a better financial position than its counterparts in Nigeria, Peru, and Venezuela and has contributed to Mexico's struggle against air pollution. (Cheap fuels not only induce greater use, but they also discourage the purchase of more energy-efficient, less polluting vehicles and machinery.) This is a clear instance in which the motive to increase government and parastatal revenues coincides with responsible resource management.

Venezuela: Another Struggle over Capitalization

Disagreement within the Venezuelan government over the pace of oil and mineral-processing development led to two clashes that ultimately left the state oil company PDVSA undercapitalized and, despite the company's relatively high efficiency and expertise, incapable of developing the technologies to exploit Venezuela's heavy oil and enormous unconventional oil deposits trapped in the "tar sands" of the Orinoco oil belt. Downstream processing initiatives also largely failed, and because the Venezuelan executive branch resorted to foreign borrowing to finance these initiatives on the strength of the country's oil-exporting potential, the fiscal crisis prompted further raids on PDVSA's investment fund. As in Peru, ultimately the undercapitalization of PDVSA forced the company to relinquish part of the cherished national autonomy that had motivated the nationalization of the oil sector in the first place.

In the late 1970s PDVSA seemed blessed with the government's strong commitment to an oil-led development strategy. Yet the rigidity of the arrangement for protecting this strategy led to its downfall, as the government's fiscal appetite prompted a raid on PDVSA's investment fund. The ferocious jurisdictional battle that followed provoked PDVSA into hasty and problematic resource development projects.

Background

Oil has dominated the Venezuelan economy throughout the twentieth century, but it has been the fulcrum of conflict between the state sector and the government for only the past twenty years. The 1976 incorporation of the full oil sector into the state was driven by two motives. The most obvious one was to capture the resource rent for government use, following decades of recriminations against the multinational oil companies for their alleged retention of excess profits. In fact, by 1948 the implementation of the 1943 Hydrocarbon Law allowed the Venezuelan government to capture roughly half of the oil company profits, and the capture of the resource rent rose steadily up to the time of expropriation; by 1970 the government-industry split was 78–22, and the effective income tax on what the companies were making was 58 percent (Coronel 1983, 19–23; Randall 1987, 175). Following the 1973–74 restructuring of the world oil industry, and the tougher terms that governments were exacting from international oil firms worldwide, the difficulty for governments of oil-producing countries to capture the oil rents from international oil companies had become a much less important problem.

Thus, while the motive to capture the oil rents was declining (despite the rhetoric of the Venezuelan nationalization), the motive to control the investment in the oil sector had become increasingly important. The multinationals had become less interested in Venezuela for many reasons: the declining prospectivity of normal oil deposits, the expense of exploiting heavy crude and tar sands, the huge discoveries in other parts of the world, and the fact that Venezuela was clearly moving toward nationalization (Coronel 1983, 221–32; Randall 1987, 47–48). The multinational oil companies began to reduce their investments as early as 1955, when the Venezuelan government decided to stop granting concessions. Some new investments came with new concessions from 1956 to 1958, but by 1960 investments were definitely in decline. Most frightening to the government, given its heavy budgetary dependence on oil, was that oil production was in decline, falling nearly 8 percent in the 1970–75 period (Boué 1993, 47). The Venezuelan government still viewed oil as the driving force of the country's growth. As a consequence, the government wanted to ensure that the oil sector would remain adequately capitalized.

These motives propelled the government to set up a structure for the new state oil company that would allow the government to capture some revenues from oil exploitation but also to foster reinvestment into oil exploration and production. However, this structure ended up exacerbating the conflict between these two objectives.

In August 1975 a law was enacted creating Petróleos de Venezuela, S.A. (PDVSA), "a company," according to President Pérez, "totally free of political interference and [that] would work with the national interest in mind without paying attention to individual interests" (Coronel 1983, 72). PDVSA's initial capital was Bs 2.5 billion, equivalent to around US$500 million. The Republic of Venezuela owned all PDVSA stock; PDVSA in turn owned all of the shares of the fourteen operating companies. These new companies were organizationally identical to the previous concessionaires (including the original, small state oil company).

A cardinal principle for the Andres Pérez government was that PDVSA should be self-financing, that is, as financially independent of the government as possible. The presidency, like the Suharto presidency with respect to Indonesian oil and timber, had no confidence that the rest of the government would permit the ambitious oil development (as well as other resource processing). Initially, the government guaranteed PDVSA's finances through mechanisms that defied conventional public finance rules by denying the central treasury the right to receive full royalties or company profits. This approach was a clear indication that the advocates of rapid oil development did not trust the central fiscal authorities to stick with an oil-led development strategy. The government decided to set up a PDVSA-controlled investment fund that would retain a 10 percent portion of net exports and profits:

> For a state-owned enterprise to be efficient it had to be self-financed . . . It could not risk going through the political system to obtain the capital required for investments because in a strongly politicized environment, such as the Venezuelan, this could probably mean long delays, distortion of original objectives, or . . . large-scale corruption. Self-financing was achieved through the retention in the financial system of [PDVSA] of 10 percent of the net value of industry exports and of the net profits of the operating companies.[10] (Coronel 1983, 92)

This arrangement certainly had the theoretical potential for PDVSA to enjoy considerable autonomy in investment decisions and to accrue significant investment capital. Compare this arrangement to that of Codelco, the Chilean state copper company, which had to surrender all profits to the government every year and then request authorization of its annual investment budget by the Ministries of Mines and Finance.

Other Off-Budget Resource Development

Oil development was not the only resource initiative that the Andres Pérez administration tried despite resistance from fiscal conservatives. The prospects of high world oil prices fueled other ambitious plans in hard-minerals exploitation. A cheap-energy strategy included the rapid development of steel- and aluminum-processing industries, aluminum smelting being even more energy intensive than steelmaking. The state metal-processing company, the Corporación Venezolana Guayana (CVG), rapidly expanded its foreign borrowing to develop the steel and aluminum complexes in the new industrial city Ciudad Guayana. With the opposition COPEI Party dominating congress, it was very difficult for the Andres Pérez government to direct fiscal spending to these downstream projects. However, as Indonesia's Pertamina had discovered a few years before, short-term foreign borrowing could circumvent the credit restrictions imposed by the Congress. Gelb notes that

> Venezuela's Public Credit Law of 1976 required that the Congress approve all public sector borrowing, except for short-term working capital, which needed only the approval of the Ministry of Finance. After 1977 the administration, seeking to accelerate public programs, facilitated such borrowing. As a result, public companies and some decentralized government agencies contributed to a massive increase in short-term debt. In the heady boom years banks lent eagerly to Venezuela with little regard for the quality of the investments financed by their loans . . . *In aggregate terms, the entire oil windfall was fully used by the domestic economy.* The structure of the Venezuelan gross debt portfolio that resulted, however, would give rise to serious problems a few years later. (1988, 301; italics in original)

Shortcomings of the Fiscal Arrangements

As well positioned as PDVSA seemed to be with the arrangement that permitted it to retain oil rents in its investment fund, the arrangement had serious flaws. First, the "profits" of PDVSA and its affiliates included the value of the oil-in-ground that the government allowed PDVSA and the affiliates to extract (i.e., the resource rent). Therefore, PDVSA retained revenues that depended much more on the world price of petroleum and the volume of Venezuelan exports than on the efficiency, true profitability, or investment needs of PDVSA and its affiliates.

Second, and related to the sensitivity of the retained "profits" to world oil prices, PDVSA's investment fund would enjoy "windfall" profits when world prices surged and retain these funds even if in following years prices dropped, oil exploration and production became less attractive, and the Venezuelan government found itself strapped for cash. Because PDVSA would not be able to claim that its higher revenues were solely or even largely from its own efforts and competence, the "windfall" nature of its retained profits would make the fund politically vulnerable to government raiding.

Third, the financial arrangement did not match the power relationship between the government and PDVSA. The bureaucratic conflicts between the government and the state oil company began almost immediately after PDVSA was established, well before the investment fund was an alluring target for raiding. The autonomy implied by the retained-profit formula was not accepted by the officials of the Ministry of Energy and Mines. Coronel, a longtime oil sector executive, describes the ambiguity and conflict: "There was no longer a clear-cut situation in which government offices (the ministry) dictated to foreign companies (the concessionaires) what to do. Now there was a fully Venezuelan managerial body in charge of contributing the leadership . . . Since the desire for power was still a fundamental ingredient of ministry's bureaucracy, there was conflict, for managerial authority could not easily be shared by the two groups" (Coronel 1983, 106).

A fundamental dispute arose between the ministry staff and the management of PDVSA regarding the effect nationalization had on the status and effect of the provisions (particularly section 832) of the Hydrocarbons Law that predated the establishment of PDVSA:

> Ministry staff argued from the very first day of nationalization that decree 832 was still in force and that, therefore, all nationalized oil-industry activities had to have their previous approval. They argued that nothing had really changed in the relationship, when in fact significant philosophical and ownership changes had taken place.
>
> Petróleos de Venezuela argued that the holding company had been created "to coordinate, supervise and control the activities of the nationalized oil industry" in accordance with the basic policies received from the National Executive through the assembly of shareholders. The Ministry of Mines and

Hydrocarbons still possessed all faculties given to it by the hydrocarbons law, essentially those of supervision and technical auditing of the operational activities of the industry.

Petróleos de Venezuela on the other hand had the responsibility of managing industry so as to fulfill the basic objectives its shareholders had asked it to pursue. Decree 832 therefore unnecessarily duplicated the effort involved in the analysis of budgets and operational programs. A managerial concern and participation of ministry staff in the activities of the industry was inefficient and would inevitably lead to confusion and friction. In the opinion of Andres Aguilar, the legal advisor of Petróleos de Venezuela, decree 832 had "automatically been rendered invalid" by the law nationalizing the oil industry. (Coronel 1983, 106)

Moreover, the establishment of a protected oil investment fund was a radical departure from the unfettered access that the presidency and the Finance Ministry had enjoyed to government oil revenues. Before nationalization, the state had to capture the oil revenues from international corporations, through royalties and taxes, but the government had full and immediate access to these captured revenues. Now the investment fund stood in their way. Therefore, once the euphoria and unity of the nationalization act faded, government officials began to reassert direct control over oil decision making. A 1979 amendment to the nationalization law called for the Ministry of Hydrocarbons and Mines to approve all PDVSA budgets. It also reduced the terms of PDVSA directors from four years to two (Lieuwen 1985, 220), hastening the government's opportunity to install directors more likely to answer directly to the ministries.

In 1979 world oil prices began to rise in the wake of the fall of the Shah of Iran and the Iran-Iraq War. This so-called Second Oil Shock kept oil prices high well into 1981. The PDVSA investment fund accumulated more than US$8 billion.

Yet by February 1982 Venezuela was in the worst economic crisis it had suffered in twenty-five years. Although the crisis was due to the decline in world crude prices, it was worsened by the politically motivated action of Minister of Hydrocarbons and Mines, Humberto Calderón Berti, to raise Venezuelan heavy crude prices following OPEC's October 1981 decision to reduce light crude prices. In the very short run, the revenue losses in light crude were offset by the heavy crude price increases, but it was clear to oil experts that the price increase would soon reduce demand for Venezuelan heavy crude.[11] The debts of CVG and other parastatal borrowing added significantly to the fiscal crisis.

Open Conflict

Faced with severe cash needs, the presidency and Finance Ministry turned to PDVSA. First, government officials charged PDVSA with mismanagement of funds, inefficiency, and corruption, even though by the standards of other state oil companies of developing countries, PDVSA was in fact remarkably well managed, professional, honest, transparent, and efficient. Then, in September 1982, the government issued a decree that assigned the Central Bank control over all state enterprises' foreign exchange earnings. PDVSA was left with the control over a US$300 million revolving fund to meet its international obligations in other currencies, with the rest of the US$8 billion account converted into public bonds. In December 1982 the government asked PDVSA to provide US$1.8 billion to bail out the bankrupt state Workers' Bank. When the board refused, the government called a special shareholders' meeting and ordered the board to acquire US$1.8 billion in public debt bonds. In the same month, the Central Bank ratified the use of up to another US$1.8 billion in the acquisition of more debt bonds to underwrite government budget deficits. As a result, PDVSA was forced to freeze its heavy crude project in the Orinoco. By April 1986, 85 percent of PDVSA's investment fund had been converted into long-term government bonds. There were strong doubts regarding the government's ability to redeem these bonds as opposed to simply rolling them over (Randall 1987, 47–48).

The peculiarity of this confrontation lies in PDVSA's being (as it still is) a wholly owned creature of the government. The government's effort to discredit PDVSA grew out of a very awkward political predicament: the post-nationalization arrangements amounted to a highly publicized commitment by the government to reserve significant funds — albeit of then-unknown magnitude — for oil investment. Prior to 1976 the government had spent all of its oil revenues; by 1982, having failed to rein in public expenditures during the 1979–81 boom, it felt a political compulsion to spend all of the accumulated oil revenues once again. According to some interpretations, the takeover of the investment fund was in violation of the 1976 legislation. To reduce the political costs of the government's failure to keep its promise to maintain adequate resource development, the government tried to lay the blame on the state enterprise. Moreover, the state enterprise, though only six years old, was clearly a separate entity, politically and organizationally, from the government. PDVSA and its affiliates had retained some of the heritage of the private oil companies that had been amalgamated into the single state company. In short, total government ownership was a financial reality but did not mean that the government and the enterprise, including its government-selected board of directors, were unified in interests or allegiance.

In essence, then, the raid on the PDVSA investment fund was the result of a faulty formula that permitted the company to retain windfalls long into the period of the government's fiscal emergency. Whether the desire of the government to spend the oil revenues rather than invest them in oil development was correct or not, the government's unilateral disregard for the formula established a mere six years earlier was clearly a violation of trust and cooperation between government and the state enterprise. The conflict was also exacerbated by the government's effort to evade accountability by blaming the crisis on the company.

Misallocation of Resource Development Investments as a Protective Strategy

To this point we cannot say definitively that a policy failure occurred, although the government's decision to spend the oil revenues rather than invest in further exploration and development may have been one. The clear policy failure came next: in PDVSA's reaction to the new reality of having no simple means to shield a highly liquid investment fund. Knowing that PDVSA had become both a cash cow and a convenient scapegoat for the government, PDVSA officials had no confidence that the government's future treatment of liquid PDVSA assets would constitute sound resource development or fair treatment of the company.

Therefore, PDVSA officials adopted the simple strategy of keeping its assets out of government hands by keeping them outside of Venezuela. In 1983 Venezuela began to implement its "internationalization program" by obtaining a 50 percent share of Germany's Veba Oil; the expense of this investment was heavily criticized. In 1986 PDVSA bought 50 percent of Citgo Petroleum Corporation, a subsidiary of Southland. This transaction was criticized on the grounds that Southland's purchase of Citgo a few years earlier had been at a much lower price (*Oil & Gas Journal* 1986a, 1986b). PDVSA also became the sole owner of the Champlin Refining Company, a Texas refinery and petrochemical complex, half-owner of the Swedish refinery company AB Nynäs operating in Sweden and Belgium, and half-owner in a half-billion-dollar joint venture with Union Oil of California involving Unocal's Lemont, Illinois, refinery, over one hundred gasoline stations, and twelve Midwest fuel distribution centers. As part of this agreement PDVSA agreed to supply light crude oil to service stations carrying Unocal's "76" brand gasoline. Because of the expenses of transporting and supplying this fuel to the American Midwest from the American Gulf

Coast, the venture has been less financially profitable than PDVSA expected (Boué 1993, 152–61). In October 1985 a PDVSA subsidiary, Refinería Isla, began start-up operations at a refinery in Emmastad, Curaçao. This refinery had been obtained from the Netherlands Antilles government because Royal Dutch/Shell — the original owner — found it impossible to operate the refinery at a profit, because of a global glut in refining capacity. By 1993 Venezuela had greater refining capacity beyond its borders than any other OPEC nation.

PDVSA officials defended each of these overseas expansions, often invoking the importance of securing demand for Venezuela's peculiar mix of light and heavy crudes. Perhaps some were ultimately justified.[12] Yet the pattern of swift movements of capital surpluses into offshore investments, often of a risky and certainly controversial nature, is problematic insofar as it has been propelled less by sound investment analysis than by the motive of defending PDVSA's control over its investment funds. Other state oil companies, with less compulsion to insulate their investment funds from cash-hungry governments, have not chosen the same risky strategy as PDVSA.

Surplus Extraction through Taxation

The Venezuelan government, as well as opposition politicians, was not inactive while PDVSA sought to shield its investment capital. As in Mexico, the Venezuelan government has imposed greater and greater royalties and taxes on PDVSA, thus capturing the crude oil revenues before PDVSA could claim and redirect them into yet other investments. Higher royalties and taxes, as well as the government's penchant for capturing liquid assets, have clouded not only PDVSA's capacity to finance domestic exploration and production but also its incentives to do so. According to Randall,

> Self-financing might not be possible in the long run because the government has levied heavy taxes on PDVSA's income and has required PDVSA to price its products on the domestic market at levels below those on the world market at times below cost, further reducing PDVSA's income below levels that would have obtained in a free market. Thus, centralization of financial management brought the affiliates under PDVSA's control but did not provide PDVSA with the financial independence sometimes attributed to state-owned enterprises in general but rarely permitted to large state-owned oil companies. (1987, 48)

Investment in exploration and new wells is very important for Venezuela's crude oil production, because production from its existing fields tends to decline by about 22–23 percent a year, causing the company to spend over 50 percent of its production budget to compensate for the drop (*Oil & Gas Journal* 1993, 50). Without new well development, capacity would halve in three years. In 1992 Robert Bottome, an economist who had been making forecasts for Venezuela's oil industry for almost twenty years, predicted that in the next thirty years PDVSA will need to invest $1 billion a year to keep production capacity at present rates, and another $4–5 billion a year to replace old fields. Bottome maintained that if the tax structure is not changed, PDVSA will not generate the cash necessary to maintain output capacity, and it will not be able to attract the private capital that it will need to finance growth after the year 2000 (Sweeney 1992, 5). In 1992 the new PDVSA president, Gustavo Roosen, warned that taxes were causing PDVSA to have a negative cash flow, and that it was more economical for the company to buy crude on the world market than to invest in boosting crude production capacity in Venezuela. He also pointed out that with debt at $3.09 billion, capacity for more borrowing was limited (*Oil & Gas Journal* 1992a, 32).

Thus, like Mexico's PEMEX, PDVSA was forced by high taxation to become a heavy international borrower despite faltering domestic exploration and production investment. In 1984, the year after the government raid on the investment fund, Minister of Hydrocarbons and Mines Calderón Berti announced that the company would have to borrow 50 percent of the funds needed for its annual investment budget of $3.4 billion (*Platt's Oilgram News* 1983, 2). Massive scale-backs of exploration and production followed from the mid-1980s through the early 1990s.[13] The company decided to stretch out or shelve many projects that it had planned to pay for from its cash flow. PDVSA had to increase borrowing on top of its already record debt and more aggressively seek foreign investors (*Oil & Gas Journal* 1992b, 41).

The combination of government attempts to capture PDVSA funds, the availability of overseas investment opportunities, and the need for domestic exploration and production investment led to a remarkable turnabout: PDVSA has effectively handed over domestic oil development and extraction to the multinationals that it was established to supplant, while transforming itself into a multinational corporation. The fiscal squeeze added to PDVSA's motivation to look abroad for investment opportunities. Its incentives to expand domestic oil production have waned insofar as the company's after-tax profits from exploration and production have sharply declined, and its interest in processing and marketing abroad, the profitability of which is far less manipulable by the Venezuelan government, has increased. Another consideration behind PDVSA's downstream acquisitions is that it can pay for new refining capacity with in-kind payments, therefore getting around its low cash ratio and avoiding taxes on production. In fact, part of the company's strategy is to go after assets that require a low up-front payment and that can be paid off with either crude supplies, the proceeds from dividends and the cash flow generated by the asset, or both (Boué 1993, 153, 173). This is a rather clear case of an investment portfolio driven by strategies to overcome governmentally imposed constraints rather than by considerations of optimizing the return on investment and resource exploitation.

Of course, domestic production is still a major part of PDVSA's responsibilities. The challenge for PDVSA, given its low profits from domestic production, its desire to shield its capital by concentrating on overseas investments, and its worry about following the PEMEX path of massive foreign indebtedness, has now become to secure the capital for domestic exploration and production from international oil companies. The *Oil & Gas Journal* (1992b) noted that

> PDVSA is homing in on an expanded role by foreign investment in Venezuela's oil sector because it assumes there will be little growth in real terms in world oil prices in the medium term as well as little likelihood of significant tax relief from the Venezuelan government in years to come . . .
>
> [PDVSA President] Roosen is advancing this politically contentious strategy with the stance that it is much more risky for Venezuela to go into debt than to accept foreign investment, particularly in the petroleum sector. He cites the debt that crippled Venezuela's economy during the 1980's . . .
>
> In the medium term, PDVSA plans to focus on investment in quicker payout projects in oil production and refining while seeking foreign capital for as many projects as possible in oil and gas exploration and development, petrochemicals, and coal. And it will continue to expand its presence in other countries, especially the U.S., to maintain market shares of crude and refined products exports . . .
>
> Roosen's new emphasis on foreign investment in Venezuela's petroleum sector is emerging amid a heightened sense of austerity at a state oil company that estimates it must spend $27 billion during 1992–1997 to meet its operating goals . . . Even with the cut, 1992 planned outlays outstrip the amount of money PDVSA spent in 1991.

Thus, PDVSA has become a multinational refining and marketing company, while multinational oil companies have been coming back into Venezuela in violation of the spirit (and, according to some critics, the law) of the 1976 nationalization. In short, the fiscal arrangements and bureaucratic-political struggles between the Venezuelan government and PDVSA have deflected the company from pursuing, for better or for worse, the main objective of the 1976 nationalization, namely, the state's control over the financing and operations of domestic oil exploitation.

Competition, Efficiency, and Accountability

It would be misleading to leave the PDVSA case without pointing out how and why the company is highly successful in other respects. Despite the frustrations of operating in an often hostile fiscal and political environment, PDVSA has escaped the rampant inefficiency and corruption that are so prevalent in state oil companies in many other countries. To be sure, PDVSA has faced its share of criticism, but it is generally directed toward strategic decisions that it has been compelled to take because of the hostile environment. Venezuela has been spared the spectacle of billions of dollars disappearing from PDVSA accounts, as has happened in Nigeria, or the completely impenetrable accounting of Mexico's PEMEX; it has not had to cope with the extravagant waste and ostentation of Indonesia's Pertamina prior to 1975, union corruption as in PEMEX, or the forays of PEMEX and pre-1975 Pertamina into investment areas totally unrelated to the core business and expertise of a petroleum company. Venezuelan oil workers are well paid, but they do not capture an outlandish share of the oil rent, nor do PDVSA operations destroy these rents through lavish spending or operational incompetence.

How can PDVSA's relative competence, cost consciousness, professionalism, and efficiency be explained? Beyond PDVSA's legacy of professionalism and efficiency of the international affiliates that were absorbed in 1976 and the impressive leadership of several PDVSA presidents, two factors stand out. First, the PDVSA structure provides for a limited but surprisingly potent form of competition among the three exploration and production affiliates. Second, the capacity of PDVSA headquarters and the governmental oversight agencies to monitor PDVSA's domestic operations and finances is significantly better than for the other state oil companies we are examining. For all of its missteps in handling PDVSA's investment fund, the Venezuelan government has not used the firm as a serious off-budget laundering mechanism. Indeed, PDVSA is often held up as a model of transparency in analyses of other state resource companies.[14]

In setting up a national oil company, the Venezuelan government wanted to avoid three pitfalls: operating numerous and redundant agencies, destroying the successful institutional structure that the private companies had created, and creating an overly powerful agency — an important consideration inasmuch as so much of the country's budget comes from oil revenue. As Calderón Berti (1978, 67–68) put it, "one should not establish a single firm for the entire nation because the magnitude of its operations would be excessive and power would be excessively concentrated." Indeed, avoiding the "Pemexization" of Venezuelan oil was an explicit concern in the debate.

Therefore, rather than immediately consolidating all the exploration and production companies into one large concern, the government merged the twenty-two prenationalization companies first into fourteen subsidiaries of PDVSA, the holding company. After a few years these fourteen were merged into four, three (Lagoven, Maraven, and Meneven) anchored by the three largest former subsidiaries, and the original state oil company (CVP). A final merger of CVP and Meneven into Corpoven brought the number down to three.[15]

Even though each of the three subsidiaries has the same overall goals, sells the same products at the same government-regulated prices, and sends all of its earnings to PDVSA, they still engage in some competition that would be absent in a monolithic company. Each has its own corporate identity. They compete for exploration rights. For example, Maraven, the successor to Shell, won exploration rights in one section of the Orinoco Belt far from its traditional area at Lake Maracaibo, by virtue of its successes in processing heavy crudes (Blank 1986, 275). To get larger exploration and production areas, and to secure PDVSA funding for their projects, they must compete with one another by demonstrating efficiency. Without this competition, Venezuela "would not have parameters for comparison, for example, of costs, profitability, and the overall well-being of the industry" (Calderón Berti 1978, 95).

PDVSA works to maintain the competitive balance for the affiliates, intervening in certain ways to prevent one from dominating over the others. For example, when PDVSA gave Corpoven control of Meneven's personnel operations, Maraven and Lagoven received some of Meneven's refining, production, and exploratory activities. Also, although Lagoven created the Orimulsion process for converting ultra-heavy crudes into usable fuel, PDVSA arranged for the other affiliates to get a share of the action (Boué 1995, 21–22). When, in the early years, the affiliates tried to underprice one another to compete for clients, PDVSA solved this problem by having the technical trading committee analyze the clients and potential markets, so that PDVSA could assign them to the different companies (Coronel 1983, 148–49).

To avoid unnecessary duplication of shareable services, PDVSA headquarters required coordinating groups to cover everything from exploration strategies to worker housing.[16] International marketing and many other global issues are handled by the PDVSA headquarters, also in the service of efficiency.

Ghana: Taxing Cocoa

The Ghana Cocoa Marketing Board fits the most common pattern of export-commodity marketing boards throughout the developing world. Beginning as an institution that defended the interests of the cocoa farmer, it was gradually transformed into a major mechanism for taxing the farmer. Rent extraction was so extreme that the dynamics of quasi-taxation through marketing boards are clearly visible, as are the consequences: rather than submit to a price regime that turned hard-earned profits into losses, the farmers often engaged in massive smuggling, and on occasion thousands of cocoa farms were abandoned, their trees cut down or left to the ravages of disease and fire. Because cocoa farming has a significantly higher economic return than other alternatives available to the farmers, this outcome qualifies as a clear policy failure: the pricing distortion has led to a deteriorated resource base rather than conversion to a better resource base.

Why did the Ghanaian government resort to extracting cocoa wealth in a way that clearly distorted the incentives for cocoa farmers to produce the country's most important crop, rather than following the Millian principle of taxing incomes or consumption separate from the cocoa-raising activity? It is not clear that there were significant disagreements within the ruling group.

The Ghana cocoa case raises perplexing questions about whether the dynamics of policy failures propelled by tax motives are at all similar to the dynamics that entail bypassing the conventional budget apparatus. Indeed, in some respects the mechanisms are inverted. First, recall that government officials with distributional motives often resort to allocations through the natural-resource exploitation process, despite the efficiency losses, because the conventional budget system would not provide such benefits. The case of the copper mine workers in India is a good example of this dilemma; central budget transfers to pensioned-off miners might make the most sense from both an efficiency and a welfare perspective, but it is simply not likely politically. Thus, the predicament that compels natural-resource abuses for the sake of distribution is that a specific group cannot be indulged without implicating the natural-resource exploitation process in the act of benefit distribution. When the taxation motive prevails, the dilemma is often how to tax differentially according to economic activity rather than on the basis of income, wealth, or consumption levels. This desire to tax differentially by economic activity can come about because the government officials give low priority to the political support of the targeted group, because they wish to undermine the economic power of the targeted group, because they believe that more can be extracted from the target group with tolerable political backlash compared to trying to extract from everyone, or because of a development strategy that they believe requires a transfer of resources from one sector to another (very often from agriculture to industry). Whatever the mix of specific motives and perceptions, the issue is the tolerance for taxation on the part of targeted economic actors and their potential to retaliate against the government, and not necessarily a conflict within the government (although it may be with the legislature, if it represents the interests of the targeted group more than the executive does).

Background

The board began in the colonial period as the Gold Coast Cocoa Marketing Board in 1947, with an explicit mandate to defend the interests of the cocoa producers.[17] To match this mandate, there was strong representation of cocoa producers on the board. Of the twelve board members, four were selected by the producers, one by the Cocoa Manufacturers Agencies, one by the Chamber of Commerce, one by the Ashanti Confederacy, one by the Joint Provincial Council, and four by the governor (Bauer 1954, 276–78). Arhin (1985, 39) points out that in the first four years of the board's operations, it made grants of more than 25 million pounds sterling to improve the infrastructure for cocoa production, investing in farm rehabilitation, harbor-facility improvement, cocoa research, and against cocoa diseases. However, with the coming of the Convention People's Party (CPP) government of Kwame Nkrumah as Leader of Public Business in 1951, the board began to be politicized in a series of steps that reduced the proportion of cocoa producers' representatives, required these representatives to be members of the CPP, and in 1954 created a state Cocoa Purchasing Company that was empowered to make Cocoa Board–financed loans to cocoa farmers. A government inquiry in 1957 revealed that these loans were predominantly made to CPP members and sympathizers (Arhin 1985, 42–43). In that year the Cocoa Purchasing Company was dissolved. However, the United Ghana Farmers' Council, an organization founded in 1953 by the CPP, was given exclusive rights to buy cocoa on behalf of the Cocoa Marketing Board. Other cocoa purchasing companies were banned, as were all other farmer organizations (Beckman 1976, 192–94; Arhin 1985, 43). In 1961 the UGFC was further transformed into the United Ghana Farmers' Council Cooperatives (UGFCC), as the state agency was also mandated to take over the entire cocoa cooperatives movement. Thus, the UGFCC had both a political and an economic monopoly, the latter covering the major producers organizations as well as farmgate purchasing and marketing. While its local-level officials and representatives were in theory chosen by local farmers, in fact the CPP dominated in these selections.

The Cocoa Board and the UGFCC took on many functions — too many to permit adequate monitoring and accountability. In addition to purchasing cocoa, they made loans, provided advances, took over the pre-existing cocoa cooperatives, provided technical assistance and area-wide treatment of cocoa-tree diseases, collected taxes, operated health centers, provided scholarships for children, and supported the University College (Arhin 1985, 43–45; Beckman 1976, 199). As with both the Sabah Foundation and the Honduran forestry enterprise COHDEFOR (see chapter 4), the commingling of functions and expenditures made it impossible to determine how much of the resources extracted by the Cocoa Board and the UGFCC were plowed back into the producing areas (the consensus of observers is that it was not a very large proportion of the total), whether these organizations were effective in accomplishing these multiple objectives, or whether they were pursuing these functions with the correct priorities.

When the government discovered in the mid-1950s that cocoa revenues could easily be captured through the Marketing Board, and that cocoa farmers could no longer defend their interests through the board, the gap between export prices and farmgate prices rose dramatically. The Cocoa Duty and Development Funds Act of 1954 froze the producer price for a four-year period, even though the government officials clearly anticipated higher international cocoa prices (Bates 1981, 109). Over the next decade, the tendency of myriad changes was to place the revenues that the Cocoa Board and the UGFCC captured into the general government coffers. In terms of the magnitude of the public capture of private cocoa revenues, Beckman (1976, 280–81) reports that the "public cocoa income" (combined Cocoa Board payments to the government and the Cocoa Board surpluses or deficits) reached 60 percent of export sales in 1953/54 and 1954/55 and remained between one-quarter and one-half of sales value up to 1964.[18] In addition, the reserves of the Cocoa Board were made available for loans and grants unconnected with cocoa production or marketing, and indeed unconnected with the welfare of the cocoa farmers. In 1957 legislation permitted broad uses of Cocoa Board funds, the government claiming that these funds "should properly be regarded as being held in trust for all the people of Ghana" (cited in Beckman 1976, 199).

The question, then, was how the government's windfall would be allocated. In 1954 the government passed the Cocoa Duty Ordinance that earmarked the difference between the farmgate price and the export price for three funds: 40 percent went into a fund to finance the national development plan, 40 percent into a fund for large-scale projects that were "beyond the scope of that Plan," and 20 percent to the central treasury. Insofar as the conventional fiscal authorities were centrally involved in the development and specific implementation of the national development plan, this arrangement meant that the central treasury captured roughly half of the producer surplus extracted by the Cocoa Marketing Board and its various instruments. The presidency, which dominated the allocation of the fund for large-scale projects, controlled the 40 percent earmarked for this purpose and obviously also had considerable influence over the central budgetary decisions as well as the national plan.

Indeed, the unity within the government, thoroughly dominated by CPP stalwarts, made policy disagreements within the government rather minor. The highly expansionist Nkrumah economic development strategy involved massive industrialization through both infrastructure expansion and import-substitution industrialization, agricultural modernization and mechanization, and expansion of social services. With the cocoa demand boom that went along with European economic recovery, the export prospects remained bright throughout the 1950s, and so then did the prospect of an investment boom financed by high cocoa export earnings. While in retrospect the economic plans appear patently unrealistic, there were enough foreign "experts" to applaud Nkrumah's boldness to keep the policies from being discredited long into the CPP's rule. Tony Killick (1978, 53) argues that the Nkrumah administration, as wrong-headed as its policies turned out to be, was following the thinking of "most development economists."

Unlike Indonesia, this was not a case of a president defying or circumventing the analysis and recommendations of his hard-nosed neoclassical experts within the planning agency and the Finance Ministry in order to pursue a nationalist development agenda. Killick demonstrates the consistency of Nkrumah's economic strategy with the development economics theories in vogue in the 1950s and 1960s; he concludes that "the mutual reinforcement of economics, socialism and nationalism gave this set of ideas an intense attraction to statesmen such as Nkrumah" (Killick 1978, 53). Moreover, the government finance experts, concerned with the prospects of inflation when high world cocoa prices could have brought greater liquidity to the Ghanaian economy, had common cause with those eager to maximize revenues in their preference to keep payments to farmers low (Beckman 1976, 194). In short, the ideological congruity within the CPP government, the legitimacy accorded by external views, and the institutional interests of government agencies produced relatively little inter-agency conflict over how to use the cocoa profits. Of course, the Agricultural Ministry would have preferred greater investment in agriculture (Killick 1978, 138–39), and there were questions raised in 1960 from the Finance Ministry as to whether the government should continue to spend on expanding the cocoa crop through disease control and agricultural extension, when it was becoming increasingly obvious that Ghana and other cocoa producers around the world were headed toward a production glut. The Ministries of Trade and Agriculture, presumably understanding the extraordinary dependence of the central budget on cocoa revenues, argued successfully for maximum production (Beckman 1976, 189–90). Nonetheless, these were not disagreements among government officials over the source and disposition of government revenues that we have seen in other chapters.

Nevertheless, the question remains as to why this rather ideologically homogeneous government did not simply impose a broader tax on income or consumption to finance its ambitious development plans and current expenditures for services, thereby avoiding the risk to Ghana's most precious export commodity. The answer seems to be a combination of political calculus, development preference for industrialization, and complacency in grabbing the easily available cocoa surpluses. The urban sectors were the core of CPP support and were to be the new industrial class manning the factories that the import-substitution industrialization strategy was to create. On the other hand, "since much of the active opposition to the CPP had come from cocoa-growing areas, especially in Ashanti, to tax the farmers was politically easier than it would have been otherwise" (Killick 1978, 49–50). Imposing higher taxes on industrial and other urban occupations would have seemed inconsistent with the strong pro-industry orientation, and this was obviously convenient from a political perspective.[19] It turned out, of course, that the entire economy, the urban sector at least as much as the rural, suffered when the deficit spending led to the economic crisis of the mid-1960s, which, in various forms and for various reasons, persisted into the 1980s. The taxation of agriculture in the name of a "self-reliance" industrial strategy created a double curse of agricultural decline and inefficient industry.[20] Finally, the long expansion in both cocoa production and world prices made the short-sighted overconfident about the capacity to squeeze the cocoa sector without provoking a serious backlash.

The unraveling began in 1960, when Ghana experienced a series of production increases that totaled more than 60 percent from 1958/59 to 1960/61, and then increased by another third in 1964/65 (Beckman 1976, 186–87). From the 1960/61 harvest through the 1962/63 harvest, the Cocoa Board had to dip deeply into its reserves to prop up farmgate prices, while still transferring nearly 18 million pounds sterling each year to the treasury (Beckman 1976, 280–82). Beckman (1976, 187) also notes that although the gross revenues remained about the same with the doubling of cocoa production and the halving of the export price, the net revenues for the farmers went down precipitously because of the greater expenses of growing twice the volume of cocoa.

Up to that time, the government had stabilized its revenues in the face of declining world cocoa prices by cutting the prices to cocoa producers. The government also borrowed heavily from the Cocoa Marketing Board reserves. In 1960 the United Ghana Farmers' Council, claiming to represent all cocoa farmers, agreed to an additional "voluntary contribution" of 17 percent of the producer price. From a farmgate price of nearly 150 pounds sterling in 1955–57, the Cocoa Board steadily reduced the price to 100 pounds for the 1961/62 to 1964/65 harvests (Arhin 1985, 44; Beckman 1976, 186–87, 282). However, with an unprecedented bumper crop harvested in 1964/65, and the collapse of world prices, the Cocoa Board ran out of reserves.[21] In 1965 the Cocoa Board cut the producer price another 26 percent in nominal currency, with an annual inflation rate of over 30 percent. The 1965/66 crop, average by previous standards, was well below the 1964/65 high; the combination of lower prices and the smaller yields resulted in the failure of many farms and the flight of crucially important non-land-owning labor (Beckman 1976, 218–20).

The pricing debacle of the mid-1960s severely damaged the cocoa industry until the late 1980s. Labor, largely originating in northern Ghana, left the southern cocoa-producing regions, often going to work in the Ivory Coast or Nigeria. Between one and two million people left Ghana in the 1970s because of the collapse of the cocoa industry (Thabatabal 1986). Cocoa trees were cut down or left to deteriorate from disease and brush fires. Roads and other infrastructure needed to bring cocoa crops to the ports also deteriorated (Pratt 1990). The independent cooperatives that tried to fill the vacuum created by the dismantling of the UGFCC had deteriorated since their banning in 1961 to the point that they could not resume their middleman role effectively; the Cocoa Board's new purchasing agent, the Produce Buying Agency, soon dominated.

Most importantly, regardless of the buying agents, the farmers still had to reckon with the Cocoa Board, which continued to set the cocoa prices. The board abandoned the policy of keeping farmgate prices constant over several years, because of the high inflation that Ghana suffered from the early 1970s through the mid-1980s. However, the farmgate prices remained low, both in real terms and in terms of the world price. The civilian government of Dr. Kofi Busia elected in 1969 was perceived as favoring the cocoa growers (Mikell 1989, 194), but in fact the proportion of total export proceeds that went to the cocoa farmers actually declined in crop years 1969/70 and 1970/71 from the levels prevailing during the early and mid-1960s under Nkrumah.[22] Under Colonel Ignatius Acheampong's government that deposed President Busia in 1972, mild efforts were initially made to raise farmgate prices, but the temptation to capture cocoa profits remained irresistible. In the period 1975–85, producer prices never exceeded one-quarter of the world market price and were frequently less than 10 percent of it (Sarris and Shams 1991, 165–66). It is striking that this pattern occurred under both military and civilian governments and under populist and nonpopulist heads of state. It is clear that public finance had come to depend so heavily on cocoa revenues that even military governments were loathe to change that dependence, despite their obvious destruction of the very industry on which they depended.

Currency Overvaluation

The worsening of the cocoa sector beginning in the late 1960s was abetted by the chronic overvaluation of Ghana's local currency, the cedi, which amounted to another, even more insidious mechanism for taxing cocoa farmers. Some observers identify the overvaluation as the most serious detriment to Ghana's long-term export performance (Coleman, Akiyama, and Varangis 1993; May 1985; Sarris and Shams 1991, 165–66). Overvalued cedis brought urban-oriented importers more dollars and pounds to purchase foreign goods, but overvaluation provided fewer cedis for cocoa producers from the export revenues of their production. Until 1967 the Ghanaian currency was exchanged at par with the pound sterling, despite higher inflation in Ghana than in pound sterling countries; even thereafter it was devalued only reluctantly by successive administrations after long periods of inflation-driven overvaluation. In addition to the pro-urban bias of overvaluation, the reluctance to devalue was motivated by the political symbolism of devaluation as a sign of the government's failure to uphold the strength of its currency. Overvaluation was allowed to grow to such high levels that when devaluation became unavoidable in 1967 and 1971, the cedi lost 30 and 42 percent of its value, respectively.

The taxation impact of overvaluation is rather straightforward. When the cedi is overvalued, the Cocoa Board's hard currency proceeds are converted into cedis at a higher dollar per cedi rate than is justified by the market exchange rate, allowing the Central Bank to pay fewer cedis back to the board and the farmers.

Smuggling

The attempt to capture such high proportions of producers' profits presumed that cocoa was an easy, "fixed" target for price manipulations and taxation. This presumption ignored the feasibility of smuggling to neighboring countries with higher producer prices paid by their marketing boards, lower export taxes, or both. The producer prices in neighboring countries were generally far higher; as early as 1954, the farmgate prices reported in neighboring countries were twice those offered in Ghana (Beckman 1976, 195), and in the 1970s farmgate prices in neighboring countries were sometimes five times higher (Mikell 1989, 198). As a consequence, the official estimates of smuggling placed it at 5–10 percent of officially recorded harvests, but other estimates have put smuggling at well over 15 percent, particularly in the late 1970s.[23] Half of the crops of border regions may have been lost to Ghanaian revenues (May 1985).

Cocoa's Recovery

In mid-1983, in the midst of hyperinflation, unmanageable debt, and economic stagnation, the Ghanaian government accepted an International Monetary Fund Economic Recovery Program that gave Ghana access to much increased IMF funds and, soon to follow, World Bank funds. Among the many reforms adopted by the government was a commitment to raise cocoa producer prices (Sarris and Shams 1991, 4–8). While the increase of producer prices as a proportion of the world market price was quite gradual (indeed, the price in 1984 was the lowest proportion since 1979), by 1988 it exceeded 40 percent and by 1989 more than half of the world market price (Sarris and Shams 1991, 165). In addition, the new arrangement provides for the farmers to be compensated for the shortfall in their share due to inflation or overvaluation of the cedi (Bulir 1996, 9).

The result of these reforms has been striking. Cocoa production, which had reached a nadir of just under 159,000 metric tons in 1983–84 — one-fifth of the production of 1964–65 — recovered to 300,000 metric tons by 1989 (Pratt 1990, 128) and reached 320,000 metric tons in 1995 (Bulir 1996, 15). Remarkably, this occurred in the face of consistently declining world prices and with the government still capturing between 20 and 40 percent of the revenues from year to year. For 1986–90 the government's revenues averaged 25 percent of total cocoa revenues; for 1991–96 they averaged 21.5 percent (Bulir 1996, 8).

In short, the stabilization of cocoa production, despite the continued decline of world cocoa prices, has been effected by the simple commitment of the Ghanaian government, albeit under some pressure by international and bilateral development institutions, to desist from trying to solve its fiscal problems by placing the bulk of the burden on the cocoa sector.

Cameroon's Forests: Parks, Roads, and Appropriation

Recall that the Honduran and Indonesian governments took the dramatic step of laying claim to all trees within their national boundaries, resulting in timber rents flowing according to the discretion of government officials. But for the development objectives that prompted certain officials to divert these funds away from the central treasury, the treasury's rent capture would have been a huge source of central-government funding. The appropriation was an enormous, immediate tax, even though in neither case did the central treasury enjoy the full measure of the captured resources.

However, the political and ideological conditions that permitted these governments to proceed so boldly are rare, and many government officials would blanch at the idea of expropriating all private and communal forests even if the government had the opportunity to do so. Therefore, the central treasury's capture of timber rents previously controlled by private or communal forest users is typically more subtle and indirect. The pattern of forest exploitation in Cameroon since the mid-1980s is in many ways a typical example of this more subtle approach. The Cameroon government has pushed further with the long-standing tendency to "nationalize" forest lands in the name of conservation and economic stewardship. While the government does not claim all forests for its own use, it does claim and exercise the right to designate who will have access to different forest tracts. This has been done by designating specific tracts as state, private, council, or communal forests (Shepherd 1993, 316) and by reserving the right to regulate forest uses on all types of forest lands (Rietbergen 1988, 2). This has opened up the opportunity for the government to extract forest rents by awarding logging concessions on lands that otherwise would have remained under more traditional use patterns. Because the government's revenues from other sources have declined precipitously since the mid-1980s, it has used the mechanism of nationalization and commercial extraction to capture timber rents that it otherwise could not have claimed. As Isaac Zama concludes,

> since the mid 1980s, Cameroon has been in the throes of an economic slump, with annual GNP having fallen by more than 30%. Unable to honour its internal and international financial commitments, the Cameroon Government

has turned to its forests as a source of revenue. Pressures on the forests by local communities and commercial loggers are causing unprecedented deforestation and degradation. A resource base that meets the needs of the people, and which provides valuable environmental and economic functions . . . is at risk of reaching the threshold of crisis. (1995, 263)

One might think that such a serious economic crisis, and the government's precarious financial position, might simply warrant liquidating the forest now to meet immediate needs.[24] However, the very low royalties charged for commercial logging make this a highly inefficient strategy for taxing forest exploitation, with a large portion of the benefits going overseas through the profits of the foreign (largely European) logging companies. In addition, the low royalties, short concession periods, and very poor enforcement of harvesting regulations induce particularly reckless logging, leading to greater collateral damage of timber that is not removed from the forest.

The objective conditions and the "technical" diagnosis of Cameroon's forestry problems are not at all complicated or unusual: underpriced and underregulated commercial logging reduces government revenues and leads to overharvesting and the construction of logging roads that draw in agriculturalists who clear more forest; subsidized wood-products processing destroys timber rents and further reduces the government's share. The government, in order to capture more revenue from the meager royalty rate assessed on the loggers, has been granting more and more concessions on land best conserved for other purposes. Deforestation outstrips afforestation by roughly ten to one; Cameroon has been losing 80,000 to 150,000 hectares of forest annually (Rietbergen 1988, 27; Horta 1991, 144; Oyog 1996), with very little to show for it.

However, the importance of international aid institutions and nongovernmental organizations (NGOs) adds considerable complexity. A financially strapped government of a low-income country facing declining terms of international trade cannot afford to antagonize either the donor agencies, which provide significant foreign assistance, or the NGOs that can shape consumer opinion about the environmental acceptability of its timber and wood-products exports. It is therefore not surprising that the Cameroon government has resorted to a curiously mixed appeal, invoking both conservation and development, for initiatives that actually are quite threatening to both the ecosystem and at least some of the poorest residents of forested areas.

While one of the main appeals invoked by the government is conservation, officials also justify the infrastructure that goes along with commercial logging in previously remote areas by appealing to the logic of majoritarian modernization: the argument is that infrastructure and greater contact with the modern-sector economy provide most residents with opportunities to improve their material well-being. This argument has been roundly criticized by advocates of the hunting-gathering populations and cultural preservation (e.g., Horta 1991; Winterbottom 1992). Yet although the Cameroon government has appropriated forest lands in ways that have both squandered economic opportunities and threatened unique ecosystems, the government has used these appeals effectively in securing international funding for its forestry initiatives.

Background

In the mid-1980s Cameroon still had roughly 40 percent of its territory in closed tropical forest, equivalent to 16.5 million hectares. The apparent primary source of deforestation was agricultural conversion, largely devoted to shifting cultivation. While agricultural conversion has been responsible for 90 percent of deforestation (Thiele and Wiebelt 1993, 502–3), much of it would not have occurred without the roads and other facilities brought by commercial forestry expansion.

Despite the deforestation, Cameroon had several heavily forested areas. The so-called Congolese forest in the Southeast had been largely untouched by logging and little affected by agricultural conversion, principally because of its remoteness to ports and population centers. The so-called Biafran forest of the Southwest had been logged over several times and was subjected to agricultural conversion and monoculture plantations, but it still had areas of dense forest of notable biological diversity.[25]

By the 1980s, the process of state appropriation of forest lands had already severely reduced the areas where communities had formal control. Although the government still retained the category of council (or community) forest, less than one-twentieth of Cameroon's forest area was so designated by 1989. State forest (*Forêt domaniale*) covered roughly one-fifth of the 22 million hectares designated as forest area; two-thirds of these state lands were designated as natural parks and reserves and the other third as "production forest" (Egli 1991, 57). However, the "reserve" designation was not permanent; the government had (and still has) the discretion to open up reserve areas for logging. Public domain forests (*Forêt de domaine national*) constituted the remaining three-fourths of the area designated as forest lands. Yet these public domain forests were largely logged-over lands, fallows, and abandoned lands. As in many other countries, the land designated as "forest," and therefore placed under the jurisdiction of the forestry department, was not necessarily forested to any meaningful degree. In Cameroon large portions of the savannas, increasingly subjected to desertification, have been included in the category of forest lands.

Like many other countries of West Africa, the government of Cameroon in the 1980s generally viewed the forest sector as a source of economic stimulus, government revenues, and foreign exchange. Forestry policy therefore entailed the typical pattern of agricultural conversion (to both tree crops such as cocoa and bananas and annual crops) and domestic wood processing (Rietbergen 1988, 28, 62). The expansion of logging was also an explicit aspect of the government's forestry policy. The fifth Five-Year Plan (1981–86) called for an extensive road network in the timber-rich, hitherto inaccessible areas, to address the problem that marketable tree species were distributed widely rather than concentrated in particular areas (Delancey 1989, 121). For this reason, Cameroon, like Brazil, had received less attention from major logging companies than the total volume of marketable trees would seem to justify. The government's desire to attract logging companies, both for the growth of the wood-products industry and to provide immediate foreign exchange through log exports, may explain why timber royalty rates were kept so low.

Yet the 1980s also brought increasing awareness and international pressures for conservation. The Cameroon government responded with greater formal attention to sustainability and the establishment of protected areas. However, financial pressures ran directly counter to the conservation goal. In the late 1970s, Cameroon had entered a short-lived oil boom that ratcheted up government spending and the economic aspirations of the urban population in particular. The government was sensitive to the limits of Cameroon's oil and recognized that oil revenues would increase the demands for government spending. Therefore, the government kept information about the levels of oil revenues secret and had the proceeds deposited in an overseas "extra-budgetary account" (*compte hors budget*). Rough estimates put 1984 revenues at $750 million (DeLancey 1989, 140–41). Despite the secrecy and the desire to save the oil wealth for the future, the president took advantage of his discretion over the extra-budgetary account to add substantially to the national budget, particularly for the investment budget and to cover the losses of state enterprises. While in 1985 the *compte hors budget* provided one-fifth of the central budget, by the end of the 1980s this was exhausted, owing to declines in oil production and world oil prices.[26] Despite major investments in agriculture, Cameroon's agricultural exports also declined in quantity (partially because of widespread drought in Central Africa), just as world prices were declining. All of this occurred just after the government unveiled its very ambitious sixth Five-Year Plan for 1986–91. Yet the economy continued to decline, reducing the gross national product 30 percent from 1985 to 1995 (Zama 1995, 264). The government was pushed into incurring its first large foreign debt, which by 1990 grew to $4 billion (Jua 1990, 42–43; Horta 1991, 142). The foreign debt, and the rising expectations of Cameroonians despite the past efforts to sterilize the oil revenues, put a much greater burden on the government to secure foreign exchange and to find new ways to increase government revenues.

In seeking support from the international community, the government did have several strong advantages. Compared to most other developing economies, particularly in Africa, the Cameroon government was favorably viewed by the official international organizations for its liberal economic policies and lack of huge distortions. For example, Cameroon was able to maintain its food sufficiency not only because of soil fertility but also because the agricultural markets were not highly distorted. The economic problems that befell Cameroon were to a large degree caused by factors beyond its control, such as declining terms of trade on the world market. Nonetheless, the government had to maintain economic policies that would not signal an abandonment of overall sound economic management.

Dealing with the "International Community"

The Cameroon government thus faced a ticklish dilemma: how to increase revenues from existing resources while placating the relevant international organizations and, indeed, enlisting their support. This was accomplished, intentionally or not, first by submitting to an internationally sanctioned forestry planning process that failed to balance economic development goals with either indigenous rights or realistic assessments of sustainability. Second, the government appropriated land in the name of conservation, expanding the national parks and buffer areas surrounding them, but used its newly acquired control to award logging concessions in some of the appropriated areas. Third, the government in effect (if not demonstrably with intent) offset questionable resource practices with impressive but largely unenforceable formal regulations.

In 1986 the government submitted its forest policy to the so-called Tropical Forest Action Plan (TFAP) process. The TFAP is a program financed by several international organizations, including the World Bank and the UN Food and Agriculture Organization (FAO), that provides technical assistance and financing for tropical countries to develop long-term forestry strategies. For Cameroon, the TFAP was financed by the UN Development Programme, with technical assistance provided by the FAO.

As Robert Winterbottom (1992, 222–23) notes, "the objective was to mobilize action to control tropical deforestation and to improve the lives of people dependent on tropical forests."

However, the Cameroon TFAP was formulated without consultation with forest dwellers, and, as Horta (1991, 145) notes, "forest-dwelling peoples are not accorded a single word in the four volume TFAP for Cameroon." Winterbottom, head of the World Resources Institute team that assessed the Cameroon TFAP, concluded that

> a retrospective review of issues related to the treatment of indigenous people in the Cameroon TFAP process is not encouraging. There were no demographic studies carried out as part of the sector review or forest policy study . . . no specific references were made to the Baka people in southern and southeastern Cameroon (estimated population of 20–35,000) or to the Bakola people in southwestern Cameroon (estimated population of 35,000), or to their customary uses of the forest resources in these areas.
>
> A small number of NGOs were involved in the TFAP planning process, but no organizations that represented the interests of the indigenous forest dwellers participated in the exercise, nor were the indigenous people able to participate directly in the TFAP process. The Ministry of Social Affairs did not play a significant role in the formulation of the TFAP strategies and proposed actions, although this ministry is proposing a government program aimed at the socioeconomic integration of the Baka and other pygmy groups.
>
> The FAO/UNDP report argues that the "unexploited" forest resources in southeastern Cameroon should be "opened up" to increase the amount of foreign exchange generated by timber exports and to help meet the projected increase in demand for tropical timber. The TFAP strategy proposes that the volume of industrial wood production be increased from 2 million cubic meters to 5.5 million m³ by the year 2010. In the absence of greatly expanded efforts to regenerate and manage logged-over areas, the higher level of timber production would likely leave little forest land untouched; logging concessions already cover more than half the remaining area of closed, productive forest. However, no proposals were made to monitor the impact of the expansion of logging and timber production on indigenous forest-dwelling people, nor to monitor the impact from associated land use changes resulting from logging-road construction. (1992, 224)

This very negative assessment by the World Resources Institute was echoed by objections from several international NGOs.[27] Nevertheless, with the implicit endorsement of the international official organizations sponsoring the TFAP process, the government's expansion of concession areas and road construction that could be defended by invoking the TFAP was less vulnerable to censure by official international organizations.

On the strength of the TFAP, the Cameroon government secured international financing for road construction into the most remote areas. The most controversial initiative was a $60 million World Bank low-interest loan approved in 1996 over the objections of French and British NGOs, the British Labour Party, the African Development Bank, and the U.S. executive director of the World Bank (Clover 1996; Oyog 1996). With the new target of 5.5 million cubic meters of timber for the year 2010, the government granted 150 logging concessions in 1989.

The Korup Park

The state's expansion of control in the name of conservation is best illustrated by the establishment of the Korup National Park, a 100,000 hectare tract of remarkable biological diversity. In 1986 the Cameroon government declared this tract a national park, the most stringent classification for forest land use, ostensibly to protect its extraordinary biological diversity. The strong international attention arose in large part because one-fourth of the world's primate species are found there, as are an estimated three thousand varieties of plants, many with pharmacological promise (Franks 1990). The park plan included the now standard provision of buffer zones designed to provide production and employment opportunities for the people living in and near the park. The park's formation brought praise from the international environmental community, which was increasingly aware that conservation efforts in Cameroon were likely to occur only if international funding were available.

It is important to understand that the Korup area was not in serious jeopardy from the actions of local people. The area had a rather stable balance of population and resource use for both agriculturalists and hunter-gatherers. Gill Shepherd describes the intricate arrangements that define the community self-discipline that accounts for this balance:

> The Korup situation is one in which the numbers of people living in the area are relatively small, and the system seems to be in equilibrium. As far as forest use and ownership is concerned, patterns of resource use between adjacent villages (and this is in an area of great ethnic heterogeneity) are so well worked out that ceremonies and actual lines of trees have gone to mark out the boundaries between them, and rules for shared or mutually exclusive hunting zones have been evolved; there are rules for the maintenance of paths and footbridges within village territories, and villagers have a way of estimating their terrain's

game resources and deciding whether or not to lease out hunting rights to outsiders. Village-specific reserves, used for religious ceremonies, exist in rich old growth forest, and no hunting or gathering is allowed in them. (1993, 316)

Moreover, efforts led by international NGOs such as the World Wide Fund for Nature were devoted to developing sustainable approaches to agriculture and agro-forestry in the areas surrounding the park, in order to reduce the activities of local people in the park itself (Franks 1990).

Nevertheless, the declaration of part of the broad Korup area as protected implicitly left the rest of it under government jurisdiction but less protected from the government's own actions. Because of the assertion of state authority over the park per se and a large area around it, the government created for itself the opportunity to have the surrounding area exploited for its own financial benefit. This vulnerability of the Korup area was clarified in 1989, when among the 150 new logging concessions awarded by the administration of President Paul Biya were several within the Korup buffer zone itself (Franks 1990). By granting the concessions, the government effectively excluded the local people from the concession areas, even though the buffers had ostensibly been designed to provide foodstuffs and income-earning opportunities for the local population in order to reduce their cultivation and hunting in the park itself.

One facet of avoiding the ire of the international organizations was the existence of apparently stringent formal conservation regulations. For example, the formal concession process has required a rather elaborate application, negotiation with local communities to determine what share of the timber taxes the communities would receive, and various deposits that the timber companies must provide as bonds for responsible logging (Gartlan 1992, 142–43). Once a concession is awarded, official approval of detailed harvesting plans and continual monitoring are formally required. Indeed, the procedures are so cumbersome that it is not plausible that logging companies would be willing to undertake or adhere to them, nor that the government's underfunded forestry agencies would be capable of enforcing them. Stephen Gartlan, scientific advisor for the World Wide Fund for Nature–UK, has concluded that "the logging companies often cut corners, do not go through all the consultative processes, often exceed quotas and cut undersized trees" (quoted in Vidal 1990, 3). Vidal concludes that

> it's easy to get a concession. Cameroonians only have to put down 5 per cent of their total expected investment and show they have not been to jail. For foreigners it's 20 per cent. When you've got the concession you must then pay 23 Cameroonian francs per year per hectare which amounts to about £8000 a year

for a 40,000 acre patch of virgin primary forest, and because just one log of veneer quality can fetch £1000 in Europe any investment can be recouped by cutting down very few trees. (1990, 3)

The Inefficiency of Capturing Timber Rents from Concessions on Appropriated Land

While the Cameroon government has awarded many logging concessions in appropriated areas, the revenue generation for the government is severely limited by the low royalties on timber harvesting. Combined forest fees constitute only 5 percent of freight-on-board prices for export logs.[28] Simon Rietbergen notes that

> indications that present forest fees and taxes are too low are numerous. For instance, the low taxes on timber volume harvested have encouraged loggers to harvest sapelli of 0.8 m diameter, which is 0.2 m below minimum exploitable diameter, and declare them as being of 1.0 m in diameter to make it appear they have complied with existing regulations. Furthermore, total forest fees are only 3 billion FCFA [Central African Francs], whereas Congolese enterprises pocket 4 billion FCFA yearly for evacuating timber from the south-east of Cameroon (20% of the country's timber exports) via the Pointe-Noire route. (1988, 34)

Moreover, as we have seen in several other cases, the government treasury does not collect royalties or taxes from illegally harvested timber, and some of the forest concessionaires have been seriously in arrears in their tax payments (Franks 1990). One might imagine that low timber rent capture would make a government less interested in expanding concessions. However, when a government is desperate for revenues, the expansion of revenue-yielding concessions, even if at low yields for the central treasury, may well still be attractive. Of course, one might also expect that fiscal authorities would simultaneously look at ways of increasing rent capture, yet this is largely a long-term effort that must entail strengthening forest administration, which is itself difficult to accomplish in the face of fiscal stringency.

The Presumption of State Competence

The Cameroon government has resorted to the common tactic of projecting the benefits of its control on the premise that it can and will enforce its forestry policies and regulations, while projecting the benefits of alternative control on the premise that alternative rights-holders will abuse the forest resources. The essential premise is that the government is more responsible and more capable than the population to husband forest resources. Wherever forest resources seem to be threatened, therefore, the presumption is that state control would improve the outlook for conservation. This presumption, dating back to colonial times, is manifest in the forestry strategy documents and long-term plans written by the Cameroon government.

Given the very poor record of the governments of developing countries in conserving forests under their control, it may seem puzzling that the international organizations and bilateral aid agencies supporting forestry initiatives in Cameroon would not reject the competence premise and put greater pressure on the government to adopt policies consistent with its obviously limited capacities to formulate and enforce forestry policies. Yet it would be very awkward for the international organizations involved directly with the government to challenge the state competency presumption. These organizations depend on the government for most of the implementation of forestry policy. To discount the government's competence in a direct and open way would risk creating breaches with the government and signaling the sometimes problematic nature of relying on the government for implementation.

However, another element of the ideology supporting Cameroon forestry policy is that when illegal or improper logging is noted, the reason is lack of capacity rather than deliberate policy. Joseph Bawak Besong, the Deputy Director of the Cameroon Forestry Department, pointed in 1990 to "over-accessibility to available forests . . . which has lead to overexploitation of these forest areas by both authorized and illegal users."[29] He also notes the failure of logged-over areas to regenerate, because of the government's failure to keep shifting cultivators from using this land; he admits that "more areas were opened up for logging than the forestry service had the personnel and means to supervise" and notes a lack of planning in the selection of sawmill sites (Besong 1992, 37). Yet Besong then identifies the main reason for these problems as "the limited means and information available at the time" (38). Even the policy failures of opening up areas for logging and failing to regulate sawmill siting are attributed to lack of information and capacity to develop sound management plans.

One may also wonder why government officials would risk the government's reputation and the general proposition of government competence in admitting to administrative weaknesses. However, at any point in time, it is possible for government officials to attribute existing administrative weaknesses to the general financial constraints of low-income countries and to past policy oversights and then argue for more international assistance to strengthen forestry administration. Most importantly, the government simply needs to maintain the image of relative competence in comparison with the traditional forest users. As long as the latter are seen as destructive of the forest, usually on the suspect grounds that shifting cultivation is in itself a root cause of deforestation, the government can appeal for support to strengthen its apparent weaknesses while still defending its status as the best resource manager.[30]

The state competence presumption is complemented by another sometimes questionable premise: that the development brought about by roads, settlements, and other infrastructure will improve the material and nonmaterial lives of the people in the "developed" area. This appeal to "economic stewardship" as a rationale for appropriating forest lands dates far back into Cameroon's colonial history under British, French, and German rule.[31] Micro-level studies of the impact of greater contact with modernity through roads and migrant settlements show very mixed results that vary from family to family.[32] Whether each of the many aspects of forest dwellers' lives are improved by closer contact with modern-sector economic activities and incoming settlers will depend on specific circumstances, and the weighing of different aspects (e.g., material wealth vs. cultural preservation) will have a huge impact on one's overall judgment. Yet the Cameroon government, like the governments of most developing countries, presents development projects such as road building as unquestionably capable of bringing higher productivity to the impoverished people living near it. The government has had the concurrence of the official international organizations, including the World Bank and the African Development Bank, in supporting road projects.

Interagency Scrambles

Rietbergen (1988, 26–30) specifies several dimensions of intragovernmental, bureaucratic rivalries and jurisdictional ambiguities in the governance of the Cameroon forestry sector. The definition of forest lands was ambiguous with respect to whether forest fallows should constitute a stage in agricultural production or should revert to public domain, making it unclear whether the Direction des Forêts (DIRFOR) or the Ministry of Agriculture and the myriad agricultural-promotion agencies and state enterprises (such as the Food Development Authority or the export-crop-oriented Cameroon Development Corporation) would be able to assume control. Therefore, as in Brazil and Costa Rica, these agencies all have had an incentive to consolidate their claims on jurisdiction by launching their sponsored activities as rapidly as possible, whether they be logging, agricultural conversion to plantation cash crops, or resettlement of small-scale agriculturalists.

Another institutional-structural problem was the separation of the general oversight for forest management and protection, which was assigned to DIRFOR, from both management plan formulation (in the hands of the National Forestry Development Center) and promotion of afforestation (overseen by the National Reforestation Office). This created an artificial division among planning, expertise and information, and implementation. In 1992 most of the forestry functions were consolidated within the Ministry of Environment and Forestry, although the transfer of authority has been very slow (Zama 1995, 266).

CONCLUSIONS

This chapter has demonstrated that government officials are often willing to distort natural-resource exploitation in order to capture greater revenues for the central treasury. They do this by infringing on private or communal resource rights, manipulating prices so that the government can capture consumer surpluses, and beggaring their own state resource enterprises.

The conflicts between government agencies and state enterprises over who controls natural-resource wealth and related funds often proceed in two stages. The first stage is the capture of control by the state enterprise and its allies in government. Resource rents make the state enterprise not only rich but also politically powerful insofar as it can provide patronage for potential allies in and out of government. The patronage leaves the state enterprise open to charges of corruption, which strengthens the hand of the central budget authorities to assert their control. Once this occurs, the central budget authorities discover that the state enterprise can be squeezed for multiple sources of revenue: oil, mineral, or forest wealth, consumer surpluses, foreign loans, and even foreign aid. The enterprises go from having too much money to use wisely to having too little to operate effectively. Because this grows out of intragovernment conflict, the technical considerations of how to balance the financial resources going to the state resource enterprise and to the central treasury are often swamped by the political battle.

Our cases reveal two political logics for raising revenues at the expense of sound resource exploitation. One logic is to target a particular producer group that lacks enough of its own power, or sympathy from other groups, to resist the capture of its resource-based wealth. In Ghana and Cameroon, the targets were the cocoa farmers and the local forest users, respectively. In Argentina, it was the beef and grain producers, previously quite powerful but clearly weakened and isolated during the Peronist years. In Ethiopia the victims were the peasants who were led to believe that land titles would bring them greater financial security, only to learn that the government could then capture the agricultural wealth that large landlords had previously controlled. These vignettes simply reflect how widespread this approach has been. The political calculation on the part of the government obviously revolves around the question of whether it can get away with a heavy burden on the producer group; the economic question is whether this burden kills off the incentive to produce.

The other logic involves extracting wealth from a much broader segment of the population: for example, all consumers or all future generations. Decapitalizing a state enterprise in order to make immediate use of its financial resources, as in the Venezuelan and Mexican oil cases, has serious costs of forgone economic growth for all. The same holds for output-pricing manipulations, such as the high copper prices in India and many cases that go beyond the scope of this book, such as high-priced petroleum-based fuels in Brazil and India. To be sure, these manipulations affect some more than others, but the government concern that typically leads to these devious forms of revenue raising is that the general population will not tolerate higher conventional taxes. It is telling that governments rarely overcharge for food in developing countries—it is too obvious a threat to the welfare of urban populations, who often can be mobilized to violence. One mystery that remains inadequately explored is why in some countries—including India and Brazil, as well as the Peruvian and Mexican cases that we have examined—oil-based fuel prices can sometimes be raised without violent urban reactions, while in other countries such as Venezuela and Nigeria, violent reactions are so predictable that the governments are often paralyzed.

CHAPTER 7

Conclusions and Recommendations

BROAD LESSONS

Before going into a detailed assessment of the lessons of our cases, and the recommendations that flow out of this assessment, it is useful to summarize the broad results that we can discern in the sum total of the case studies.

Something Really Is Afoot

We have seen how natural-resource exploitation can be badly distorted through government policy failures. It is abundantly clear that the natural-resource policy failures examined in this book are not due to simple ignorance or weak governmental capacity to develop and enforce resource policies. Such interpretations are quickly dispelled by the elaborateness of the manipulations of resource regulations.

Government officials frequently use or allow distorted resource policies to serve as instruments for accomplishing other objectives. I have examined sixteen cases, chosen because of the importance of the resources rather than because they were known to illustrate particular strategies. In all sixteen we have discovered that the three programmatic motives of promoting development initiatives, redistributing wealth, and capturing revenues for the central treasury are clearly at play. Simple blunders and weak capacity are clearly not root causes, even if the policy failures seem at face value to be technical mistakes. Certainly the top government leaders of Indonesia are aware that the commercial loggers are paying too little, that the forests are suffering as a consequence, and that the president can direct some of the loggers' income to his favored projects. Certainly the officials of the Mexican Finance Ministry have long been aware that the state oil company PEMEX has been pushed into debt through high taxes, and that this indebtedness has both enriched the treasury and hampered PEMEX's efficiency. They were also aware for decades that low water charges were destroying the irrigation system. In fact, for all the examples covered in this book, unsound resource policies have been introduced or sustained because they fit the interests of certain government officials to pursue at least one, and often several, of the programmatic strategies. To be sure, the examples were not selected randomly, so it cannot (and in any event would not) be argued that every resource policy failure encountered in developing countries is either intended or deliberately perpetuated. Yet the cases certainly attest to the prevalence of these motives in the exploitation of nationally significant resources. This makes good sense, because the high stakes involved in exploiting a country's most important natural-resource endowments make casual or inadvertent errors most unlikely.

Furthermore, the political strategies of establishing rent-seeking exchanges, evading accountability, and capturing more control over the financial flows are very common. These strategies make the policy failures even worse. They increase the likelihood that resources will be squandered to benefit small groups of powerful people, reduce the visibility of resource-depleting maneuvers, and worsen the infighting among government agencies that shape resource policies and practices.

Resource Exploitation Involves Much More than Resource Rents

We have also discovered that the apparently simple task of converting natural-resource wealth into financial capital is greatly complicated by the fact that so many different sources of wealth may be involved:

- natural-resource rents;
- flows from the central treasury dedicated to resource development;
- consumer surpluses captured by high output prices;
- producer surpluses captured by low prices offered by government;
- borrowed capital; and
- foreign assistance.

State resource exploiters, in particular, face an enormous challenge in dealing with several of these financial sources at the same time. In every case of state resource exploitation encountered in this book, the government agency or state enterprise has been confronted with a financial balancing act that is highly distracting from the main tasks of exploiting natural resources responsibly. Thus, the state oil company PEMEX has been saddled with the role of borrowing for the Mexican government; the perverse pricing policies and unproductive operations of the Indian copper company Hindustan Copper Limited grow out of the scheme to capture consumers' wealth for the central treasury through high copper prices. Similarly, the Cameroon national park authority is not simply creating national parks but also attracting foreign aid and maneuvering property rights so that the treasury can capture more revenues. Chile's state copper company Codelco has had most of its problems in securing investment funds from the central treasury.

The Irresponsibility of State Resource Control

One enormously important conclusion is that government appropriation of natural-resource endowments is generally unlikely to safeguard the resources. Recall that governments typically invoke the conservation motive when they wrest control over natural resources from former owners and users. The obvious premise for believing that conservation would be best served by state control is that private and communal resource exploiters cannot be trusted to use natural resources responsibly. Yet we have seen, time and time again, that influential government officials have many reasons to exploit resources irresponsibly themselves. The fact that state resource exploiters face the difficult distractions of juggling many sources of financial flows is just one part of the explanation for why state resource exploitation has not been the answer to the conservation problem. One can go much farther in arguing that state resource control makes it easier for government officials to engage in the manipulations that result in unsound resource exploitation. Clever policy maneuvers may be able to accomplish officials' objectives at the expense of sound resource exploitation, but direct control simply puts government officials in the position to dictate resource-exploitation practices. We have seen that these directives may be vigorously resisted, sometimes in ways that make resource exploitation even more perverse (e.g., the hasty investments for Venezuela's state oil company to avoid the government's further raids on its investment budget). Nevertheless, the temptations and opportunities to manipulate natural-resource exploitation when resources are under direct government control are very high.

The Weakness of the Equity Rationale

We have also discovered very few instances in which the sacrifice of the efficiency of resource exploitation can be justified by the achievement of greater equity. Of course, it remains true that an efficient economy is not necessarily a fair and equitable one. Yet the one argument in favor of sacrificing efficiency, namely, that institutional limitations leave only inefficient resource exploitation as a way of benefiting needy people, holds for at the most one case among the sixteen examined here. Arguably, the miners of Hindustan copper's money-losing operations are better off than they would be without the mines, even if one could argue that other desperately poor Indians would have benefited more if the wealth squandered through unproductive copper exploitation were devoted to their welfare. Yet in the other cases in which distortions in resource exploitation led to significant transfers of income, the very wealthy (commercial logging-firm owners in Costa Rica, Indonesia, and Malaysia; large-scale ranchers in Brazil; large-scale Mexican farmers) and the relatively well-to-do (the oil labor elite in Mexico and the copper labor elite in Chile) were the clear winners. In all of the cases involving land and forests (Brazil, Cameroon, Costa Rica, Ghana, Honduras, Indonesia, and the Malaysian states of Sabah and Sarawak), the resource manipulations hurt the most economically vulnerable local people, in particular the indigenous people whose user rights were appropriated.

CASE-BY-CASE ANALYSIS

Specific Policy Failures

A wide range of natural-resource policy failures was found among the cases examined in this book:

Country and Sector	Policy Failures
Brazil (land and forests)	credit underpricing; erosion of property rights; insufficient government charges for negative externalities; insufficient incentives for preserving positive externalities; underpricing of outputs (log export ban)
Cameroon (forests)	underpricing of access to forests; erosion of property rights; insufficient government charges for negative externalities
Chile (copper)	early inappropriate use of proceeds; later underexploitation due to undercapitalization
Costa Rica (land and forests)	underpricing of access to forests; erosion of property rights; insufficient government charges for negative externalities; excessive but ineffective government transfers for positive externalities

Country and Sector	Policy Failures
Ghana (cocoa)	underpricing of outputs
Honduras (forests)	early overexploitation; unsound investments; inappropriate use of proceeds; erosion of property rights; insufficient government charges for negative externalities; insufficient incentives for preserving positive externalities
India (copper)	excessive exploitation; overpricing of outputs; unsound investments; undercapitalization of potentially productive new deposits
Indonesia (forests)	underpricing of access to forests; erosion of property rights; insufficient government charges for negative externalities; insufficient incentives for preserving positive externalities; suppression of information; inappropriate use of proceeds; underpricing of outputs (log export ban)
Indonesia (oil)	unsound investments; early underpricing of outputs; inappropriate use of proceeds; failure to minimize costs; lack of accountability
Malaysia: Sabah (forests)	underpricing of access to forests; over-exploitation by state; erosion of property rights; insufficient government charges for negative externalities; insufficient incentives for preserving positive externalities; inappropriate use of proceeds
Malaysia: Sarawak (forests)	underpricing of access to forests; erosion of property rights; insufficient government charges for negative externalities; insufficient incentives for preserving positive externalities
Mexico (oil)	unsound investments; early underpricing of outputs; inappropriate use of proceeds; failure to minimize costs; lack of accountability; later underexploitation due to undercapitalization

Country and Sector	Policy Failures
Mexico (water)	underpricing of water; initial overexploitation; later underexploitation due to under-capitalization
Nigeria (oil)	unsound investments; inappropriate use of proceeds; failure to minimize costs; lack of accountability
Peru (oil)	unsound investments; underexploitation due to undercapitalization
Venezuela (oil)	underexploitation due to undercapitalization; unsound investments

In the forestry and land cases six policy failures are highly prevalent. First, governments do not charge high enough royalties or sales prices for the resources on government lands or for the land itself. Second, they undercharge for negative externalities (such as collateral damage to unharvested trees). Third, they fail to provide effective incentives to preserve forests and other living endowments for the sake of their positive externalities. Fourth, through logging concessions and land giveaways, governments create uncertainty regarding property rights, and they often promote non-viable wood-products industries, sometimes through wasteful state spending. Also, when state entities receive the profits, they often waste the proceeds through overspending and unwise investments that go beyond even the forest sector. Another common pattern is reckless resource development and extraction that occurs when agencies compete for jurisdiction over the same land and resources.

In the oil and mining sectors, six policy failures predominate: very low accountability, unwise investments within the sector, failure to minimize costs by state entities, inappropriate use of proceeds outside of the sector, underexploitation by state entities due to their undercapitalization, and (with the exception of Indian copper) underpricing of outputs when the product has significant domestic sales. It should be noted that the undercapitalization that plagues so many state oil and mining companies does not lead just to undercapitalization and incapacity to respond to high world prices when they occur but also to inefficient exploitation and avoidable environmental damage. The sequencing of policy failures in the oil and mining sectors shows a fairly common pattern of profligate spending and "laundering" that eventually gives way to undercapitalization of state resource enterprises due to rather heavy-handed efforts by fiscal authorities to wrest control of natural-resource rents away from these enterprises and their allies. In several cases, the resource exploiters themselves are provoked into unwise investments and expenditures in order to fend off fiscal authorities' efforts to gain control over the surpluses.

The variations are also revealing. Whereas Mexico, Nigeria, Peru, and Venezuela have sold petroleum products at far below market prices, the Indian copper price has been too high; this can be explained by the obvious fact that the lack of rents in Indian copper exploitation requires either subsidizing copper consumption through the treasury's coverage of the state company's losses or charging higher prices to make the company profitable on paper. The Indian government has used both financing mechanisms over time. In Venezuela the questionable investments came during the period of fiscal authorities' efforts to wrest control over the financial flows, whereas in the other cases, unsound expenditures and investments prompted the fiscal authorities' efforts to take control.

The single water case involving Mexican irrigation bears strong similarities to forest and lands cases, in that the government provided unwarranted subsidies through both its investments and water underpricing, leading to the undercapitalization of the irrigation system and its physical decay. Yet the appropriation of water from those with traditional user rights has not been an issue for many decades (although it certainly is for other water cases, for example, India and Thailand).

The Ghana cocoa case is unusually simple compared to the other cases: forcing cocoa farmers to sell their output at artificially low prices to the government accounts for the disaster in that sector. The case was simple because resource control remained formally in private hands. However, that there was a single policy failure in this case does not diminish the disaster for cocoa farmers and the Ghanaian economy.

Patterns of Improvement

Although I have concentrated on unsound resource policies in order to understand the dynamics of policy failures, the cases do reveal numerous instances of pitfalls avoided and reversals of policy failures:

Country and Sector	Avoidance or Improvement of Policy Failure
(Better overall performance than comparable cases in **boldface**, reversals and reforms in *italic*.)	
Brazil (land and forests)	*elimination of Amazonian subsidies*
Chile (copper)	**wise investment decisions compared to other oil and mining state enterprises**

Country and Sector	Avoidance or Improvement of Policy Failure
Costa Rica (land and forests)	*elimination of reforestation subsidies*
Ghana (cocoa)	*reduction in unusually high cocoa taxes*
Honduras (forests)	*reduction in harvest rate; elimination of downstream emphasis*
Indonesia (forests)	*occasional increases in timber royalties*
Indonesia (oil)	*drastic reduction in state off-budget manipulations; greater accountability*
Malaysia: Sabah (forests)	**avoided log export bans; avoided low royalties**
Malaysia: Sarawak (forests)	**avoided log export bans**
Mexico (oil)	*drastic reduction in state off-budget manipulations; greater accountability; increase in output pricing*
Mexico (water)	*increase in water pricing*
Peru (oil)	*reduction in state off-budget manipulations; increase in output pricing*
Venezuela (oil)	**high relative efficiency and cost minimization**

These cases tell us something about how reform comes about. In some cases the reversal of unsound policies and practices came only after it was patently obvious that the policy could not even achieve its other objectives. For example, the ranching and resettlement subsidies in the Brazilian Amazon were not terminated because of their gratuitous damage to the forests, but rather because so many of the ranches and small-scale farms failed. Similarly, the profligate borrowing and spending of Indonesia's state oil company Pertamina in the early 1970s ended only after the country was brought to the edge of bankruptcy, making it impossible to continue Pertamina's off-budget investments. In Peru the distributive rationales for low domestic fuel prices became too costly when Peru ceased to be a significant oil exporter. Even so, it is noteworthy that even in these cases the increasing visibility of the damage done by faulty policy helped push the government into the policy reversal.

In other cases, unsound resource policies were reversed when the tide of market-oriented liberal economic thinking rose high enough to make government officials sufficiently intolerant of egregious price distortions. In Mexico the prior near-collapse of the irrigation system was not enough to precipitate the reforms until the ideology of attending to market forces and cost recovery gained enough strength in the late 1980s. Mexican fuel prices were also brought much more closely in line with international prices only when the government experienced a radical shift from its previous statist perspective on energy pricing.

Unsound policies are sometimes reversed when the officials responsible for the policies, and their agencies, are defeated in partisan or bureaucratic politics. The early policy failures of excessive spending and lack of accountability of Chile's copper company and Mexico's oil company were reversed when the companies and their allies were defeated by budget authorities — although the undercapitalization that followed was also a policy failure. In the Mexican irrigation sector, the subsidies for large farmers were cut back when administrations favoring small farmers came to power, and vice versa, although the use of water subsidies for both objectives relied on the same policy failure of underpricing water.

Other patterns provide insights into how the policy failures can be avoided in the first place. In Chile and India the state copper enterprises have avoided the large-scale failures of accountability that have plagued other state oil and mining companies,[1] reflecting the general professionalism of public institutions in those countries and the effectiveness of monitoring institutions. In Chile the chaos within government during the Allende years (1970–73) was the exception, not the rule, and the state copper company Codelco has paid dearly for its failure to fulfill its function of ensuring the government its revenues from copper exploitation. In Venezuela, despite the problematic management of many government agencies and state enterprises, the state oil company PDVSA has maintained much of the professionalism established by the multinational oil companies that preceded PDVSA. In short, competence, accountability, and professionalism within the public sector, the industry, or both can mitigate against state abuses.

EVALUATION OF TRADEOFFS

The findings summarized above provide some insights into the costs and benefits of government reliance on the natural-resource exploitation process for the pursuit of other objectives. When political and institutional factors preclude the theoretically optimal approach of pursuing these other objectives apart from the productive process, we must weigh the costs of unsound resource exploitation against the potential gains with respect to these other objectives.

Considerations of Efficiency

The efficiency concerns prevalent in this book have obviously focused on natural-resource exploitation. Yet there is another notion of efficiency that emerges from many of the cases: how well these other objectives are served by relying on natural-resource maneuvers to pursue them. In other words, given that sound resource exploitation is often sacrificed in order to pursue other objectives, we may also ask how well these other objectives are achieved through maneuvers in the resource sectors. Does this success make up for the waste of natural resources?

The general answer is that the pursuit of these other objectives has been highly inefficient. We have seen in many cases that the resource rents and other funds are first diverted from their proper paths in the resource-exploitation process, but they are then diverted again from the objectives of the government officials responsible for the original manipulation. In Indonesia, for example, President Suharto was able to direct significant funds into the political projects and economic activities he has targeted for investment by the private loggers. Yet these loggers also retained billions of dollars, some of which have been removed from the Indonesian economy because of the perfectly understandable desire of the loggers to diversify their wealth and reduce the possibility of future confiscation. Recall also that in Cameroon the quasi-taxation strategy of appropriating forest lands to the state and then leasing them to commercial loggers brought in quite low revenues, because of low royalty rates. In other instances, particularly when state enterprises are involved in resource manipulations, the resource extractors who face losing control over resource rents have their own capacity to reduce the funds that the government officials are trying to divert. For example, hasty overseas investments that the Venezuelan oil company PDVSA made in the mid-1980s kept a large part of its investment fund out of government hands. State enterprises set on development tasks, such as the Indonesian oil company Pertamina, the Mexican oil company PEMEX, the Sabah Foundation in Malaysia, and the Honduran forestry enterprise COHDEFOR, have squandered resources to achieve their own goals of aggrandizement, falling far short of the development goals for which natural resources were sacrificed.

One problem that governments face in pursuing other objectives through natural-resource exploitation is that the actors who collaborate with them through access to the various financial flows often can create leakages for their own personal or institutional benefit. The Mexican government certainly succeeded in using PEMEX as a magnet for foreign borrowing and thus a means of taxing future generations for the sake of immediate consumption, and yet some of these resources leaked away through PEMEX's corruption and inefficiency. If the remoteness of the resources is an advantage for the government officials in obscuring the abuses of natural resources for the sake of other goals, it is also a disadvantage for the government officials in controlling their agents, whether in the state or private sectors. Thus, President Suharto could rely on the private-sector logging concessionaires to finance some of his favorite projects, but he could not know just how much illegal logging, removal of capital to overseas havens, and other maneuvers were undertaken by the concessionaires.

On the other side, the actors who oppose the maneuvers by a particular set of government officials are also likely to take actions that diminish the effectiveness of pursuing objectives through natural-resource exploitation. The hasty investments by Venezuela's state oil company PDVSA, the abandonment of cocoa farms by disillusioned Ghanaian farmers, and even the forest fires set by Honduran farmers in revenge for the government's appropriation of forest rights have all sapped the effectiveness of the governments' strategies.

In sum, the effectiveness and efficiency of directing financial resource flows through natural-resource exploitation maneuvers seem quite compromised. This makes it all the more dubious that unsound natural-resource exploitation is a fair price to pay for pursuing other objectives.

The Principle of Accountability

Yet some might still argue that despite the inefficiency of pursuing other objectives through unsound natural-resource policies, and the rarity of accomplishing progressive distribution through such policies, circumventing government officials through resource maneuvers is sometimes defensible because of the irresponsibility, malintent, or otherwise reprehensible characteristics of these officials. For example, what if the officials controlling the central budget process are not serving the people, or what if they are highly responsive to the public, but the public (or at least the public that counts politically) is eager to create economic injustices or squander the nation's wealth? One often hears appeals from admirable agency officials that they would like to help neglected groups, clean up the environment, pursue worthy development projects, or keep some financial resources away from the pressure groups that often seem to dominate the budget outcomes, if only they had a way to wrest control over some resources from the central budget authorities.

Our cases reveal that while it is true that the central budget process can produce outcomes that a particular observer may regard as horrible, this is a risk to both conventional budgetary allocation and off-budget subsidization. We certainly have no way of knowing, a priori, whether the scoundrels who wish to manipulate off-budget slush funds are better or worse than the scoundrels who wish to manipulate the central budget for objectionable ends. The one thing we do know is that the latter type of scoundrel is more likely to be taken to task for his or her sins. Short of judging each official and each policy, the most that can be done is to suggest arrangements wherein bad or selfish decisions are more likely to be punished. The central budgeting process is clearly superior in this respect. Moreover, if an open, fully debated, transparent budget fight among popularly elected representatives yields a bad budget, the reforms necessary to turn the situation around are much deeper (including probably fundamental changes in political attitudes and possibly in the nature of representation) than any fiscal manipulations could accomplish.

Motives of Policy Failures

Programmatic Motives

The most basic finding regarding the dynamics behind these policy failures is that in every case examined here, natural-resource policy failures have served identifiable programmatic objectives and preferences of important government officials. The variety of motives is quite striking.

Country and Sector	Programmatic Objectives or Preferences
Brazil (land and forests)	national security, regional development
Cameroon (forests)	foreign assistance inflows, tax revenues
Chile (copper)	income redistribution
Costa Rica (land and forests)	income redistribution (largely temporal)
Ghana (cocoa)	tax revenues
Honduras (forests)	downstream industrialization
India (copper)	income redistribution, national security, regional development, tax revenues
Indonesia (forests)	industrial development, downstream industry
Indonesia (oil)	industrial development
Malaysia: Sabah (forests)	industrial development, downstream industrialization, social services
Malaysia: Sarawak (forests)	income redistribution

Country and Sector	Programmatic Objectives or Preferences
Mexico (oil)	income redistribution, industrial development, tax revenues
Mexico (water)	agricultural development, income redistribution
Nigeria (oil)	income redistribution, industrial development, national security
Peru (oil)	national security, regional development, tax revenues
Venezuela (oil)	industrial development, tax revenues

Common Political Motives

In addition to these programmatic and often explicit objectives, three other motivations of a more generic, political nature are present in most cases.

Control of Exploitation Patterns and Resource Flows

First, the motivation to gain control over the resource flows constitutes a "meta-motive," inasmuch as having discretion is necessary to pursue the programmatic objectives. Moreover, controlling how the natural-resource base is exploited and the relevant financial flows is also the essence of institutional strength and standing for many of the agencies involved. The struggles within government to gain or maintain control over resource flows have led to many natural-resource policy failures:

Country and Sector	Policy Failures Due to Conflict over Flow Control
Brazil (land and forests)	reckless land allocation and subsidies due to agencies' competition for jurisdiction over land
Cameroon (forests)	reckless land allocation and subsidies due to agencies' competition for jurisdiction over land
Chile (copper)	undercapitalization when fiscal authorities rein in the state enterprise; unwise expenditures and investments by state enterprise to maintain control

Country and Sector	Policy Failures Due to Conflict over Flow Control
Costa Rica (land and forests)	reckless land allocation and subsidies due to agencies' competition for jurisdiction over land
Honduras (forests)	reckless land allocation and subsidies due to agencies' competition for jurisdiction over land
India (copper)	undercapitalization due to fiscal authorities' efforts to rein in the state enterprise
Indonesia (forests)	underpricing of timber to circumvent fiscal authorities' control over resource rents
Indonesia (oil)	reckless borrowing to evade limits imposed by fiscal authorities
Malaysia: Sabah (forests)	overharvesting by quasi-governmental Sabah Foundation to fund off-budget spending beyond control by national or state fiscal authorities
Mexico (oil)	undercapitalization when fiscal authorities rein in the state enterprise; unwise expenditures and investments by state enterprise to maintain control
Mexico (water)	water underpricing due to competition over agricultural development and incomes strategies
Peru (oil)	undercapitalization when fiscal authorities rein in the state enterprise; unwise expenditures and investments by enterprise to maintain control
Venezuela (oil)	undercapitalization when fiscal authorities rein in the state enterprise; unwise expenditures and investments by the state enterprise to maintain control

Rent-seeking

The second highly prevalent pattern is the creation of rent-seeking opportunities that permit government officials to gain the political support and policy cooperation of key actors outside of government. Here I distinguish the creation of rent-seeking opportunities for specific individuals, firms, or organizations from the programmatic objective of income distribution for significant segments of the population (e.g., urban dwellers, small farmers, mineworkers, people of particular regions). The creation of rent-seeking opportunities is often a matter of tactics to elicit support and cooperation rather than a programmatic policy objective in its own right.[2]

The creation of rent-seeking opportunities at the expense of sound natural-resource exploitation arises for at least three reasons. First, government officials may offer rent-seeking opportunities in order to enlist the cooperation of state or extra-governmental actors in pursuit of ulterior objectives. In exchange for actions that help the policymaker accomplish programmatic goals, the extra-governmental actors receive benefits as rewards and incentives. Second, the financial flows with which the state or extra-governmental actors are involved may give them the opportunity to capture some of the surplus. Consider the Indonesian Chinese loggers, who help the so-called nationalists accomplish development objectives through their own investments but also keep a portion of the timber rents that passes to them because of the low timber royalty rates. Similarly, many wealthy Brazilians who received government subsidies to establish ranches in the Amazon added to their wealth even though their ranches failed; in many cases part of the subsidy was diverted from the ranching ventures. Government machinations to allocate oil rents outside of the central budget in Indonesia, Mexico, and Nigeria, which involved low transparency and accountability, gave state officials the opportunity to capture rents for the enterprises and often for personal aggrandizement. Third, programmatic distribution often drifts into rent-seeking. Even if subsidies or other special treatments are designed for a broad segment of potential beneficiaries, the best-connected actors often end up with the bulk of the benefits. Recall that despite the invocation of poverty alleviation to justify the overextension and low water prices of the Mexican irrigation system, these subsidies often benefited the most politically powerful large-scale farmers in each irrigation district.

The prevalence of rent-seeking that distorts resource exploitation in countries governed by authoritarian regimes is very striking. One might assume that subsidies and resource giveaways would be a vice of democratic governments desperate to win electoral support, as in the cases of Costa Rica and Sarawak. Authoritarian governments (the Brazilian military and the Suharto administration in Indonesia, for example) seemed equally eager to use unsound resource policies to enrich particular groups in order to gain their political cooperation, even when elections have been absent or insignificant.

Evasion of Accountability

The third common, if not universal, motive is to reduce the political costs of pursuing ulterior objectives and of abusing natural resources to do so. Policymakers intent on pursuing controversial objectives, such as building petrochemical plants when the economic analysis indicates that they would be moneylosers, are potentially vulnerable to criticism. Resource exploitation is sometimes the "cover story," as in the case of oil exploration in the Peruvian Amazon geared partially to subsidize the military, that achieves the objective so circuitously that the officials' accountability is minimized. This helps to explain why the path of distorting the natural-resource exploitation process is so often chosen. In the cases of underpriced timber on government-controlled land, neither the inadequacy of the timber royalty nor the fact that the privileged logging concessionaires are prepared to help their allies within the government has been readily apparent to the general population. In the cases of state exploitation of oil and minerals, the site selections for exploration, production, and processing have not been easy to condemn as suboptimal without a large amount of technical information. This is also true of the schemes involving resource development (Costa Rican and Indonesian reforestation programs, the establishment of ranches in Brazil and Costa Rica) and downstream processing (Honduran timber, Indonesian timber, Nigerian oil, Sabah timber).

In addition to choosing the natural-resource exploitation process because of the low transparency of these maneuvers, further policy failures have been introduced in order to reduce accountability even more. Reducing awareness of the maneuvers by suppressing information, as in the minimal reporting requirements for timber companies in Indonesia, or by making financial transactions and accounting so opaque that monitoring becomes virtually impossible, as in the cases of the Nigerian and Mexican oil companies, has its own costs in reducing the accountability of state agents and increasing the uncertainty of everyone involved in resource exploitation. Another tactic for evading accountability has been to distract attention away from contestable distributional implications of resource policies by invoking politically popular rationales of secondary significance. The appeals to national security (Indian copper, Indonesian and Nigerian oil), conservation (Cameroon, Costa Rican, and Indonesian forests),[3] and poverty alleviation (Mexican water and Sabah's forests) have obscured the damage to natural-resource endowments caused by the policies rationalized by these appeals.

Understanding "Motives"

In tracing out how deviations from sound resource policies help certain government officials achieve other objectives, the issue inevitably arises as to whether the officials consciously intended to manipulate resource exploitation in order to pursue these objectives. Ascribing conscious intent to the adoption of poor policies obviously runs the risk of cynicism, which in turn implies that little can be done about policy failures because officials are too self-serving, ruthless, or indifferent toward the natural-resource endowment to care. It also runs the risk of depicting government officials as more Machiavellian — and clever — then they really are. The reality is much more complex: our cases reveal a complicated set of intended and unintended outcomes.

In some cases, actions leading to destructive resource exploitation were taken with the clear intent to achieve other objectives. For example, the increasingly onerous burden on Ghanaian cocoa farmers was imposed for no other reason than to fill government coffers, and it is hardly plausible that government officials did not know that the farmers' shrinking incomes were a risk to the continued viability of the cocoa sector. The gifts of logging concessions to unqualified individuals in Sarawak, the overpricing of Indian copper, and the domestic underpricing of gasoline and other petroleum products in the oil-exporting countries were all undertaken with widespread understanding that these actions would distort resource exploitation.

In other cases the policymakers must have known that experts had warned of the unsoundness of the policies with respect to natural-resource exploitation, but whether the policymakers fully appreciated or believed the warnings is difficult to ascertain. Thus, the Brazilian military leadership, under the sway of an interventionist, statist ideology that generated considerable optimism in the capacity of a military-led transformation of the economy, may have initially dismissed the risks of heavy subsidization as unwarranted negativism. However, this reaction became increasingly untenable as evidence of land abandonment mounted. One may also argue that the governments of Brazil, Honduras, and Indonesia did not appreciate the highly negative consequences of appropriating huge forest tracts under state control.

In yet other cases, policies became unsound with the passage of time. First, new information sometimes emerged that revealed serious problems of a policy that had been sound on the basis of pre-existing information. In the Indian copper case, the initial assessments of the ore grades at Khetri were much greater than the actual ore grades turned out to be. Second, changing economic conditions can make initially sound policies into unsound policies, especially when inflation changes the significance of nominal prices. In the oil cases, low fuel price levels, designed to spur energy-intensive industry and to benefit urban consumers, became even lower in real terms in the face of inflation. In the Ghanaian cocoa case, government prices did start out at fair levels for the farmers and only later deteriorated in the face of inflation. The policy failure was in not adjusting the farmgate price in reaction to real-price changes. In all of the forestry cases, inflation certainly has exacerbated the underpricing of timber. However, none of our forestry cases shows evidence that royalty and taxation rates were ever close to the full stumpage value.

In short, many resource-policy failures occur when government officials learn that they can take advantage of an emerging or growing policy failure in order to pursue other objectives. The problem, therefore, is not so much that officials initiate policies and practices that intentionally distort resource exploitation in order to accomplish other ends, but that they maintain these policies and practices even when their consequences prove to be unsound for resource exploitation.

The Prevalence of Multiple Motives

Although the case studies have been organized in chapters to highlight how each major programmatic motive (development-strategy financing, distribution, and revenue collection) drives natural-resource policy distortions, multiple motives are the rule rather than the exception. The multiplicity of objectives arises for several reasons. Sometimes the officials try to pursue several objectives at the same time through manipulations of natural-resource exploitation. We have seen that even when development objectives are pursued, some petty rent-seeking and even more massive redistribution are often present. Indeed, some development strategies that favor a particular sector or region would qualify almost automatically as distributive as well as developmental. We have also seen, for example, in the Hindustan Copper Limited case, that an alliance can be forged among officials concerned with taxation and officials interested in distribution (and even national defense).

A special case of multiple motives arises when a politically popular objective is invoked to justify a resource policy or practice that is truly motivated by another objective. Of course, it is not always possible to determine which motive is the driving force when the same action pursues several objectives. However, in several of our cases the popular objectives have been specious, as indicated by the questionable linkages between the policy and the objective, or by later events that reveal that the actions did not further these objectives. For example, the Indonesian Forestry Ministry's "reforestation fund" was certainly not dedicated to reforestation, and the national security appeal of subsidizing Indian copper production was suspect both on practical grounds (India could have stockpiled copper much more cheaply than producing it) and because the Defense Ministry was not definitively involved in making the decision.

A third and crucial scenario for multiple objectives comes about when different officials and agencies have conflicting motives. Indeed, the core of my argument is that the conflict among motivations held by different government and state officials lies at the root of many natural-resource abuses, in that faulty resource exploitation is the means by which some officials either circumvent the opposition of others or try to reduce the conflict within the government and state. And, of course, even if many government officials believe that resource exploitation can be sacrificed for other objectives, someone in government will — and certainly should — defend the objective of efficient and equitable resource exploitation.

The prevalence of multiple motives is significant not only because of its implications for conflict but also because of the ambiguity that surrounds resource policy deliberations in so many cases. It becomes very difficult to answer such questions as Is the resource depletion caused by policy X justified by objective A? Should the agency's emphasis be so strongly oriented toward achieving objective A rather than its other objectives? What is the optimal policy when objectives A, B, and C are all affected in different ways? When these questions cannot be definitively answered, the accountability of government officials declines, inasmuch as their performance cannot be easily evaluated.

Common Transition Patterns in Dominant Motives

Although many cases reveal simultaneous motives of distribution, development financing, and revenue collection, it is also common to see shifts in the dominance of one motive to another, as different factions within the government succeed in controlling the flows of natural and financial resources.

For state resource exploitation in the oil and mining sectors, the most common pattern revealed by our cases is the transformation of state enterprises from accomplices in off-budget financing to undercapitalized victims of the budget authorities' efforts to tax and control. Chile's state copper company and the oil companies of Mexico, Peru, and Venezuela were initially beyond the control of the budget authorities, but eventually, as sound public finance theory requires, the Finance Ministry officials prevailed.

Unfortunately, these officials clamped down on the enterprises' discretion and investment budgets so vigorously that their control has severely weakened the enterprises' capacity to pursue resource extraction in a timely and efficient manner.

In the sustainable resources cases, a strangely obverse pattern often holds. The government first took control of the resources, giving it the capacity to control the resource rents. Yet the state apparatus created by the government to control the resource then initiated activities, such as downstream processing, that destroyed rents or diverted them from the government coffers. The initial appropriation of lands by the governments of Brazil, Honduras, Indonesia, Sabah, and Sarawak would seem at first glance to mean vast enrichment for the central treasuries. Instead, the resource rents were dissipated through poor investments and simple rent-seeking. Of course, part of the reason for these diversions was the motivation of top government officials to favor particular groups or development projects.

Institutional Roots of Natural-Resource Policy Failures

These patterns of failures and reforms provide several insights into the relationships between institutional structures and the soundness of natural-resource policies and practices.

Disunity

The relationship between disunity within government and resorting to maneuvers that abuse natural resources emerges as particularly strong. First, we must recognize that certain institutional arrangements within governments make it difficult to resolve intragovernmental conflicts in priorities; as a consequence, government officials are moved to circumvent the opposition of other officials through natural-resource maneuvers. We have seen from our cases that intragovernmental conflicts arise and persist because of four conditions.

Lack of Clarity in Land-Use Jurisdictions

The opportunities for greater agency power and standing induce several agencies to compete for control. Clashing motives among government agencies, if left unresolved by compromise or by judgment of jurisdiction imposed by higher authority, often put resource bases into "open access" status, which provokes hasty and reckless resource exploitation not only by private exploiters but also by state and governmental actors. In Brazil, Costa Rica, and Honduras conflicts among land reform agencies, forestry agencies, infrastructure agencies, and agencies defending indigenous rights induced unsound resource extraction and land conversions.[4] These countries lack a tradition of cabinet-level or legislative resolution of such jurisdictional disputes.

Lack of Clear and Consensual Assertions of Scientific or Technical Judgment

Governments may be deterred from pursuing particular resource-exploitation approaches if they and the public are told in no uncertain terms that the approaches are technically unsound, and yet this happens surprisingly rarely. The scientific community is often an unwitting accomplice to the government's excuse that there is no scientific agreement on technical issues of land-use classification, soil assessments, regeneration of renewable resources, optimal extraction rates of nonrenewable resources, downstream industrialization, and a host of other issues on which experts share enough consensus on what are clearly unsound policies even if they do not agree on all matters. Of course, there is always a degree of scientific disagreement, but the scientific community often allows this to convey an impression that generally high scientific and technical uncertainty prevails, and therefore one policy is just as plausible as another. The questionable soil quality of the Amazon, the problematic list of tree species permitted under the Costa Rican reforestation scheme, ambiguous and conflicting land classification schemes in Brazil, Cameroon, Costa Rica, Honduras, and Indonesia, the unlikely success of downstream wood-products processing in countries with very poor processing facilities (such as Honduras, Indonesia, and Malaysia), and the dubious contribution of copper production to Indian national defense were not emphasized by respected experts to pose enough embarrassment to government officials for pursuing these courses. Especially when popular objectives are invoked to justify unsound resource policies, the lack of healthy skepticism expressed by the scientific community (both in the natural sciences and the social sciences, including, of course, economics) has often allowed questionable schemes to go largely unchallenged.

Absence of Intragovernmental Transparency

The basic strategy of circumventing intragovernmental opposition often depends on the difficulty of opposing officials to get rival information to recognize and react effectively to these maneuvers. This is true for both resource exploitation patterns (e.g., the early excessive logging promoted by COHDEFOR in Honduras, or the settlement of farmers on poor soils in Brazil) and financial strategies (e.g., Pertamina's financial manipulations prior to Indonesia's 1975 debt crisis probably would not have been allowed to go on for so long if the Finance Ministry had better information).

Political Culture That Prevents the Resolution of Intragovernmental Policy Conflicts

While intragovernmental disunity seems to be a key institutional factor in provoking maneuvers that rely on unsound resource policies, it is a peculiar form of intragovernmental conflict that is not so severe or open that it comes to a head and forces top government leadership to resolve it. It typically revolves around differences in objectives that, for various reasons, government officials do not want to bring to public attention. It thrives where open conflict within government is politically, ideologically, or culturally unacceptable, but officials can fight silent battles against other priorities and agencies.

The Virtues of Disunity

We must acknowledge, however, that divisions within government may be crucial for natural-resource policy reform. For almost all natural-resource policy failures, some government agencies and individual officials have reason to oppose the unsound policies. Sometimes this is because the policy failures divert resource control away from these actors; sometimes it is because of commitment to sound policy. It is important to note, for example, that Finance Ministry officials in Indonesia have been among the staunchest allies with environmental groups for charging appropriate royalties for timber harvesting; the higher royalties would give the central budget authorities more resources and more control. In India the Ministry of Industry favors eliminating the very costly price supports for copper, for the obvious reason that it would help Indian industry not to have to pay inflated copper prices. This general pattern of opposition within government means that extra-governmental actors who wish to influence government policy can usually find allies within government.

Finally, it is very important to note that the problem of resource distortions emerging from intragovernmental disunity is not resolved through dictatorship. Disunity is not simply a matter of democratic squabbling, although one might expect coalition governments to harbor more differences in priorities and development perspectives on the cabinet level than would a "strong man" government. The Brazilian, Nigerian, and Peruvian military governments and the Suharto government in Indonesia provide ample proof that nondemocratic governments have their share of intra-governmental rivalries and infighting.

Ambiguous and Muddled Mandates

Many of the cases involve ambiguous and muddled mandates of both agencies and policies. When agencies are mandated to pursue several, sometimes conflicting, objectives, their prioritizing of objectives is often inconsistent and self-serving. Honduras's COHDEFOR has neglected conservation and poverty alleviation objectives to concentrate on pine-forest exploitation, which is the backbone of the enterprise's budget. Hindustan Copper Limited and the Indian Mining Ministry have maintained high levels of copper production to address employment and national security objectives, at the expense of what many consider to be the most important mission of a copper-producing state enterprise: to produce copper efficiently.

When an agency or enterprise has a complicated mandate, its responsibilities become muddled as well. If an agency or enterprise is to pursue different objectives that are under the jurisdiction of several ministries, ambiguity prevails as to which ministry is the true master of the agency or enterprise. Agency or enterprise officials may be paralyzed knowing that any action will disappoint one ministry or another, or they may be clever enough to play one off against the other and avoid control by any ministry (Aharoni 1982).

Ambiguous mandates also leave little chance for a technical assessment of whether the policies are optimal and therefore little accountability. Is the conservation of existing forests worth the lower rate of forest development and the poverty of families with traditional user rights in the forest? Is Costa Rican reforestation, albeit limited, worth the destruction of natural forest and the loss of revenues for the central treasury? Is the sustainability of pine harvesting in Honduras worth the loss of biodiversity and the neglect of low-income forest dwellers? The typical agency or enterprise mandate is currently structured in ways that make these questions extremely difficult to answer in a definitive fashion.

Lack of Internalization of Damage or Benefits

Many cases also involve incomplete internalization of the costs of poor policy on the part of the responsible politicians and administrators. For example, forest depletion and environmental degradation do not typically impinge upon leaders and subordinates in forestry agencies, any more than they impinge directly or obviously on other citizens besides those who depend directly on the forests, particularly low-income forest users who often lack a voice within the political system. The displacement of the indigenous peoples in Indonesia, Malaysia, Brazil, and Honduras hardly impinges upon the officials responsible for their travails, even if the officials are personally sympathetic with their plight.

The dilemma is that requiring agencies to internalize the costs of their actions could be addressed by assigning an agency with responsibility to deal comprehensively with both its programs and their consequences. For example, for Honduras this would imply that the state forestry enterprise would be responsible not only for harvesting timber but also for maintaining the ecosystems of the areas where harvesting is undertaken. If the agency and its leadership could be rewarded or deprived according to the quality of its conservation programs, as well as its performance as a timber exploiter, then the agency could find an appropriate balance. In the very special circumstances of a top leadership that is ideologically committed to balance, such an approach could conceivably work. However, without this ideological commitment, a multiple mandate is likely to provoke a policy approach that sacrifices one or more objectives for the sake of the objective that serves the agency and its officials best. Experience shows quite clearly that agencies with multiple-objective mandates tend to put much greater emphasis on the objectives that most strongly enhance the agency's standing and resources.

Government-State Enterprise Arrangements

Another set of institutional problems relates to the arrangements between governments and their state enterprises in the natural-resource sectors. We have seen in the cases of Chile, India, Mexico, Nigeria, Peru, and Venezuela that major tensions emerge between the state enterprise officials and certain government officials over a host of issues: wage levels, employment levels, scope of diversification, investment prerogatives, transparency, facility location, foreign borrowing, the reporting and approval processes, availability of foreign exchange, and taxation. It is striking how deeply the issue of control over rents is at the heart of these disputes. It is even more striking that the egregious resource practices that seem at first glance to be the doing of the state enterprises are compelled by strategies of top government officials, with which the enterprises either collude — seen most obviously in the cases of Mexican oil during the López Portillo administration and the Ghanaian Cocoa Marketing Board during Nkrumah's administration — or conflict (as seen in the struggles of the Chilean copper company and the Venezuelan oil company with their respective finance ministries).

The government's capacity to judge the effectiveness of state enterprise resource management is also hampered by the misleading information that the typical accounting and fiscal-transfer arrangements impart. The typical accounting system for state oil or mining enterprises defines the difference between revenues and operating and financing costs as "profit" but does not subtract the preprocessed, intrinsic value of the resource (i.e., the resource rent) as a cost.

Many government officials dismiss the importance of charging the state enterprise for the resource rent, on the grounds that the central treasury will eventually capture the rent through the profits tax or dividends from the enterprise to its "owner," the government. However, the behavior of the state enterprise under these scenarios is likely to be quite different. If the enterprise officials are trying to pursue profit and are not charged for the resource rent, then they will opt to exploit resources beyond the point where the full marginal costs of exploitation (including the cost of the resource itself) exceed marginal gains. The result is overexploitation from the perspective of society, even though the enterprise will show a higher profit when overexploiting. If the enterprise officials are interested in high spending for the aggrandizement of the enterprise, themselves, or workers within the enterprise, then the failure to charge for the resource rent will protect them from appearing to be as inefficient as they really are. In short, by failing to charge the enterprise for the resource rent, the government provides a perverse incentive for the enterprise to increase the rent extraction and puts these resources into the hands of the enterprise. As we have seen in Chilean copper, Honduran forestry, and all of the state oil company cases, exploitation proceeds without taking into account the costs of depletion, apparent profits can mask serious inefficiencies, and the enterprises can channel the rents to myriad purposes without full accountability.

Lack of Enforcement Capability

The weak capacity of the government to enforce natural-resource regulations and guard against illegal exploitation is an obvious factor in many of the cases reviewed. In every case of land and forest use, illegal extraction and failure to abide by conservation regulations reduce the costs to the resource exploiter and induce overexploitation, while failing to make the exploiter internalize the costs of resource depletion and pollution. Even when the exploiter is a state institution, whether an oil or mining company of Chile, India, Mexico, Nigeria, and Venezuela or a state forestry enterprise in Honduras and Malaysia, weak government monitoring and enforcement permits pollution and reckless exploitation.

It is important to keep in mind that apparently weak enforcement "capacity" is as much a choice as a "given," and lack of enforcement capability is often part of the strategy of resource maneuvers. For example, in Costa Rica the quiet depletion of so much of the forests outside of the national park system during the 1980s and early 1990s was hastened by minimal oversight and enforcement by the Dirección General Forestal (DGF). Yet instead of regarding the DGF's weakness as an inevitable feature of the Costa Rican government, we should recognize that the Costa Rican executive and legislature chose to deny the DGF sufficient budget even to pay for gasoline for forest guards to drive through the forest. The budgets for the national parks were more reasonable in terms of the capacity of park guards to enforce land uses.

RECOMMENDATIONS

The patterns summarized above point to many paths for improving the exploitation of natural resources. The following recommendations are directed to government officials who wish to prevent current or future government officials and state managers from sacrificing the soundness of resource exploitation, activists who can mobilize public support for such reforms, and officials of bilateral and international institutions that have some impact on policy reforms in the relevant countries. The fact that some government officials may intend to sacrifice resource-exploitation soundness for other objectives does not mean that they will necessarily have their way, even if they are chiefs of state. Prior arrangements, public outcry, and adverse reactions by international institutions can raise the political or economic costs too high. Other officials may be in a position to block their actions, especially if the structures of natural-resource policymaking reveal policy failures for what they are.

Restoring Nongovernmental Resource Control

Turning first to the fundamental question of who controls natural resources, it is clear that government appropriation of natural-resource control has not been a solution to the problem of unsound resource exploitation, and in many instances the restoration of private or communal re-source ownership has strong potential to improve resource management. Of course, the soundness of private and communal resource management is a very complicated issue; sometimes nongovernmental resource manage-ment produces good results and sometimes disasters. This is partly because of the fact that private and communal resource exploiters can be short-sighted and incompetent; and even when the government does not directly control natural-resource exploitation, its policy influences on nongovern-mental exploitation can distort the incentives of private and communal resource exploiters. Therefore, shifting to private or communal resource exploitation may not solve the problem of governmental machinations that end up abusing natural resources, as the cases of Indonesian and Costa Rican forestry, Ghanaian cocoa, and Brazilian ranching painfully illustrate. In all of these cases, private resource control did not save natural resources from damage by perverse resource policies.

Nevertheless, private and communal resource exploitation has several advantages in terms of the factors found to be related to resource abuse. First, having nongovernmental actors involved in the system of resource policy and resource exploitation may increase the public's awareness of gov-ernment efforts to manipulate resource exploitation. It is often the closed loop of state resource exploitation, in which only government and state-enterprise officials have access to in-depth information, that allows govern-ment officials to engage in blatant manipulations with little transparency.

Second, this combination of nongovernmental resource exploitation and governmental regulation has greater potential to address negative spill-over effects in a serious fashion. When a governmental or state institution is both exploiter and regulator, the regulatory effort is often weakened by intragovernmental agreement that enriching the state is worth disregard-ing the environment or by intragovernmental conflict between the ministry overseeing the state resource-exploiting agency and the ministry in charge of the environment. In the case of nongovernmental resource exploitation, in many instances the regulatory agency would have fewer qualms about enforcing environmental regulations and less intragovernmental opposi-tion to doing so.

Third, nongovernmental resource exploiters have greater intrinsic in-centive to care about long-term sustainability of resource exploitation, as long as the policy environment does not force them into short time hori-zons. While some progress can be made to get public officials to care about long-term consequences of resource policies and practices (as we will see), the arrangements necessary to accomplish this progress are very often difficult to establish and quite fragile. In contrast, the self-interest of private and communal resource exploiters to maximize their returns over the long run, when the policy environment makes this attractive, is a reliable anchor for sounder resource management.

Resource experts and social scientists have made great strides in understanding the requirements and strategies for restoring natural-resource rights to private and communal resource exploiters (Bromley 1992; Ostrom 1990, 1992; Ostrom et al. 1993; Schlager and Ostrom 1992). These restorations, which dovetail into worldwide trends toward privatization, community empowerment, and decentralization, may hold the greatest promise for taming government resource abuses.

Restructuring State Resource Exploitation

Turning next to the institutional structures of the government and the state, the four avenues of reform are (1) simplifying the mandates of agencies and policies, (2) clarifying jurisdictions among agencies, (3) prioritizing through the central budget, and (4) reforming the arrangements between government and state enterprises.

Simplifying Mandates

The ambiguity that allows top government leaders, agencies, and state enterprises to avoid careful assessments of their performance and to evade accountability can be directly reduced by tightening the mandates for specific agencies and policies. Agency leaders and personnel should be held accountable for their performance in pursuing highly simplified, differentiated, single-objective mandates. Each agency should have one function. If the Honduran government wishes to have a state forestry enterprise, it should mandate the state enterprise to pursue profitable forestry development and extraction, while assigning another agency to regulate forest uses and another to pursue poverty alleviation among people living in and near the forest. The top government officials must be sure to clarify which agency has jurisdiction in each contingency; for example, if forest-conservation principles cover state as well as private forest uses, then the regulatory agency must be able to fine the state forestry enterprise for infractions and pursue legal actions against state officials who defy the regulations. In parallel fashion, the Mexican irrigation system was saved by the simplification of its mandate to provide water for farmers whose productivity permits the farmers to pay for the costs of providing the water—not to fight poverty, promote particular types of crops, and the like. If the government wishes to support these other pursuits, it should do so through additional government spending channeled through different institutions, each held accountable for its performance in pursuing its single mandate.

By simplifying the mandates of particular agencies, these reforms push decisions on priorities among objectives up to the highest levels of government, where decisions are made on creating agencies and their mandates, assigning them authority, and allocating financial resources. Thus, Hindustan Copper Limited should not be in the position of having to provide for the national defense of India: it should produce copper as efficiently as possible, sell it to any willing customers, and stay in business if it is truly profitable. The Indian Defence Ministry should determine whether domestic copper production is a good use of its own budget, and the cabinet and parliament should decide how much to spend for defense straightforwardly through their budget allocations rather than through the convoluted exercise of subsidizing a money-losing copper company.

Lest this principle seem obvious, it should be noted that it is completely opposite from the prevailing conventional wisdom of "integrated" or "system" management, which attempts to give agencies jurisdiction over as many aspects of the activities and outcomes in a particular sphere or geographical area as possible.

Clarifying Jurisdictions among Agencies

One approach to prevent the clash of objectives among government agencies and enterprises from triggering hasty and reckless resource exploitation is for the government, at the cabinet or legislative levels, to establish clear jurisdictional rules binding on all government agencies. One component would be a uniform land-use classification system. Such a system implicitly clarifies the jurisdictions of relevant government agencies, thereby reducing the land-grabbing competition that in cases like the Brazilian Amazon and Costa Rica have devastated natural forest lands in the clash between promoting ranching and small-farmer resettlement.

Another component of an improved allocation of jurisdictions would be a thorough review of resource legislation to identify conflicting jurisdictions. In many countries the legislation governing resource management is fraught with inconsistencies regarding the roles of government and state agencies.

Of course, chief executives, cabinets, and legislatures are often loathe to force a resolution of intragovernmental jurisdictional disputes; they may wish to avoid antagonizing whichever agencies and constituencies that would lose. Yet efforts to reduce jurisdictional ambiguity may be supported by government officials who welcome the opportunity to accomplish their objectives openly.

Prioritizing through the Central Budget

Once the mandates and jurisdictions of agencies and enterprises have been streamlined and clarified, prioritization of objectives should be accomplished through the main budget of the national, provincial, state, or local government. The level of government depends on the degree of decentralization chosen to provide government services and regulation,[5] but the core of this recommendation is that financial resources should be allocated by the highest officials within that level of government.

Recall that John Stuart Mill's approach to addressing distributional and noneconomic objectives apart from the processes of production was intended to avoid inefficiencies in the productive sphere. But it is also remarkably effective in terms of transparency and accountability. The central budget is the legitimate locus of government efforts to alleviate poverty, defend the nation against outside enemies, enhance culture, and so on. Only at the level of the central budget, the apex of the allocation of national resources for national interests, can the relative merits of devoting the nation's wealth be weighed holistically; only through the central budget can the "rates of return" for society be considered in a transparent and accountable way. By the same token, the central budget defines the resources that the top government officials place into the hands of each agency to pursue its mandate.

A crucial implication is that other sources of funds should not be available to deploy for the pursuit of costly objectives other than through the central budget. This reform would force the most accountable officials to make decisions on priorities in what is typically the most transparent arena. It is, of course, conventional wisdom that each ministry or agency should have to make the case for spending to pursue its mandate and objectives in the central budget arena, in competition with the needs and rationales of other government units. The key point here is that restricting government resource flows that are outside of the central budget process would reduce both the incidence of nonaccountable expenditures and the temptation to distort the natural-resource exploitation process for the sake of off-budget financing.

Reforms of Government-State Enterprise Arrangements

The arrangements between government and state enterprises can be reformed to increase transparency and accountability, reduce conflict, and provide greater incentives for responsible resource management. The three issues of greatest relevance for these reforms are accounting conventions, interministerial oversight, and fiscal arrangements.

Accounting Conventions. Accountability and transparency begin with accounting. It should be apparent that the state-owned enterprise ought to operate within a regime of full disclosure in which all involved have full and accurate information. The question is how to accomplish this in situations marked by bureaucratic politics and incentives to evade accountability. Three avenues are promising.

First, if contesting the control over surpluses is such an important root of the problems of state oil and mining companies, then the key principle of reform ought to be a clear and precise definition of the accounting rules that would allow a distinction between resource rents and true business "profits." Natural-resource rent can be measured either by its auction price or by calculating the difference between the sale price of the extracted resource and the costs of extraction, the latter including a "normal profit" for that particular industry. The resource rent is the major surplus available when resource exploitation is profitable.

Second, prioritizing through the central budgetary allocations to agencies with simpler, differentiated mandates also implies that government ministries must pay the full economic costs of their directives to state enterprises. If a ministry places an enterprise in a money-losing situation by requiring it to employ certain persons, exploit unproductive resources, or sell outputs at below market price, that ministry should finance the costs from its own budget. The decisions do not have to be based on sophisticated cost accounting or complex cost benefit analysis: they can simply be based on a willingness-to-pay principle. Any government ministry advocating a policy should inform the government and the enterprise how much it is willing to pay. The enterprise management would have to decide whether, given the transfer, the proposed policy is feasible. Another possibility is to develop a system of auctions for carrying out national objectives that would be open to all state (or even private) enterprises.

Third, joint ventures with private-sector enterprises put a reporting requirement on government or state entities that often yields better accounting information than is widely available. In our oil and mining cases, the transparency of state enterprise cooperation with international oil or mining companies in full-fledged joint ventures is consistently greater than it is in the state companies' solo operations.

Interministerial Oversight. While each agency and state enterprise should have a simple approval relationship with the most relevant ministry, interministerial oversight is important for keeping all top-level government officials aware of resource manipulations. The much more disciplined management of Indonesia's Pertamina under the post-1975 interministerial commission is an excellent example. The distinction between monitoring and approval mechanisms is thus very important, because the arrangements should provide for transparency across the whole government but not put an agency in the position of having to answer to multiple authorities. For example, the investments of Hindustan Copper Limited should be known to the whole range of Indian ministries, but HCL should not be burdened with the currently cumbersome requirements to seek approval from so many ministries, commissions, and agencies.

Fiscal Arrangements and Incentives for the State Enterprise. Insofar as dynamic agency leaders are likely to be motivated by the desire to enhance the authority and standing of the agency, good performance should be rewarded by greater jurisdiction and greater budgetary discretion.[6] The soundness of performance evaluation and rewards depends on according sufficient discretion for enterprise leaders and rank-and-file personnel to be legitimately held accountable. Discretion serves two crucial functions. First, it is essential for meaningful accountability, because criticism of judgment is sensible only if policymakers can exercise their judgment. Accountability for simply carrying out specific orders is an almost trivial form of accountability. Second, discretion is a powerful incentive for many of the most desirable agency leaders. Competent agency heads want to have enough rope to either hang themselves or show off their competence and dynamism.

When state enterprises have discretion, the institutional interests of the state enterprise, and the personal interest of its leadership and staff, ought to be rewarded for good, business-like performance. By identifying the true profitability of the enterprise, the government is in a stronger position to reward good management. Profit-maximizing behavior ought to result in the enterprise gaining, at least to a moderate degree, greater discretion over part of the surplus or other enhancements to the enterprise's status or capacity. A dynamic, ambitious chief executive officer of a state enterprise — and that is the preferred type of leader — will typically want as much discretion as he or she can get. Therefore, good performance should be linked to greater discretion, greater certainty that the enterprise's plans can be financed, or both. For example, greater profitability and efficiency (e.g., less downtime of machinery, higher physical yields in refining) can be set as the conditions for guaranteeing that the enterprise can count on receiving at least a certain percentage of its capital budget proposals in future years (e.g., if targets are met with excellent results, the company may receive a government commitment that, say, at least 80 percent of its capital budget projections outlined in its three- or five-year plan will be forthcoming). The government may also raise the ceiling on the value of goods that the enterprise can import without having to go through lengthy government approval procedures.

A small proportion of true profits can provide monetary incentives for managers and workers to perform well. Some may argue that it is not advisable to allow substantial profits to remain with enterprises for the purposes of capitalization, especially in the nonrenewable resource sectors that will eventually have to be liquidated. The risk therefore is that highly profitable state enterprises in oil or mining might use retained profits to expand their production facilities just when dwindling supplies call for decapitalization. This argument is much less relevant once true profits are distinguished from surpluses, because the portion of profits retained would be taken from a smaller surplus base.

Both this strategy and that of allowing for greater discretion require explicit agreements — "performance contracts" or "memoranda of understanding" — between the government and the state enterprise. Such agreements work only if the relevant government agencies are involved and the performance targets are realistic (Nellis 1989). In India the memoranda of understanding between the government and the state mining enterprises were hardly meaningful, because the government signatory was the Ministry of Mines rather than the Finance Ministry and the latter controlled the promised access to foreign exchange. As a consequence, the targets have been too lenient, and government commitments to provide foreign exchange have often been unfulfilled because the Ministry of Mines does not control foreign exchange licenses (Aharoni and Ascher 1991).

If the central budget is the proper mechanism for determining whether state resource enterprises should undertake nonbusiness objectives, then the enterprises must be paid to pursue these objectives rather than accumulate chronic deficits. Any deficit-producing activity that is worth continuing ought to be financed by a transfer from whichever government agency is mandated to pursue the objectives served by these activities. A deficit that persists beyond the typical fluctuations that could bring temporary losses to a business is a sign that the state enterprise is pursuing activities that are insufficiently profitable from both a market perspective (as indicated by its business loss) and a social perspective (as indicated by the unwillingness of government agencies to make transfers to alleviate its losses).

Finally, incentive systems work best in competitive environments. Competition reveals competence, commitment to cost consciousness, and sound business performance. The possibility that an agency may expand its jurisdiction through good performance opens up very promising possibilities for introducing competition within government, whereby the better managed agencies will be rewarded with more responsibility and resources. This would not necessarily entail more elaborate and remuddled mandates. Consider, for example, the three more or less separate affiliate exploration and production companies of Venezuela's state oil-holding company, PDVSA (see chapter 6). As entities that exploit somewhat different but partially overlapping areas of Venezuela's land and offshore oil areas, the affiliates compete for the mother company's decision to award exploration and production rights in the areas where more than one affiliate could develop the fields without undue transport and control costs. This simple arrangement makes PDVSA one of the few state enterprises with an effective form of competition and incentives for efficiency and cost consciousness.

Actions by Extra-governmental Actors

Individuals and organizations outside of government have five important potentials for reducing the incidence of government maneuvers that sacrifice sound resource policy. First, in light of the key role played by transparency, extra-governmental actors can increase the political costs of these maneuvers simply by publicizing any such maneuvers that they can uncover. The political advantage of relying on obscure natural-resource manipulations obviously diminishes when the manipulations are heavily publicized. The Indonesian environmental umbrella group WALHI has done a great service to conservation and sustainable development in Indonesia simply by revealing the inadequacy of timber rents. Many organizations, alerted by WALHI's analyses, have pressured the Indonesian government to raise timber rents, with at least modest success.

Among these organizations has been the World Bank, which demonstrates a second role for extra-governmental actors. Any organization that is committed to sustainable development and is involved in an exchange relationship with a government has the option of making its support contingent on sound natural-resource policy. When these organizations are international, they often have greater latitude in publicizing the policy fail-

ures encountered in analyzing the government's resource policies. Therefore, they can contribute to transparency even as they are pressing for
policy reforms.

The finding that policy failures related to important resource endowments are unlikely to be simple technical mistakes has very important implications for the tack that international donors ought to take in trying to
promote sounder policies. The rather common impulse to instruct and
enlighten the officials responsible for the faulty policies, as if they were
simply ignorant of sound resource economics, is dangerously naive. It is
dangerous not only because it insults the intelligence of government and
state officials who know full well what tradeoffs they face but also because it
lulls the donor agencies into thinking that a bit of instruction and admoni-
tion will turn things around. This may reduce the donor agencies' resolve
to devote their resources only where the government makes commitments
to adopt responsible resource and environmental policies.

Third, the groups outside of government can often provide support to
those within government who oppose natural-resource policy abuses. As
mentioned above, pessimism based on the premise that government is a
monolithic actor has been shown, in case after case, to be unfounded. Because some government officials and agencies are likely to oppose each policy failure, extra-governmental actors can coordinate pressure with these
officials, provide outlets for the release of official data, and provide information to strengthen the hand of these officials in the intragovernmental
policy debates.

Fourth, the community of scientists and experts can assert its provisional consensus on sound and unsound natural-resource policies. Soil scientists, botanists, geologists, and meteorologists do not have to lay to rest
all of their disagreements about the optimal soil and land classification systems to form a provisional consensus around one system that all government agencies should adopt for the time being. Silviculturalists do not have
to agree on the precise regeneration cycle for a given tree species to be able
to let the government, the public, and the international community know
when harvesting policies are inconsistent with even the minimal estimates
of regeneration periods. Economists do not have to agree on the optimal
incentives for reforestation or mitigation of mining damage to join to-
gether in condemning subsidy schemes that are clearly unsound from an
economic perspective. There is a host of issues on which scientific opinion
is unified enough to play a much greater role, both to educate policymakers
and to increase the political penalties of relying on unsound natural-
resource policies.

Fifth, there is great virtue in a skeptical public that is intolerant of special subsidies, suspicious government accounting, grandiose policy claims, ambiguous mandates, and rosy optimism. The rising tide of democracy in developing countries has certainly enhanced the importance of public disappointment with government resource abuses, but ironically it has also made it more tempting for governments to provide immediate benefits, and sometimes to tax deviously, at the expense of largely hidden damage to the natural-resource endowment and the ecosystem in general. A responsible and independent press is crucial for unveiling resource abuses and their consequences.

The most difficult adjustment for the public and extra-governmental organizations is to accept the principle that subsidizing economic activities is generally very damaging to the economy and the resource endowment. Apart from encouraging precisely defined public goods (positive externalities) through the minimum support necessary for these activities to occur, the justification for economic subsidy is without merit, and yet interest groups are understandably enamored with the prospect of obtaining subsidies for themselves. The public must understand that rejecting economic subsidies does not mean abandoning redistribution, poverty alleviation, and noneconomic objectives; it means reserving these objectives to the process of taxing and budgeting.

Finally, the broadest lesson is that the use of natural-resource abuses to subsidize any of the programmatic objectives has both a political and an economic logic. Addressing either one without the other is likely to fail. Yet appreciating political leaders as people who need to balance a broad range of motives and interests will often yield the countermeasures for combating unsound resource policies, whether by increasing the political costs through transparency or by changing the incentives for government and state officials. As natural resources dwindle, these countermeasures become more and more crucial in the struggle for sustainable development.

Notes

Chapter 1. *Introduction*

1. Other cases assessed by the Center for International Development Research at Duke University include Indian and Sri Lankan hydroelectric and irrigation projects; Brazilian, Indian, and Indonesian resettlement projects; Mexican, Central American, and Korean agricultural development; comparative community-forestry policies in a large number of countries; Zambian copper development; and many individual analyses conducted by the fellows of the Program in International Development Policy. It must be stressed that no case was excluded from the present analysis because it failed to fit the theory and interpretations of this volume.

2. "Sustainable yield" of a renewable resource is the approach of keeping the harvest rate as high as possible without reducing the total resource stock. The premise is that if the stock remains constant, the new growth can indefinitely supply a constant yield.

3. Projections by the World Energy Council, the International Energy Agency, and the U.S. Department of Energy, summarized in World Resources Institute (1996, 280).

4. The key to understanding these figures is to note that they encompass the SITC three-digit categories that cover crude raw materials, processed materials that are not final products, and final products whose value is predominantly from the raw material itself. This provides a reasonably conservative measure of natural-resource reliance, without introducing the arbitrariness of separating processed materials (such as copper) from the original resource (such as copper ore), while avoiding the trap of including highly processed goods whose value may be largely from capital and labor and whose raw-material inputs may actually be imported. Therefore, cocoa is included but not chocolate confections; all hydrocarbons are included but not plastics; iron ore and raw iron and steel are included but not specific products; logs and "wood simply worked" are included but not furniture; and all tobacco products are included.

5. More valuable local currencies mean that for a given sale price abroad, the foreign currency earnings will fetch fewer units of the local currency. Because the producer has to cover local costs, such as wages and locally produced inputs, with these local currency earnings, this decline may make it difficult or impossible for the producer to make a profit without raising the export price. When this occurs, the volume of sales is likely to decline. Even if the producer does not raise the price, the attractiveness of investments in that sector will diminish. This is the so-called Dutch disease, so named because of the problem that the Netherlands faced during the North Sea oil boom.

6. Gelb (1988) and Auty (1990) provide very good analyses of how governments have tried to cope with export booms in the oil sector.

7. The Mexican case is developed in this book, but because of an extensive analysis of the Mahaweli case in Ascher and Healy (1990), the Sri Lankan case is not.

8. The decline of agriculture comes from diminished capacity to deliver water through irrigation systems that have greater and greater water leakage as the physical structures deteriorate. In addition, soil degradation occurs through salinization, water-logging caused by low water prices and poor irrigation administration that allows some farmers to overuse water, and soil poisoning from water-borne pesticides and fertilizations.

9. This figure is based on Haughton et al.'s (1992) estimate that the private loggers were retaining 75 percent of the timber rent, which in the early 1990s was roughly US$1.6 billion.

10. The wild fluctuations in oil prices are well known; however, such fluctuations are common for numerous commodities. For example, copper prices surged 30 percent from 1996 to late 1997, without a major world conflict.

11. For an excellent survey of rent-seeking behavior, see Tollison (1982).

12. Dove's argument is that swidden (i.e., "slash-and-burn" or "shifting") agriculture has been falsely "found" to be generally unsustainable as an excuse for governments to deny swidden agriculturalists their land-use rights (see Dove 1983).

CHAPTER 2. *Anatomy of Resource Policy Failures and Their Linkages to Programmatic Strategies*

1. Note that any individual can legitimately assert a preference for a particular distribution of income or wealth. Yet the question is whether policies that establish a different distribution can usefully be labeled as policy failures. Unlike policy failures defined in terms of inefficiency (i.e., the failure to achieve the greatest total societal welfare), policy failures defined in terms of distributions that a given individual condemns are not subject to technical consensus.

2. The theory of monopoly focuses not so much on the wealth of the monopolist — a distributional issue — but rather on the fact that under monopoly conditions the seller maximizes his or her income by charging a higher price for fewer units. In short, there is less production in a monopoly situation.

3. These are sometimes called "Pigovian taxes" or "Pigovian charges," after the British economist Arthur Pigou (1920). Environmental damage is distinct from the cost of making the resource scarcer by its depletion. In a competitive free market, scarcity will be reflected in the prices of inputs and outputs and are thus internalized by the private resource exploiter.

4. This is often called the "principal-agent problem"; in this instance, the society is the "principal," while its "agent" is the state entity.

5. This is because the rent, as profit in excess of the normal competitive profit, will not arise under competitive circumstances even if the sector receives a general benefit such as low prices for government-provided inputs. Competition would transform this into a benefit for the consumer.

CHAPTER 3. *Oil and Timber Abuses to Fund Off-Budget Development Programs in Indonesia*

1. In contrast to Venezuela's PDVSA, which retained a large cadre of expatriate managers and well-trained local managers, Pertamina lost most of its expatriate managers and technicians.

2. Nevertheless, the boundaries of the "oil and gas sector" are fuzzy enough to have allowed Pertamina to keep its Pelita airline and part of the petrochemical industry.

3. The traditional fear of governments of developing countries in dealing with international oil companies is that the companies will capture more of the resource rent than if government entities were exploiting the oil.

4. The World Bank (1990) estimated that Indonesia was losing forest at a rate of 1 million hectares annually as of 1988. Since the more accessible, higher-yielding areas are targeted for logging before the less accessible ones (such as the relatively low-quality, inaccessible forests of Irian Jaya), the loss of 1 percent of the total forested area is of much greater economic significance for future supplies of timber than it might appear at first glance. There are estimates that all commercial timber will be gone by 2020 at present rates of exploitation (Schwarz 1990, 62). Some prized furniture woods, such as ramin, have already become scarce. Depletion of the Sumatran forests has resulted in the need to import logs from Kalimantan to supply the Sumatran mills; interviews with executives in the forest-products industry reveal that some supplies have been faltering even in Kalimantan. Some government officials estimated in the mid-1990s that throughout the country, sawmills were operating at only an average

of 40 percent of capacity (although this is a reflection of poor siting of the mills and the growth of plywood manufacturing, as well as overall problems of supply). Nongovernmental sources estimated commercial logging rates at around 44 million cubic meters of wood annually (WALHI 1991). This far exceeded the government's own calculation of the maximum sustainable yield of 31 million cubic meters (FAO and Ministry of Forestry 1990).

5. The particular policy failures were the following:

(1) The formal harvesting system that has prevailed throughout most of Indonesia's nonplantation production forests (the so-called Indonesian Selective Logging and Regeneration System) leaves the harvester essentially free to remove the best trees, has not prevented relogging within five to ten years rather than the thirty-five years formally required by the policy (Gillis 1988a, 100), and encourages very high collateral logging damage that can affect nearly 40 percent of standing stock (World Bank 1990, 10).

(2) The practice of granting huge concessions (some over 1 million hectares) has made it impossible for the government and concessionaires to police the larger concessions, while the concessionaires have no responsibility to permit local people access to concession areas when active logging is not occurring. Gillis (1992, 149) points out that government regulation of a few huge concessions may or may not be more difficult than regulation of many smaller concessions; however, huge concessions are difficult for the concessionaires themselves to police in terms of invasion by shifting cultivators or poachers. He also points out that "restriction of concession size will discourage speculation in the form of 'stockpiling' of desirable tracts to keep them out of the hands of other firms." The concession policy also has vague renewal criteria that permit political considerations to enter and leave the concessionaires with little incentive to manage their concessions sustainably.

(3) The royalty and taxation system, based largely on an ad valorem royalty, captures far too little of the natural-resource rent (roughly 20 percent of declared rents) and also encourages high-grading, the practice of removing only the most valuable trees. It is a problematic practice because (1) greater areas suffer collateral damage to obtain the target volume of timber, and (2) forest stands become degraded as the best specimens are removed. The low level of rent capture encourages overharvesting, puts considerable resources in the hands of individuals and companies with no incentive to reinvest them in the Indonesian economy, and undermines the timber estate initiative.

(4) The reforestation subsidy policy, financed by a large reforestation

fee on the volume of timber removed, was ostensibly designed to encourage loggers to replant in order to receive refunds of their reforestation deposits, but the government rarely provided the refunds for qualifying concessionaires. The fee was effectively a volume tax (Gillis 1992, 161–62), nearly of the same magnitude as the normal ad valorem royalty, and therefore induced high-grading, because the removal of more valuable trees did not incur a higher tax, thus effectively reducing the tax rate. The retention of the reforestation fees by the Forestry Department provided an enormous fund, equivalent to around US$1 billion, with no external controls or monitoring on its disposition of the funds. There has been much speculation that the funds have been used for political purposes; it is no surprise that the monitoring of the fund has been inadequate.

(5) The promotion of downstream wood products, including a ban on round-log and rattan export and substantial subsidies to the processors, has led to inefficient processing vulnerable both to international competition and to the reduction in inputs from domestic logging (see Kuswata, Riswan, and Vayda 1984; Gillis 1988a, 56–57). The export ban, enacted in 1980 with a five-year phase-in period, was an extension of the 1978 policy for promoting the domestic forest-products industry through higher export taxes on round logs than on sawn timber or plywood. In mid-1992 the outright ban was replaced by an export tax, not to increase log exports but simply to redirect the jurisdiction over the ban from the Ministry of Industry to the Finance Ministry. This was not a very significant change in terms of the possibility of exporting round logs, since the export tax is prohibitively high. Gillis (1988a, 95–97) estimated that in 1981 and 1982 alone, the Indonesian economy lost over US$400,000,000 of foregone revenues, equivalent to 27 percent of the timber rent, largely because of inefficiencies of processing. Fitzgerald (1986) found that US$4 in log exports were sacrificed for every US$1 gained in plywood exports. It was not until 1988 that the value of plywood exports exceeded the 1979 log export earnings of US$2.1 billion (Schwarz 1989, 86).

(6) Inconsistencies in land classification have both detracted from optimal land use and weakened conservation regulations. Different agencies use different classifications, resulting in suboptimal land use and confusing information. The Forestry Ministry has clung to its jurisdiction over some land of relatively high agricultural potential and already deforested (the World Bank [1990, 31] study estimates that 30 percent of Sumatra's land within forestry boundaries is unforested);

other areas, classified as conversion forests though of poor soils, have been barred to the Forestry Ministry, because they have been classified as conversion forests.

(7) The timber estate promotion policy, impelled by growing concern over supply shortages for the wood-products industry, subsidized questionable plantations. The World Bank estimated the subsidy at US$425 per hectare (World Bank 1990, 14). The money came from the Forestry Ministry's reforestation fund, and the claimants were largely already-established, vertically integrated timber companies. The lack of subsidy beyond the third year encouraged the planting of inexpensive species and minimal maintenance, leading to stands of little value at harvest time. Prohibitions against foreign ownership of concessions effectively deterred the multinational companies with sufficient capital and technology for successful plantations (Gillis 1987; 1988a, 75), but the main problem was that low timber rent capture from concession areas made the logging of natural forests more economically attractive than plantations to the forestry industry. There was an incentive to capture the benefits of the zero-interest loans by diverting the funds to other projects and then walk away from the plantations because even successful production would be difficult to sell in light of the low price of logs from natural forests.

6. According to Gillis (1988a, 55), this ban curtailed logging very rapidly in 1981 and 1982, because sawmill capacity could not increase rapidly enough to handle the nonexportable logs.

7. These developments are analyzed with great insight in Ross (1996, ch. 5).

8. Schwarz (1994, 28) notes that two of today's biggest ethnic Chinese logging entrepreneurs, Liem Sioe Liong and "Bob Hasan," were allied with Suharto in the mid-1950s.

9. Personal interviews, Pontianak, West Kalimantan, July 1992.

10. In 1991 WALHI calculated, based on the government's own figures, that prevailing royalty rates were one-fifth of actual stumpage values. Even after the rise of royalties from 1987 to the present, and by the most generous estimates, the government has captured no more than 40 percent of the timber rents on declared felling.

11. As of mid-1992, private sources and interviews estimated the Forestry Ministry's deforestation fund at US$800,000,000; some interviewees believed that it had exceeded US$1 billion.

12. Government equity participation is considered an advantage, because the operation is more likely to receive fair or even favored treatment, rather than a disadvantage because of the risk of government interference.

13. Interviews. See also Scarsborough (1992, 14) and WALHI (1991, 4, 8).

14. However, it is by no means the only case of suboptimality in resource policy that can be linked to the pursuit of such programmatic objectives. Other examples are reviewed in chapter 4.

CHAPTER 4. *Development Programs through Natural-Resource Abuses*

1. If we recognize energy inputs as important to many manufacturing processes, we can see that energy-intensive industrialization is itself a form of downstream promotion. However, I treat energy-intensive industrialization separately because of its somewhat different political dynamics.

2. Yergin (1991) documents many nationalizations in the petroleum sector.

3. This has been analyzed for the Peruvian rural areas in Ascher (1984).

4. This section on Sarawak follows closely on the interpretation in Mochida (1996). The most useful general treatments of politics and economics in Sarawak and Sabah are to be found in Means (1991) and Crouch (1996).

5. Hurst (1989, 105) and Stesser (1991, 62–63) also report on such arrangements.

6. The Melanaus are a coastal, largely Muslim people living predominantly in the Mukah region of Central Sarawak. Because they are Muslim and share many Malay cultural characteristics, they are typically grouped with the Malays. The Chief Ministers Abdul Rahman Ya'akub and Abdul Taif Mahmud are of this group.

7. The *New Straits Times* reported in March 1995 that a "Price Waterhouse investigation into Innoprise revealed that it was independent from the Foundation with differing objectives and priorities. The investigation also uncovered that ICSB has introduced a diverse corporate structure with no defined corporate focus and overdependence on timber. There was also no clear guidelines whether or not it was necessary for all decisions made by the Innoprise BOD to be referred to the foundation's BOT for approval. The 'loopholes' came to light after Innoprise entered into a timber sale and purchase agreement with Crocker Range Timber Sdn Bhd (CRT) and Peluamas Sdn Bhd (PSB) without getting the approval of the foundation's BOT" (Bangkuai 1995, 8).

8. Crouch (1996, 64) points out that the Berjaya administration also hobbled opposition parties, for example, by not permitting certain national leaders into Sabah to campaign.

9. Crouch (1996, 51) judges that the "by the mid-1980s [the Berjaya administration's] reputation for corruption and mismanagement of resources rivaled Tun Mustapha's."

10. Utting (1993, 10). From 1974 to 1989, forest area has decreased from 7.4 million hectares to less than 4.8 million (Secretaría de Planificación 1990).

11. For example, in 1993 the Inter-American Development Bank made a US$110 million loan conditional on the passage of legislation to open up timber concession bidding to international firms (*Inter Press Service* 1993).

12. Of course, there have been some recognitions of this fact, and occasional policy responses. In the 1960s a reforestation plan allowed forestry companies to retain up to half of their income tax obligations for the purpose of replanting. Official sources claimed that 1.8 billion trees were replanted on 820,000 hectares between 1970 and 1975, although questions were raised as to whether plantations or natural forest restoration was actually accomplished (Gillis 1992, 166).

13. In a solid analysis of the Brazilian Amazon's economic potential, Browder (1988, 248–49) points out that "the industrial wood sector plays a small but growing role in the Brazilian economy . . . In the Amazon, . . . four of the region's six states and federal territories depend on wood products for more than 25 percent of their industrial output . . . In Rondonia and Roraima, wood products account for more than 60 percent of industrial output. However, industrial output in the Amazon is quite small compared to crop and livestock production. Thus, Browder (1988, 250–51) concludes that "notwithstanding this tremendous industrial growth potential . . . Brazil's stewardship of its tropical forest patrimony has allowed, in fact promoted, its destruction."

14. In a sense, both were extensive compared to agriculture found in most developing countries, because the poor soils of the Amazon required that even the family farm holdings had to be in the range of 100 hectares. See Hecht (1984, 381–88).

15. Ronald Schneider (1995) argues that there have been several phases and dynamics of land use in the Brazilian Amazon triggered by differential profitability of land exploitation. In the 1970s, land was granted to higher-income, often urban-based recipients who had a short-term interest in the tax credits offered by the government and at least a theoretical interest in the long-term profitability that the land would yield with the eventual extension of infrastructure and population growth. The tax credits and worries about losing claims through inaction prompted what Schneider calls premature exploitation. The problem was that the remoteness of much of the frontier left the profitability of land exploitation lower than the opportunity costs of the new landowners. Therefore, despite their officially recognized property rights, many of these landowners lacked economic incentive to do anything beyond clear their land, as they saw more ambitious initiatives fail because of the combination of distance from markets and the poor land quality. Many cattle ranches failed even with the tax credits and subsidies; some failed because the tax credits and subsidies made it attractive to keep the transfers rather than invest them. In general, little exploitation occurred, until in the 1980s lower-income settlers with

lower opportunity costs "invaded" these marginal lands for whatever meager incomes they could yield. The nominal title holders found that the government was not prepared to enforce exclusion of squatters, and the title holders found it too expensive, in relation to the value of the land, to enforce their own property rights. Many landowners abandoned the land, as the low-income settlers either gradually gained recognition of their occupancy or were simply ignored because of the still-marginal value of the land to anyone else. A third phase has been emerging as the Amazonian frontier "matures" and the profitability of land rises enough to revive the interest of higher-income people even without subsidization. Schneider (1995, 28–30) demonstrates that higher-income landowners with access to their own capital or bank credit can clear substantially higher profits than can low-income settlers who must rely on more expensive informal credit. The consequent difference in the value of the land to those with and without access to less expensive capital motivates the wealthier to buy out the poorer.

16. If workable land had been given to the settlers, it would be a case of rent transfer, but not necessarily a poor context for sustainable resource use, since the private owner would have the incentive to manage the land and the resources thereon to get the greatest value out of both present and future use, as long as tenure were secure. Instead, the poor-quality land in most of the Amazon has to be abandoned after a few agricultural seasons (and then often converted to pasture that may be permanent because of the low probability of forest regeneration on heavily grazed land). Because settlers can start over on other lands within the Amazon, the initial holding is not generally regarded as warranting the extra effort and the income delay that disciplined exploitation requires.

17. The "North" states of Acre, Amapa, Amazonas, Para, Rondonia, Roraima, and Tocantins and the "Central West" states of Goias, Mato Grosso, and Mato Grosso do Sul, excluding the Federal District of Brasilia.

18. The nationalization entailed by the confiscation of Standard Oil of New Jersey's Peruvian oil fields was a partial nationalization, in that other foreign-owned facilities operated there until their gradual buyout, and the government sanctioned numerous production-sharing arrangements between international companies and the state oil company thereafter.

19. Stallings (1983, 170–71) reviews the divisions within the government and the generally more conservative position of the Finance Ministry.

20. Cleaves and Pease García (1983, 229) point out that roughly three hundred officers served in the civilian government and bureaucracy.

21. This theme is reviewed intensively in Stepan (1978).

22. This was a peculiar inversion of the tactic used by Chile's state copper company Codelco, which developed a deposit adjacent to an existing mine by

accounting investment costs as operating expenses, when its investment budget was restricted by the Finance Ministry (see chapter 5).

23. In 1989 Peru's Prime Minister Juan Carlos Hurtado, who at the time also held the portfolio of Minister of Economy and Finance, argued for higher fuel prices on the grounds that

> a short-sighted economist, concerned only with monthly survival, would recommend maintenance of the price of fuel in dollars at the level set by the government last August. This, however, would mean condemning PetroPerú to the permanent agony of financing its operational deficit with a growing accumulation of debts, of not having resources to replace its production and exploration investments, of paralysing the profitable projects of Chambira and Lot 42 south, of not adequately maintaining its industrial plants and refineries, of not offering an appropriate oil pipeline service and of not establishing a complete communication system that will allow it to face the threat of subversion. In such a case, PetroPerú would live from day to day trying to pay yesterday's bills without thinking of tomorrow. As a result of the Persian Gulf crisis, 1991 will be very difficult and unstable for all oil companies. If we want PetroPerú, our largest national company, to survive this enormous challenge, we must give it resources. (Televisión Peruana, Lima 0205 gmt 17 December 90; monitored by the British Broadcasting Corporation, January 1, 1990)

24. The following historical interpretation closely follows Wionczek (1982), which is the best short analysis of the political economy of Mexican irrigation. Orive Alba (1960) is essentially the official history of Mexican irrigation, written by the longtime head of the irrigation authority. Tamayo (1946) and Tamayo (1964) are more critical contemporary accounts. Support for the political analysis can be found in Sanderson (1986) and Castro (1995).

25. "Agricultural modernization" has meant building up largely export-oriented nontraditional crops, including poultry, vegetable oils, fodder crops such as soya and sorghum, green vegetables, strawberries and other fresh or frozen fruits, and frozen orange juice concentrates. These products all depended on intensive application of water. To meet the rising demand for staple foods, the Mexican government also emphasized wheat production, because of the greater success of increasing wheat yields than corn yields through improved varieties and greater inputs of fertilizer and water. Mexico's wheat farms are of larger scale than the farms devoted to more traditional food crops. See Sanderson (1986) for the most thorough discussion of the components of agricultural modernization in Mexico.

26. Calles's concerns over consolidating the political support for the regime were not paranoid in the least: in 1929 he had to quell a military uprising.

27. Cummings and Nercissiantz (1992, 739) point to the fact that "large parts of the newly developed irrigation lands were used for the formation of farm cooperatives (*ejidos*) populated with previously landless farmers." Castro (1995, 464) points out the enduring interest of *ejiditarios* in having the state maintain its rights and control over the national irrigation system.

28. The precise figures reported by Sanderson (1986, 47) are

1940	80.0%	1955	99.2	1970	92.5
1945	95.8	1960	85.5	1975	76.0
1950	72.1	1965	98.4	1980	59.2

These percentages represent the proportions of federal expenditures on irrigation to total federal expenditures on agriculture and livestock (Sanderson 1986, 47).

29. Tamayo (1964, 141) reports payments of 45 percent of operating costs for the period 1947–59.

30. Wionczek (1982, 401). Hewitt de Alcantara (1976) and Sanderson (1986) also point to the many other subsidies provided to export-oriented farming, the focus of agricultural research on innovations that could most easily be adopted by large-scale, export-oriented producers, and the concentration of new irrigation in the states dominated by large-scale agriculture.

31. This was the *Plan Nacional de Pequeña Irrigación*. See Secretaría de Recursos Hidráulicos (1968).

32. This phenomenon has come to be called the "Dutch disease," with an abundant literature beginning in the early 1980s (e.g., Corden and Neary 1982; Harberger 1983) that assessed how currency appreciation and investment diversion from an export boom makes it more difficult to export other commodities. The interpretation here is not that the Mexican government officials in the mid-1970s fully appreciated all of the nuances of this phenomenon, which were largely discovered later, but rather that some officials certainly recognized that the appreciation of the peso was making it more difficult to sell Mexican agricultural produce abroad at prices that would allow for production costs to be covered.

33. This topic is elaborated more generally in Ascher and Healy (1990, ch. 5).

34. Wionczek (1982, 397) writes, "The mere construction of irrigation dams and canals did not appear to offer in themselves great attraction to the potential users. A few years after its founding the National Irrigation Commission discovered that it was not only necessary to cover the total cost of infrastructure works with state funds, but also to sell irrigated lands to the new owners at prices below their actual value" (my translation).

35. From Enríquez (1909), cited in Wionczek (1982, 395); my translation.

CHAPTER 5. *Distribution through Resource Abuses*

1. According to reasonable land-use analyses, roughly 60 percent of Costa Rican territory ought to be maintained as forest land; forests currently cover less than 20 percent of Costa Rica's territory. See Abt Associates (1990) and Lutz and Daly (1990).

2. This clash is examined in more detail in Ascher (1993b).

3. Codelco's costs averaged 44 cents/lb in the early mid-1980s, rising to 50 cents/lb (40 cents/lb for the average direct cost) by 1989, largely because of the fall in the grade of available copper ores. Yet the average direct cost of American competitors was 85 cents/lb in 1982, dropping to 50 cents/lb by 1989.

4. The most comprehensive treatment of the nationalization of Chilean copper can be found in Allende (1985). The best summaries of post-nationalization issues can be found in Fortín (1984) and Tironi (1977).

5. The local currency revenues from copper were negligible, amounting to only 1,000 pesos in 1970. The figures are given in Méndez (1979, 311).

6. One confidential account states that analysts of the international organizations pressed for a US$350 million limit for 1985 and that underruns in other investment areas eased the pressure for restraint.

7. Purchases could have been canceled or delayed, albeit at some cost. In addition, given the nature of the existing mining operations and the expansions, production would not have collapsed if the expansion components had been delayed, although future production expansions would clearly have been postponed, as subsequent events demonstrated.

8. The richness of the privately developed Escondida deposit exceeded the Tironi ore-quality expectations.

9. Statement of Juan Villarzú, executive vice president of Codelco, as reported by Newsfile, July 15, 1996.

10. This triggers a particularly painful result: the ten biggest money-losers, like the ten biggest profit-makers, are featured at length in the annual "Public Enterprises Survey" of the Bureau of Public Enterprises.

11. The figures in rupees were Rs. 933,000,000, Rs. 451,000,000, and Rs. 290,300,000, respectively.

12. As of 1987, ICC's output per man-shift for ore production was 1.2 MT; Khetri's was 2.0 MT, and Malanjkhand's was 37 MT, compared to an underground mine average in the United States of 16 MT and an open-pit average of 45 MT. Malanjkhand's output per man-shift has since increased to the U.S. level as its capacity utilization has increased to around 100 percent. In smelting, the Indian facilities at Khetri and ICC required 60 man-hours per MT of copper, compared to 18 man-hours for the United States (Rao and Vaidyanath 1987, 79).

13. The Rao-Vaidyanath report recommended that once the price of copper was set to allow for the target rate of return on investment, subsequent increases in copper prices should be permitted at only half the rate of increase in input costs (which had been running at 10 percent a year in nominal terms) (Rao and Vaidyanath 1987, 138).

14. HCL officials do not participate in the functioning of the Commerce Ministry's pricing committee, which fixes the price of imported copper monthly, by calculating the landed cost of imported copper, the service charges of the state minerals-importing company MMTC, and the customs duty. There is very little flexibility in this formula. HCL's copper must be sold at this price or lower; in practice, the imported copper price is the price at which HCL sells its supply.

15. This estimate is based on copper imports of around 90,000 tons in 1990, with a cost difference of 40,000 rupees per ton between HCL and the London Metal Exchange price, and an exchange rate of 20 rupees per U.S. dollar.

16. The international cost of converting concentrates into wirebars is approximately US$450 per MT. By processing imported concentrates, HCL could save part of the US$450 of foreign exchange per MT (since foreign equipment would have to be imported, not all of the US$450 would be saved), but at a cost of Rs. 25,000 under current conditions (equivalent to US$1,000 at the current exchange rate) and at no less than Rs. 20,000 (equivalent to US$800) with greater throughput. It is again hard to imagine the Indian government according such a high premium for foreign exchange to justify this approach on economic grounds. Only the fact that the customs duty on concentrates is only 30 percent makes such a proposition profitable for HCL.

17. The oversight arrangements that prevail for Hindustan Copper Limited are elaborate and vary according to which facet of the enterprise's operations are involved. HCL is formally under the jurisdiction of the Department of Mines of the Ministry of Steel and Mines. The chairman/managing director of HCL reports directly to the Secretary of the Department of Mines. In addition, adherence to the regulations for public undertakings and completion of targets are monitored by the Finance Ministry's Bureau of Public Enterprises, while financial operations are scrutinized by the comptroller and auditor general of India.

On investment issues, the Finance Ministry (in addition to the Ministry of Steel and Mines) reviews and has to approve all investments of government funds and all company-financed investments above the ceiling of Rs. 500,000,000 (or roughly US$20,000,000) that could be approved at the discretion of the board of directors. HCL would require permission from the Ministry of Finance to borrow from nongovernmental sources; the Finance Ministry's Department of Economic Affairs must approve all transactions involving foreign exchange. The Finance Ministry also has the critical responsibility of setting the customs duties on copper (on average once a year, but the frequency varies according to the volatility in the world price of copper), in part taking into account HCL's cost of production. Since HCL investment plans are elements of the Five-Year Plan, the Indian Planning Commission also participates in clearing significant investment policies. Every year the Finance Ministry and the Planning Commission determine HCL's budget allocation. They also determine the company's obligations for repayment of its capitalization loan. Thus, the Finance Ministry and the Planning Commission exercise control over HCL's discretion even to invest its own surplus through their authority to decide how much of HCL's profit will have to go toward repayment of the enterprise's outstanding debt with the government.

Neither the Finance Ministry nor the Planning Commission is mandated to approve the specific projects in HCL's budget. Once the Planning Commission approves the consolidated budget of the Department of Mines in line with the broad spending and investment guidelines formulated by the Planning Commission and the Finance Ministry, the Department of Mines can transfer funds among its various public undertakings. The Planning Commission indeed scrutinizes the consolidated budget carefully and usually makes substantial cuts, but the emphasis is on economizing rather than on particular project evaluations.

18. Parliamentary oversight through the Committee on Public Undertakings and ministerial monitoring through a quarterly performance review may be largely pro forma, but virtually every aspect of HCL operations is overseen by some combination of ministries and bureaus that require constant communication from the company and many stages of consultation and approval. The introduction of a Memorandum of Understanding (MOU) process for 1990–91 was intended, in part, to enable HCL to become more autonomous by clarifying the targets by which it should be evaluated and held accountable. Yet except for having a higher ceiling on investments that the HCL board can authorize without formal government approval, the company has not been relieved from any of the approval requirements or from exposure to intervention into its operations.

19. The defense industry uses approximately 12 percent of India's total copper consumption, while the entire electrical equipment subsector uses 43 percent (Rao and Vaidyanath 1987, 122), of which a relatively small proportion is devoted to electricity-generation equipment.

20. Because of the great variation in the geological conditions and ore grades among the currently operating HCL mining installations (Mining, Geological, and Metallurgical Institute of India 1989, 93–94), costs vary greatly

as well. It follows that closing some of the currently operating facilities would reduce HCL's average costs considerably. The least efficient mines of the Indian Copper Complex in Bihar would be the first target; its ore grade and efficiency are low, and ICC has the smallest production of ore and copper metal content of the three installations (less than 25 percent), with Khetri accounting for 36 percent and Malanjkhand for 39 percent of milled copper metal (Hindustan Copper Limited 1991, 2). If domestic production in a given year is, say, 35 percent, even the closure of all ICC mines (a 25 percent reduction in HCL production) would still provide HCL more than one-quarter of total supply, while both reducing the average cost of HCL copper and increasing its profitability substantially.

21. For the sake of illustration, if the government had loaned HCL the full Rs. 3,000,000,000 in equal tranches from 1986 through 1990, with payback beginning in 1991, then the roughly Rs. 4,000,000,000 debt as of 1991 would require a combined annual principal and interest payment of around Rs. 500,000,000 if the loan were on comparable terms to HCL's Rs. 2,000,000,000 debt actually outstanding as of 1991. With a capacity of 100,000 MT of copper, or 220,460,000 pounds, the capital costs would be Rs. 2.27/lb, or less than 10 U.S. cents/lb. If the Malanjkhand facility could produce copper at around the international operating costs, then the capital costs could easily be justified by virtue of the elimination of international transport costs and consideration of the foreign exchange premium.

22. A few production-sharing contracting arrangements do exist, but they constitute less than 10 percent of Nigerian production. See Ahmad Khan (1994) for a detailed analysis of the various types of arrangements.

23. Roughly 70 percent of Nigeria's oil is produced from on-shore sites in the Niger delta; 30 percent is from off-shore sites.

24. "The Government sets the price of all petroleum products in Nigeria. In nominal terms, the price of gasoline has increased from Naira 115.68 per ton of oil equivalent (TOE) in 1965 to N197.98/TOE in 1981. The price pattern has been a nominal (pump) price which stays constant for three or four years at a time, followed by a price change. While in nominal terms the pump price has increased, in real terms the price of gasoline has been decreasing since 1965 with the exception of a modest increase in 1979, followed by a decline thereafter" (Adegbulube and Dayo 1986, 132).

25. The lack of unity is described succinctly by Dafe Otobo (1995, 50): "We are left with a military organization that is divided internally because it is controlled by a few military officers and their 'boys,' and in Nigerian elite's lexicon, the northern minorities feel discriminated against, just as the southern and Christian officers do. There is thus a consequent loss of legitimacy/loyalty and corporate pride inside the military organization. Power and patronage

system having been personalized, institutional avenues for replacing military leadership become blocked."

CHAPTER 6. *Raising Revenues through Resource Abuses*

1. See Ascher (1994; 1997) for greater elaborations on this strategy.

2. Characterizing these benefits as "excessive" is justified by noting that workers with comparable levels of training, skill, and experience earned considerably less than the organized oil workers.

3. In a study of "tax capacity" of developing countries, Chelliah (1971) found Mexico to be among the very lowest in terms of taxes collected as a proportion of potential taxes, the latter based on predictions essentially depending on GDP levels.

4. As Guzman (1988a, 395) notes,

> The federal government's policy was to appropriate most of PEMEX's international earnings and redistribute them according to the priorities established in government programs; thus, the oil industry's remaining profit, which was to be used for investment, was severely reduced. In 1982 the government again increased its tax on the sale of refined products to 27 percent; for petrochemicals it was set at 15 percent and exported crude at 58 percent plus 3 percent ad valorem. Consequently, the federal tax PEMEX had to pay in 1982 amounted to 91 percent of its before-tax profits, that is, around $11.724 billion (US$), which was 5.4 times more than it had paid in 1979 in constant 1977 currency.

Similarly, when the Mexican government finally decided in the early 1980s to limit the expansion of energy use by raising the domestic prices of petroleum products, it did so largely by increasing energy taxes rather than PEMEX's base prices (Guzman 1988b, 410–11), again enhancing the government's access to resources.

5. Guzman (1988a, 395) notes that "although PEMEX's before-tax profits grew substantially, the fiscal cuts left very little margin for financing the oil industry's development and operations; so, the financial policy that had been elaborated in 1973 lingered on. However, by the end of the 1970s the oil industry's growth and the amount of revenue in circulation reached such unprecedented dimensions that the whole country's economy was brought into play. PEMEX's borrowing for financing purposes represented 28.3 percent of its total income in 1980, that is, 5.4 times more than during the first half of the 1976–82 administration."

6. A U.S. General Accounting Office study of spring 1992 (excerpted in *Mexico Trade and Law Reporter* 1992, 3) concluded that

Pemex faces a number of limitations while trying to meet the goals of the national energy program. Pemex currently does not have adequate accessible oil reserves to meet the long-term goals of the program without substantial new capital investment. In addition, Pemex cannot raise all the necessary capital internally . . . Pemex must undertake a major investment program in order to offset the effects of investment reductions in the 1980s . . . Pemex plans to obtain the US$20 billion necessary for its investment through a combination of increasing its sales revenues and raising foreign capital . . . Pemex has limitations on its ability to meet its goal of raising US$20 billion, however . . . [A] senior official from the Ministry of Planning and Budget explained that Pemex's five-year plan has not been officially sanctioned by the government. Rather, the Pemex budget is approved year by year, based on overall Mexican economic policy, and Pemex must operate within the government budget goals, which are to reduce inflation, balance the budget, and reduce the national debt.

7. The logic of lending to a state enterprise beyond the credit ceiling of its government "owner," despite the fact that all of the debt involved is "sovereign debt" owed by the government, is that (1) assets of the state company may be attachable; (2) the bank may believe that the government would choose to keep the state enterprise solvent even if the government itself is in default, because the government may wish the state enterprise to continue to be able to do business and bring in hard currency (as occurred in the case of the Zambian Consolidated Copper Mines); and (3) the bank officers may have incentives to increase total lending even if it puts the bank as a whole in jeopardy.

8. A typical example is recorded by *Platt's Oilgram News* (1989, 1):
[President] Salinas acknowledged the debilitating effect of the company's shrinking budget, saying there would be efforts to increase investment in production, exploration and maintenance. Director General Francisco Rojas said during the ceremony that crude and natural gas reserves had dropped by 2% to 67.6-billion bbl as of Jan. 1, 1989 from the prior year. This represents a drop of almost 7% from Dec. 31, 1983, when hydrocarbon reserves stood at 72.5-billion bbl, and the fifth consecutive year that Pemex has reported a decline in proven reserves.

9. The 1997 investment budget was authorized at US$5.9 billion. Typically half of the investment budget is expended in the last quarter. Therefore, inasmuch as only US$1.5 billion was expended in the first half of 1997, a reasonable forecast of 1997 investment would be US$4 billion.

10. According to Coronel (1983, 77), the law creating PDVSA required the operating companies to "pay a sum of money to the holding company equiv-

alent to ten percent of the net income originating from their petroleum exports during the preceding month." In addition, they were subject to taxation and also required to make "contributions established for hydrocarbon concessions."

11. Coronel (1983, 212) notes that "at the level of the operating companies, this increase was seen as a purely political maneuver designed to make the government bureaucracy look good after the October OPEC meeting . . . Oil experts knew that the market would not accept an increase and that such an increase would simply serve to weaken further the position of Venezuelan oil in the world markets. The measure was perceived as short-term oriented."

12. To justify these acquisitions, the company put forth four main arguments; Boué (1993, 164–69) argues convincingly that none of them was based on sound financial theory. The first argument was that PDVSA will maximize revenue and fully utilize its assets by being involved in all aspects of the oil industry. However, this policy was not a good long-term strategy. The company can only maintain gains if it works "in a counter-cyclical manner," because if the strategy is successful other companies will adopt it, making success harder to achieve. Second, PDVSA maintained that integration allowed it to avoid price-cutting wars without reducing production. But in a price war, if PDVSA does not cut production, it will lose money at the refining end, when it sells its products in a glutted market. This strategy could work only if they could keep other producers from gaining access to refinery space. Venezuela's experiences in joint ventures prove the point. All of these are based on a netback-type arrangement, for which PDVSA has been roundly criticized for having undervalued its oil. In the cases where PDVSA is the sole owner of the refinery, losses can be hidden in the company's consolidated income statements. Third, PDVSA argued that integration could take advantage of any fluctuations in crude prices: "by controlling all the segments of the industry, volume can be maintained and revenues maximized, either from the production segment or from the refining and retail sales, according to the conditions of the market" (CEPET 1989, 2:175). However, these gains are short-lived, because competition will cause refining margins to fall in line with crude prices eventually. Refining margins that are higher than the average will bring more capacity online, which in turn will bring the margins down. Finally, overseas refineries were supposed to provide secure outlets for Venezuela's heavy crudes, which are unattractive to refineries, because of their viscosity and sulphur and metal contents. But instead of using the overseas refineries in this manner, PDVSA uses much of its capacity to run some of its lightest crudes in the United States and medium crudes in its Ruhr Öl plants.

13. In 1987 PDVSA had to order its exploration and production affiliates, Maraven, Lagoven, and Corpoven, to cut operating costs by 5–15 percent and cut investment expenditures by 30 percent. In all, PDVSA cut spending by 22

percent that year (Sweeney 1987, 3). The year 1992 brought a reduction of 7 percent, ordered by the government, mostly from capital projects that were intended to lift capacity by about 117,000 barrels/day that year; by the end of the year PDVSA had cut US$1 billion from its US$5 billion capital investment budget. In 1992 PDVSA also slashed its five-year capital spending plan by about US$6 billion, down to about US$20 billion, in response to weak prices and high taxes.

14. For example, Auty (1990, 142–44) judges PDVSA management (as opposed to some of the uses to which oil revenues were put by the Venezuelan government) as relatively solid. Not infrequently, discussions of state oil companies in other countries invoke PDVSA as an example to be emulated.

15. PDVSA has also set up specialized subsidiaries — Pequiven to handle petrochemicals, Intevep for technology, Bariven for imports, Interven to manage foreign refineries and distribution systems, and Corpozulia for coal development. Yet the essential issue of competition concerns the three exploration and production affiliates.

16. In 1976 PDVSA required the affiliates to establish coordinating groups for computing and telecommunications, control and finances, domestic marketing, exploration, housing, materials and technical services, organization and human resources, planning, production, refining, technology, and trade and supply. In 1977 PDVSA organized coordinating groups for the Faja Petrolífera del Orinoco, information and public relations, and petrochemicals. Cooperation on medical affairs, organizational development, relations with the comptroller general, and urban development and environment began in 1980, security in 1984, and loss prevention and control in 1985 (PDVSA 1976–85; Randall 1987, 45).

17. Ordinance 16 establishing the board stated "It shall be the duty of the Board to secure the most favourable arrangements for the purchase, grading and selling of Gold Coast cocoa, and to assist in the development, by all possible means, of the cocoa industry of the Gold Coast for the benefit and prosperity of the producers."

18. The only exception was the 1956/57 harvest, for which the low world price required the Cocoa Board to deplete its reserves to cover the farmgate price (Beckman 1976, 279).

19. It is true that by 1964, the Nkrumah government was prepared to raise other taxes, but that was because it was desperate to maintain government spending levels in the face of depressed world cocoa prices and a severe domestic recession.

20. Sarris and Shams (1991, 2) conclude that

although worse was to come in the nineteen-seventies, it is important to understand that the economic crisis then was due to the relative neglect of the agricultural sector in the nineteen-sixties. Ghana's post-independence economic strategy emphasized rapid industrialization by state-owned enterprises (SOEs) at the expense of agriculture. This resulted in lower export production and export earnings. Industrial strategy opted for self-reliance, and established import-substitution industries behind highly protective trade and nontrade barriers. This caused further economic deterioration during 1973–83: GDP fell by 1.3 percent per annum, industrial output by 7 percent, exports by 6.4 percent, imports by 8 percent, cocoa output by 7.1 percent and food production by 2.7 percent. The annual rate of inflation rose from about 6 percent during 1965–73 to 50 percent overall in the following decade. During the period 1973–83 annual inflation rates of 53.2 percent for food prices and 46.5 percent for nonfood prices were registered . . . In 1970–81, cereal output fell by 2.3 percent per annum and that of starchy staples by 3.7 percent. The decline in agricultural output was the result of policy choices based on incorrect signals in both factor and produce markets, resulting in domestic distortions inimical to growth, equity and poverty alleviation.

21. The world price collapse should not be considered as simply an external event. As the world's leading cocoa producer, Ghana's output had a significant effect on the world supply, and the government had rebuffed overtures from Brazil for all major cocoa exporters to "coordinate" marketing operations (Beckman 1976, 190).

22. For crop years 1969/70 and 1970/71, the cocoa farmers' payments were 50 percent and 37 percent of total export proceeds, compared to 59 percent for the period 1960/61 to 1966/67 (calculated from figures given in Killick 1978, 119).

23. May (1985, 69) cites estimates ranging from 8,000 to 21,000 MT annually for the 1960s, with total production averaging around 400,000 MT; and between 30,000 and 50,000 MT in the 1970s, when total production averaged roughly 350,000 MT. When production was lowest, dipping below 300,000 MT in the late 1970s, smuggling was highest, reaching 45,000 MT in 1977/78 and 50,000 in 1978/79.

24. In the language of economics, the government's (and people's) "discount rate," or preference for receiving income now rather than later, may be very high. When this occurs, a more rapid time path of resource extraction is not a policy failure per se.

25. Rietbergen (1988). The biological diversity has been recognized by the International Union for the Conservation of Nature in including Cameroon on its list of "megadiversity" countries (Horta 1991, 142).

26. DeLancey (1989, 141–43). He notes that oil income dropped in 1986 alone by 60 percent from 1985 levels.

27. A more detailed critique by the World Resources Institute staff can be found in Halpin (1990).

28. According to the governmental Centre National de Developpement des Forêts, cited in Rietbergen (1988, 34).

29. Published in Besong (1992), as one paper presented at a World Bank conference on forestry in West and Central Africa.

30. The government's interest in ignoring the sustainability of shifting cultivation arises in our cases of forestry in both Indonesia and Malaysia.

31. Perhaps the most overt example was the Cameroon Development Corporation, established in 1947 under the British colonial administration of West Cameroon, which was essentially mandated to transform uncultivated areas into plantations, primarily in export crops such as palm oil, rubber, tea, bananas, and pepper. In establishing processing operations for these crops, the CDC became a major employer, with twenty thousand employees by 1980 (Ndongko 1986, 112–13). These operations were also a major source of financing for the government.

32. It is important to recognize that the issue is not whether there will be any contact between remote forest dwellers and "modernized" agriculturalists. Bailey, Bahuchet, and Hewlett (1992, 204) point out that "there are no people living today in central Africa independently of agriculture as pure hunter-gatherers, and all evidence suggests that this has been true for many hundreds of years . . . if indeed pygmies *ever* lived in the forest without access to agricultural foods." The issue is whether particular forms of contact, changes in the ecosystem, and increasing population will have positive impacts. Musa (1997) surveys some cases of "pygmy" families gaining greater access to cash-earning opportunities, education, and health care, but also suffering from demeaning labor opportunities. According to Ngangoue (1995), "pygmies" from Cameroon, Gabon, Congo (Brazzaville), and the Central African Republic are often materially better off, through labor with the logging companies or as contract hunters, but women's workloads have increased because of the shift to cultivating staple and cash crops, and working arrangements bordering on forced servitude sometimes prevail.

CHAPTER 7. *Conclusions and Recommendations*

1. This is not a peculiarity of copper companies. Zambian Consolidated Copper Mines has been one of the least accountable and most corrupt parastatals anywhere. See Aron (1991).

2. It must be acknowledged, however, that the boundary between the creation of rent-seeking opportunities and income redistribution as a programmatic objective can be fuzzy. For example, many governments subsidize particular population segments, such as residents of the capital city or of an especially powerful labor union, in order to enlist their political support and quell their dissatisfaction. There may be nothing inconsistent about arriving at a convergence of programmatic objective to improve the incomes of a particular sector, income stratum, or region, while also enjoying the increased cooperation of the beneficiaries.

3. Referring here to the so-called reforestation fund ultimately used to finance the state aerospace industry rather than tree planting.

4. Similar patterns occurred in Indonesia, as summarized in Ascher and Healy (1990, ch. 4), pitting the *transmigrasi* resettlement agency against the Forestry Ministry.

5. Thus, my principle does not imply centralization of all activities under the national government operating through its central budget. Subnational governments should follow the same logic of making expenditure decisions at a high enough level to promote a healthy discourse and accountability of public officials.

6. Note that parallel arrangements can be implemented for mainline government agencies. It may not seem feasible or wise to provide budgetary discretion; after all, the central budget each year is supposed to cover the programmatic and administrative costs of the priorities chosen at the highest levels. However, there can be sensible arrangements whereby the agency can have a stronger guarantee that its budget for the following year will be predictably close to the medium-term (one-to-three-year) budget planning that virtually all agencies undertake. There can also be sensible arrangements to allow well-performing agencies to enjoy greater latitude in how they allocate their budgets.

References

Abt Associates. 1990. *Costa Rica Natural Resource Policy Inventory. Vol. 2: The Inventory.* Bethesda, Md.: Abt Associates.

Adegbulube, A. O., and F. B. Dayo. 1986. Demand analysis of gasoline consumption in Nigeria. *OPEC Review* 10 (summer): 131–41.

Adesina, Jimi. 1994. *Labour in the Explanation of an African Crisis: A Critique of Current Orthodoxy: The Case of Nigeria.* Oxford: Council for the Development of Social Science Research in Africa.

Adlin, Tengku. 1988. A view on forest conservation. *Berita IDS* (Kota Kinabalu) 3 (2) (March/April): 21–22.

African Development Consulting Group. 1996. *Nigerian Oil Industry: A Survey.* Lagos: ADCG Publications.

Aharoni, Yair. 1982. State-owned enterprise: An agent without a principal. In *Public Enterprise in Developing Countries*, edited by Leroy Jones. Cambridge: Cambridge University Press.

Aharoni, Yair, and William Ascher. 1991. *Indian Copper Policy and the Protected Niche of Hindustan Copper Limited.* November. Durham: Center for International Development Research Report for the World Bank.

Ahmad Khan, Sarah. 1994. *Nigeria: The Political Economy of Oil.* Oxford: Oxford University Press.

Allende, Juan. 1985. State enterprises and political environments: Chile's National Copper Corporation. Ph.D. dissertation, Department of Political Science, University of North Carolina, Chapel Hill.

Arhin, Kwame. 1985. The Ghana Cocoa Marketing Board and the farmer. In *Marketing Boards in Tropical Africa*, edited by Kwame Arhin, Paul Hesp, and Laurens van der Laan. London: KPI.

Aron, Janine. 1991. *Political Mismanagement of a Mining Parastatal: The Case of Zambia Consolidated Copper Mines Limited.* Oxford: Oxford University Centre for the Study of African Economies.

Ascher, William. 1984. *Scheming for the Poor: The Politics of Income Redistribution in Latin America.* Cambridge: Harvard University Press.

——. 1993a. "Political Economy and Problematic Forestry Policies in Indonesia." September. Durham: Duke University Center for Tropical Conservation.

——. 1993b. "Science and Forestry Policy in Costa Rica and Honduras." February. Durham: Duke University Center for Tropical Conservation.

——. 1994. *Communities and Sustainable Forestry in Developing Countries.* San Francisco: ICS Press.

——. 1997. The politics of rent distribution and Latin American resource policy. In *Latin American Environmental Policy in International Perspective*, edited by Gordon MacDonald, Daniel Nelson, and Marc Stern. Boulder: Westview Press.

Ascher, William, and Robert Healy. 1990. *Natural Resource Policymaking in Developing Countries.* Durham: Duke University Press.

Auty, R. M. 1990. *Resource-Based Industrialization: Sowing the Oil in Eight Developing Countries.* Oxford: Clarendon Press.

Bailey, Robert, Serge Bahuchet, and Barry Hewlett. 1992. Development in the Central African rainforest: Concern for forest peoples. In *Conservation and West and Central African Rainforests*, edited by Kevin Cleaver, Mohan Munasinghe, Mary Dyson, Nicolas Egli, Axel Peuker, and François Wencelius. World Bank Environment Paper no. 1. Washington, D.C.: World Bank.

Baker, George. 1981. The eclipse of Mexican light. *Oil & Gas Journal* 79, no. 23 (12 June): 83–86.

Baklanoff, Eric. 1983. *Copper in Chile: The Expropriation of a Partially Nationalized Industry.* Technical Papers Series no. 38, Office for Public Sector Studies, Institute of Latin American Studies. Austin: University of Texas.

Baltodano, Victor, Roberto Chávez, Francisco Sequeira, and Laureano Montero. 1988. *FODEA.* Heredia, Costa Rica: Universidad Nacional.

Bangkuai, Joniston. 1995. Revamp for Sabah Foundation. *New Straits Times*, 23 March:8.

Barkin, David, and Gustavo Esteva. 1981. *El papel del sector público en la comercialización y la fijación de precios de los productos agrícolas basicos en México.* Mexico City: UN Economic Commission for Latin America.

Barnes, Philip. 1995. *Indonesia: The Political Economy of Energy.* Oxford: Oxford University Press.

Bates, Robert. 1981. *Markets and States in Tropical Africa.* Berkeley: University of California Press.

Bauer, Peter. 1954. *West African Trade: A Study of Competition, Oligopoly and Monopoly in a Changing Economy.* Cambridge: Cambridge University Press.

Bautista, Romeo, and Alberto Valdez, eds. 1993. *The Bias against Agriculture.* San Francisco: ICS Press.

Beckman, Bjorn. 1976. *Organizing the Farmers: Cocoa Politics and National Development in Ghana.* Upsalla: Scandinavian Institute of African Studies.

Benítez P., Andres. 1990. Codelco: palos de ciego? *El Mercurio* (Santiago, Chile), 1 July: F1.

Besong, Joseph Bawak. 1992. New directions in national forestry policies: Cameroon. In *Conservation and West and Central African Rainforests,* edited by Kevin Cleaver, Mohan Munasinghe, Mary Dyson, Nicolas Egli, Axel Peuker, and François Wencelius. World Bank Environment Paper no. 1. Washington, D.C.: World Bank.

Bienen, Henry. 1985. *Political Conflict and Economic Change in Nigeria.* London: Frank Cass.

Bingkasan, Joseph, and Joniston Bangkuai. 1995. Sabah State Assembly. *New Straits Times,* 11 August: 9.

Binswanger, Hans. 1991. Brazilian policies that encourage deforestation in the Amazon. *World Development* 19 (7): 821–29.

Bitar, Sergio. 1979. The interrelationship between economics and politics. In *Chile at the Turning Point: Lessons of the Socialist Years,* edited by Federico Gil. Philadelphia: Institute for the Study of Human Issues.

Blaikie, Piers M. 1985. *The Political Economy of Soil Erosion in Developing Countries.* London: Longman.

Blank, David. 1986. Petroleum: The community and regional perspectives. In *Venezuela: The Democratic Experience,* edited by John Martz and David Myers. New York: Praeger.

Boado, Eufresina. 1988. Incentive policies and forest use in the Philippines. In *Public Policies and the Misuse of Forest Resources,* edited by Robert Repetto and Malcolm Gillis. Cambridge: Cambridge University Press.

Boué, Juan Carlos. 1993. *Venezuela: The Political Economy of Oil.* Oxford: Oxford University Press.

Brenes, Lidiette. 1991. La política económica en los 80 y el programa de ajuste estructural. In *Historia de Costa Rica en el siglo XX,* 3d ed., edited by Jaime Murillo and Astrid Fischel Volio. San José, Costa Rica: Editorial Porvenir.

Bresnan, John. 1993. *Managing Indonesia: The Modern Political Economy.* New York: Columbia University Press.

Broad, Robin. 1995. The political economy of natural resources: Case studies of the Indonesian and Philippine forest sectors. *Journal of Developing Areas* 29 (April): 317–40.

Bromley, Daniel, ed. 1992. *Making the Commons Work.* San Francisco: ICS Press.

Brossard, Emma. 1993. *Petroleum Research and Venezuela's INTEVEP: The Clash of the Giants.* Houston: Pennwell.

Browder, John. 1988. Public policy and deforestation in the Brazilian Amazon. In *Public Policies and the Misuse of Forest Resources,* edited by Robert Repetto and Malcolm Gillis. Cambridge: Cambridge University Press.

Bruenig, Eberhard. 1993. Integrated and multi-sectoral approaches to achieve sustainability of ecosystem development: The Sarawak forestry case. *Global Ecology and Biogeography Letters* 3 (4–6): 253–66.

Bruggermann, J., and E. Salas Mandujano. 1992. *Population Dynamics, Environmental Change and Development Processes in Costa Rica.* Geneva: United Nations Research Institute for Social Development.

Buliř, Aleš. 1996. Impact of cocoa taxation on cocoa supply in Ghana. In *Ghana: Selected Issues and Statistical Annex.* IMF Staff Country Report no. 96/69, November. Washington, D.C.: International Monetary Fund.

Bunker, Steven. 1985. *Underdeveloping the Amazon: Extraction, Unequal Exchange, and the Failure of the Modern State.* Urbana: University of Illinois Press.

Burgess, Peter. 1989. Asia. In *No Timber without Trees,* edited by Duncan Poore, Peter Burgess, John Palmer, Simon Rietbergen, and Timothy Synnott. London: Earthscan.

Business Times (Malaysia). 1995. Malaysia: New, better chapter for NBT. 24 April: 5.

Calderon Bertí, Humberto. 1978. *La nacionalización petrolera: Visión de un proceso.* Caracas: Graficas Armitano.

Campódonico, Humberto. 1986. *La política petrolera 1970–1985: El Estado, las contratistas y PetroPerú.* Lima: DESCO, Centro de Estudios y Promoción del Desarrollo.

Cárdenas, Marta, Hernán Dario Correa, and Mauricio Gómez Baron, eds. 1992. *Derechos territoriales indígenas y ecología en las selvas tropicales del América.* Bogotá: Gaia Foundation.

Castro, José Esteban. 1995. Decentralization and modernization in Mexico: The management of water services. *Natural Resources Journal* 35 (summer): 461–87.

CEPET. 1989. *La industria venezolana de los hidrocárburos.* Caracas: Ediciones del Centro de Formación y Adiestramiento de Petróleos de Venezuela y sus Filiales.

Chelliah, Raja. 1971. Trends in taxation in developing countries. *International Monetary Fund Staff Papers.* Washington, D.C.: International Monetary Fund.

Chemical Week. 1988. Forecast 1988: Mexico: Dealing with an economic crisis. 27 January: 30–31.

Cleaves, Peter, and Henry Pease García. 1983. State autonomy and military policy making. In *The Peruvian Experiment Reconsidered*, edited by Cynthia McClintock and Abraham Lowenthal. Princeton: Princeton University Press.

Clover, Charles. 1996. Britain backs "damaging" road plan in rainforest. *Daily Telegraph* (London), 9 September: 4.

Codelco (Chile). 1989. *El cobre en imágenes*. Santiago: Corporación Nacional del Cobre.

———. 1992. *Memoria anual 1992*. Santiago: Corporación Nacional del Cobre.

Coleman, Jonathan, Takamasa Akiyama, and Panos Varangis. 1993. *How Policy Changes Affected Cocoa Sectors in Sub-Saharan African Countries*. World Bank Policy Research Working Paper no. WPS 1129. Washington, D.C.: World Bank.

Corden, Max, and Peter Neary. 1982. Booming sector and deindustrialization in a small open economy. *Economic Journal* 92 (December): 825–48.

Coronel, Gustavo. 1983. *The Nationalization of the Venezuelan Oil Industry*. Lexington, Mass.: Lexington Books.

Crouch, Harold. 1988. *The Army and Politics in Indonesia*. Ithaca: Cornell University Press.

———. 1996. *Government and Society in Malaysia*. Ithaca: Cornell University Press.

Crow, Patrick. 1996. Rising tide of U.S. oil imports sparks debate on energy. *Oil & Gas Journal* 94, no. 24 (17 June): 16.

Cummings, Ronald, and Nahram Nercissiantz. 1992. The use of water pricing as a means for enhancing water use efficiency in irrigation: Case studies in Mexico and the United States. *Natural Resources Journal* 32 (fall): 731–55.

DeLancey, Mark. 1989. *Cameroon: Dependence and Independence*. Boulder: Westview Press.

Dove, Michael. 1983. Theories of swidden agriculture and political economy of ignorance. *Agroforestry Systems* 1 (3): 85–99.

The Economist. 1981. Pertamina: The profligates return? 20 June: 85.

———. 1990. The dwindling forest beyond Long San. 18 August: 23–24.

Egli, Nicolas. 1991. Summaries of country case studies of selected West and Central African countries. In *Forest Pricing and Concession Policies: Managing the High Forests of West and Central Africa*, edited by Mikael Grut, John Gray, and Nicolas Egli. World Bank Technical Paper no. 143. Washington, D.C.: World Bank.

Enríquez, Andrés. 1909. *Los grandes problemas nacionales*. Mexico City: A. Carranza e hijos.

ESMAP (Energy Sector Management Assistance Programme). 1993. *Nigeria Energy Assessment*. Washington, D.C.: World Bank.

FAO (Food and Agriculture Organization of the United Nations). 1994. *Current World Fertilizer Situation and Outlook*. Rome: FAO.

FAO (Food and Agriculture Organization of the United Nations) and Directorate General of Forest Utilization, Ministry of Forestry, Government of Indonesia. 1990. *Situation and Outlook of the Forestry Sector in Indonesia*. Jakarta: FAO.

Fearnside, Philip. 1985. Deforestation and decision-making in the development of Brazilian Amazonia. *Interciencia* 10 (September-October): 223–47.

Fitzgerald, Bruce. 1986. *An Analysis of Indonesian Trade Policies: Countertrade, Downstream Processing, Import Restrictions and the Deletion Program*. CPD Discussion Paper 1986–22. Washington, D.C.: World Bank.

Forrest, Tom. 1995. *Politics and Economic Development in Nigeria*. Updated version. Boulder: Westview Press.

Fortin, Carlos. 1984. Copper investment policy in Chile 1973–1984. *Natural Resources Forum* 8 (4): 315–25.

Franks, Alan. 1990. An axe over nature's nursery. *The Times* (London), 2 March.

Gallegos, Armando. 1985. *Mapa económico financiero de la actividad empresarial del estado peruano*. Lima: Escuela de Administración de Negocios.

Gartlan, Stephen. 1992. Practical constraints on sustainable logging in Cameroon. In *Conservation and West and Central African Rainforests*, edited by Kevin Cleaver, Mohan Munasinghe, Mary Dyson, Nicolas Egli, Axel Peuker, and François Wencelius. World Bank Environment Paper no. 1. Washington, D.C.: World Bank.

Gasques, J., and C. Yakimoto. 1986. *Resultados de 20 anos de incentivos fiscais na agropecuaria da Amazonia*. Brasilia: ANPEC.

Gelb, Alan. 1988. *Oil Windfalls: Blessing or Curse?* Oxford: Oxford University Press.

Geller, Lucio, and Jaime Estevez. 1972. La nacionalización del cobre. In *La economía chilena en 1971*, edited by Universidad de Chile. Santiago: Universidad de Chile.

Gieseke, Carlos. 1991. PetroPerú: A case study. Durham: Duke University Center for International Development Research. Duplicated.

Gil Díaz, Francisco. 1990. Tax reform issues in Mexico. In *World Tax Reform: Case Studies of Developed and Developing Countries*, edited by Michael Boskin and Charles McClure. San Francisco: ICS Press.

Gillis, Malcolm. 1987. Multinational enterprises and environmental and resource management issues in the Indonesian tropical forest sector. In *Multinational Corporations, Environment, and the Third World: Business Matters*, edited by Charles Pearson. Durham: Duke University Press.

———. 1988a. Indonesia: Public policies, resource management, and the tropical forest. In *Public Policies and the Misuse of Forest Resources*, edited by Robert Repetto and Malcolm Gillis. Cambridge: Cambridge University Press.

———. 1988b. West Africa: Resource management policies and the tropical forest. In *Public Policies and the Misuse of Forest Resources*, edited by Robert Repetto and Malcolm Gillis. Cambridge: Cambridge University Press.

———. 1988c. Malaysia: Public policies and the tropical forest. In *Public Policies and the Misuse of Forest Resources*, edited by Robert Repetto and Malcolm Gillis. Cambridge: Cambridge University Press.

———. 1992. Forest concession management and revenue policies. In *Managing the World's Forests*, edited by Narendra Sharma. Dubuque: Kendall/ Hunt Publishing for the World Bank.

Gillis, Malcolm, and Robert Repetto. 1988. Conclusion: Findings and policy implications. In *Public Policies and the Misuse of Forest Resources*, edited by Robert Repetto and Malcolm Gillis. Cambridge: Cambridge University Press.

González, L., E. Alpizar, and R. Muñoz. 1987. *Problematica del sector forestal.* San José, Costa Rica: Centro Científico Tropical.

Gorriz, Cecilia, Ashok Subramanian, and José Simas. 1995. *Irrigation Management Transfer in Mexico.* World Bank Technical Paper no. 292. Washington, D.C.: World Bank.

Government of India, Planning Commission. 1993. *Report of the Expert Group on Estimation of Proportion and Number of Poor.* New Delhi: Government of India.

Grayson, George. 1980. *The Politics of Mexican Oil.* Pittsburgh: University of Pittsburgh Press.

———. 1993. Will PEMEX follow YPF to the auction block? *Wall Street Journal*, 17 September: A11.

Greenberg, Martin. 1970. *Bureaucracy and Development: A Mexican Case Study.* Lexington, Mass.: D. C. Heath.

Grupo de Minería del CED. 1985. La Gran Minería del cobre y Codelco. In *Desarrollo Minero: evolución y desafíos para Chile*, edited by Centro de Estudios del Desarrollo. Santiago: Centro de Estudios del Desarrollo.

Guzman, Oscar. 1988a. PEMEX's finances. In *Energy Policy in Mexico*, edited by Miguel Wionczek, Oscar Guzman, and Roberto Gutiérrez. Boulder: Westview Press.

———. 1988b. Domestic oil policy. In *Energy Policy in Mexico*, edited by Miguel Wionczek, Oscar Guzman, and Roberto Gutierrez. Boulder: Westview Press.

Halpin, Elizabeth. 1990. *Indigenous Peoples and the TFAP.* World Resources Institute Report. Washington, D.C.: World Resources Institute.

Harberger, Arnold. 1983. Dutch disease: How much sickness, how much boom? *Resources and Energy* 5:1–20.

Haughton, Jonathan, Darius Teter, and Joseph Stern. 1992. Report on forestry taxation. Memorandum to Minister Saleh Afiff, 8 September, Jakarta.

Hecht, Susanna. 1984. Cattle ranching in Amazona: Political and ecological considerations. In *Frontier Expansion in Amazonia*, edited by Marianne Schmink and Charles Wood. Gainesville: University of Florida Press.

———. 1992. The logics of livestock and deforestation. In *Development or Destruction: The Conversion of Tropical Forest to Pasture in Latin America*, edited by Theodore Downing, Susanna Hecht, Henry Pearson, and Carmen Garcia-Downing. Boulder: Westview Press.

Hecht, Susanna, and Alexander Cockburn. 1989. *The Fate of the Forest: Developers, Destroyers and Defenders of the Amazon.* London: Verso.

Helsingin Sanomat. 1984. Enzo-Gutzeit of Finland will shortly complete a sawmill in the Olancho Province of Honduras. 24 March: 34.

Hepburn, A. 1979. The possibility for the sustained yield management of natural forest in Sabah with reference to the Sabah Foundation. *Malaysian Forester* 42 (4): 400–408.

Hewitt de Alcantara, Silvia. 1976. *Modernizing Mexican Agriculture: Socioeconomic Implications of Technological Change 1940–1970.* Geneva: UN Research Institute for Social Development.

Hindustan Copper Limited. 1991. Report of the Board of Directors, August 5. Calcutta: Hindustan Copper Limited.

Hindustan Copper Limited and Ministry of Mines, Government of India. 1991. Memorandum of Understanding for 1991–92, September. New Delhi: Government of India.

Horta, Korinna. 1991. The last big rush for the green gold: The plundering of Cameroon's rainforests. *Ecologist* 21 (May/June): 142–47.

Hunt, Shane. 1975. Direct foreign investment in Peru: New rules for an old game. In *The Peruvian Experiment: Continuity and Change under Military Rule*, edited by Abraham Lowenthal. Princeton: Princeton University Press.

Hurst, Philip. 1989. *Rainforest Politics: Ecological Destruction in South-east Asia.* Atlantic Highlands, N.J.: Zed Books.

IBGE (Instituto Brasileiro de Geografia e Estatistica). 1992. *Censo demografico 1991.* Brasilia: Government of Brazil.

Ikein, Augustine. 1990. *The Impact of Oil on a Developing Country: The Case of Nigeria.* New York: Praeger.

Inter Press Service. 1993. Honduras: IDB forces forest auction, lumber companies claim. 4 May: 1–2.

Iyer, Ramaswamy. 1990. *A Grammar of Public Enterprises*. Jaipur: Rawat Publications.

Jakarta Post. 1994. IPTN's loans converted to equity. 7 July: 1.

Jua, Nantang. 1990. *Economic Management in Neo-colonial States: A Case Study of Cameroon*. Research Report no. 38. Leiden: African Studies Center.

Killick, Tony. 1978. *Development Economics in Action: A Study of Economic Policies in Ghana*. New York: St. Martin's Press.

King, Victor. 1993. Politik Pembangunan: The political economy of rainforest exploitation and development in Sarawak, East Malaysia. *Global Ecology and Biogeography Letters* 3 (4–6): 235–44.

Kosmo, Mark. 1987. *Money to Burn? The High Costs of Energy Subsidies*. Washington, D.C.: World Resources Institute.

Kumar, Raj. 1986. *The Forest Resources of Malaysia: Their Economics and Development*. New York: Oxford University Press.

Kuswata, Kartawinata, Soedarsono Riswan, and Andrew Vayda. 1984. The impact of man on a tropical forest in Indonesia. *Ambio* 10 (2–3): 115.

Lasswell, Harold. 1936. *Politics: Who Gets What, When, How*. New York: McGraw-Hill.

Latin American Energy Alert. 1996. Mexico plans to boost public Pemex capital spending in 1997. 15 November: 2.

Latin American Weekly Report. 1989. Peru: Deal with Mobil. 28 September: 12.

Lewis, Peter. 1996. From prebendalism to predation: The political economy of decline in Nigeria. *Journal of Modern African Studies* 34 (1): 79–103.

Lieuwen, Edwin. 1985. The politics of energy in Venezuela. In *Latin American Oil Companies and the Politics of Energy*, edited by John D. Wirth. Lincoln: University of Nebraska Press.

Lutz, Ernst, and Herman Daly. 1990. Incentives, regulations, and sustainable land use in Costa Rica. Environment Working Paper no. 34, July. Washington, D.C.: World Bank.

Mahar, Dennis. 1989. *Government Policies and Deforestation in Brazil's Amazon Region*. Washington, D.C.: World Bank.

Mannion, A. M. 1997. *Global Environmental Change: A Natural and Cultural Environmental History*. Harlow, England: Addison-Wesley Longman.

Martínez, Aníbal R. 1989. *Venezuelan Oil: Development and Chronology*. London: Elsevier Applied Science.

May, Ernesto. 1985. *Exchange Controls and Parallel Market Economies in Sub-Saharan Africa: Focus on Ghana*. World Bank Staff Working Paper no. 711. Washington, D.C.: World Bank.

Mayorga Alba, Eleodoro. 1987. The social and economic effects of petroleum development in Peru. In *Social and Economic Effects of Petroleum Develop-*

ment, edited by Normal Gall and Eleodoro Mayorga Alba. Geneva: International Labour Office.

McDonald, Hamish. 1981. *Suharto's Indonesia.* Honolulu: University of Hawaii Press.

Means, Gordon. 1991. *Malaysian Politics: The Second Generation.* Singapore: Oxford University Press.

Méndez, Juan Carlos, ed. 1979. *Chilean Economic Policy.* Santiago: Ministry of Finance Budget Directorate.

Mengisteab, Kidane. 1990. *Ethiopia: Failure of Land Reform and Agricultural Crisis.* New York: Greenwood Press.

Mexico Trade and Law Reporter. 1992. Pemex's recent production history and future goals. Vol. 2, no. 5 (1 May): 1–8.

Mikell, Gwendolyn. 1989. *Cocoa and Chaos in Ghana.* New York: Paragon House.

Mill, John Stuart. 1848. *Principles of Political Economy, with Some of Their Applications to Social Philosophy.* London: Longmans, Green.

Mining, Geological and Metallurgical Institute of India. 1989. Hindustan Copper Limited: A profile. In *Indian Mining Directory.* 3d ed. Calcutta: Mining, Geological and Metallurgical Institute of India.

Ministry of Mines (Chile). 1990. *Analysis of the Current Situation at Codelco and Its Future Plans.* Santiago: Ministry of Mines.

Miranda, Marie Lynn, Olga Corrales, Michael Regan, and William Ascher. 1992. Forestry institutions. In *Managing the World's Forests,* edited by Narendra Sharma. Dubuque: Kendall/Hunt Publishing for the World Bank.

Mochida, Tomoo. 1996. Forestry policies and rent-seeking in Sarawak. Durham: Duke University Center for International Development Research. Duplicated.

Mora, Juan. 1982. *Esto nos dió López Portillo.* Mexico City: Anaya Editores.

Moran, Theodore. 1974. *Multinational Corporations and the Politics of Dependence: Copper in Chile.* Princeton: Princeton University Press.

Morris, James. 1984. *Honduras: Caudillo Politics and Military Rulers.* Boulder: Westview Press.

Musa, Tansa. 1997. Cameroon: Indigenous pygmies face challenge of integration. *Inter Press Service,* 3 August: 1–3.

Ndongko, Wilfred. 1986. *Economic Management in Cameroon: Policies and Performance.* Leiden: African Studies Center.

Nellis, John. 1989. *Contract Plans and Public Enterprise Performance.* World Bank Discussion Paper no. 48. Washington, D.C.: World Bank.

New Straits Times. 1996a. Foundation and Kitingan settle suit out of court. 7 March: 9.

——. 1996b. Sabah Foundation abolishes cash dividend payment. 15 August: 4.

——. 1996c. NBT takes steps to buy Sabah Softwoods. 21 December: 23.

Newswatch (Lagos). 1993. The oil subsidy trap. 15 March: 25–30.

Ngangouie, Nana. 1995. Congo: Culture: Pygmies lose out in modern world. *Inter Press Service*, 10 September: 1–2.

Nuhu-Koko, Abubakar. 1993. Redefining the role of government in domestic pricing policies: Some policy issues. Durham: Duke University Center for International Development Research. Duplicated.

Oil Daily. 1984. Nigeria cracks down on crude oil smuggling. 19 June: 10.

Oil & Gas Journal. 1986a. PDVSA's Citgo deal probed in Venezuela. Vol. 84, no. 22 (2 June): 26.

——. 1986b. PDVSA signs final accord to acquire Citgo stake. Vol. 84, no. 38 (22 September): 22.

——. 1992a. PDVSA's new president warns the Venezuelan government's onerous tax take is causing the state oil company to have a negative cashflow. Vol. 90, no. 19 (11 May): 32.

——. 1992b. PDVSA seeks foreign investment hike. Vol. 90, no. 31 (3 August): 41.

——. 1993. The role of state oil companies: Venezuela. Vol. 31, no. 33 (16 August): 50–54.

——. 1994. Pemex operating results slip amid restructuring. Vol. 92, no. 50 (12 December): 21.

Orive Alba, Adolfo. 1960. *La política de irrigación en México.* Mexico City: Fondo de Cultura Económica.

Ostrom, Elinor. 1990. *Governing the Commons: The Evolution of Institutions for Collective Action.* New York: Cambridge University Press.

——. 1992. *Crafting Institutions for Self-governing Irrigation Systems.* San Francisco: ICS Press.

Ostrom, Elinor, Larry Schroeder, and Susan Wynne. 1993. *Institutional Incentives and Sustainable Development: Infrastructure Policies in Perspective.* Boulder: Westview Press.

Otobo, Dafe. 1995. *The Trades Union Movement in Nigeria.* Lagos: Malthouse Press.

Oyog, Angeline. 1996. Cameroon: Transport plan threatens virgin rainforests. *Inter Press Service*, 21 August: 1–2.

Pascó-Font Quevedo, Alberto, and Arturo Briceño Lira. 1992. *La política de precios de los combustibles y la distribución del ingreso en el Perú: 1985–1990.* Lima: Grupo de Análisis para el Desarrollo.

PEMEX [Petróleos Mexicanos]. Various years. *Memoria de Labores.* Mexico City: PEMEX.

Petróleos de Venezuela, S.A. Various years. Annual report. Caracas: PDVSA.

Peluso, Nancy. 1992. *Rich Forests, Poor People: Resource Control and Resistance in Java*. Berkeley: University of California Press.

Pickles, David. 1989. Honduran forestry lumbers into crisis. *Financial Times*, 28 April: 42–43.

Pigou, Arthur. 1920. *The Economics of Welfare*. London: Macmillan.

Pinstrup-Andersen, Per, ed. 1988. *Food Subsidies in Developing Countries*. Baltimore: Johns Hopkins University Press.

Platt's Oilgram News. 1983. Venezuela expected to soon disclose aid plan for PDVSA. 6 July: 2.

——. 1984. Products smugglers persist in Nigeria. 11 September: 3.

——. 1989. Mexican president defends government policies on private investment in oil industry. 21 March: 1–2.

Pompermayer, Malori José. 1979. The state and frontier in Brazil. Ph.D. dissertation, Department of Political Science, Stanford University.

Pratt, Kwesi, Jr. 1990. Battle of the bean: Cocoa industry's new initiative. *West Africa*, 29 January: 128–29.

Pura, Raphael. 1990. Battle over forestry rights in Sarawak pits ethnic groups against wealthy loggers. *Asian Wall Street Journal*, 26 February: 16.

Radetzki, Marian. 1977. Where should developing countries' minerals be processed? The country view versus the multinational company view. *World Development* 5 (4): 325–34.

——. 1985. *State Mineral Enterprises*. Washington, D.C.: Resources for the Future.

Ramírez, Carlos. 1981. Las finanzas de PEMEX a punto de estallar por corrupción e incapacidad. *Proceso* 238 (25 May): 6.

Randall, Laura. 1978. *An Economic History of Argentina in the Twentieth Century*. New York: Columbia University Press.

——. 1987. *The Political Economy of Venezuelan Oil*. New York: Praeger.

Rao, M. V. N. R. S., and L. R. Vaidyanath. 1987. Copper in India: Survey, analysis and outlook. Calcutta: Bureau of Industrial Costs and Prices, Department of Industrial Development, Ministry of Industry, Government of India. Duplicated.

Républica de Chile. 1976. *Diario oficial*. Santiago: Government of Chile.

Républica de Honduras. 1974. *Ley forestal*. Tegucigalpa: Government of Honduras.

Rietbergen, Simon. 1988. Africa. In *Natural Forest Management for Sustainable Timber Production, Pre-project Report*, edited by Duncan Poore, Peter Burgess, John Palmer, Simon Rietbergen, and Timothy Synott. London: International Institute for Environment and Development.

Ross, Michael. 1996. The political economy of boom-and-bust logging in Indonesia, the Philippines and East Malaysia, 1950–1994. Ph.D. dissertation, Department of Politics, Princeton University.

Ross-Larson, Bruce. 1976. *The Politics of Federalism: Syed Kechik in East Malaysia*. Singapore: Bruce Ross-Larson.

Royaards, Albert, and William Hui. 1977. Indonesia struggles to recover from the Pertamina affair. *Euromoney* (March): 37–42.

Rutledge, Peter. 1976. Letter from Jakarta. *Business Week*, 25 October: 26.

Ruzicka, I. 1977. Rent appropriation in Indonesian logging: East Kalimantan 1972/3–1976/7. *Bulletin of Indonesian Economic Studies* 13 (July): 45–74.

Sanderson, Steven. 1986. *The Transformation of Mexican Agriculture*. Princeton: Princeton University Press.

Sarris, Alexander, and Hadi Shams. 1991. *Ghana under Structural Adjustment: The Impact on Agriculture and the Rural Poor.* New York: New York University Press.

Scarsborough, Erik. 1992. Some initial thoughts on long term forestry development objectives and policies in the context of the second long-term development plan. Natural Resources Management Project, Jakarta. Duplicated.

Schlager, Edella, and Elinor Ostrom. 1992. Property-rights regimes and natural resources. *Land Economics* 68 (3): 249–62.

Schneider, Ronald R. 1995. *Government and the Economy on the Amazon Frontier.* World Bank Environmental Paper no. 11. Washington, D.C.: World Bank.

Schramm, Gunter, and Fernando Gonzales. 1977. Pricing irrigation water in Mexico: Efficiency, equity and revenue considerations. *Annals of Regional Science* 11 (1) (March): 15–35.

Schwarz, Adam. 1989. Timber troubles. *Far Eastern Economic Review*, 6 April: 86–88.

———. 1990. A saw point for ecology. *Far Eastern Economic Review*, 19 April: 60.

———. 1994. *A Nation in Waiting: Indonesia in the 1990s.* St. Leonards, Australia: Allen & Unwin.

Schwarz, Adam, and Jonathan Friedland. 1992. Green fingers: Indonesia's Prajogo proves that money grows on trees. *Far Eastern Economic Review*, 12 March: 42–44.

Searle, Peter. 1983. *Politics in Sarawak: The Iban Perspective.* Singapore: Oxford University Press.

Secretaría de Planificación (Honduras). 1990. *Perfil ambiental de Honduras 1989.* Tegucigalpa: Government of Honduras.

Secretaría de Recursos Hidráulicos (Mexico). 1968. *Plan nacional de pequeña irrigación.* Mexico City: Government of Mexico.

Sharma, Narendra, Raymond Rowe, Keith Openshaw, and Michael Jacobson.

1992. World forests in perspective. In *Managing the World's Forests*, edited by Narendra Sharma. Dubuque, Iowa: Kendall/Hunt Publishing for the World Bank.

Shepherd, Gill. 1993. Local and national level forest management strategies—competing priorities at the forest boundary: The case of Madagascar and Cameroon. *Commonwealth Forestry Review* 72 (4): 316–20.

Smith, Wesley. 1992. Liberalizing the Mexican oil industry. *Mexico Trade and Law Reporter* 2, no. 12 (1 December): 1–15.

Solórzano, Raul, Ronnie de Camino, Richard Woodward, Joseph Tosi, Vicente Watson, Alexis Vásquez, Carlos Villalobos, Jorge Jiménez, Robert Repetto, and Wilfrido Cruz. 1991. *Accounts Overdue: Natural Resource Depreciation in Costa Rica*. Washington, D.C.: World Resources Institute.

Stallings, Barbara. 1983. International capitalism and the Peruvian military government. In *The Peruvian Experiment Reconsidered*, edited by Cynthia McClintock and Abraham Lowenthal. Princeton: Princeton University Press.

Stepan, Alfred. 1978. *The State and Society: Peru in Comparative Perspective*. Princeton: Princeton University Press.

Stesser, Stanley. 1991. A reporter at large in the rainforest. *New Yorker*, 27 May: 42–68.

Sweeney, John. 1987. PDVSA orders planners to slash operating, investment costs for 1987. *Platt's Oilgram News*, 23 April: 3.

———. 1992. PDVSA investments: Few dollars; tough choices. *Platt's Oilgram News*, 31 August: 5.

Synnott, Timothy. 1989. South America and the Caribbean. In *No Timber without Trees*, edited by Duncan Poore. London: Earthscan.

Tamayo, Jorge. 1946. La administración de los distritos de riego. *Trimestre Económico* 13 (July-September): 249–71.

———. 1964. *El problema fundamental de la agricultura mexicana*. Mexico City: Instituto Mexicano de Investigaciones Económicas.

Teichman, Barbara. 1988. *Policymaking in Mexico: From Boom to Crisis*. Boston: Allen & Unwin.

Thabatabai, Hamid. 1986. *Economic decline, access to food and structural adjustment in Ghana*. World Economic Programme Research Working Paper, 10-6/WP80. Geneva: International Labour Organisation.

Thiele, Rainer, and Manfred Wiebelt. 1993. National and international policies for tropical rain forest conservation: A quantitative analysis for Cameroon. *Environmental and Resource Economics* 3:501–31.

Tietenberg, Tom. 1992. *Environmental and Natural Resource Economics*. 3d ed. New York: HarperCollins.

Timmer, C. Peter, ed. 1991. *Agriculture and the State*. Ithaca: Cornell University Press.

Tironi, Ernesto. 1977. Issues in the development of resource-rich LDCs: Copper in Chile. In *Mineral Resources in the Pacific Area: Proceedings of the Ninth Pacific Trade and Development Conference*. San Francisco: Pacific Trade and Development Conference.

Tironi, Ernesto, and Grupo de Minería CED. 1985. Prioridades para la expansión del cobre: Empresas extranjeras o Codelco? In *Desarrollo minero: Evolución y desafíos para Chile*, edited by Ernesto Tironi, Jorge Bande, Ivan Valenzuela, Victor Zuniga, and José Miguel Vivanco. Santiago: Editorial Universitaria.

Tollison, Robert. 1982. Rent seeking: A survey. *Kyklos* 35:575–602.

Tsuruoka, Doug. 1991. Cutting down to size. *Far Eastern Economic Review*, 14 July: 43–46.

Utting, Peter. 1993. *Trees, Power and People*. London: Earthscan.

Vidal, John. 1990. Cameroon: The Korup project in Cameroon is regarded as an environmental priority for Africa. *The Guardian*, 2 March: 1–7.

Wakker, E. 1993. Mitsubishi's unsustainable timber trade: Sarawak. In *Restoration of Tropical Forest Ecosystems*, edited by Helmut Lieth and Martina Lohmann. Dordrecht: Kluwer.

WALHI. 1991. Sustainability and economic rent in the forestry sector. Jakarta: WALHI. Duplicated.

Walton, John. 1990. The economic structure of Sarawak. In *Margins and Minorities: The Peripheral Areas and Peoples of Malaysia*, edited by Victor King and Michael Parnwell. Hull, England: Hull University Press.

Werner, Johannes. 1993. A lack of refineries creates shortfall of unleaded fuel. *Business Mexico*, June: 1–6.

West Africa. 1994. Fuel price crisis. 10 October: 1752–53.

Wilson, Edward O. 1998. Back from chaos. *Atlantic Monthly*, March: 41–62.

Winterbottom, Robert. 1992. Tropical forestry action plans and indigenous people: The case of Cameroon. In *Conservation and West and Central African Rainforests*, edited by Kevin Cleaver, Mohan Munasinghe, Mary Dyson, Nicolas Egli, Axel Peuker, and François Wencelius. World Bank Environment Paper no. 1. Washington, D.C.: World Bank.

Wionczek, Miguel. 1982. La aportación de la política hidráulica entre 1925 y 1970 a la actual crisis agrícola mexicana. *Comercio Exterior* 32 (April): 394–409.

Wood, Charles, and John Wilson. 1984. The magnitude of migration to the Brazilian frontier. In *Frontier Expansion in Amazonia*, edited by Marianne Schmink and Charles Wood. Gainesville: University of Florida Press.

World Bank. 1989. *Chile Mining Sector Memorandum, June 15*. Report no. 7509-CH. Washington, D.C.: World Bank.

——. 1990. *Indonesia: Sustainable Development of Forests, Land, and Water.* Washington, D.C.: World Bank.

World Resources Institute. 1996. *World Resources: A Guide to the Global Environment.* New York: Oxford University Press.

Yates, P. Lamartine. 1981. *Mexico's Agricultural Dilemma.* Tucson: University of Arizona Press.

Yergin, David. 1991. *The Prize: The Epic Quest for Oil, Money & Power.* New York: Simon & Schuster.

Zama, Isaac. 1995. Achieving sustainable forest management in Cameroon. *Review of European Community and International Environmental Law* 4 (3): 263–70.

Index

AB Nynas, 217

Abt Associates, 150–51, 292

Accountability, 16, 23, 26, 38, 46–47, 55–57, 60, 217, 254

Acheampong, Ignatius, 229

Adegbulube, A. O., 295

Adesina, Jimi, 181

Adlin, Tengku, 99

Africa, 235, 301

African Development Bank, 237, 241

African Development Consulting Group, 185

Agricultural conversion, 110

Agricultural development, 4, 11–14, 86, 94–96, 130, 132, 137, 140, 290; Africa, 95; Amazonia, 85–86, 117–21; Argentina, 195; Asia, 95; Cameroon, 234; Colombia, 95; Costa Rica, 150–53; Egypt, 86, 94; Ethiopia, 195–96; extension, 86; Ghana, 227; India, 86; Irian Jaya, 72; Kalimantan, 72; Latin America, 95; Mexico, 94; 130–41; Nigeria, 180; Sumatra, 72; Agricultural strategies, 86, 96, 132, 290; Amazonia, 117–21; Costa Rica, 150; Egypt, 86, 94; extensification, 86; Ghana, 227; intensification, 86; Mexico, 94, 130–41; Nigeria, 180

Aguilar, Andres, 215

Aharoni, Yair, 266, 276

Ahmad Khan, Sarah, 179, 182, 295

Air pollution, 10; Mexico, 210

Ajaokuta Steel Mill, 16, 179

Allende, Juan, 292

Allende, Salvador, 153–55, 252

Alpizar, E., 152

Aluminum processing, 8, 11

Amazon, 8, 15, 116–23, 288–89

Andres Pérez, Carlos, 212–13

Apkindo (Indonesian Wood Panel Association), 78

Appropriation of forests: Cameroon, 233; Honduras, 111; Indonesia, 72

Aquifer depletion, 11; Mexico, 130

Aral Sea, 11

Argentina, 5, 195

Argentine Institute for Trade Promotion, 195

Arhin, Kwame, 224, 225, 228

Arias, Oscar, 149, 152

Aron, Janine, 301

Arthur Young & Associates, 66

Ascher, William, 11, 79, 115–16, 120, 155, 195, 276, 282, 287, 291–92, 296, 302

Association of Amazonian Entrepreneurs, 118

Auty, R. M., 10, 16, 63, 87, 179, 282, 299

Bahuchet, Serge, 301

Bailey, Robert, 301

Baklanoff, Eric, 155

Baltodano, Victor, 150

Bangkuai, Joniston, 108, 287

Bank Bumi Daya, 76
Bank Duta, 76
Bank Indonesia, 66
BAPPENAS (Indonesian National Planning Agency), 59, 62, 65, 70, 78, 83
Bariven, 299
Barkin, David, 140
Barnes, Philip, 67, 69, 70, 71
Barra del Colorado Wildlife Refuge, 151
Bates, Robert, 225
Bauer, Peter, 194, 224
Bautista, Romeo, 41
Beckman, Bjorn, 224–28, 230, 299–300
Belaúnde Terry, Fernando, 126, 127
Benítez P., Andres, 163
Besong, Joseph Bawak, 240, 301
Bienen, Henry, 180–81
Bingkasan, Joseph, 108
Binswanger, Hans, 14, 122, 123
Biodiversity, 122, 237
Bitar, Sergio, 155
Biya, Paul, 238
Blaikie, Piers, 11, 27
Blank, David, 222
Boado, Eufresina, 91
Bolivia, 5, 7
Bottome, Robert, 219
Boué, Juan Carlos, 211, 217–18, 220, 222, 298
Bratanata, Slamet, 64
Brazil, 1, 4–5, 9, 11, 86, 115–17, 281, 288–89, 300; afforestation, 123; Agency for Research in Agriculture and Cattle Ranching (EMBRAPA), 120; Amazon, 115–24; cattle ranching, 150–52; colonization of frontiers, 117; conversion of forest lands, 119; deforestation, 116, 120, 122; forest value, 118; geopolitics, 115; hardwood exports, 119; INCRA, 118–20; land claims, 116; land giveaways, 115–22; log-export ban, 118; March to the West, 117; National Indian Foundation (FUNAI), 120; National Integration Program, 118;

Operation Amazonia, 118; population, 115, 122; Program for Amazonian Development, 118; Rondonia, 117, 120, 288–89; Transport Ministry, 142
Brenes, Lidiette, 149
Briceño Lira, Arturo, 128
Broad, Robin, 27, 72–74, 82–83
Bromley, Daniel, 271
Brossard, Emma, 92
Browder, John, 91, 116, 119, 121, 288
Bruggerman, J., 151
Buliř, Aleš, 230
Bunker, Steven, 119
Burgess, Peter, 105
Busia, Kofi, 229

Calderon Bertí, Humberto, 215, 219, 222
Calles, Plutarco Elías, 132, 139, 290
Cameroon, 1, 5, 9, 20, 300–301; agricultural exports, 234; Baka, 236; Bakola, 236; commercial logging, 231; conservation, 233–34, 238; Direction des Forêts (DIRFOR), 241–42; FAO/ UNDP report, 236; fifth Five-Year Plan, roads, 234; Food Development Authority, 241; forest appropriation, 241; forest protection, 242; Forestry Department, 240; forêt de domaine national, 233; forêt domaniale, 233; intragovernmental rivalries, 241; Korup National Park, 235–38; national park initiative, 20; NGO involvement, 236, 238; Tropical Forestry Action Plan, 236
Cameroon Development Corporation (CDC), 241, 301
Cameroon National Forestry Development Center, 242
Campódonico, Humberto, 124
Carbon sequestration, 7
Cárdenas, Lázaro, 133–34, 193
Cárdenas, Marta, 193
Castro, José Esteban, 290–91
Cattle-ranching, 189; in Brazilian Ama-

zon, 118; subsidies in Brazil, 150–52; subsidies in Costa Rica, 150–52

Center for International Development Research, Duke University, 281

Central Africa, 13, 301; drought in, 234

Central African Republic, 5, 301

Central America, 112, 281

Central Asia, 11

Central budget process, 24–25, 54

Centromin, 16

CEPET, 298

CFA states, 184

Chambira, 290

Champlin Refining Company, 217

Chandra Asri Petrochemical Complex, 76

Cheap energy, 11, 12. *See also* Energy-intensive industrialization

Chelliah, Raja, 296

Chicontepec oil fields, 201–2

Chile, 1, 5, 6, 7, 21, 32, 155, 289, 292; budget process, 165; collective state societies, 155; copper, 11, 123, 153–65, 189, 205, 252, 289, 292; diversification, 11; Escondida deposit, 159, 292; Finance Ministry, 156–61, 189–90; foreign debt, 160, 164; inflation, 155; Santiago, 158; Unidad Popular, 154; wage levels, 168. *See also* Codelco Chilean Confederation of Copper Workers, 156, 161–62

Chilean Copper Commission (Cochilco), 156

Chilean Copper Corporation, 155

Chilean National Copper Corporation. *See* Codelco

Chin, S. C., 103

China, 4, 5, 6, 12

Chinese: in Indonesia, 74–78, 82–83; in Sabah, 107; in Sarawak, 100, 102

Chuquicamata Mine, 159–61. *See also* Codelco

Citgo, 213

Cleaves, Peter, 126, 289

Clover, Charles, 237

CNI (Comisíon National de Irrigacíon), 134, 141

Cochilco. *See* Chilean Copper Commission

Cockburn, Alexander, 117, 121

Cocoa, 95; Ghana, 196, 225–30, 299; world prices, 228–30. *See also* Ghana Cocoa Marketing Board

Cocoa Purchasing Company, 224

Codelco (Chilean National Copper Corporation), 11, 17, 123, 153–65, 189, 252, 289, 292; accountability, 153, 162; autonomy issues, 156–65; budget and finances, 154–65; Chuquicamata mine, 159–60; cost advantages, 153, 164; efficiency, 153, 158, 161–62; El Teniente Mine, 161–63; ghost workers, 203; history, 153; joint ventures, 164; labor and wage issues, 161–63; Las Pampas deposit, 159; management selection, 158, 161; and military, 165; new deposit development, 158–59; presidential oversight, 157; privatization, 163; relations with government ministries, 155–65, 213; revenues, 156; undercapitalization, 157–61

COHDEFOR (Honduran Forestry Development Corporation), 89, 110–15, 253, 265; downstream diversification, 110–15; history, 110; international borrowing and debt, 113–15; mandate, 111; reserve management, 112; Siguatepeque mill, 112–13; Yoro mill, 112–13

Coleman, Jonathan, 229

Competition, 34, 36–37, 43; within Venezuela's PDVSA, 222

Confiscation: of private or communal property, 192; of resource access, 52

Conservation, 3, 8, 12; Cameroon, 234, 238; Costa Rica, 152

Copper, 1, 6–7, 15, 30, 154–56, 165–77, 188–89, 293–95; Canada, 165; Chile, 11, 123, 153–65, 189, 252, 289, 292;

Copper (*continued*)
India, 147, 165–77, 293–95; United States, 165; world prices, 34, 155, 167; Zambia, 5, 165, 281, 297
Corden, Max, 291
Corfino, 89, 112. *See also* COHDEFOR
Coronel, Gustavo, 92, 211–12, 214–15, 222, 297–98
Corporación Forestal Industrial de Olancho (Corfino), 112
Corporación Nacional del Cobre. *See* Codelco
Corporación Venezolana Guayana. *See* CVG
Corpoven, 298. *See also* PDVSA
Corpozulia, 299
Correa, Hernán Dario, 193
Corruption, 15, 185; and Nigerian oil, 178, 185
Costa Rica, 1, 5, 9, 20, 148–53, 292; agro-exporters, 149; Caribbean Basin Initiative, 149; debt-rescheduling, 150; export-promotion strategy, 148–49; forestry policies, 148–53; Instituto de Desarrollo Agrario (IDA), 152; land reform, 112, 152; Ley Fodea, 150; liberalization, 148–49; reforestation-incentive program, 20, 151–52; rent-seeking, 151–52; unrest, 149
Crocker Range Timber (CRT), 287
Crouch, Harold, 77, 105, 107, 287
Cummings, Ronald, 137, 142, 291
CVG (Corporación Venezolana Guayana), 196, 213, 214
CVRD (Companhia Vale Rio Doce), 11

Daly, Herman, 91, 93, 150, 292
Dams, 8, 11; Mexico, 130
De la Madrid, Miguel, 209–10
Deforestation, 9, 13; agricultural conversion, 72; Brazil, 116, 122; Cameroon, 232–33, 241; cattle ranching, 116; commercial logging, 149; plantations, 72; Costa Rica, 148–49; Honduras,

113–14; Indonesia, 103, 119–22; Laos, 13; Malaysia, 99, 103; Sabah, 99; Sarawak, 99, 102–03; shifting cultivation, 72; causes of, 72; Thailand, 13
DeLancey, Mark, 234, 301
De Oteyza, Jose, 205
Díaz Ordaz, Gustavo, 136
Díaz Serrano, Jorgé, 200–6
Dirección General Forestal (DGF), 151–53, 269
Domestic fuel prices: Cameroon, 184; Indonesia, 60, 69–70; Mexico, 198, 208–10, 252; Nigeria, 178, 180–84, 209; Peru, 127–28, 251; reform, 209–10; subsidies, 10–11, 34; Venezuela, 209–10
Dove, Michael, 28, 103, 282
Downstream diversification, 86–88, 173; minerals processing, 88; Nigeria, 178; wood-products, 87
Downstream industrialization, 87–90, 110–12, 178
Drought: central Africa, 234; Ethiopia, 196; Mexico, 130
Dutch disease, 180, 282, 291
Dynamic efficiency, definition of, 33

Echeverría, Luis, 198–9
Economically marginal populations, low extractive potential of, 192, 194
Ecosystems, 2, 8; collapse, 12; management, 83
Efficiency, defining, 33
Egli, Nicolas, 233
Ejidos, 133–35, 138–40, 291
Energy, 3, 39, 70, 94, 178, 198; conservation, 4; consumption, 12; entitlement nature of, 70; hidden costs of production, 39; prices, 12, 17, 70; subsidies, 12
Energy-intensive industrialization: Mexico, 86; Nigeria, 86; Peru, 123; Venezuela, 86, 213
Enríquez, Andrés, 291
ESMAP, 182

Estate crops, 95
Esteva, Gustavo, 140
Estevez, Jaime, 154
Ethiopia, 195, 196
Etibet, Don, 183
Europe, 204; economic recovery, 226
Exports, 6, 10; boom, 7; earnings, 4, 7; promotion in Costa Rica, 148–49. *See also* Dutch disease; Oil boom effects
Externalities, 38. *See also* Negative externalities; Positive externalities

FAO. *See* UN Food and Agricultural Organization
Fearnside, Philip, 120
Fertilizer, 4, 14; pricing, 34
Financial resources, categories, 8, 20
Fiscal resources, categories, 11
Fitzgerald, Bruce, 285
Food, 3–4; price ceilings, 34; prices in Nigeria, 180
Forest fires, Honduras, 113
Forest rents: Cameroon, 231; Indonesia, 77–78
Forest, 1–2, 8–9, 12, 33–35, 72. *See also* Logging
Forestry policies, 10, 99, 149, 152, 234–35, 241; Brazil, 152; Cameroon, 231–35, 239, 241; Costa Rica, 149, 152, 186; Honduras, 115; Indonesia, 75, 99; Sarawak, 99
Forrest, Tom, 184–86
Fortin, Carlos, 292
Forward integration, 86
Franks, Alan, 237, 238, 239
Frei, President Eduardo, 154–55, 165
Friedland, Jonathan, 76
Fuel conservation, 10
Fuel prices. *See* Domestic fuel prices
FUNAI. *See* Brazil, National Indian Foundation

García, Alan, 128
Gartlan, Stephen, 238

Gasoline, 10, 12; as luxury good in Mexico, 210; pollution taxes, 34
Gasques, J., 116
Gazetting of forest lands, 35
Gelb, Alan, 179, 180, 213, 282
Geller, Lucio, 154
General Agreement in Tariffs and Trade (GATT), 5
Germany, 217
Ghana, 1, 5, 223–29, 300; Agricultural Ministry, 227; Ashanti Confederacy, 224, 227; Central Bank, 229; Chamber of Commerce, 224; Cocoa Duty and Funds Act of 1954, 225; Cocoa Duty Ordinance, 226; cocoa farming, 223–31; Convention People's Party (CPP), 224–27; currency overvaluation, 229–30; economic crisis, 227; Finance Ministry, 227; government unity, 226; import-substitution industrialization, 227; Joint Provincial Council, 224; Produce Buying Agency, 228; University College, 225; vertical integration, 90
Ghana Cocoa Marketing Board, 196, 223–29, 299; mandate, 225; pricing policies, 230; relations with farmers, 228; relations with government ministries, 241; reserves, 225, 228; revenues, 225; transparency, 225
Ghanaian Cocoa Manufacturers Agencies, 224
Ghatsila copper deposit, 168. *See also* HCL
Gieseke, Carlos, 124–25, 127–28
Gil Díaz, Francisco, 198–99
Gillis, Malcolm, 9, 14, 80, 87–90, 100, 107, 118, 284–86, 288
Golbery do Couto e Silva, General, 117, 122
Gold Coast Cocoa Marketing Board, 224. *See also* Ghana Cocoa Marketing Board
Gold Coast, 299. *See also* Ghana
Gómez Baron, Mauricio, 193

Gonzales, Fernando, 135, 136
González, L., 152
Gorriz, Cecilia, 130, 137, 138
Government-controlled lands, rent capture by treasury, 190
Government-provided inputs, 34
Grayson, George, 202, 208
Grazing lands: erosion, 41; fees, 11
Green Revolution, 4
Greenberg, Martin, 134
Grupo de Minería del CED, 15, 92, 163–64
Gulf War, 207
Guzman, Oscar, 15, 199, 201, 203–6, 209–10, 296

Halpin, Elizabeth, 301
Harberger, Arnold, 291
Harun, Tun Mustapha, 104–6, 287
Haryono, Piet, 65
Hasan, Mohamed (Bob), 78–79, 286
Haughton, Jonathan, 75, 80, 282
HCL (Hindustan Copper Limited), 165–72, 293–95; accounting, 174; downstream diversification, 173–74; energy conservation, 175; finances, 170–71; history, 168; import rent capture, 173; inefficiency, 175; international borrowing and debt, 171, 175, 177; labor relations, 169; mandate, 168; pricing, 165–77; relations with government ministries, 166–72, 175–76; Taloja, 173
Healy, Robert, 11, 115, 116, 120, 282, 291, 302
Hecht, Susanna, 27, 116, 117, 118, 119, 121, 122, 288
Hepburn, A., 106
Hernández Galicia, Joaquín, 208
Hewitt de Alcantara, Silvia, 291, 301
Hindustan Copper Limited. See HCL
Honduran Foresty Development Coporation. See COHDEFOR
Honduras, 1, 5, 9, 110; deforestation, 114; forestry, 89, 110–15, 231, 253, 265;

land reform, 112; military, 111; National Agrarian Institute (INA), 112–13; wood-products industry, 89, 98, 112; Yodeco Timber Company, 112–13; Yoro Department, 113. See also COHDEFOR
Horta, Korinna, 232–36, 300
Hui, William, 66
Hunt, Shane, 124
Hurst, Philip, 99, 108, 287
Hurtado, Juan Carlos, 290

ICC. See Indian Copper Corporation Limited
Ikein, Augustine, 179
Import-substitution, Ghana, 227
Income redistribution, 30, 147
India, 1, 4, 5, 6, 30, 165, 281, 292, 293; Bihar 168, 295; copper mining, 30, 165–78; Congress Party, 169; Defence Ministry, 167, 176–77, 262, 272; employment policy, 167–68; Finance Ministry, 166, 170–73, 177, 276, 293–94; Labour Ministry, 167, 170, 172, 175; Maharashthra, 169, 173; military conflicts, 168; Planning Commission, 294; Taloja, 173–74; tariff barriers, 166; wage levels, 167
Indian Copper Corporation Limited (ICC), 166, 168–69, 177, 292, 295
Indian National Metal Workers Federation, 169
Indonesia, 1, 4–5, 9–10, 13, 29, 59–62, 64–65, 82, 88, 184, 281, 283–84, 301; aircraft industry, 29, 80; BAPPENAS (Planning Agency), 59, 62, 65, 70, 78, 83; Chinese in, 74–78, 82–83, 86; civil service efficiency, 63; Commission of Four, 64–65, 71; Communist insurrection, 61; Domestic Investment Law of 1968, 72; Finance Ministry, 59, 62, 64–65, 262; food riots, 61; forestry, 71–84; Forestry Ministry, 71, 75, 78–80, 83–84, 104, 226, 265, 285–86; Golkar Party,

79; international debt, 65; Irian Jaya, 283; military, 61–62, 184; National Energy Coordinating Board, 69; nationalist development agenda, 80, 226; oil, 59–71, 212; Outer Islands, 60; Pancasila, 83, 102; petrochemical industry, 76; political culture, 83, 102; Pontianak, 286; Pribumi, 74, 76–77; separatism, 61; Sumatra, 13, 283, 285; technocrats, 70, 80; timber, 71–84, 212; Timber Cess Fund, 104; vertical integration, 90; West Kalimantan, 286; wood-products industry, 81, 83, 88; yayasans, 74

Indonesian Chinese, 74–78, 82–83, 86

Industrialization strategies, 86, 96

Infant industry logic, 87

Inflation, 7, 12, 26; Ghana, 226, 228–30; Mexico, 199, 203, 208

Information, 9, 21, 35–37, 44, 50, 56, 85

Innoprise Corporation, 106–8, 287

Input underpricing, defined, 39

Institute for the Defense of the Forest (IBDF), 120

Institutional strengthening, 28

Interagency scrambles: Brazil, 119, 241; Cameroon, 241–42; Costa Rica, 241

Inter-American Development Bank, 288

International aid organizations, 232

International community, and Cameroon conservation, 235

International Energy Agency, 281

International mining companies, Chile, 153

International Monetary Fund (IMF): Chile, 159, 164; Costa Rica, 148–51; Ghana, 230; Indonesia, 61; Nigeria, 182; Peru, 127

International oil companies: Indonesia, 60; Nigeria, 179–80; Peru, 123–26, 128; Venezuela, 121

International Petroleum Corporation (IPC), 124, 126

International Tropical Timber Organization, 99

Interven, 299

Intevep, 299

Intragovernmental disagreement, 144, 242; Brazil, 143; Costa Rica, 152; Ghana, 223; Peru, 143; Venezuela, 210

IPTN (Indonesian State Aircraft Industry), 80

Irrigation, 1, 4, 8, 11, 139; Mexico, 130–42

Irrigation system, Mexico, 130–42; cost recovery, 138; deterioration, 13, 130; financing, 130–42; institutions, 141–42; liberalization, 137; maintenance, 136; policy failures, 245; reforms, 132; subsidization, 130–31, 138; underpricing, 130; water charges, 137, 141; water districts, 138; Water Resources Ministry, 135; water users, 137–38

Ivory Coast, 88, 228

Iyer, Ramaswamy, 174, 175

Japanese Ministry of International Trade and Industry, 76

Joint ventures, 274–75; Codelco, 164; NNPC, 179–80, 185; Pertamina, 68–69; PetroPerú, 124

Jua, Nantang, 235

Kadazans, 107

Kalimantan. *See* Indonesia

Kerosene, 10; Indonesia, 69

Keynesian economics, 155

Khetri copper mine, 168, 177, 292, 295. *See also* HCL

Killick, Tony, 226–27, 300

King, Victor, 100–101

Kitingan, Jeffrey, 107, 109

Korea, 281

Kosmo, Mark, 12

Krakatau Steel, 62–63, 69

Kumar, Raj, 100

Kuswata, Kartawinata, 285

Labor, 6, 21, 162. *See also* Codelco; HCL; PEMEX; Pertamina

Lagoven, 298. *See also* PDVSA
Land, 1–2, 6, 8, 41, 153, 188; classification, 41, 153; conversion, 12; government-controlled, 24; open access, 52; regulation, 52
Land appropriation, 121
Land giveaways: Brazil, 121–22, 187; Costa Rica, 258; Sarawak, 258
Land use: Brazil, 116, 121; Costa Rica, 148; distortions, 12, 41, 152; land clearing, 119, 122; policy, 28
Lasswell, Harold, 144
Latin America, deforestation in, 148
Laundering of funds: Indonesia, 142; Nigeria, 178; resource exploitation, 192; resource rents, 187; treasury funds, 187
Lewis, Peter, 182, 184
Liberalization of oil prices, 69–70
Liberia, 49
Liem Sioe Liong, 76, 286
Lieuwen, Edwin, 215
Log exports, 10; bans, 10, 34, 41, 72–73, 77; taxes on, 73
Logging, 9, 13, 23, 110, 114, 119, 188; Brazilian Amazon, 119; Cameroon, 232–240; Costa Rica, 151, 186; Honduras, 110–14; illegal, 21, 28, 40, 72; Indonesia, 71–84, 244; loss of forested area, 110; Malaysia, 100; Sarawak, 99–104, 187. *See also* Logging concessions
Logging concessions, 72, 80, 101, 187, 236–39; Brazil, 119; Cameroon, 236–39; Indonesia, 72–74, 81; Sarawak, 102, 187
London Metal Exchange, 293
Lopez Arellano, Oswaldo, 111
Lopéz Portillo, José, 136, 199–201, 203–4, 209
Lutz, Ernst, 91, 93, 150, 292

Mahar, Dennis, 14, 119, 122
Mahaweli Dam, 8, 115, 282
Mahmud, Abdul Taib, 101–2, 287

Malaysia, 1, 5, 9, 100, 106, 109, 189, 287, 301; Berjaya Party, 106–7, 287; bumiputra, 100; Internal Security Act, 109; Kuala Lumpur, 107; Malaysian Borneo, 99–109; National Front (Barisan Nasional), 106; oil, 109; Petronas, 109; timber wealth, 109; UMNO Party, 108; University of Malaysia, 103. *See also* Sabah; Sarawak
Maraven, 298
Marketing boards, 52, 91, 194–96. *See also* Ghana Cocoa Marketing Board
Martínez, Aníbal, 92
Material wealth, vs. cultural preservation, 241
May, Ernesto, 229–30, 300
Mayorga Alba, Eleodoro, 125
McDonald, Hamish, 61–65
Means, Gordon, 99–102, 105, 287
Melanaus, 287
Memorandum of Understanding (MOU): India, 294
Méndez, Juan Carlos, 292
Mengisteab, Kidane, 195, 196
Mexican National Irrigation Commission (CNI), 291
Mexican National Water Commission (CAN), 142
Mexican National Water Plan Commission, 134
Mexican Petroleum Workers Union (STPRM), 203, 208
Mexico, 1, 4–5, 8, 10, 11–12, 20, 68–69, 130–43, 197–204; 206, 210, 281, 282, 290–91, 296–97; agricultural modernization, 133; Chicontepec oil fields, 201–2; commercial agriculture, 136; economic growth alternatives, 198; export revenues, 205; foreign debt, 198–204; inflation, 136, 197; land consolidation, 135; nationalism, 198; public spending, 199; redistribution to industry, 132; revolution, 132, 140; state enterprises, 199; taxation, 198; urban

workers, 140; water, 13, 17, 130–43, 197–99. *See also* Irrigation system, Mexico; PEMEX

Mikesell, Raymond, 229, 230

Military budget, 181–82

Mill, John Stuart, 29–30, 147, 167, 223, 273

Mineral exploitation, 11, 24. *See also* Codelco; Copper; HCL

Minerals and Metals Trading Corporation. *See* MMTC

Minerals, 2, 8, 10–12, 86; ore grades, 15. *See also* Copper; Mining

Mineroperu, 16

Mining, 1, 12, 21, 29, 167, 294. *See also* Codelco; CVG; CVRD; HCL

Mining, Geological, and Metallurgical Institute of India, 294

Miranda, Marie Lynn, 100, 105, 112–13

MMTC (Minerals and Metals Trading Corporation), 171–73, 175, 293

Mobil Oil Company, 60

Mochida, Tomoo, 287

Molina Enríquez, Andres, 140

Monge Alvarez, Luís Alberto, 149

Monopoly, 9, 34–35, 44, 155

Mora, Juan, 203

Moran, Theodore, 92

Morris, James, 113

Multiple oversight, 85

Multiplicity of financial services, 20

Muñoz, R., 152

Musa, Tanza, 301

Muslims, 287

National Association of Copper Supervisors, 156

National Department for Roads and Highways (DNER), 119

Nationalization: Cameroon forests, 231; Chilean copper, 153–54, 168; Mexican oil, 179; Nigerian oil, 179; Venezuelan oil, 153, 211

National security, 30; India, 176

Ndongko, Wilfred, 301

Neary, Peter, 291

Negative externalities, 34–35, 40–42, 52

Nellis, John, 276

Nercissiantz, Nahram, 137, 142, 291

Netherlands, 282

Netherlands Antilles, 218

Ngangoue, Nana, 301

Nglobo Oil Mining, 60

NGOs (Nongovernmental organizations), 232, 236–38

Nigeria, 1, 10, 12, 178–86, 226–28, 295; Biafran Civil War, 180–83; bureaucracy, 178; ethnic conflict, 180; federal budget, 180; financial management, 178; deficits, 183; fuel shortages, 178, 182–84; Ibos, 180–83; industrialization strategy, 178; interregional distribution, 183; Lagos, 179, 183–84; military, 181–85; Niger delta, 181, 183, 295; oil, 89, 124, 178–85; River State, 183; urbanization, 179; Yoruba, 179

Nigerian Labour Congress, 182

Nigerian National Oil Corporation, 179

Nigerian National Petroleum Corporation. *See* NNPC

Nkrumah, President Kwame, 224, 226, 229, 299

NNPC (Nigerian National Petroleum Corporation), 89, 124, 178–85

Nongovernmental organizations. *See* NGOs

Nonrenewable raw materials, 3, 6

North Borneo Timber Corporation, 109

Norway, 4

Nunu-Koko, Abubakar, 182

Occidental Petroleum, Peru, 124

Off-budget investments: Indonesia, 59, 64, 100, 143; Sabah, 100; Sarawak, 100; Venezuela, 213

Off-budget subsidization, 255

Oil and mining policy failures, 249–50

Oil boom effects, 136; Cameroon, 234; Mexico, 200; Venezuela, 215. *See also* Dutch disease

Oil product subsidies. *See* Domestic fuel prices

Oil, 1–2, 4, 8, 10, 12, 15, 70–71, 188–89, 209–10. Cameroon, 233; consumption growth, 70; Indonesia, 59–71, 212; Mexico, 64, 68, 70, 115, 185, 197–209, 219–21, 244, 253–54, 296–97; Nigeria, 89, 124, 178–87; Peru, 93, 123–29, 143, 197–98, 290; refining, 10; smuggling, 183–84; Venezuela, 69, 154, 210–23; world prices, 199, 204, 215, 220, 234. *See also* NNPC; PDVSA; PEMEX; Pertamina; Petronas, Petro-Perú

Olancho Forest Reserve, 112; paper mill, 113

OPEC (Organization of Petroleum Exporting Countries), 61, 207, 215, 218, 298

Open-access resources, 44, 152

Orimulsion process, 222

Orive Alba, Adolfo, 134, 290

Ostrom, Elinor, 271

Otobo, Dafe, 295

Output pricing, 34, 37, 48–49

Output underpricing, 48–49

Overcapitalization, 9

Overexploitation, 12, 27. *See also* Deforestation; Soil, erosion

Overgrazing, 11–12

Overpricing of resource outputs, 42–43

Overproduction of oil; Nigeria, 178; as result of low fuel prices, 42

Overspending on inputs, 49

Oversubsidization, 40, 41

Oyog, Angeline, 232, 237

Paraguay, 5, 7

Parti Bersatu Sabah, 107

Pascó-Font Quevedo, Alberto, 128

Pasture, 8; Brazilian Amazon, 119

PDVSA (Petróleos de Venezuela, S.A.), 10, 68, 89, 197, 210–22, 252–54, 283, 297–99; autonomy, 212–14; bailout of Workers' Bank, 216; capital, 212; competition among subsidiaries, 222; control over funds, 212–18; corporate identity, 222; efficiency, 216, 221, 223; government raids on funds, 210–11, 216; history, 211; international borrowing and debt, 219; investment fund, 212–13, 215–17, 219; jurisdiction, 211; merging of subsidiaries, 222; mismanagement of funds, 216; off-budget spending, 221; Orinoco heavy crude project, 216; overseas operations, 218–19; oversight, 221; professionalism, 221; refining capacity, 218; revenues, 214; taxation, 219; transparency, 216, 221; undercapitalization, 197

Pease Garcia, Henry, 126, 289

Pelita Airline, 283

Peluamas Sdn Bhd (PSB), 287

Peluso, Nancy, 194

PEMEX (Petróleos Mexicanos), 64, 68, 115, 185, 197–209, 219–21, 244, 253–54, 296–97; accounting, 203, 211, 221; corruption, 208, 221; efficiency, 203; expansion strategy, 200; finance and budgets, 197–209; Guadalajara gas explosion, 208; history, 197; international borrowing and debt, 115, 199–206, 219–220; jurisdictional battles, 201, 204; labor and wage issues, 203; policy failures, 244; public image, 197; restructuring, 208; taxation of, 200–202; transparency, 185, 208; undercapitalization, 185, 197–99, 205–7

Pequiven, 299

Pérez, Carlos Andres, 212

Performance contracts, 276

Permigan, 60

Permina, 60–61, 64

Perón, Juan, 195

Pertamina, 46, 59–71, 76, 79, 179, 185,

196, 206, 213, 253, 265, 283; access to capital, 63; accounting, 66; bankruptcy, 64–65, 70; community projects, 62; as development agency, 79; efficiency, 71; exploration, 68; history, 60–61; inter-ministerial management, 205; international borrowing and debt, 64–65, 70, 196, 206, 213; investments, 70–71, 221; joint ventures, 68–69; lack of expertise, 60; off-budget spending, 62, 71; overexploitation, 71; as patronage employers, 67; pricing policies, 68, 71; reform, 66–67; relations with international oil companies, 60, 64, 66, 68; revenues, 61, 63; transparency, 61, 64, 71, 185; vertical integration, 60; waste, 221

Peru, 1, 5, 8, 10, 16, 123–29, 287–90; Amazonian initiatives, 123; Finance Ministry, 126–28; Lima, 290; oil exploitation, 93, 123–29, 143; peasant leagues, 126; Revolutionary Government of the Armed Forces, 126. *See also* PetroPerú

Petróleos de Venezuela, S.A. *See* PDVSA

Petróleos Mexicanos. *See* PEMEX

Petroleum. *See* Oil

Petronas, 109

PetroPerú, 96, 123–29, 143, 197–98, 290; Amazonian expansion, 124–25; bankruptcy, 128; debt, 127–29; domestic fuel pricing, 127; exploration costs, 124; inadequate manpower, 125; international borrowing and debt, 128; losses, 127; pipeline, 127–28; privatization, 123, 129; revenues, 127–28; taxes, 127; undercapitalization, 123–24, 127–28, 190, 197

Philippines, 5, 82; deforestation, 13

Pickles, David, 14, 113

Pigou, Arthur, 283

Pigovian charges or taxes, 283

Pinochet, Augusto, 155–57, 161, 163

Pinstrup-Andersen, Per, 41, 97

Plantations, 80; on Sumatra, 72

Policy failures, 8–9, 12, 28, 31–32, 110, 123, 129, 164, 178, 223, 240, 255–59. *See also specific cases*

Political motives, of officials, 19

Pollution charges, 34, 38, 43

Polonoroeste project, Brazil, 120

Pompermayer, Malori José, 120

Population, 3, 4; Amazon, 116–17, 122

Positive externalities, 34

Prajogo Pangestu, 76

Pratt, Kwesi, Jr., 14, 228, 230

Presumption of state competence, Cameroon, 239

PRI (Partido Revolucionario Institucional), 137

Price Waterhouse, 66–67, 108, 287

Prices, 8, 10; ceilings, 34, 41; collapse, 12; subsidies, 70

Principal-agent problem, 283

Production-sharing arrangements: Indonesia, 68, 124; Middle East, 68; Nigeria, 179; Peru, 124

Programmatic motives, categories, 26, 29–30, 244

Property rights, 9, 11, 35–37, 44–45, 50–52, 54, 73, 192; the Andes, 50–51; Brazil, 121; as bundle of user rights, 193; confiscation, 52; encroachment, 44, 52; government role, 35, 37, 42; impact on resource exploitation, 44–45; violence, 36

Public Enterprises Survey, 292

Public lands, 9, 11, 16, 26, 35; communal, 11; Mexico, 135

Pura, Raphael, 102

Radetzki, Marian, 86–88, 129

Ramírez, Carlos, 15, 203

Ranching: Brazil, 119–23; Costa Rica, 186–88; subsidies, 34, 122, 152, 186

Randall, Laura, 92, 195, 211, 216, 218, 299

Rao, M.V.N.R.S., 167–76, 292–94

Raw materials, 3–7; exports, 6–7; inputs, 4; processing, 23; underpricing, 40. *See also under specific materials*

Recommendations, 269–79; clarifying jurisdictions, 272; for extra-governmental actors, 277; fiscal reforms, 275–76; government-state enterprise arrangements, 274–77; joint ventures with private-sector enterprises, 274–75; prioritizing through central budget, 273; restoring nongovernmental resource control, 270; restructuring state resource exploitation, 271; simplifying mandates, 271–72

Reforestation, 8–9, 34, 151–52, 186–89; fees, 42, 79; fund in Indonesia, 73–74, 79–81; subsidies in Costa Rica, 147, 186–87

Regional development, 11, 86, 95–96; Brazilian Amazon, 86, 95, 143; Costa Rica, 95; India, 86, 95–96; Nigeria, 180–83; Peru, 95–96

Renewable resources, 3, 6–7

Rent-creation strategies, 31, 53

Rent destruction, 100, 115

Rent-seeking, 26–27, 31, 78, 187, 258; creating opportunities for, 52–53, 257–58

Repetto, Robert, 87

Resource-based industrialization, 10

Resource development, 8; African, 178; motives for manipulation, 86, 146

Resource policy failures: costs of, 12–16; as pricing violations, 39; and property right, 39; as strategies, 47; upstream expansion, 93; violations of accountability, 39

Resource rent capture, 19, 27–28, 85, 172, 192–95, 242

Resource-use regulations: implementation of, 28; manipulations of, 244

Rietbergen, Simon, 231–32, 234, 239, 241, 300–301

Riswan, Soedarsono, 285

Rojas, Francisco, 297

Roosen, Gustavo, 219–20

Ross, Michael, 27, 74, 286

Ross-Larson, Bruce, 105

Royaards, Albert, 66

Royal Dutch Shell, 218

Royalties, 10, 26; Costa Rican public forest reserves, 150; private oil exploiters, Peru, 128

Rukmana, 76

Rural water management, Mexico, 130. *See also* Irrigation system, Mexico; Water

Rutledge, Peter, 66

Sabah Foundation, 104–9, 142, 253

Sabah, 1, 14, 99, 104, 107–8, 186, 287; deforestation, 99, 104, 107; downstream wood-product industry, 108; geopolitics, 104; illegal logging, 107; Pekemas, 105; rent seeking, 104; resistance to log-export ban, 107; royalty rates, 107; strongman politics, 104; timber rent capture, 107–9; United Sabah Party (PBS), 109

Sahabat Alam Malaysia, 103

Said, Datuk Salleh Tun, 108

Salas Mandujano, E., 151

Salinas Galtieri, Carlos, 208, 297

Salleh, Harris, 106

Sanderson, Steven, 27, 130, 136–37, 290–91

Sarawak, 1, 99–104, 107, 143, 186, 287; Barisan Nasional (National Front), 101; Chinese in, 102; deforestation, 98–99; government relations with Dayaks, 102; Ibans, 104; logging concessions, 99–104; Mukah, 287; multi-ethnic coalitions, 101; PBB Party, 101; political exchange, 99; political parties, 101; value of timber concessions, 99

Sarawak Foundation, 104

Sarawak Timber Industry Development Corporation, 100

Sarris, Alexander, 229, 230, 299–300
Scarsborough, Erik, 287
Schlager, Edella, 271
Schneider, Ronald, 91, 116, 119, 288–89
Schramm, Gunter, 135, 136
Schwarz, Adam, 14, 61, 76, 78, 283–86
Searle, Peter, 104
Second Oil Shock, 215
Self-reliance, defined by Indian government, 176
Shah of Iran, 215
Shams, Hadi, 229–30, 299–300
Shell Oil Company, 60
Shepherd, Gill, 231, 237–38
Shifting cultivation, 17, 103, 241, 282
Simas, José, 130
Sindicato de Trabajadores Petroleros de la República Mexicana (STPRM). *See* Mexican Petroleum Workers Union
Slash-and-burn agriculture. *See* Shifting cultivation
Small-scale farms, sustainability, 120
Smith, Adam, 36, 207
Smuggling, 196; Ghanaian cocoa, 196, 230, 233; Nigerian oil, 183–84
Soil, 7, 12–13, 33; erosion, 11, 36
Solórzano, Raúl, 14, 189
Sources of wealth, categories, 245
South Africa, 5
Southeast Asia, 13, 118
Southland Corporation, 217
Spillover effects, 38. *See also* Negative externalities; Positive externalities
Sri Lanka, 5, 8, 281, 282
Stallings, Barbara, 289
Standard Oil of New Jersey, 60, 124, 289
State copper enterprises: Chile, 11, 17, 123, 153–65, 189, 252, 289, 292; India, 165–77, 191, 293–95; Zambia, 17
State enterprises, 10–12, 16–17, 39, 242; accounts, 35; autonomy, 16; complexity, 16; efficiency, 129; undercapitalization, 17, 68. *See also under individual entries*

State oil enterprises, 8, 11, 16, 17, 24, 35; inefficiency and corruption, 13; investment budgets, 35; Malaysia, 109; Mexico, 64, 68, 115, 185, 197–209, 219–21, 244, 253–54, 296–97; Nigeria, 89, 124, 178–85; operating costs, 51; Peru, 96, 123–29, 143, 197–98, 290; pricing limitations, 42; Venezuela, 10, 17, 68, 89, 197, 210–22, 252–54, 283, 297–99
State resource enterprises, 35, 38, 245–46; accountability, 46; decapitalization, 54; irresponsibility, 246, managers, 54; price ceilings, 41; pricing, 54; profit, 206; royalties, 40; undercapitalization, 35
Steel industry, 16; Brazil 11; Indonesia, 62–63; Venezuela, 196, 213, 215
Stepan, Alfred, 289
Stern, Joseph, 75
Stesser, Stanley, 102, 287
STPRM. *See* Mexican Petroleum Workers Union
Subramanian, Ashok, 130
Subsidies, 9–11, 34, 122, 136–37, 152, 186; Brazilian Amazon, 187; Costa Rica, 187; land giveaways, 38, 258; for positive externalities, 38
SUDAM (Superintendancy of the Amazon), 116, 118
Suharto, President, 29, 59–64, 72, 74, 76–80, 83, 85, 190, 212, 253–54, 266, 286
Sukarno, President, 61, 74
Superintendency for the Development of the Amazon. *See* SUDAM
Surplus capture, 54–55; through taxation, Venezuela, 218
Sustainable development, 32, 114
Sustainable yield strategy, 2–3, 281
Sutowo, Ibnu, 61–64
Sweden, 217
Sweeney, John, 219, 299
Swidden agriculture. *See* Shifting cultivation
Synnott, Timothy, 114

Taman Mini Theme Park, 76
Tamayo, Jorge, 134, 290, 291
Taxation, 10–12, 30, 224
Technology, 3, 90
Teichman, Judith, 15, 27, 198–205
Teter, Darius, 75
Texas, 217
TFAP (Tropical Forestry Action Plan),
  Cameroon, 235–36
Thabatabai, Hamid, 228
Thailand, 5; deforestation, 13
Thiele, Rainer, 233
Tietenberg, Tom, 33
Timber, 1, 4–10, 21; booms, 13; estates,
  79. See also Logging
Timber Marketing Board, 89
Timber rents: Cameroon, 232, 239; Indo-
  nesia, 72, 74, 82; Sarawak, 100–102
Timber shortages, 13; Honduras, 112;
  Indonesia, 71
Timber taxes, 100. See also under specific
  countries
Time horizon, uncertainty, 45
Timmer, C. Peter, 41, 97
Tironi, Ernesto, 15, 163, 164, 292
Tollison, Robert, 83, 282
TransAmazon Highway, 118
Transfers of wealth, 145–47
Transmigrasi, 79, 302
Tree burning, Brazil, 119
Trihatmodjo, 76
Trinidad and Tobago, 5
Tropical Forest Action Plan. See TFAP
Tsuruoka, Doug, 99

UGFC. See United Ghana Farmers'
  Council
UGFCC. See United Ghama Farmers'
  Council Cooperatives
UN Conference of Trade and Develop-
  ment (UNCTAD), 5
Undercapitalization, 9–10; Chile's
  Codelco, 157–60, 190; Mexico's
  PEMEX 185, 197–99, 205–7; Nigeria's

NNPC, 178, 182, 185; Peru's Petro-
  Perú, 123–24, 127–28, 190, 197; state
  oil enterprises, 197; state resource
  exploiters, 45; Venezuela's PDVSA,
  190, 210
Underdevelopment of resources, 35, 42,
  45
Underexploitation of resources, 9, 34, 36,
  40, 42
Underpricing, 11; Cameroon timber, 232;
  resource exports, 41; resource outputs,
  41, 191; and weak enforcement, 40. See
  also Domestic fuel prices
UN Development Programme, 235
UN Food and Agricultural Organization
  (FAO), 4, 235–36, 284
UN International Trade Centre, 5
Union Oil of California, 217
United Ghana Farmers' Council
  (UGFC), 224
United Ghana Farmers' Council Cooper-
  atives (UGFCC), 224–25, 228
United Kingdom, 301; British Labour
  Party, 237
United Malays National Organization,
  107
United States, 4, 6, 148, 204, 217, 220,
  292, 298; Agency for International
  Development, 78; Department of
  Energy, 281; General Accounting
  Office, 296–97
Unocal. See Union Oil of California
Upstream expansion, 91–92, 97–98;
  Mexico, 179; Nigeria, 179; Venezuela,
  179
Urban riots, Nigeria, 180, 182–83
Utting, Peter, 27, 112, 113, 287

Vaidyanath, L. R., 167–76, 292–94
Valdez, Alberto, 41
Value-added strategy, 23, 87–88
Varangis, Panos, 229
Vargas, Getulio, 117
Vayda, Andrew, 285

Veba Oil, 217

Velasco Alvarado, Juan, 124–26

Venezuela, 1, 5, 8, 10, 12, 68–69, 210–23, 283, 298; COPEI Party, 213; economic crisis, 215–16; Finance Ministry, 215–16; Hydrocarbons Law, 211, 214–15; Lake Maracaibo, 222; oil production, 210–23; Orinoco oil belt, 210; potential oil reserves, 69; Ruhr Öl, 298; tar sands, 210; Workers' Bank, 216. *See also* PDVSA

Vertical diversification, 46

Vidal, John, 238

Villarzú, Juan, 292

WALHI, 277, 284, 286–87

Walton, John, 103, 109

Water, 1, 2, 4, 11–12, 24; overuse, 14; pollution, 41. *See also* Irrigation system, Mexico; Mexico, water

Werner, Johannes, 207

West Africa, 182–83, 234, 301; logging, 13

Wiebelt, Manfred, 233

Wildlife, 2, 7, 12; habitat destruction, 13

Willingness to pay, 176

Wilson, Edward O., 122

Winterbottom, Robert, 233, 236

Wionczek, Miguel, 131, 133–35, 139, 141, 290–91

Wong, James, 103

Wood, Charles, 122

Wood-processing industry, 13, 77, 112–13; Ghana, 90; Honduras, 112–13; Indonesia, 77, 90

World Bank, 14, 148–50, 155, 159–60, 164, 283–86, 301; Brazil, 122; Cameroon, 237, 241; Costa Rica, 148; Ghana, 230; Indonesia, 78–79; Nigeria, 178, 182

World Bank–UN Development Programme, 14, 178

World Energy Council, 281

World Resources Institute, 12–13, 236, 281, 301

World Wide Fund for Nature, 238

Ya'akub, Abdul Rahman, 101–2, 287

Yakimoto, C., 116

Yates, P. Lamartine, 130

Yergin, Daniel, 287

Zama, Isaac, 231–32, 235, 242

Zambia, 5, 281

Zambian Consolidated Copper Mines, 297, 301

Library of Congress Cataloging-in-Publication Data

Ascher, William.
   Why governments waste natural resources : policy failures in developing
countries / William Ascher.
      p.   cm.
   Includes bibliographical references and index.
   ISBN 0-8018-6095-4 (alk. paper). — ISBN 0-8018-6096-2 (pbk. : alk. paper)
      1. Natural resources — Government policy — Developing countries.   2. Natural
resources — Developing countries — Management.   I. Title.
HC85.A83   1999
333.7'09172'4 — dc21   98-51020
                                                                             CIP